PUBLICITY
FOR SOCIAL WORK

BY

MARY SWAIN ROUTZAHN

AND

EVART G. ROUTZAHN

Department of Surveys and Exhibits

RUSSELL SAGE FOUNDATION

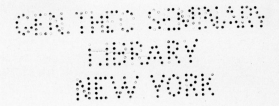

NEW YORK
RUSSELL SAGE FOUNDATION
1928

Copyright, 1928, by
RUSSELL SAGE FOUNDATION

PREFACE

PUBLICITY may be broadly defined as the act of making information public. As a rule its purpose is to gain some end. As a part of a movement to improve living conditions, its aim can be realized only as it succeeds in effecting changes in human thought and action. Although the term is at times used to describe unscrupulous methods, publicity is none the less a good word and the only one we have to present an important phase of social, religious, and civic work.

Whereas classroom education is a course of training directed to persons who can be individually identified and who undertake to complete a prescribed term of study, publicity is commonly addressed to people reached through newspapers, pamphlets, meetings, exhibits, and other mediums which do not permit of continuous relations such as obtain in schools and colleges. Because of the uncertain and intermittent nature of its audience, publicity is best suited to make known easily comprehensible or at least non-technical information; to remind people of familiar but unheeded situations deserving attention; and to prod them to acts which they are inclined to postpone.

A characteristic of publicity for social work is that it urges information upon people who do not seek it. An effort to induce them to give money or service to relieve suffering, to change personal habits, or to acknowledge and correct injustice must often be unwelcome. To secure their attention under these circumstances necessarily requires an aggressive process of overcoming indifference and of creating a desire for understanding.

On this interpretation of the nature of publicity for social work, namely, that it consists in disseminating information directed toward human betterment; that it has no certain, constant audience; and that it is purposeful and aggressive, we base the discussion of its technique in this book. The method of presentation here chosen is largely the setting forth of accepted principles, or, where these are lacking, of the best judgment we could obtain in regard to the process, illustrated by examples drawn from the practices of social agencies.

iii

The preparation for the task began in a study of the methods employed by organizations engaged in the public health field. We found the logical starting point for our inquiry in the work of the national health organizations, since much of the material used throughout the country is prepared in their offices. These offices, through their field workers, as a rule, keep fairly well informed about the work being done by affiliated or branch agencies in local communities. While information was secured from all of the leading national health organizations, detailed examination was confined to the operations of the National Tuberculosis Association, the American Social Hygiene Association, and the Division of Venereal Diseases of the United States Public Health Service.

The National Tuberculosis Association, together with its state and local branches, supplies a greater volume and variety of publicity material than any other single organization known to us, and we have drawn very freely upon it for examples. During the early period of our study the American Social Hygiene Association and the United States Public Health Service were jointly conducting a vigorous campaign of education in regard to social hygiene in which they not only tried out many interesting, and, at that time, unusual experiments, but also examined critically their own methods of propaganda.

State departments of health and state public health associations are usually the chief administrative and distributing centers for the exhibits and literature originating in national offices. They also produce a great deal of material of their own and actively engage in local undertakings. Their work presented therefore an important body of information about current methods.

The main part of our field work was an inquiry into the educational work of the North Carolina State Board of Health. Visits were made also to the state health departments of New Jersey, Ohio, Michigan, Illinois, Indiana, and New York. Our observations in North Carolina covered not only the headquarters of the State Board of Health but also a number of towns and rural districts where the Board was carrying on some special project, and a few selected counties which were doing unusually good work in health education.

In addition, our study consisted of the examination here and

iv

there of particular forms of publicity. For example, we kept closely in touch with the preparation for Health Week in a certain New Jersey city and its celebration; visited a dozen or more state and county fairs in New England and the Atlantic states; attended health expositions in Louisville, Scranton, Boston, and New York, as well as many other expositions held in the vicinity of New York; and followed closely a series of health talks given under the auspices of the New York County Chapter of the American Red Cross in stores, factories, and churches, as well as similar meetings in other cities.

For material outside the health field, we have drawn extensively upon the annual campaigns of the safety movement, the community chests, and, indeed, upon practically every other branch of social work. A considerable number of social workers have supplied valuable material in response to our requests for information. They have reported on particular campaigns and have furnished outlines of procedure, as well as thousands of specimens of printed publicity material. Still another source of help in collecting material for this book has been our own participation in many projects, especially in the publicity "clinics"[1] which have for several years been features of the annual programs arranged by the Committee on Publicity Methods in Social Work[2] and also of meetings of the Section on Public Health Education of the American Public Health Association.[3]

To examine this great volume of effort and achievement, and to select out of it all that seemed applicable to our purpose has been an important part of our task. A comparatively small part only of the material has found its way into the text of the book in the form of reports of specific projects.

[1] These clinics consist of discussion by appointed critics to whom examples of publicity material are submitted by social agencies and by members of the audience. The examples include newspaper articles, letters of appeal, posters, printed matter, public addresses, motion pictures, and plays.

[2] The Committee on Publicity Methods in Social Work is an informal organization of persons responsible for or engaged in publicity work. Organized in 1921 in connection with the National Conference of Social Work, it has continued to meet annually. A news bulletin is published at intervals during the year for the exchange of ideas and information among the members. The headquarters of the Committee are at 130 East 22d St., New York.

[3] The Public Health Section of the American Public Health Association, 370 Seventh Ave., New York, conducts a group of meetings as part of the annual con-

As our study progressed, we realized that unconsciously we had been relying too much on the actual practice of social organizations to reveal the principles and technique of publicity. We had expected their procedure to be based on more or less well-defined standards and carefully developed plans. It soon became apparent, however, that in the majority of cases, the choice of a method was determined by economy, imitation, or habit, rather than by deliberate judgment. The quality of the work, too, depended in many instances upon the chance possession by a staff member of talent or experience in some one line, for instance, news writing, exhibit designing, or public speaking. Again, the work was often being carried on by persons without either training or experience in any of the approved methods of presenting information. Usually the duties were combined with others so that the person who performed them had no time to make up for his lack of training by study and experimentation. Except in rare instances, we had no means of determining in any given case the relation between the methods used and the results achieved.

This situation led us to search outside the social work field for reasonably practical standards by which to judge the merits or suitability of the examples of publicity which we had assembled. The sources upon which we drew for a final workable technique are so fully acknowledged in the various chapters that we do not need to list them here. On such topics as journalism, printing, and public speaking a considerable body of literature was available, as well as a generally accepted practice directly applicable to the problems of social publicity. To authorities in each of these pursuits we submitted parts of the manuscript and we have besides consulted them on specific questions.

In other branches of publicity, however, especially in those pertaining to meetings, distribution of printed matter, the employment of dramatic methods, expositions, and fairs, there seemed to be no recognized standards. Practically none of the principles that governed the persons who have used these methods success-

vention of the American Public Health Association, and a department on "Education and Publicity" in the monthly issues of the American Journal of Public Health.
  Both the Committee and the Section invite the affiliation of those who are interested.

fully has been set down in print. In these departments we depended upon conferences with individuals, as well as upon our own observation and experience. We offer our conclusions frankly as opinions and will welcome criticism and suggestions from those who differ with us.

For reasons which we state below the book does not pretend to be a complete and well-rounded handbook of publicity methods for social work. Indeed, a discussion of the topics omitted would make a second volume of the size of this one. Some of these omissions deserve a word of explanation.

In the first place, we have arbitrarily confined our discussion to publicity addressed to adults and to its presentation outside of classrooms. In other words, we have considered the school and its methods as beyond the province of this book.

Again, the reader will find no discussion of books as mediums to disseminate social information. Important as they are in spreading a knowledge of social problems, we believe that our readers are likely to be those who find less permanent and substantial forms of publicity, such as exhibits, booklets, and public speaking more suited to the work they are carrying on. Excellent advice, however, about popularizing information in book form may be found in such a book as The Humanizing of Knowledge.[1]

The publication of periodical bulletins or house organs is, on the other hand, a method very widely used by social agencies and one which we have regretted our inability to include as a separate topic. Much of what we have to say about printed matter applies as well to these publications, but much more needs to be said. A careful study to determine the real field of usefulness of such bulletins or house organs, as well as their definite limitations as a method of spreading information about social work, is greatly needed.

Still another topic of considerable significance not fully treated is the use of motion pictures for social propaganda. There is, at this date, much experimenting and little specialization in the production of such films; and the matter of non-theatrical film distribution is in a chaotic condition. The whole problem should be

[1] Robinson, James Harvey, The Humanizing of Knowledge. Geo. H. Doran Co., New York, 1923.

studied, since the demands of social agencies for assistance in producing and in obtaining motion pictures are growing more pressing.

The organization of a publicity department within a social agency is another topic deserving attention. This would include a discussion of the training, ability, and experience which should constitute the equipment of the publicity worker, the budget required for maintenance, and the administration of the publicity office.

At the time of writing, we can only report that no training course[1] which prepares students to engage in publicity work exists; that the qualifications of those now engaged in this task, as we have already indicated, are largely accidental and without general significance; that the turnover in the comparatively few positions known by the title of publicity director or secretary is very high; and that it is not possible to compare the budgets of social agencies for this purpose because scarcely any two are undertaking work similar in scope and purpose. Under these circumstances any suggestions we might offer would be either without basis in actual experience or of such limited application as to be valueless.

The reader may feel, perhaps, that in the discussions throughout this book we have taken too much for granted that the publicity worker has his information well in hand, and that it deserves to be presented. We do offer a word of warning to those who prepare publicity not to become so absorbed in getting information into use as to grow careless about the accuracy of the facts or the value of the ideas underlying their presentation, since authenticated facts, truthful statements written or spoken, clear thinking, and sound social programs are fundamentals of good publicity. However, the function of this book is primarily to discuss the technique of imparting information about social facts and ideas already gathered and appraised.

To many of our fellow workers who have read and criticized our manuscript in whole or in part, and who have supplied illustrative material we wish to express our sincere appreciation. Especial acknowledgments are due to Willard G. Bleyer, who, through

[1] Courses in publicity have been introduced in several schools of journalism and schools of social work, but these are too limited in scope to be regarded as training for publicity work.

personal conference and criticism, has made an important contribution to our discussion of the Newspaper; to Louis Resnick,
for criticisms on the same part; to James A. Winans, who criticized in detail the chapter on Public Speaking; to J. Howard Fell
for much practical help in revising the part on Printed Matter
and in making up illustrations for it; and to Austin Pierpont,
who did important field work for us.

TABLE OF CONTENTS

xi

TABLE OF CONTENTS

TABLE OF CONTENTS

PUBLICITY FOR SOCIAL WORK

LIST OF ILLUSTRATIONS

2   xvii

PART I: ANALYSIS OF THE TASK

INTRODUCTION TO PART I

PUBLIC understanding of social work usually lags years behind current practice. Methods of dealing with old and familiar problems of poverty and disease are continually improving. At the same time social research is uncovering new situations that call for treatment and is pointing the way to the application of remedies, developments with which the general public does not keep pace. Publicity aims to close the gap. The skill and persistence with which its task is performed largely determine how extensively the results of social research and experience will be used.

The ends for which social organizations, both official and private, seek public understanding are in the main to obtain the necessary support to carry on their work; to bring about changes in personal conduct, especially in matters affecting health or safety; and to secure new laws, or the enforcement of old ones, for improving social conditions and protecting the exploited classes. Often a given effort of publicity is intended to take a single step toward one of these objectives. In any case, the task in hand is not merely to impart information, but to impress it upon the minds of persons who, it is hoped, will act upon it.

In developing a plan of procedure, one should remember that the persons for whom information is designed are not seeking enlightenment. Therefore, the starting point is in creating the desire to receive it. To attract attention, to arouse and hold interest, to be understood, to create goodwill or favorable opinion, and to provoke responsive action constitute a formula that well enumerates the consecutive steps in the whole process of imparting information.

The practical application of this formula to the preparation of various kinds of social publicity is realized if we observe the aimlessness and futility of efforts which lack this orderly development of steps. For instance, a specialist in some branch of social work is

3

very likely in speaking or writing about his subject to assume that those who are ignorant of it compose a waiting and eager audience. Filled with a sense of the dignity and importance of his theme, he believes, no doubt, that his information would be cheapened by efforts to draw attention to it, or else he is unaware of the indifference of those addressed. Yet his speech or article is wasted if no one listens to or reads it.

On the other hand, it is easily possible for the publicity worker to become too greatly absorbed in the first stage of the task. Realizing that attention is difficult to secure, especially if the purpose is to interest one class of society in the welfare of another, he may drift into a continuous and restless search for new schemes to attract. These become ends in themselves, while clear and convincing exposition is neglected.

Again, action is sometimes sought on the basis of emotional appeals which may seem effective for the moment, but not being based on understanding, do not produce lasting results. The lobbyist, impatient to push his bill through the legislature, has omitted to educate public opinion on the subject and later is disappointed to find the new law unsupported and generally evaded. He has tried to jump to the end without taking the intermediate steps.

The amount of time required to accomplish the task of obtaining a response to publicity varies greatly. When the aim is to persuade people to undertake some simple act easily understood and arousing no opposition, the formula as a whole may be applied to a single process, such as designing a poster or drafting an appeal. For instance, the exhortation to avoid danger is so urgent in the "Stop, Look and Listen" sign of a railway that it commands both attention and immediate response. On the other hand, if the ideas presented involve a radical change of thought or habit, each step may require the use of varied forms of publicity over a period of months or even years. When this is true, one must continue to address the same individuals until the message is heeded and acted upon. In a small community the task may not be difficult, but a social agency that wishes to reach thousands or millions of persons distributed over large geographical areas is likely to be obliged to tax all its resources in the effort to spread information so widely.

4

While it may be able to reach these large numbers once, no time or money is left with which to follow them up and secure their interest and response.

Thoroughness in carrying out any project of educational publicity may be achieved by breaking up a large and miscellaneous audience into smaller groups made up of persons with similar interests who can be identified sufficiently to be reached many times. If it is not possible to address all these groups at the same time, each in turn may become the objective of a concentrated effort during a given period. Thus, fairly constant audiences, to whom one may repeatedly address information, may be found in the regular readers of newspapers or popular magazines, members of fraternal organizations, the persons who ride regularly over a given route, or workers in the same factory or type of industry. Sometimes, however, it is desirable to identify the individuals to whom publicity is addressed. This is the case in building up and maintaining a list of members or contributors to an organization.

The suggestions as to methods of attracting and holding attention and provoking action contained in the chapters that follow are merely applications of general principles which tell us how the human mind works. They cannot be used successfully unless one bears in mind the nature of the people to be reached by a given project. Therefore, the more we know about the degree of education, racial traits, financial status, social background, and present interests of the particular persons addressed in any given effort, the greater our chances will be of causing the information and advice presented to them to be noticed, understood, and adopted.

CHAPTER I

ATTRACTING ATTENTION

LATE in the afternoon during the baseball season in almost any American city a crowd of men and boys may be seen gathered around a baseball score board outside a newspaper building, on which each move in the game of the day is registered as it is made. An eager propagandist might suppose that so large a crowd would furnish an excellent audience for a talk about the frightful conditions existing in the state tuberculosis sanatorium or the seriousness of the housing shortage. If, however, he began to make a speech on these subjects or to distribute literature, he would no doubt quickly discover that a crowd is not necessarily an audience.

Just such a situation as this exists, in lesser or greater degree, in relation to every attempt to attract attention. Mere accessibility to people—a crowd that passes a given corner, a mailing list of names and addresses, or the readers of a newspaper or magazine—does not automatically provide listeners or readers for the subject one has in hand. Even if the accessible group is not absorbed in anything so exciting as the baseball score board, most of its members usually have some other preoccupations which fill their minds, excluding less personal or urgent matters. A man walking down the street in tight shoes may be too absorbed in his discomfort to notice one's window display. A woman whose morning mail has brought letters from friends and relatives lays aside, and possibly loses or throws away, the campaign folder delivered in the same mail. In addition to such immediate and more or less trifling matters, each of us has a fairly well-established set of interests which determines what we will notice and what we will pass over out of the many things which come within range of our consciousness at any given moment. Walter Lippmann has put it, "We are concerned in public affairs, but immersed in our private ones."[1]

Then, too, there is always a host of claimants for whatever atten-

[1] Public Opinion. Harcourt, Brace and Co., New York, 1922, p. 57.

6

tion we may have to spare, offering us suggestions for spending our money, advice about our health, our duties, or our pleasure, and appeals for aid.

Therefore, in seeking to secure attention we must recognize that we shall have to divert people from what already absorbs them, and that we shall have many competitors also trying to attract them.

How Attention Is Sought

Whatever represents the first point of observation, whether it is the cover-page of a folder or booklet, the headlines of a news story, the opening sentence of an article or speech, the conspicuously placed object or placard in an exhibit, or the slogan of an intensive campaign, should have one or several attention-getting qualities.

Among the many qualities and conditions mentioned by psychologists as contributing to the power of any object to catch attention, the following seem especially applicable to the problems of social publicity:

Absence of counter attraction

Intensity

Contrast

Familiarity

Ease of comprehension

Absence of Counter Attraction

Other things being equal, the probabilities that any particular thing will catch our attention are in proportion to the absence of competing attractions.[1] Releasing news items for Monday morning newspapers on the assumption that on Monday there is likely to be little important news, and mailing printed matter to people who presumably receive few letters are two ways to take advantage of comparative lack of competition.

Advertisements are displayed in railway or street cars in the expectation that they will be read because there is little else for passengers to do. People who are obliged to wait in places such as dispensaries, employment offices, or railroad stations often lack

[1] Scott, Walter Dill, The Psychology of Advertising in Theory and Practice. Small, Maynard and Co., Boston, 1921, p. 262.

occupation and their attention is obtainable for literature or posters which they might fail to notice under ordinary conditions.

Large advertisers often overcome the obstacle of counter attraction by taking a whole page in a newspaper or a double page in a magazine, thus obtaining assurance that anyone turning to that page will notice nothing else. The use of a whole tent or building for one's exhibit at a fair insures that once people are inside their attention will be focused only on what one has there. The generous use of blank space around a block of type and the display of a single poster on a wall are other applications of the principle of eliminating counter attraction.

Through a mistaken effort to crowd as much as possible into a single occasion, counter attractions to the subject for which interest is sought are often unfortunately introduced into publicity. Too many different ideas are set forth in a leaflet or poster. An exhibit may be so crowded that the eye cannot rest anywhere. Several different good causes are pressed upon the attention of citizens in the same week. Some organizations are recognizing the value of reducing competition for attention by agreeing not to infringe upon one another's campaign periods. The American Red Cross and the National Tuberculosis Association, for instance, have an agreement that there shall be no overlapping of the annual Roll Call and the Christmas Seal Sale, one coming in November and the other in December.

INTENSITY

Brightness, color, size, and movement attract attention through the intensity of the sensation they arouse. Brilliantly lighted windows and street signs are sure to be noticed. Among colors, red is generally regarded as having the greatest attention value, and is much used in posters and on covers of booklets and folders. Large type in headlines and large display space are examples of the use of magnitude to draw attention. During an intensive campaign, the great size of conspicuously placed signs causes people to notice the announcement of the event. That movement attracts attention is amply demonstrated by the tendency of exposition visitors to crowd around exhibits in motion and by the drawing power of animated displays in store windows.

8

The danger in attempting to attract attention by using sensational devices is that they often draw it to themselves rather than to the objects for which interest is sought. A person may stop to look at a highly colored, unusually large, or unexpectedly animated display without giving any heed to the subject it is supposed to introduce or interpret. Indeed, his attention frequently ends where it began, with a passing interest in the striking nature of the device. Dazzling light or color is especially treacherous in that it frequently repels almost as quickly as it attracts.

Movement, if rightly used, will not only secure but hold attention. In exhibits, lights flashing at regular intervals, bars on diagrams moving into position, a series of pictures automatically succeeding each other in a stereopticon machine, and other mechanisms are ingeniously devised to convey an idea or tell a story.

The suggestion of life and activity found in pictures or in the phrasing of headlines is also effective in attracting attention. In the cover design of a folder, a boy appears to be running pell-mell down an indicated road in his haste to reach a tuberculosis dispensary which is pictured in the lower opposite corner. The eye is at once arrested by the figure. Titles or headlines worded to suggest action are quoted on page 190.

CONTRAST

A striking difference between two objects or ideas encountered at the same time or in quick succession causes us to notice them.

The attention value of an object depends upon the contrast it forms to the object presented with it, preceding or following it.

The contrast produced by a flash of lightning on a dark night, or by the hooting of an owl at midnight, is so strong that the attention is absolutely forced, and there is no one who can disregard them. Novel things and sudden changes of any sort are noticed, while familiar things and gradual changes are hardly noticed at all.[1]

Strong contrast makes the silhouette in solid black on a white ground arresting. On maps picturing the progress of labor legislation in the United States, those states which have not yet passed good labor laws are often colored black in contrast to the white

[1] Scott, Walter Dill, The Psychology of Advertising. p. 267.

9

states which have such laws. Blue on yellow, and red on green are color combinations in which strong contrast is obtained.

"Before" and "after" pictures showing striking transformations have been the great standby of welfare organizations. For instance, pictures may show a group of forlorn and neglected children on their reception by a child-placing society, and the same group of children after they had blossomed out in foster homes. The wretchedly dirty and poverty-stricken kitchen as found by the family case worker and the same place made clean and comfortable through her assistance are frequently reproduced in exhibits of family welfare societies.

At the top of a Boy Scout letterhead a picture of a crowd of boys shooting craps behind a freight car appeared beside another of Boy Scouts in uniform setting up camp. The letter begins as follows:

> There isn't anything I can add to the above pictures, except to say that the Boy Scout organization in Queens is taking boys out of picture number one and putting them into picture number two.

The Unusual or Novel. The examples just cited illustrate contrast between two objects or ideas presented together. The same principle is applied when the novel form or content of a design or announcement places it in contrast with its surroundings. A striking drawing or color scheme makes a poster stand out from its mates on the crowded bulletin board. The gigantic double-barred cross shown on page 11 attracted notice partly because of its great size, but also because of the novelty of producing the design by illuminating some of the windows of a tall building.

As stated in the passage quoted from Walter Dill Scott, sudden changes are noticed while gradual changes are not. This is illustrated by the shock felt when 100 lives are lost in a disaster, whereas there is indifference to the gradual day-by-day piling up of the same number of deaths. Occasionally a health organization tries to startle people out of their complacent acceptance of gradual losses, as in the following statements:

> You were shocked to hear that the number of deaths resulting from the influenza epidemic in 1918 was greater than the total losses among the American troops during the war. Is it any less a shock to know that the army lost more days of service on account of venereal disease than from any other group of diseases?

What great pains we take in building some things,
and what little pains in building others!

A STRIKING AND THOUGHT-PROVOKING CONTRAST

A SPECTACULAR DEVICE

A gigantic double-barred cross, emblem of the tuberculosis campaign, which illuminated the windows of the American Radiator Company's building on West 40th Street, New York, attracted the attention of amusement-seeking crowds to the Christmas Seal Sale.

During the Great War the United States lost about 80,000 soldiers. During the same two years 180,000 people died of cancer in this country. Cancer is now killing one out of every 10 persons over forty years of age.

An unexpected form of statement occurring in a headline or title is perhaps the commonest way of employing novelty to get an article, an advertisement, or a booklet noticed. "Six Thousand Miles Alone at Five Years" is the headline of a folder of appeal distributed by the National Association of Travelers Aid Societies. The text relates the true story of five-year-old Peggy who traveled safely from California to England under the supervision of the Association. Other examples of striking titles are given in Chapter XI, Copy.[1]

Novelty is frequently introduced into money-raising campaigns to attract attention. The Girl Scouts at one time sold bricks at $10 each to obtain funds for a new national headquarters building. Playgrounds have been financed through auction sales of small plots of the land included in the playground space, each purchaser being expected to make out a deed of gift of his land to the responsible organization. The Children's Year, a period during which a group of women's organizations led by the Children's Bureau of the United States Department of Labor united in an endeavor to save 100,000 babies who otherwise would probably have died in that time, was an unusual method of attracting attention to an effort to secure more public health nurses and to establish more child hygiene departments. Many examples of novel ways of attracting attention are described in Chapter XV, Dramatic Methods.[2] The large scale on which a campaign is undertaken or the fact that the public has never been appealed to before on the subject is put forward in seeking interest and support. Figures or statements showing the extraordinary gravity of a situation or the large numbers of people affected by it are also much used.

FAMILIARITY AND ATTENTION

The apparent contradiction in suggesting both the strange and the familiar as means of attracting attention disappears when one

---

[1] See p. 189.   [2] See p. 259.

realizes that the arresting force in both instances is the union of the usual with the unusual. We do not notice familiar things in their accustomed places; we may, indeed, fail to see them even when we

"Sure! I'm all right—
I eat right"

Do you?

New York Tuberculosis Ass'n. Inc.
Ten East 39" Street   New York City

RECOGNITION A FACTOR IN ATTENTION

This poster is intended to catch the eye of the industrial worker by picturing men of types well known to him.

are looking for them. But a well-known person, object, or idea in a new or unusual situation easily attracts our attention.

People known to us, either personally or by reputation, attract our notice more quickly than do strangers. This power of attraction accounts for the frequent appearance of their names in the headlines of newspapers. If names or pictures cannot be appropriately used, the information or appeal may, perhaps, be presented through its connection with familiar types. In the poster shown on page 12, the artist has with great care reproduced the position, clothing, and expressions of men like those to whom the information on the poster is directed.

Allusion to a common experience is another use of the familiar as an attention-getting device. In a booklet of the United Hospital Fund of New York, called "Folks Around the Corner," the universal experience of illness is used to show the need of hospitals.

That family next door—the man who sits beside you in the theatre—the Browns, Caseys, Cohens—and Van Rocks too.

They have a common denominator. Illness. It levels as does no other factor in the complex existence of a great city.

If Tommy Casey gets tonsillitis, it becomes the concern of the Browns, the Cohens, the Van Rocks.

Why is this so? Because "bugs"—the tonsillitis brand, the influenza variety and a host of other destructive bacilli—travel. It's seldom they confine themselves to one home.

That is why the United Hospital Fund has adopted this slogan: "The Health of Each Is the Concern of All."

A series of posters on the avoidance of accidents issued by the Employers' Mutual Liability Insurance Company of Wausau, Wisconsin, attempted to attract the notice of factory employes by describing forms of carelessness in which they could recognize their own habits or impulses.

Saved a Minute

Olaf Olson, a La Crosse workman, was in a hurry to get home. Instead of going around through the door he took a short cut through the elevator pit. The descending elevator struck him.

Used Pin to Remove Splinter

George S. . . . was piling wood parts and ran a sliver into his finger. He picked it out with an ordinary brass pin and blood poisoning resulted.

Publicity workers trying to get attention for conditions in another part of the world find that unless the situations described

13

are very terrible or picturesque or dramatic they have great difficulty in overcoming the indifference due to lack of familiarity with the place and the people. Those who have visited a foreign country often return ardent supporters of work on its behalf and are much disconcerted to find that they cannot immediately interest persons who have never been there. When we are trying to promote a movement which relates to territory reaching far beyond the limits of our own neighborhood, we should do well in introducing the subject to show how the movement is related to local interests as well.

The greater news value of local information is indicated by the preference given to local news in the small city or country newspapers,[1] where it frequently takes precedence even over events of national importance.

Familiar phrases are also effective in arresting attention. "Once upon a time" begins the story teller, and the child's interest is immediately caught by the phrase which he has come to associate with pleasant anticipations. "Mother and Child Doing Well," the headline of an advertisement of the Metropolitan Life Insurance Company, is a common expression used to draw attention to information on how to protect maternity. The adaptation of fables, proverbs, and nursery rhymes combines admirably the old and the new. "A Salesman Is Known by the Customers He Keeps" was the prize-winning slogan in a contest for sayings to use in teaching salesmanship.

EASE OF COMPREHENSION

The first glance at a group of charts hanging on a wall may deter many persons from giving further attention to them or to the exhibit of which they are a part, because they seem hard to understand. The pamphlet received in the mail which appears to contain highly technical or difficult reading matter is laid aside until the recipient can find time to study it.

Methods of securing ease of comprehension form so large a part of the discussion throughout this book that we need not go into them here. It is perhaps enough to point out that the attention of most people is more readily obtained when their initial contact

[1] See p. 74.

14

with publicity, in whatever form it is presented, causes them to anticipate no difficulties in grasping its meaning.

STUDYING HABITS OF ATTENTION

In an earlier paragraph we referred to the fact that people acquire interests which largely determine what they will notice voluntarily. They not only form habits of paying attention to certain kinds of information, but they also look for it habitually in certain places. The reading habits of any group to be addressed offer a fruitful field of study for the publicity worker. So also do the meetings they attend.

A book recently published reported the successful working out of a plan of employe representation in industry.[1] Some of the employers for whom the volume contains important suggestions are the type of men who would pay little attention to ideas on this subject presented to them in book form, but who are regular readers of their trade papers; therefore abstracts of the report were supplied to leading trade journals.

The choice of a place for displaying exhibit material or for holding a meeting or an exposition may sometimes depend on whether or not people are accustomed to going there. Certain store windows are much noticed, perhaps because they have acquired a reputation for attractive displays. Certain buildings, because of the convenient location or the pleasant associations attached to them, gain popularity. A child welfare exhibition once held in an unused railway station several blocks from the busy center of an eastern city was poorly attended in spite of generous advertising, partly no doubt because people were not accustomed to go to this building, and partly because its location was off the beaten track.

Not only the place where people are likely to encounter information but also the circumstances are factors in planning its method of presentation. Almost always, there is some topic of the day which is receiving much newspaper attention and is a general subject for conversation. Bringing out the relation of one's information to this timely subject helps to get attention for it. The title, If Winter Comes, was used at the height of the popularity of the book

[1] Selekman, Ben M., Sharing Management with the Workers. Russell Sage Foundation, New York, 1924.

in an appeal for funds to aid an unemployed group during cold weather.

ATTRACTING ATTENTION ONLY THE FIRST STEP

For convenience we have discussed attracting attention as a distinct and independent procedure, but it should not be regarded as such in planning publicity. There is a tendency on the part of those who become absorbed in this first stage in the task to make cleverness or novelty an end in itself while the purpose for which attention is sought is forgotten. The search for unusual forms of expression, spectacular stunts, or striking designs may lead far afield from the simplicity and directness of approach to public interest which should be the main reliance of the social agency.

The safeguard of the publicity worker is in keeping always in mind that whatever device is employed for attracting attention must be appropriate to the purpose for which it is used, and must tie up directly with the method used in the second stage of the task, namely, holding attention.

CHAPTER II

HOLDING ATTENTION

THE distinction between attracting and holding attention with which we are concerned in this discussion involves the practical problem of keeping up the interest aroused by the initial contact; of writing our stories and articles so well that people will read them to the end instead of being satisfied with the headlines; of making the annual report so interesting that those receiving it will do more than glance hurriedly through it. Holding attention means keeping an audience from lapsing into drowsiness or thoughts of their own affairs; it means retaining the interest aroused by the spectacular nature of the drive, for example, so that people will continue throughout the year to read what appears in the newspapers on the subject of the campaign.

Some of the methods described as effective in attracting attention—for example, recognition of the familiar—are equally effective in holding it, while others—such as mechanical movement—quickly lose their power after curiosity about the device has been satisfied. The means which seem to us especially adapted to securing sustained interest are the creation of clear mental pictures, personal application of ideas, suspense, light or humorous treatment, personal contact, and variety or change.

CLEAR MENTAL PICTURES

Ease of comprehension is one of the biggest factors in sustained attention. In order to understand social information, the public must have clear and vivid mental pictures of the people, situations, and processes described. Attention quickly lapses when the phrases used are so unfamiliar or the ideas so obscure that the audience cannot turn them into mental pictures.

Often the persons who are to be benefited by social work belong to another world from that of those asked to help them. Jacob Riis recognized this separation by naming his book about New York's East Side, How the Other Half Lives. Many married

17

mothers suppose that the girl who has an illegitimate child is another kind of human being from themselves. The situations dealt with by social work are often unreal to the people to whom publicity is addressed. To many persons the term "child labor" creates a mental picture of nothing more arduous than running errands and performing other household chores; the life of a child working in a cotton mill or in the beet fields is beyond their imagination. Night work for women and overcrowded tenements are phrases bringing vivid pictures of misery to the minds of the initiated, but only blankness, or vague and distorted images to those who have not seen at first hand the unhappy existence of families burdened by these conditions.

Again, the methods and aims of social work and the phrases used to describe them are meaningless to many persons. "Rehabilitation of families," "occupational therapy," and "prevention of delinquency" are terms implying a number of concrete activities, yet wholly mysterious to the outsider.

Visualization. Skilful portrayal by means of pictures and demonstrations on the part of the social worker offers one way of making the conditions and causes with which he is concerned take the form of clear and accurate mental pictures.

The speaker and exhibitor may use models, slides, maps, motion pictures, or diagrams for this purpose; for printed matter we have photographs, cartoons, and sketches. All these mediums are discussed in this volume.

The motion picture has made a valuable contribution to the art of visualization, not only in presenting people and places, but in making otherwise incomprehensible processes easy to understand. Unhooking the Hookworm, produced by the International Health Board of the Rockefeller Foundation, and used with great success wherever hookworm disease is prevalent, is an excellent example of what the film can do to make a physical condition understandable.

Beginning with remarkable pictures of the embryo breaking out of the hookworm egg, the film next shows the scattering of embryos and eggs on the ground around privies and the larvæ entering the heel of a barefooted boy who happens to be walking where they are. Animated diagrams trace the progress of the larvæ through the body until they reach the intestines, where they attach themselves to the intestinal

18

There Must Be The Right Job For Us In This Big City
BUT HOW CAN WE FIND IT?
Vocational Service for Juniors
122 EAST 25th STREET

SKILFUL VISUALIZATION OF A PROBLEM

wall and grow to full size. Another picture shows the effect of the parasites on the blood. Then there are scenes in a physician's office, where a hookworm patient goes for examination and treatment; next the patient is shown in his home, taking the medicine that cures the disease. The film closes by emphasizing the rôle of the sanitary privy as the means of prevention.

In Baltimore, where an additional public playground was needed, a film was used as a means of presenting the situation to the City Council. It showed the congested section with children playing amid the dangers of the street, and in contrast, a public playground with children playing safely. Presented at a meeting of the City Council, it caught and held the attention of the members, and the playground appropriation was granted; whereas without the vivid portrayal of actual situations the project might have been postponed for consideration and possibly shelved altogether.

Conditions may be visualized by enacting them in play or exhibit form. Daddy Long Legs, a play dealing with the institutional life of children, has given thousands of persons a picture which has since become synonymous with the word "orphanage." At the time when a movement was on foot to abolish the inhuman cell block at Sing Sing, an exhibit taken around the state contained a life-sized model of a cell, and visitors consenting to be locked into it were able to realize its cramping dimensions and its insanitary and wretched furnishings.

Visual forms, however, are at best a small part of the means of giving information or championing a cause. Words are the tools employed most commonly and it is well worth while to cultivate the habit of selecting picture-making words and phrases. "It's a long rough road to motherhood down here" is the picturesque beginning of a description of the treatment from midwives before and during confinement endured by women in a rural district of the South. An article on the conquest of scarlet fever, carrying the vivid title "Another Germ Bites the Dust!" holds attention by such word sketches as this:

> Each child in the line—of assorted sizes and haircuts—held up a bared forearm. The school nurse helped the smaller ones roll up obstinate sleeves. Most of the arms showed a reddish spot, dime to dollar size. Into them the doctor injected a few drops of clear fluid.

"Now, that didn't hurt," he said, with a pat on a chubby cheek. About one child in seven who had no spot or a tiny one got only the pat. "We won't need you again," and to his secretary busily jotting down names and results, the doctor said, "negative."[1]

Specific versus General Information. The substitution of specific for general information sharpens the outline of the mental picture. If general statements are needed, then they should be accompanied by specific examples. When we read a few years ago the news that $4,000,000 was voted by Congress to send medical supplies to Russia, it probably made only a vague and fleeting impression on most of us because we cannot think in terms of such large cost for commodities we are accustomed to seeing or using in small quantities. The itemized description in the paragraphs below holds our attention and stirs our imagination.

Yesterday I saw a "prescription" sent over from Russia by the American doctor who directs the medical work there for Mr. Hoover's relief organization. The first item on it called for 300,000 small glass bottles for prescriptions. I asked the man in charge about it. "Haven't they got to have medicine bottles to put medicine in?" he growled reproachfully. That hadn't occurred to me. Everyone, I thought, had bottles.

You'd be interested in that prescription. Besides the bottles there were 140 tons of disinfectant, 6,000,000 aspirin tablets, 80,000 pounds of castor oil, 20,000 pairs of surgical forceps, 2,000,000 vaccination units, 9,000 hot water bottles, 350,000 safety pins, 18,000 hospital thermometers, 50,000,000 units of diphtheria antitoxin, 15,000 sets of baby clothing, 30,000 medicine droppers, 4,000,000 quinine pills.

That was the first prescription. The second was more simple. There was only one item on it—"150 complete drugstores."[2]

In its account of the case of Martin Taber, some time ago the New York World presented the horrors of peonage in convict camps so vividly that readers seemed almost to be seeing and hearing the travesties on justice, the brutality, and the coarseness that prevailed among them.

[1] Gruenig, Ernest, "Another Germ Bites the Dust!" *In* Collier's, New York, Oct. 4, 1924.

[2] Storey, Harry Powers, The You and Me in Russia. Russian Famine Fund, New York, 1922 (Out of print).

When we are dealing with abstractions it is worth searching for concrete expressions or examples that will make them real. A living wage for a factory girl, for example, in itself means nothing to the ordinary person, but when the sort of living possible on $8.00 a week is described, the shoddy clothing which quickly falls to pieces and has little warmth, the cheap, badly fitting shoes to stand in during eight or nine hours of hard work, the thin soup which her lunch money will buy, a "living wage" is no longer merely an abstract and uninteresting phrase.

PERSONAL APPLICATION OF IDEAS

Most people are practical in their thinking and grow impatient if a speech or article continues to discuss ideas at any great length without coming to some concrete application of the material either to their own interests or to some plan of action in which they can participate. In the midst of so much more distress and injustice than any one person can give attention to, people as a rule become interested more readily in the problems that are closely related to their own experience or affect the welfare of those in their immediate circle.

It is difficult to arouse interest in insanitary and demoralizing conditions in jails, partly, no doubt, because of a widespread belief that wrong-doers deserve to suffer. If once it is brought home to those who are indifferent about the matter that the safety of their families and their community is endangered by these crime-breeding conditions, they may be aroused sufficiently to go to see for themselves what their local jail is like, and to listen to the details of plans for reform. Once they have come directly in contact with the situation, they are more likely to become interested in the prisoners on their own account.

The New York Times, in reporting the response of the public to its Christmas appeal for the " 100 Neediest Cases," says:

> Some of the letters disclosed that a certain case would strike an instant response, even though others seemingly were in distress more dire, because of some parallel in the life of the contributor or in the life of a friend. Often a writer would tell of a fact in his own experience and in so doing would say that he forwarded his donation specifically for "Dan" or "John" or for a widowed mother of three because the reading

21

of the particular case had conjured out of the past some episode in the life of the writer. . . .

The social worker's own vision of the particular end toward which he is working often blinds him to the fact that people with other interests cannot see the practical application of the idea as easily as he can. One of the problems, then, in holding attention is to show a definite connection between the subject of the publicity and the interests of the audience.

THE ELEMENT OF SUSPENSE

"How will it turn out?" We follow the development of story, play, or contest until we obtain the answer to this question. One way, then, of holding attention is by introducing the element of suspense or by taking advantage of it, if it already exists.

Suspense in Stories. The experiences occurring in social work are full of suspense. Tangles in family situations are seldom straightened out instantly and often in the course of the process both workers and clients wonder if they ever will be unraveled. Yet in most of the stories and plays based on social work the difficulties presented are solved with a too remarkable speed and smoothness. The interest of listener or reader is not sufficiently held by uncertainty as to the outcome. The element of suspense which is lacking might in many instances have been easily introduced. How effectively it can be used is shown in the following story of "Samuel" circulated by the National Kindergarten Association.

> Samuel was four, and he was going to kindergarten in the morning. He was in bed now, but he was too happy to go to sleep just yet. Clutched tightly in his arms were his new brown shoes. It had been an exciting moment when Daddy had handed him the package. He had been waiting and hoping for a long time. Boys didn't go to school without shoes, his mother had said. How hard it had been to wait! But now, tomorrow, O, tomorrow!

There follows the description of a dream in which one of the new brown shoes is confused with a rabbit. Samuel has heard that sometimes there are rabbits in kindergartens. In his dream he hopes there will be one in the kindergarten to which he is going. The reader hopes so too.

22

The morning sun was shining when the boy awoke. A yellow beam fell across a brown shoe. He saw it. O, joy! Kindergarten! Had he been there? No, that must have been a dream; but he was going. Two hours later the little brown shoes were carrying a beaming Samuel up the stone steps of an imposing building.

The reader is glad he is there. He reads on to see how the child likes it; to see if there is a rabbit.

Across the street the big clock stared at the doorway through which they had passed, struck nine, and ticked on with perfect unconcern until the quarter hour was reached, when the door again opened. Well might the clock stare now, for the pair of brown shoes reappeared. Why were they coming out? And why did their little owner and his mother look so depressed? What had happened? Just this: Some one had said, *"We have no more room."*

Samuel had seen the happy children but had not been invited to join them; he had gazed upon the flowers, the gold fishes, and the little white rabbit, but had not had a chance to go near them; he had listened to the song of the Flag but had not been allowed to stay to learn it. He could not understand. The door had been opened for him to go, but he did not want to go. His mother had taken him by the hand and led him out. Now they had shut the door. He looked down at his little brown shoes, his lip quivered, and the tears came.

Yet it was just as the people of our country have decreed. Only one child in nine may go to kindergarten. Little Samuel was one of the four million who may not have that privilege.

The reader is greatly affected by little Samuel's bitter disappointment and it is safe to assume that he does not put the booklet down until he has read the final sentence asking his support for a bill to make possible more kindergartens.

Suspense in Meetings. Stories used as illustrative material in speeches are usually too short to admit of any great degree of suspense. However, suspense may be brought into a talk by some such simple means as withholding promised information until the end; by presenting some striking result and then showing how it was obtained; or even by stating the number of reasons for certain deductions and checking off each point as it is made. A method pursued by Dr. W. W. Peter in a talk to a Chinese audience on health is given below:

Dr. Peter introduced suspense into his talk by putting together a mechanical device to illustrate the growth of an idea. He showed first a glass box in which, he said, the light of National Health would shine as soon as the box was placed on the proper foundation. "Can you name one stone?" he asked. "Money," the audience replied. A box labeled with the Chinese character for money was brought out and the glass box placed upon it, but no light appeared. So a box labeled "Special Health Laws," which Dr. Peter explained briefly, was brought to place under "Money." Still no results. Next came a larger, heavier box labeled "Education," explained as meaning trained leadership. Still the light did not appear. But when the fifth box, "Public Opinion," was brought and set in place as the base for all the others, the light of National Health shone at the top as promised.[1]

The program of a meeting can be arranged to create expectancy by keeping the best feature until the end.

At a dinner meeting where the winners in a contest were to present to the audience the plans for which they had been awarded prizes, the chairman reversed the usual order of procedure by calling first upon those who received honorable mention; then in order, the third and second prize winners, reserving for the last speech of the evening that of the winner of the first prize. Very few persons left before the end of the program although it lasted several hours. If a program includes taking a written vote on some subject, the announcement of the result may be withheld until the close of the meeting.

Suspense in Campaigns. When campaign leaders set a goal to be reached within a given number of days, the public is curious to know whether it can be achieved. The huge clock face or thermometer used to record the progress of collections and pledges is a familiar object. Throughout Safety Week, when a city proposes to finish the week without the occurrence of a single death from a street accident, we read the campaign news each day to make sure that so far nothing has happened to defeat this purpose. Newspaper readers follow with keen interest the doings of a weight-reducing squad, to learn whether or not the members will succeed in losing the number of pounds set as the objective. A sum of money offered to some cause on condition that an equal sum be

[1] Routzahn, Evart G., The Health Show Comes to Town. Russell Sage Foundation, New York, 1920, pp. 19–20.

raised adds dramatic interest to the task of raising the required amount.

We do not mean to say that setting a goal will of itself produce the thrill of suspense. Success in keeping up suspense requires that the campaign shall have life and activity, that something shall happen, and that the public be kept informed about the details. Also, it is necessary that the proposed objective shall be possible of attainment yet difficult to reach. Recently an objective was announced for a year's campaign, and later acknowledged to have been proposed not with any hope of reaching it but in the belief that merely naming an impressive goal would stir people's imagination. But people are not easily stirred by ideals which they consider visionary. Many of the aims toward which social movements are directed, such as completely to wipe out a disease, seem too hopeless or too far distant to arouse interest through suspense.

When the probability of complete attainment is too remote to hold attention, interest may well be centered on some intermediate objective which can be realized in a comparatively short time. An ambitious purpose is by all means worth presenting as an inspiration but it needs to be approached by milestones along the way, each one being made the goal of a particular effort. We may not believe, as a recent slogan prophesied, that tuberculosis will be the next disease to go, but we may enter with enthusiasm into a campaign to discover all the existing cases in our town and get them under treatment.

Light or Humorous Treatment

The funny picture or story used to attract attention also arouses the expectation of continued entertainment. So long as the humor is sustained, people will continue to pay attention. Irrelevant humor used to introduce the subject does not hold attention long.

Unless the story or witty saying serves the purpose of the speech, it is likely to distract attention. The practice of dragging in stories without connection, or with only a fictitious connection, though very common, is one to "make the judicious grieve." . . .

Young speakers will do well to note that the repetition of "stories" is not the only way to add humor to a speech. It may spring from the

25

whimsical turn of a phrase, from placing in juxtaposition an opponent's incongruous arguments, from a comical bit of narration or description, without going at all outside the proper materials of the speech, or checking its movement.[1]

A similar warning about the use of humor is given in the following:

Humor for our purpose may be defined as a light and good-natured way of making a point, but bear in mind that it must make the point. It is the kind of advertising that should be done only by those who know how to do it, for nothing is so lamentable as a humorous ad gone wrong.[2]

Light and good-natured treatment is appropriate to otherwise unwelcome advice or warnings, especially in matters of disease and accidents, subjects from which people turn away as not being pleasant to think about. "The Wisdom of Professor Happy," made up of droll health epigrams and illustrations, issued by the American Child Health Association, is used in calendars and booklets for young people. A certain group of high school students, who would probably have become bored by too much serious preaching about hygiene, enjoyed these sayings so much that they were inspired to try their skill at similar cartooning and pun making about open windows, daily exercise, and wholesome food.[3]

The pictures on page 27 show two pages from a primer issued by the People's Institute of Brooklyn, which tell in light vein of the work of a community center.

Whimsical characters are sometimes introduced into cartoons, stories, or motion pictures to enliven otherwise dull subjects. The Health Twins at Work is the name of a cartoon film produced by the American Social Hygiene Association. Two sprightly and absurd little figures attack the problem of disease. They drag the culprits, representing various diseases, into court and have them sent to prison. The prison bars fade into a conventional diagram with bars of different heights to represent mortality rates.

---

[1] Winans, James A., Public Speaking. Century Co., New York, Revised 1917, pp. 131, 133.

[2] Calkins, Ernest Elmo, "How Calkins and Holden Use Humorous Advertising." *In* Direct Advertising, Boston, vol. 9, no. 3, 1923, p. 8.

[3] "The Sayings of Three Wise Schools," by students of Central, Humboldt and Johnson High Schools, St. Paul, Minn.

Here are The People, their day's work is
through:

Hundreds of thousands with nothing to do:

People   People   People

"   "   "

"   "   "

Nothing provided, then where will they roam?

One thing is certain, -- but few will stay home!

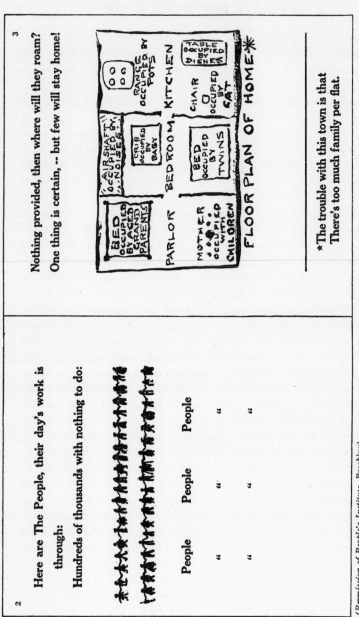

*The trouble with this town is that
There's too much family per flat.

(Permission of People's Institute, Brooklyn)

LIGHT AND HUMOROUS TREATMENT OF A RECREATION PROBLEM

The droll rhymes and pictures in the Community Center Primer from which these pages were taken amuse us and hold our interest to the end.

27

By vigorous hammering the twins reduce considerably the bars representing tuberculosis, infantile diarrhea, and diphtheria. The bar representing venereal diseases is so high that the top is out of sight. The twins scurry about trying all sorts of implements to break it and finally climb to the top and pound it down with the hammers of "Public Opinion."

Social workers often find humor in their own experiences, many of which can be used without any violation of confidence. It is nearly always safe to repeat the amusing sayings of children. Clare M. Tousley has used in talks the story of a boy to whose mother a district visitor had promised a skirt. The mother sent the boy to the Charity Organization Society of New York to tell the visitor the proper size. The visitor was out when he called, but when she returned she found his message. A long, grubby top string lay in a perfect circle on her desk and written on the blotter beneath was the boy's note: "Dear Missus, Please this is the size of me mudders shape." Jane Addams, whose good sense of humor never fails her, frequently points and enlivens her talks with amusing stories drawn from her own experience.

Personal Contact

First-hand knowledge gives a sense of reality to situations, people, and places, which telling about them, or even showing pictures of them cannot produce. Persons who have had some form of direct contact with social work are more likely to pay attention continuously to information about it than those who have not.

The New York State Department of Markets in an effort to interest a group of women in better terminal market facilities has at different times conducted tours at night of the docks and warehouses where food supplies are received. Those who went on these excursions saw endless carloads of vegetables being unloaded on the piers, and the inadequate facilities for distributing such enormous quantities of perishable food at the required speed were pointed out to them.

Prison conditions in Georgia were made vivid to a group of almost 300 citizens of that state a few years ago through a well-worked out plan of visits by which committees in each county actually saw the inside of the jails.

28

Similar in purpose and effect are the come and see tours, know your city tours, and school visiting days sometimes included as features of intensive campaigns for civic betterment.[1]

Demonstrations are methods of bringing processes or situations to the audience instead of taking the audience to see the processes. Babies are examined at a county fair or an exposition in a series of rooms constructed of glass so that visitors may watch and have explained to them the weighing, measuring, and testing which go on daily in community health stations. In remote rural districts implements for more efficient housekeeping and farming are carried in trains or trucks to one community after another and demonstrations given of their use.

Volunteer service, since it keeps the volunteer and usually his or her family too in actual touch with social problems, is also effective in holding interest. In one instance, a large number of women took part in an effort to check up all the unregistered births in a city, through the search of the parish registers and house-to-house visits. Other groups of women have made studies of school buildings in their communities, filling out questionnaires which sought information in regard to the position of blackboards, the relation of windows to desks, sanitary conditions in toilets, and so on. A men's club assigned its members to interview the boys in a graduating class regarding their plans for continuing in school or going to work.

Variety or Change

Along with whatever else is done to hold interest, change or variety in presentation is essential. This need for variety is complicated by the fact that the problems requiring the aid of social publicity recur constantly. Attacks must be renewed on insanitary conditions; repeated efforts must be made to form right habits in eating or in taking daily exercise. Organizations giving service or relief have much the same story to tell each year in annual reports or in their appeals for funds. The delays in reaching any objective—in obtaining the passage of a law, for example—make it necessary to explain many times about the extent of the situation and its evils. Woman suffrage was so many years in coming that the ingenuity of the leaders of the movement was

[1] For further discussion, see p. 273.

taxed to find varied ways in which to create new interest in propaganda for its support.

Another point to be taken into account is that repetition is needed to get information remembered. We may hear a name or see a face several times before the impression becomes fixed so that we will recognize either again. If publicity deals with more or less complex ideas or new ones, repetition is doubly necessary.

Yet continuous harping on the same tale of suffering, reiterations of the same slogan, the same arguments, dull the sensitiveness of the public. How then can we repeat facts and pleas over and over again, and still vary our presentation so as to hold interest?

Change of Emphasis. By shifting the point of attack from one aspect of a subject to another, we may keep it before the public without monotonous repetition. In the child labor campaign, for instance, we may at one time place the emphasis on the situation of the child himself—the cruelty of robbing him of the chance to play, of confining him for long tedious hours at monotonous toil; at another time on the menace to the state because of the ignorance and illiteracy which inevitably accompany child labor and render men and women unfit to become good citizens; again, the effect of child labor on the health of the children may be described. We may publish the names of prominent supporters and opponents of the child labor movement, telling of their personalities, their activities for and against child labor laws, and the reasons they give for taking the stand which they do.

In a continuous campaign to make the streets safe we may center attention for a time on the way in which pedestrians cross the street; another period may be devoted to campaigning against speeding by motorists on city streets; another to instruction in getting on and off cars and buses. Certain information which needs repeating may be included incidentally with whatever aspect of the subject is under consideration.

Familiar ideas dressed in new clothing take on a new interest. Safety is presented now as the subject of a poster contest; again in dramatic form in a motion picture, play or parade; at another time in a series of stories from real life. In the intensive campaign there is a new event featuring the same idea every day. In meet-

30

ings, people will pay attention to the same facts told by different speakers, then pictured in a series of slides, and afterward printed in the folders distributed at the door. Each form of presentation gives the information the appearance of freshness.

A change in the style of writing also gives variety. This is illustrated by the different form in which the same subject is treated in various sections of the newspaper in news stories, editorials, and special articles.

Changing the form does not mean a mere search for novelty. Restless and meaningless change from one device to another is largely a waste of effort.

CHAPTER III

OBTAINING GOODWILL

THE service rendered by a social agency is the soundest basis of public approval. Favorable opinion of a proposed course of action is most worth having when it rests on conviction that the proposition deserves support. The part of publicity in seeking this well-grounded goodwill is to secure intelligent understanding of the service or the program for which approval is sought. The process involved, is, in the main, one of making information so interesting that it holds attention, and of presenting it so clearly that distinct mental pictures result. The means of thus getting information understood have already been described.

Consideration of facts is, however, only part of the basis of public opinion. Indeed widespread goodwill may exist in relation t⌐ ⌐ome movement to which its well-wishers pay slight attention. The warmth of feeling held by the public toward an organization is often based on little besides a vague realization that it is doing good. Conversely, many prejudices against organizations and ideas are firmly held by persons not at all well informed about them. These factors in opinion also need to be reckoned with in planning publicity.

Because people are so often thoughtless or hurried in forming their judgments, social agencies have an added obligation to interpret their work to the public with scrupulous honesty and frankness.

Publicity workers, quite unintentionally, sometimes publish inaccurate or exaggerated statements. Dr. Charles V. Chapin warns public health workers that in their eagerness to influence public conduct, they make absurd claims: "A wash pail and scrubbing brush are pictured as keeping tuberculosis from the house. Breathed air is represented as being loaded with poison."[1]

A wrong impression may be given by presenting only one side of a situation or by unduly emphasizing that phase of it which most easily wins sympathy. Because people contribute money more

---

[1] "Evolution of Preventive Medicine." *In* Journal of American Medical Association, Chicago, vol. 76, Jan. 22, 1921, p. 222.

readily for cure than for prevention, a health organization making an appeal describes only its care of those who are sick, even though the solicited funds are largely intended for preventive work.

Annual reports and letters of appeal sometimes cite exceptional cases and achievements as though they were typical. Again, a success is too often reported with no hint of the struggle and ineffectual efforts that preceded it. To the listener or reader such a glowing and unrelieved account of achievement may seem unreal.

In the process of reducing a considerable volume of information to a few statements, it is easy to fall into exaggeration. This is especially likely to happen when a writer is striving for dramatic effect as in the following:

> Again we bring to you the cry of the children! the soul famished little ones of our great city who live in the midst of ignorance, sin and degradation.

The personified symbol of a health association is made to express these extravagant and wholly unjustified claims:

> I am the bond that keeps intact the home, and within my protecting arms are kept safe the lives of little children.
> I am the guaranty of the morale of a united people.

In an attempt to create a sense of personal responsibility in each reader, the writer of an appeal for vacation funds follows his description of the yearning of a child of a city's tenement district for the country by the imperative suggestion, "Just dreams, that's all—unless *you* make them come true." The reader of this appeal knows that hundreds of copies have been distributed and he may feel that that child's holiday could not possibly depend solely upon his personal gift.

We should, of course, strive for accuracy of statement and sincerity in the form of expression as a matter of principle. Moreover, while undoubtedly exaggeration is sometimes effective in winning a favorable response, simplicity, frankness, and moderation are more likely to be convincing.

The Need of an Organization to Be Known

While it does not and should not always follow that to be known is to be approved, obviously an organization or movement must become known before it can be favorably regarded. Making a name, a phrase, or a slogan familiar to the public is one of the functions of publicity and is accomplished chiefly by causing it to be seen or heard frequently.

Short names are most likely to be used in newspaper headlines where they have an excellent chance to be seen. A newspaper man has called attention to the tendency of newspapers to use short names and when possible to substitute nicknames or abbreviations for long names. Thus Theodore Roosevelt was called "T.R." Headlines referred to our soldiers in the World War as "The Yanks." The Republican party is the "G.O.P."

The Red Cross, Boy Scouts, Hull House, Near East Relief, Salvation Army are examples of short, distinctive, and easily remembered names of social organizations. Many with longer names are known by initials as: Y.M.C.A., W.C.T.U., C.O.S., and S.P.C.C. Those who have much occasion to speak of the Y.M.C.A. shorten the title still further, calling it the "Y."

On the other hand, names like the Society for the Prevention and Control of Communicable Diseases are distinct liabilities in so far as publicity is concerned. The National Association for the Study and Prevention of Tuberculosis found it advantageous to shorten its name to the National Tuberculosis Association. One important state organization engaged in public health work is handicapped by a name containing 13 words and 76 letters. A name easy to remember, if otherwise suitable, is an asset in obtaining recognition.

Slogans. Slogans, catch phrases, or words that stick in the mind help to make ideas familiar and also to create associations that may be favorable or unfavorable. "A Safe and Sane Fourth," "Every Child in School," "Golden Rule Sunday," "The Short Ballot" are phrases having an easily recognized significance, and likely to be remembered. Slogans should be selected with caution because an interpretation not intended may color the public's whole attitude toward the movement for which they stand. Thus "The City Beautiful," a phrase used in the earlier days of town improvement and city planning, still confuses some people who think that a city plan is largely concerned with the improved appearance of streets, homes, and open spaces, and not with such primary elements as

34

the laying out of streets, transit facilities, the location of parks, public buildings, and industries.

Emblems. The publicity value of an emblem or symbol lies in its ability to catch the eye and to fix itself permanently in the memory. Striking in color and design, it is more conspicuous than the name and so is noticed more easily. An emblem may be used on posters, letterheads, poster stamps, advertisements, uniforms, and banners. When it is seen it tends to call to mind whatever is believed or felt about the movement for which it stands.

Emblems may establish their significance solely by long use and association, but in choosing them it is often possible and always desirable to select something symbolic of the work of the organization. The ship on the cover of the Survey is a symbol of exploration, typifying observations in the world of social service.

INSPIRING CONFIDENCE

People of prominence, who at the same time have the confidence of the public, give prestige to whatever cause they endorse and their names carry to many persons the assurance that the project is a sound one. Busy persons, finding it impossible to inform themselves fully about all the causes they are asked to support, are likely to run over the list of the sponsors of each enterprise to see "who is for it."

Publicity can do much to inspire confidence in an organization by making it known that trusted and competent persons are responsible for its policies and work. The methods of doing this are so generally known that they need only be mentioned: names of boards of directors and honorary committee members are listed on letterheads and other printed matter; well-known leaders of a movement are made its spokesmen at meetings and in published interviews; official proclamations and letters expressing approval are issued by the President, governors, and mayors in connection with intensive campaigns.

Under the headline "Famous Men Lend Support to Boy Scout Organization" the New York Times tells of well-known men actively interested in the movement.

To the long list of distinguished honorary members of the Scout organization there have recently been added notable names from varied

EMBLEMS THAT TYPIFY THE SERVICES OF SOCIAL ORGANIZATIONS

36

Yes, Sara, "Quite Glad"

Sara, in her quaint, grown-up way said: "Things don't seem fair very often, do they? But you do help to even them up. I hope you're quite glad of that."

She really was saying that to *employes here* who helped the hospitals to back Sara — and a good many others, when they gave to the 1925 Community Fund.

July, 1925

Harrisburg Welfare Federation and Community Fund

Welfare Building   ::   ::   ::   Second and South Streets

EXPRESSION OF APPRECIATION TO INCREASE GOODWILL

One of a series of posters displayed in a factory to thank the workers for contributions to a community fund and to show them some of the results toward which they have contributed.

House organs or news bulletins are sent by some organizations to members or givers. These publications go to people whose sympathetic understanding of social work is as greatly to be desired, and not so easy to secure, as their occasional gifts of money. They best serve their purpose of maintaining goodwill if they are brief and well written.

Annual reports also keep supporters in touch with an organization and are more generally used than house organs for this purpose. Those who issue annual reports appear to waver between making them an accounting or progress report addressed to friends, or an explanation of aims and methods addressed chiefly to strangers. The reports best suited to fostering goodwill are friendly and somewhat informal in manner. They tell the news of the year as though to members of the family circle, yet so clearly and untechnically that it is of interest to outsiders as well.

Including the names of givers makes reports seem more personal to those who appear on the lists. More personal and gratifying to the giver, however, than the appearance of his name in a report is the friendly letter of thanks which tells a little of what his own gift accomplished. Family welfare societies sometimes address appeals by mail to limited lists of persons who are asked to help a particular family. Those who respond receive letters some months later telling them of the progress made in re-establishing the independence of the family. The District Nurse Association in Providence, Rhode Island, invites individuals and firms to pay for the service of a single nurse or of all its nurses for one day, suggesting the selection of the birthday of the donor or some other anniversary that he would like to commemorate. A report of the work accomplished on the day chosen is then sent to each donor. These are ways of building goodwill which do more than merely please contributors, since the reports increase their understanding of the work itself.

OVERCOMING PREJUDICE

As has been said, it is the ideas people associate with a movement that count most in building up lasting goodwill. Social workers are trying to gain public approval for probation as a method of treating certain types of offenders; for placing dependent children in private homes rather than in institutions; for improving stan-

39

dards of living by providing living wages, more leisure time, and proper housing.

These proposals are opposed to long-established ways of thinking; loss of freedom is regarded as a just punishment for law breakers; adopted children are not supposed to turn out well; the individual is expected to rise above his circumstances and environment.

Almost every social movement has some misunderstanding to overcome! Organized charity is accused of being mechanical, of spending too much for overhead expenses. A reporter for a New York paper asked five persons whom he chanced to meet their opinion of organized charity. Four out of the five said there was too much red tape, echoing without doubt, a widely held belief. A sanatorium is sometimes thought of as "a place where you go to die." Work with immigrants encounters the argument that "nobody made them come here and if they can't get along they ought to go back where they came from." Attempts to abolish child labor bring out the assertion that work keeps boys and girls out of mischief, and the fact that many wealthy men got their start in street trades is supposed to prove that it is a good thing for boys to be newsboys or bootblacks. The effort to raise the scale of wages for girls has been met by the claim that they work only for pin money.

Some of the prejudices which social workers encounter have been deliberately created by opposing propagandists. One method used is the subtle and effective one of causing people to associate an organization or movement with something generally disapproved. A proposed legislative measure needs only to be referred to as Bolshevist to be regarded with suspicion. At a time when people were greatly shocked by newspaper reports that women had been made national property in Russia, a proposed child labor amendment was said by its enemies to be intended to bring about "the nationalization of children" in the United States. The persons who support a welfare measure are described by the opposition as "well meaning," a term which has become equivalent to impractical and visionary. "Uplifter" is a word that carries an implication of self-righteousness and an attitude of superiority which is generally resented. Opponents of social legislation often apply the term derisively to those who are trying to promote good measures.

Changing Bad Impressions to Good. It becomes necessary, then, to substitute new ideas for those already fixed in the public mind— a task much more difficult than that of establishing associations where none has yet been formed.

We cannot get far in the effort to obtain goodwill without recognizing how important these associations are, whether they are deliberately created or whether they come about through misunderstandings.

A method of changing opinion about social work is to show that aims which the public already approves may be achieved by the means which social workers employ. Social service exchanges have been trying to persuade schools, churches, Sunday schools, and various clubs to avoid duplication in their Christmas giving to needy families by registering with the exchange the names of families on their lists. The proposal is regarded with disfavor because it sounds like substituting cold efficiency for the friendly spirit of Christmas. "After all," people say, "what does it matter if a family gets two baskets at Christmas when they don't have enough to eat most of the time?" A letter addressed by the New Haven Social Service Exchange to school principals, ministers, and others urging them to register with the Exchange recognizes and sympathizes with this attitude. The opening sentence disarms the critics by showing that to use the Exchange will "make this the merriest Christmas for all the boys and girls that they have ever known." The writer explains that "It isn't so bad that some get more than they need, as it is that some do not get enough," and adds, "Let's try to even things up a bit better."

The Charity Organization Society of New York, accepting the current belief that there is much red tape connected with relief, published an article called "Red Tape to the Rescue," in which this same red tape was shown to have saved lives and restored unfortunate families to self-support. The people who think immigrants ungrateful and indifferent to our institutions are reminded that the immigrants are "Americans by choice and not by chance"; that they came here believing in our ideals and wishing to become good Americans.

41

Misunderstandings such as we have enumerated have become crystallized because we have not taken the trouble to find them out and correct them early enough. Sometimes they can be anticipated. The Cleveland Community Fund in one of its campaigns forestalled criticism of the increased amount of money for which it asked by adopting the slogan "The Community Fund Serving More Needs More." Remedies advertised by quacks cannot easily gain wide credence in communities where sound health education has taught the public to distrust exaggerated claims of miraculous cures.

The methods of the "inquiring reporter" who asks citizens chosen at random for expressions of opinion on questions of general interest might well be applied or adapted on a larger scale in an effort to find out what opinions are commonly held in regard to a given movement. In Ohio a few years ago, in an attempt to discover the attitudes of different sorts of people in regard to social work, about 100 persons were interviewed who had no affiliations with social organizations.[1] This same inquiring method might perhaps be applied more profitably to getting information about a more specific topic. The weeks following an intensive campaign which has brought an idea or a movement before many people would be a good time during which to make a canvass of public sentiment and intelligence regarding it. Certainly, any scheme successful in obtaining a genuine cross-section of opinion, uncolored by the desire to be polite, will be of inestimable value in helping to decide what information and what methods of presentation will do most to establish the basis of understanding essential to intelligent goodwill.

[1] For both questions and answers, see Bing, Mrs. Lucia Johnson, "What the Public Thinks of Social Work." *In* Proceedings of the National Conference of Social Work (Fiftieth Anniversary Session held in Washington), Columbus, Ohio, 1923, pp. 483–487.

CHAPTER IV

OBTAINING A RESPONSE

AN AUDIENCE of high school girls, interested in a demonstration of the merits of proper shoes, may agree heartily that the shoes are sensible; but they are not fashionable nor attractive, and that settles the matter. The girls will not wear them. "Mrs. Brown" has heard with approval the arguments against night work for women presented by a speaker at her club; yet in spite of her serious intention to do it, she fails to carry out the speaker's suggestion to write a letter to her legislator urging the passage of a night work law. "Mr. Brown" has read various publications advising him to have an annual health examination and is convinced that it is a good idea, nevertheless he makes no appointment with his physician.

It does not necessarily follow, then, that when publicity has aroused interest and approval it will also win a favorable response. Yet this is, after all, its main task. While taking a particular step toward the goal, such as getting people interested or obtaining their approval, may be all that is required of a given speech or article or even of a given year's work, the thing that counts ultimately is that those who are inclined to follow advice or respond to appeals do so without delay; that girls shall *wear* sensible shoes, not merely approve them; that women aroused over evils like night work will make their indignation count by urging their representatives to enact measures to abolish them.

PLANNING THE APPEAL

In order to obtain a response after a person has been convinced of the value of an appeal, it is necessary to stir the emotions or the intelligence strongly enough to touch the springs of action. While we cannot foresee all of the many and complex elements which may enter into the response to a given suggestion, we do know something of the ways in which conduct is motivated. We know that it is influenced by such factors as age, habit, occupation, nationality, and experience. A group of young girls will probably

43

care more about their appearance than about their health, and good looks and style rather than common sense are the qualities that influence them in the selection of shoes. We know that habit is one of the strongest of the controlling forces in conduct, and that a great deal of prodding may be necessary before Mr. Brown will be stirred to change his custom of going to the doctor only when ill. We know that unless people are eager to follow a particular course of action they will allow even quite simple obstacles to stand in their way. It might be an effort for Mrs. Brown to compose a letter to her representative—perhaps, too, she may have to go to some trouble to learn his name. If the social agency making the appeal offers to give in writing to her and the other clubwomen the information they need to use, they are much more likely to send the suggested letter.

The examination of printed matter—letters, cartoons, posters, and campaign plans—shows what appeals to action are used in social publicity. Unfortunately we have but little tested evidence of the effectiveness of any particular appeal in obtaining results. We may, however, venture opinions or quote those of others as to whether or not present practice agrees with what is known about motives of conduct.

FEAR AS A MOTIVE

The fear of disease, accident, and death naturally suggests itself as a motive which will induce people to strive to avoid such calamities.

"On Guard against Your Deadliest Enemy—Pneumonia" is a warning on a placard telling how to prevent this disease. A widely used window display produced by the Illinois Tuberculosis Association read as follows:

The Chances Are

20 to 1   You have an unsuspected tuberculosis infection.
1 to 9   You will be killed by tuberculosis.
1 to 6   You now have tuberculosis in an active form.
75 to 1   You will recover from tuberculosis if you begin the fight in time.
1 to 3   You will die of tuberculosis if you die between the ages of 15 and 40.

"They Are Dead" is the gloomy title of a black bordered folder giving death-rates from avoidable diseases. Formerly, in the tuberculosis movement, it was common to display disease-ravaged lungs preserved in alcohol. Hideous pictures of persons with small-pox are used in booklets advising vaccination. A state department of health sent the following grim warning to mothers of new born babies:

> Every year in this state almost 10,000 babies under one year of age sicken and die. Think what this means!

The figures quoted on page 11 are used not only to attract attention by their unusual size, but also to arouse in readers the fear that they, too, if they are not careful, may become victims of these widespread diseases.

Disadvantages of Using Fear as a Motive. Under some circumstances an appeal to fear may be the only means of overcoming indifference to danger, but there are valid objections to its use. The attempt to arouse fear is often unsuccessful. We question the effectiveness of the cartoon showing death lurking behind the spitter to suggest that he scatters destruction wherever he goes, and of another in which a large fly with death-dealing bombs attached to its feet hovers over the baby's crib. Such suggestions must seem either ludicrous or puzzling to those who regard spitting as a commonplace act and to whom the presence of house flies is a familiar condition survived by countless babies.

Again, the appeal to fear is generally useless in cases where the dire consequences are in the future, as they are so often in disease producing conditions. Dr. John H. Stokes says in regard to the appeal to fear in the campaign against venereal diseases:

> The belief is exceedingly common that the fear of acquiring syphilis or gonorrhea, if widely enough spread, will deter those who would otherwise seek unsocial sexual gratification. No unequivocal answer to the argument can be offered. On one side of the question, however, it can be given as the experience of many workers in this field, myself among the number, that the popular impression is a delusion. As a student of this question for a number of years, and at times a speaker upon it, I have been unable to convince myself that fear stands effectively between a man and the gratification of his sexual desire. Of many well-informed sexual offenders that have passed through my

45

hands, I can scarcely recall one who did not believe himself skillful enough to evade trouble, or the possessor of some talismanic key to a situation or who did not go ahead, risk or no risk, in response to imperious desire.[1]

Aside from its doubtful efficacy, there is a positive objection to the implanting of fear. There is always a danger that instead of arousing a sense of caution, which is desirable, one may cause morbid fears not easily overcome. The writer who appeals to fear as a motive usually offers what he considers to be adequate means of removing the cause; but actually, the remedies offered are not always available to every person in whom fear is aroused.

PLEASURABLE FEELING

Harry L. Hollingworth speaks of the "feeling tone," by which he means "the pleasantness or unpleasantness which accompanies our perception of objects."

> The feeling of pleasantness is accompanied by expansive, open, appropriative bodily attitudes, and by actual movements toward the agreeable stimulus. Under these conditions stimuli effect easy entrance to the higher levels, make strong impressions and are long remembered. The pleasant impression tends to persist in consciousness, long after the original stimulus has been removed.
> The feeling of unpleasantness, on the contrary, is accompanied by refractile, conflicting, or evasive movements, the organism tends to shrink away from the stimulus rather than move toward it. . . . The feeling tone of an advertisement, as of any other object, will influence not only the amount of attention it receives but its persistence in consciousness as well, and it follows that the reaction to the appeal will also involve the article in the interest of which the appeal is made.[2]

That social workers are beginning to realize this difference in the effects of pleasant and unpleasant impressions is indicated by the decrease in the tendency to try to frighten people into doing what they should. The earlier literature of advice on health was full of "Don'ts" and these are still used in circumstances where positive suggestions which would be more efficacious are available.

[1] Today's World Problem in Disease Prevention. U.S. Public Health Service, Washington, 1919, pp. 106–107.
[2] Advertising and Selling. D. Appleton and Co., New York, 1913, pp. 139–140.

A COMPELLING APPEAL

The joyous note in this illustration of crippled children who have been cured or improved is a spur to giving because it suggests that a gift brings not only health but happiness.

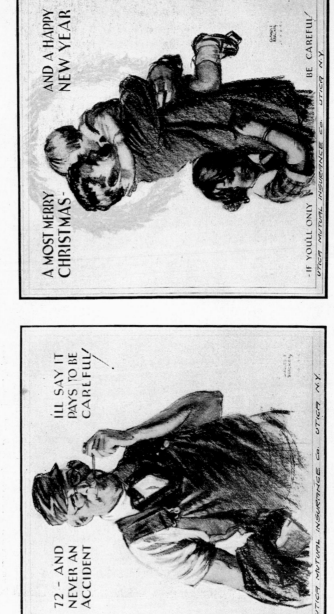

POSTERS THAT OFFER STRONG INCENTIVES TO PRACTICE CAUTION

Whereas in the past solemn warnings have been issued to mothers that the summer is a dangerous time for babies, a folder of the Toledo District Nurse Association called "Summer Time Is Health-building Time," takes the opposite tone:

Of all the seasons of the year the good old summer is the time for babies and young children to grow strong and healthy. How this statement would have shocked our grandmothers, for when they were the mothers of young children, didn't the dreaded "summer complaint" pluck off hundreds of babies and children? But today we know how to prevent this unnecessary children's disease.

Following this hopeful beginning are the practical and definite health hints that formerly accompanied the statistics of summer death-rates.

A safety appeal draws upon the joy of sport to inspire boys to avoid accidents:

Listen!

Nobody wants to get hurt at this time o' year. What with summer comin' on and the sun shinin' thru the pines and the trout risin' to the fly. Oh, Boy!

"Sure, I'm All Right, I Eat Right," says the sturdy, finely built workman shown in the poster on page 12, addressing the uncomfortably fat man and the nervous, thin man who sit beside him. And for a moment other workers picture themselves becoming "all right" by eating the same kind of wholesome, strength-giving food.

Boys who do not respond to any argument in favor of drinking milk and eating whole wheat bread are told of famous athletes who live on this kind of diet, and accept it gladly because they imagine themselves becoming like their heroes. A sense of security is a pleasurable feeling. The poster shown opposite suggests to industrial workers the satisfaction and pleasure to be had from taking precautions to be safe. The lure that soap-flake advertisers give to fine laundering might be applied to washing the hands before meals. Or better, picture the pleasant feeling of clean hands when one sits down to eat.

The suggestion of a simple, but immediate satisfaction that will result from the proposed action is sometimes more persuasive than

5

the assurance of a more important, but nevertheless remote benefit. A reminder that opening the windows at night means increased vigor the next morning may bring a readier response than the continued emphasis on the relation of lack of fresh air to disease.

PRIDE IN APPEARANCE

A motive recognized by commercial advertisers but seldom appealed to in social publicity is the desire of persons to look well. Advertisers of tooth paste, soap, and medicines try to make us want to look like the handsome young men and women in the pictures, who, we are told, have taken precautions to keep their teeth clean, and their skin clear. The opticians are waging a campaign to prove to us that glasses are becoming.

Among the comparatively few examples of the use of this appeal in social publicity, we may cite the poster of the American Social Hygiene Association on page 54. "Happy's Vanity Case" is the title of a popular booklet for girls prepared by the American Child Health Association. "Stand Tall—Correct Position Is Attractive," reads a placard urging young men to good posture. That the appeal of improved appearance would be effective in health advice, is indicated by the large number of questions on the subject sent to the conductors of newspaper health columns.

Pride in the beauty of their children is natural to parents, to mothers especially; and in the health talks and literature addressed to mothers more emphasis might be laid on what the proper care of children's health means in the way of straight backs and legs, good color, clear eyes, and beautiful teeth.

"IT PAYS"

In health campaigns, activity is often stimulated by showing that to support the campaign is sound business. "Saving Millions for American Industry" is the caption of an appeal of the American Social Hygiene Association in The Saturday Evening Post and other periodicals which reads as follows:

> During the war a great corporation built an industrial plant and manned it with 10,000 workmen. . . . Production . . . dropped far below what had been expected. . . . It was found that 68% of the workers on the non-effective list each day were listed because

48

of the venereal diseases. Measurements of output showed that a man so infected was 33% below normal in production. Scientific treatment facilities were introduced at small cost by the corporation and 2,000 employees were treated during the year. Every man's output returned to normal after treatment was concluded and the men were returned to health! The company estimates that the work was worth at least $150,000 net for the year in increased production.

The corporation was urged to these measures by the national agencies at work on the American Plan to combat venereal diseases. Today more than 2,000 other corporations have found that it pays. They are conducting educational campaigns and are providing treatment facilities.

It has been said that the temperance movement really began to take long strides ahead when business men were convinced that they were losing dollars and cents because of drinking on the part of their employes. Workers are told as a reason for wearing goggles "Your eyes are your breadwinners." The opportunity to give a city child a week's vacation in the country for only $2.00 was offered to a radio audience as a "bargain in giving" by the financial secretary of the Chicago United Charities, and many checks for that amount were received, some from as far away as New England and Canada, together with letters expressing appreciation of "the bargain opportunity."

Saving one's own money is a much more compelling motive for economy than saving public money. The latter motive is not ignored, however, nor should it be. Many measures for which social agencies are working, such as prison reform, health, public recreation, and vocational training, are really sound investments for taxpayers. Proof is often offered that it costs less to support playgrounds than jails and that the two may sometimes present an alternative.

PUBLIC SPIRIT

The appeal to public spirit is an effective spur to action if used under the right conditions. The slogans "Help Show That Toledo Has a Soul," "Make Framingham the Health Town," and "Dayton, the City with a Heart," made a distinct appeal to local pride and, after having been used as campaign slogans, they were reinforced by a great deal of publicity aimed to give the townspeople

While Washington holds the World's Championship for Baseball. she's down at the bottom of the list in the support given her Public Nursing Service—down where her baseball standing used to be!

Baseball Standing

WASHINGTON
New York
Pittsburg
Detroit
Cincinnati
St. Louis
Philadelphia
Cleveland
Boston
Chicago

Nursing Standing

Boston
Cleveland
New York
Detroit
Cincinnati
Pittsburg
Philadelphia
St. Louis
Chicago
WASHINGTON

Washington spent $523,346 during the World Series to see the Nationals beat the Giants—and this was all right—

But—how much is Washington now going to spend to beat disease and poverty, by backing the Visiting Nurses?

The *quality* of Washington's nursing service equals that of any other American city, but Washington fails in the number of nurses maintained per 100,000 population

WHY NOT PUT WASHINGTON AT THE TOP IN BOTH BASEBALL AND NURSING SERVICE?

"I'm strong for the Visiting Nurse Society—and I'm going to do my best to put 'it into the championship class.'"— BUCKY HARRIS, Chairman Men's Committee, Instructive Visiting Nurse Society's 1924 Campaign

A CHALLENGE TO CIVIC LOYALTY

A timely effort by a visiting nurse society to take advantage of local pride already aroused is seen in this folder which was distributed immediately after Washington had won the baseball championship in the world series in 1924. The strength of the appeal is further reinforced by quoting a popular baseball hero in support of the campaign.

of each place a feeling of unity and to lend personality to the town itself. We doubt that much sense of responsibility is roused by the placards "Promote the Health of Your Community by Exterminating Flies" or "Wipe This Disgrace (Tuberculosis) Off the Map of Your State," such as one sees in local public buildings. They are writen so impersonally that they do not even carry the name of the town where they are posted.

Placing a town in competition with other towns, or getting it interested in proving its superiority, offers one means of creating a favorable condition for arousing public spirit. The enthusiastic rivalry among cities to secure one of the various health demonstrations offered by national agencies is a good illustration of this.[1]

Superiority in industry and in the beauty of public buildings and residences seems quite possible of attainment to cities going through the stage of rapid growth or change, and under such circumstances local pride can easily be awakened. Towns both young and old, which are on main traveled automobile routes seem to gain a new or increased self-consciousness because they have so many visitors. Whether this town pride can be turned to account for other purposes as well as that of maintaining the safety and good looks of Main Street is a question which social agencies might do well to look into.

Duty

Duty is another motive for action sometimes held up before the indifferent and procrastinating. The imperative tone of the following paragraph, another appeal of the American Social Hygiene Association that appeared as an experiment in The Saturday Evening Post and other periodicals, is not unusual:

> Every man and woman must help. The Government has declared it a duty of citizenship for everyone to know about the American Plan of action. Send today for Will Irwin's absorbing booklet, "Conquering an Old Enemy," a stirring book that should be read by the millions. It explains social and economic reasons that obligate you as a citizen to back up the campaign.

Most of us will accept dictation without resentment when it comes from recognized authority. The President of the United

[1] See p. 277.

States or the governor of a state may make a proclamation calling upon us to do our duty. The clergyman also may preach duty to the members of his church. During times of aroused public feeling, as in war, it often makes a powerful appeal. But as a rule people do not respond very readily to an imperative reminder of moral obligation. The publicity of social agencies is full of commands— to give money, to be careful, to obey rules. In the quotation above the writer says "Every man and woman *must* help." Many commands are not intended to be peremptory, the terse form being used to save space. Perhaps they are accepted in this spirit. Yet the dislike of an assumption of superiority on the part of others and the desire to follow our own ideas are sufficiently general to make it worth while to substitute indirect suggestions for the direct command.

The following paragraphs from a circular describing Clean-up Week issued by the Cleveland Health Council do not insist upon action but instead make it seem desirable by suggesting the pleasant results of cleaning up:

> How does your yard look? Does your fence, or your house, need a coat of paint? Besides being a good preservative, fresh paint gives your place a prosperous look.
>
> And what about the garden? Are you letting your back yard go to waste when you might be planting bright flowers, or green vegetables for crisp summer salads? Perhaps a window box will suit your needs, if you are an apartment dweller. Here's a planting schedule that will help you.

RESPECT FOR SOCIAL CUSTOM

The tendency to conform to custom, which is so often an obstruction to getting new ideas accepted, may be turned to account by making the proposed act "the thing to do." The aim of much social publicity is to cause a given course of action to become so generally accepted that it ceases to be spasmodic or occasional and becomes automatically part of our plan of living.

Visiting teachers, public health nurses, and probation officers are gradually becoming a recognized part of the machinery of city government, although a long period of public education and private demonstration is needed in any community before an appropriation for their services is granted without opposition. The Christmas

Seal Sale has already benefited by a fairly well-established idea that putting seals on Christmas mail is the thing to do, and the increasing success of the sale probably depends on extending more and more the custom of using, as well as buying, the seals.

In some community fund campaigns, the position of team captain in the drive is regarded as such an honor that what would otherwise be merely thankless drudgery becomes a pleasure. So effective, indeed, is social approval in guiding conduct that it may

About Feet Again

Hundreds of people have asked us again to request you not to sit with your legs crossed and your feet extended into the aisle. We are making some headway. Thank You!

Theodore P Shonts
President
Interborough Rapid Transit Company

RIDICULE TO SHOW PUBLIC DISAPPROVAL OF AN UNSOCIAL ACT

amount to compulsion. The element in money-raising drives which provokes criticism is that the pressure of public opinion created by the campaign publicity is in some instances so strong as to make giving practically obligatory.

This brings us to the use of public disapproval of an unsocial act as a deterrent which can be brought to bear as effectively as its opposite in controlling conduct.

At present people do all sorts of things that they shouldn't and wouldn't if public opinion were against them. They evade their taxes, spoil beautiful public places with litter, allow flies to carry infection, forget that their old age may need provision.[1]

Is it not likely that the campaign against spitting in public places would make greater headway if the spitter were presented as an object of public disapproval?

NEIGHBORLINESS

Being a good neighbor is an old-fashioned but widely approved virtue, although because of conditions of modern life it is becoming harder, in cities, at least, to practice it. In several community fund campaigns, the slogan "Be a Good Neighbor" has been used. The following paragraphs from a folder issued by a family welfare society, recognize that people appreciate the opportunity to be neighborly:

> Have you ever been disturbed because the family in the alley is often hungry? . . . Have you pictured what the future must look like to the discouraged widow with many children who does your family laundry? Does it bother you that in these days of cities and complex industrial life you cannot lend a helping hand to every neighbor in distress? . . .
>
> The Good Neighbor represents the spirit of helpfulness of the whole community. The United Charities undertakes to serve those whom the good neighbor finds to be in need of service. This means that it is your agency and represents you in a most vital and serious way.
>
> Your sympathetic understanding and personal support are more essential even than funds if constructive service is to be rendered to every neighbor who needs a friend.

The spirit of neighborliness was the chief motive appealed to in a campaign in Pennsylvania to get aliens to register for citizenship.

> "Every Resident a Citizen" was the battle cry, and every man and woman went in heart and soul to make everybody a Homebody. . . .
>
> A week was set aside in which to invite the alien 2,500 into partnership, without thought of partisanship. . . . "What are *you* doing to help *your* neighbor become a citizen?" was the question asked from poster, pamphlet, and newspaper. . . .
>
> Not only were the advantages of citizenship explained and the ad-

[1] Higham, Sir Charles, Advertising. Henry Holt and Co., New York, 1925, p. 223.

Beauty Comes From Within

By courtesy of St. Nicholas

Paint Your Cheeks From the Inside Out

Outdoor exercise, baths, regular meals, and plenty
of sleep will help

Most girls could be prettier than they are because
most girls could be healthier

(Permission of American Social Hygiene Association)

PRIDE IN APPEARANCE AS A MOTIVE FOR OBEYING HEALTH LAWS
The red cheeks of the girl in the original picture, which was in colors,
added to its attractiveness.

Let's Give Them a Chance

THE APPEAL OF CHILDHOOD

This jolly picture of a lovable youngster appeared on the cover of a booklet distributed by the Harrisburg Welfare Federation in its appeal for support of social work for the benefit of both young and old.

vantages of helping to make a richer, better town, but everyone desiring to become a citizen had a *neighbor* to go with him to court. . . .

As a result of the week's campaign about 1,000 of the 2,500 took the initial step towards full citizenship.[1]

The citizenship campaign offered an exceptional opportunity for the literal practice of neighborliness. About many kinds of social service, however, the feeling prevails that the methods are too impersonal to be really neighborly. It is the part, then, of social propaganda to prove that the help social agencies give is genuine neighborliness and is the kind generally best suited to present conditions.

LOVE AND PROTECTION OF CHILDREN

The appeal of children is so fundamental and so generally recognized that it seems scarcely necessary to dwell on it. We find pictures and stories of children used in all forms of printed publicity, and children themselves take part in pageants, parades, and motion pictures. Baby weeks and boys' weeks are planned to turn the widespread sentiment to account.

Parents to whom a picture is presented of children in distress imagine such a calamity befalling their own children and their parental instinct of protection is aroused in behalf of dependent, neglected, or crippled children. The right of childhood to happiness, health, and training for the future is generally conceded and social programs which provide these things for children otherwise deprived of them have the least difficulty of any movements in obtaining financial support.

Observation of the appeals most successful in raising money for child welfare work indicates that a request on behalf of a single child is more effective than one seeking aid for many children. We can be made to see the picture of one child's suffering so vividly that we cannot endure the thought of it, but it is more difficult to grasp a situation involving large numbers of children.

This susceptibility to the appeal of one child when children in mass fail to move is well put by a writer in Collier's:

If a man comes up to me and says "70% of the children of middle

[1] "Home, Sweet Home," a magazine advertisement of the Metropolitan Life Insurance Company.

55

Europe are starving to death," I am likely to reply: "That's too bad. Did you know I made the fifth hole in three yesterday?"

But suppose he says: "I want to tell you about little Felix Popoff of 1872 Main Street, Vienna, Austria. Felix is nine years old, looks about five, and has the weazened face of an old man. . . . He took me home with him to a bare room without any fire, and on a pile of straw in a corner his little sister . . ." But by this time I am walking the floor shouting that something has got to be done.[1]

CHALLENGE

Challenge, as Harry A. Overstreet pointed out in his discussion of Influencing Human Behavior, has great power to stir us.

Ghandi flings a challenge to the British Empire and becomes a figure of foremost interest in the world. . . .

Challenge . . . is most powerful when it enlists others in the fight. Not, "Come, see me wipe up the earth with this false prophet"; but, rather, "Come, let's join in the fight."[2]

Social situations, if presented so compellingly that we see that something must be done about them, challenge our fighting spirit. The terms of combat are much used in calling on the public to join in getting rid of disease. "The fight against tuberculosis," "the first line of defense against typhoid," and "the war on cancer," suggest that these diseases are enemies that can and must be defeated. In the passage quoted below, the very difficulties of the situation presented awaken a desire to attack the problem. The writer, after telling the story of four subnormal girls incapable either of holding jobs or of keeping out of trouble, put the problem up to her readers, thus:

Yet Tilly and Lulu, Elda and Sadie all are here and all must earn their livings. . . . They must have a room to live in, and they must live with other girls so that they will not be lonesome. They must have a place to entertain . . . and some one to show them how to do it suitably. They must be helped patiently in the long task of paying their bills. They must be encouraged to refrain from quarrels and lies and profanity and light-fingeredness and dirty stories, and to substitute for these good manners, truth-telling, honesty, and an ap-

[1] Biggers, Earl Derr, "Here Is a Thing Worth Fighting For." *In* Collier's, New York, May 5, 1923.

[2] Influencing Human Behavior. W. W. Norton & Co., New York, 1925, pp. 21, 23.

preciation of wit that is not obscene. This is an uphill road for girls who did not learn such lessons in their childhood and who are not very quick and adaptable at getting new ideas, and it is often up-hill work for their teachers.

Many are the places of refuge for the girl who is rich and dull, and the girl who is poor, but bright, is finding more open roads every year. But the girl who is not gifted either in her mind or in her purse, and whose environment has steadily exploited all her weaknesses, needs a consideration that she has seldom received because she could never pay for it. Yet she and her brothers are with us in vast numbers. Have they a right to live? If so, how can we help them to live safely?[1]

An inspiring purpose fires the imagination, and if presented by a leader in whom the public has confidence, is likely to obtain support. In a call to the nation to join in a May Day celebration, Herbert Hoover challenges our best efforts by setting before us a picture of great achievement:

The ideal to which we should strive is that there should be no child in America that has not been born under proper conditions, that does not live in hygienic surroundings, that ever suffers from undernutrition, that does not have prompt and efficient medical attention and inspection, that does not receive primary instruction in the elements of hygiene and good health.[2]

USE OF ARGUMENTS

Making people realize the acuteness of a situation is a more effective method of persuasion than arguing the matter with them. Lists of arguments are used on posters under such headings as "Why Your Child's Birth Should Be Registered" and "Why Every Citizen Should Vote 'Yes' on the Bond Issue." The writer who composes such a list probably first enumerates his points to clarify his own mind, and finding that he has a strong case, presents them to his imagined opponents. However, those addressed may be indifferent rather than antagonistic, and the mere piling up of reasons is too wearisome to arouse their interest. On the other hand, if people are actively opposed, arguing with them may stiffen their resistance.

[1] Wembridge, Eleanor Rowland, "The Development Battalion." *In* Mental Hygiene, New York, vol. 8, Jan., 1924, p. 25.

[2] "May Day—Child Health Day—1925. A Message from Herbert Hoover." *In* Child Health Magazine, New York, vol. 6, Jan., 1925, p. 26.

Under some circumstances, reasoning may be the right approach. In legislative campaigns it may be necessary to reply to the claims of one's opponents. If the debate becomes vigorous, people give attention to it because conflict is interesting.

Stating one's own reasons for believing in or actively supporting a cause is, of course, an entirely acceptable form of exposition; but most people like to make their own decisions and the argumentative form of presentation does not seem to allow for one's own initiative.

Clearing Away Obstacles

In the beginning of this chapter, it was brought out that possibly more people would follow the suggestion to write letters to their representative if they were given his name and a memorandum of what to say to him.

Political leaders, recognizing that ignorance of how the act of voting is performed is a deterrent to voting, send to their constituents sample ballots showing just how the ballots will look when marked. Frequently, they meet the obstacle of inconvenience or inertia by sending automobiles to take voters to the polling places. The mail-order house supplies the prospective customer with an addressed envelope and an order blank with a space in which to fill in size and other specifications or to place a check mark.

The social agency usually encloses with an appeal letter a return envelope and coupon. Still another help to the hesitating contributor may be the suggestion of specific sums which would accomplish certain results:

$25.00 will give 5 weeks' care to a sick child.
$10.00 will pay a baby's expenses for 2 weeks.
$5.00 will care for one baby for one week.

A suggestion sometimes given to former contributors is the reminder "you gave $100 last year." While in some cases one may obtain more by leaving the amount to the discretion of the giver, it often happens that the mention of a specific sum will help persons who would otherwise postpone action to decide promptly how much they will give.

Making It Easy to Come to a Clinic or Meeting. A notice inviting people to come to an unfamiliar place needs especially to be planned so as to make attendance easy. The health folder some-

58

times ends with "go to your doctor or to the nearest clinic." Who among its readers will know where the nearest clinic is to be found? And yet that knowledge may have more to do with the response to the suggestion than all the arguments given in its favor. If exact directions cannot be given, a source of information should be named, or, if possible, a map should be included. When a certain place is designated, the card or letter may include a picture of the building or directions for reaching it. One side, to be shown when asking street directions, may carry merely the location; the other side could carry an introduction to the clinic that would help to overcome the timidity people often feel about going to a strange place for assistance.

Suggesting a Specific Time. To have a health examination is an excellent example of something which people may thoroughly approve and yet fail to do. One of the reasons for failure is that it may be done at any time and so continues to be postponed. The slogan "Have a Health Examination on Your Birthday" was devised to set a definite time for everyone. Come and See Week makes an occasion which will be remembered as a time for visits which under ordinary circumstances might be put off indefinitely. Parents are permitted to visit schools any day, but many will go only during School Week, partly because of the special program then, but partly also because a time is set for them to make the visit.

TESTING APPEALS

Appeals, however effectively presented, may encounter an attitude of aloofness or indifference because they are not applicable to the persons approached. Much time and energy might be saved by experiments to determine what is likely to succeed in a particular instance.

Advance tests are increasingly used in the advertising field to determine this matter. Several designs for a box or other container will be submitted to a number of consumers to ascertain the one likely to be the most pleasing to customers. Several pieces of copy will be tested in the same way to learn which will make the strongest impression.[1]

[1] For detailed accounts of such investigations, see Starch, Daniel, Principles of Advertising. A. W. Shaw Co., Chicago, 1923.

Efforts to determine what information on the subject under consideration a particular group of individuals needs most and in what form it can be most readily understood have preceded a few educational campaigns. Preliminary to an anti-typhoid campaign in a rural district, the United States Public Health Service canvassed the householders of a community to find out how many had any idea of the causes of the disease. Of 2,500 who replied, about half named water, dirt, germs, or flies; more than one-third said "I don't know"; while the replies of the remainder ranged from "The Lord sends it" to "crabs," "going barefoot," and "heredity." With this picture of widespread ignorance and uncertainty to guide them, the campaigners knew that their "talking points" must be elementary.

As to the motives for giving or for acting on advice about health or safety, very little investigation has been made. A preliminary step to discover prevailing beliefs in regard to social questions which might be developed into a more thorough kind of inquiry is described on page 42. A study in the political field which analyzed the appeals that influenced about 1,000 voters in their selection of a candidate for president suggests one way of going about such studies.[1]

Two investigations that have a bearing on this subject were made by psychologists for the American Social Hygiene Association; the first being an evaluation of a motion picture called Fit to Win, and the second, an evaluation of certain pamphlets. Both took account of the effectiveness of the material in conveying information, changing mental attitudes, and influencing conduct. The methods used in both studies are described in published reports.[2]

There are indications that this type of investigation is likely to be further developed by psychologists and sociologists.

[1] Meier, Norman C., "Motives in Voting: A Study in Public Opinion." *In* American Journal of Sociology, Chicago, vol. 31, Sept., 1925, pp. 199–212.

[2] Lashley, Karl S., and Watson, John B., A Psychological Study of Motion Pictures in Relation to Venereal Disease Campaigns. U.S. Interdepartmental Social Hygiene Board, 1922. (Available only through American Social Hygiene Association, New York.)

Achilles, Paul S., The Effectiveness of Certain Social Hygiene Literature. American Social Hygiene Association, New York, 1923.

Technical Skill the First Need

Some few of the larger social agencies appear to have reached the stage in the improvement of their technique when advance tests to determine the best methods for presenting their information to the public ought to be practicable and helpful. But the majority of those who prepare publicity for social work have not yet brought their skill beyond the point where much of the weakness or strength of their efforts can be easily discovered by consulting a qualified critic. Many of them have still to realize that there is an orderly process to be carried out in getting information understood and acted upon and that each effort, whether it is a speech, an exhibit, or an intensive campaign, should be part of a well thought out plan directed toward a sound objective. Examples of good writing, pleasing design, attractive pictures, and judicious selection of facts and ideas in social publicity to illustrate this book were hard to find. Higher standards need to be achieved in all of these lines before scientific testing is called for.

This preliminary task of bringing about a wider familiarity with recognized technique in writing, printing, speaking, and other major forms of expressing and circulating information in connection with social work is undertaken in the remaining chapters of the book.

PART II: SOCIAL WORK AND THE NEWSPAPER

INTRODUCTION TO PART II

WE RANK the newspaper first in importance among avenues of public information because a large percentage of the population in any community, whether urban or rural, habitually read daily or weekly newspapers. We cannot assume, however, that articles about social work, or indeed, any topics, will be read by everyone merely because they are published where the majority of the population have an opportunity to see them.

Two studies of newspaper readers' habits[1] brought out the information that about 70 to 75 per cent of those replying to questionnaires estimated that they spent an average of fifteen minutes a day reading newspapers. The returns from a third study[2] among Chicago business and professional men were practically the same.

Fifteen minutes divided between morning and evening newspapers does not allow time for reading a very large percentage of the 20 or more pages which a city newspaper contains, and even though this evidence need not be considered typical, it is safe to say that average readers do no more than scan the headlines and read in detail such articles as especially attract their interest. The story is told of a man who, on hearing of an exciting riot which had occurred the day before, complained that the newspaper that he read had not reported it. When he was shown the front-page article with three-column spread reporting the event, he recalled that on that day he had turned first to the sporting page and had not even glanced at the rest of the paper.

Taking reading habits into account, it becomes clear that getting social information into the newspapers is not enough. Each item must compete for attention with others in the same issue.

[1] Hotchkiss, George Burton, and Franken, Richard B., Newspaper Reading Habits of College Students. Bureau of Business Research, New York University, New York, 1920.
——— Newspaper Reading Habits of Business Executives and Professional Men in New York. Bureau of Business Research, New York University, New York, 1922.
[2] Scott, Walter Dill, The Psychology of Advertising in Theory and Practice. Small, Maynard and Co., Boston, 1921, p. 380.

Social work appears to be fairly well established as a source of news which editors sometimes gladly, and at other times, no doubt, reluctantly find space for in their columns. To get an idea of the importance of social publicity in an average day's grist of news and features, we obtained, on a day when there were no national events sufficiently spectacular to crowd out minor items, four morning and two evening newspapers published in six widely separated cities ranging in population from 50,000 to 150,000. Altogether we found in the newspapers 20 items about such social welfare topics as public health, recreation, family welfare, foreign relief, juvenile courts, safety, and city planning. They ranged in length from a "stick"—the printer's term for about two and one-half inches of space—to a full column.

The experiment was repeated on another occasion, newspapers from 10 cities with populations ranging from 200,000 to 500,000 being examined. Again, social work was found to be well represented in news, pictures, and editorials, one newspaper containing as many as 11 and none less than two separate items bearing on this topic.

Nevertheless, the items found in both lists were nearly all brief and inconspicuously placed. Such mildly interesting headlines as "Humane Society Has Busy Month," "Social Workers Hear Expert at Temple Dinner," and "Treat Teeth of 10,948 Children" were in competition with "Collapse in Stock Prices in Largest Trading in History," "Forecast Severe Winter in America," "Mitchell Hurls New Sensation at Trial Court," and "Blazer Denies He Murdered His Daughter."

Holding no illusions about the possibilities of putting social material into competition with news of great importance or sensational interest, we may nevertheless hope to obtain for it a better position, more attractive headlines, and more readers, if we study how to make the most of what we have to tell.

We need to understand better what is meant by news value, especially as it applies to our own material; how to give facts a news shape; and how to write in newspaper style.

The first requisite of successful newspaper publicity is an understanding of what editors are likely to want and how they like to have it prepared. The second is the ability to find in the field from which the information is drawn material which meets their requirements. The third is a familiarity with the methods of getting news articles into print.

In the following chapters these questions are discussed in terms of what social organizations have done and can do about them.

CHAPTER V

THE NEWSPAPER

EACH department of a newspaper affords the social agency an opportunity for publicity. Besides the news, which is commonly divided into general, local, society, financial, sporting, and so on, there are features, syndicated articles or columns, editorials, letters to the editor, photographic sections, and advertising. The first thing to determine with regard to any piece of information which we want to get into the newspapers is the department for which it is suited.

THE NEWS COLUMNS

For the news columns the editor requires that an event or a situation shall take what we may call a "news shape," that it shall have news value, and that the story of it shall be written in good newspaper style.

News Shape. John L. Given[1] supposes the case of John Smith, a broker, who "for ten years pursues the even tenor of his way— and to the newspapers he is as if he were not." In the eleventh year he suffers heavy losses and has to make an assignment, and with the making of the necessary entries in the county clerk's office, "in step the newspapers." Walter Lippmann, borrowing the illustration to assist him in explaining the nature of news, comments as follows:

> That overt act "uncovers" the news about Smith. . . . Before a series of events become news they have usually to make themselves noticeable in some more or less overt act.[2]

Mr. Lippmann points out that, although there may have been rumors about Smith, they could not be published because there was "nothing definite on which to peg a story."

> Something definite must occur that has unmistakable form. It may be the act of going into bankruptcy, it may be a fire, a collision, an as-

[1] Making a Newspaper. Henry Holt and Co., New York, 1907.
[2] Public Opinion. Harcourt, Brace and Co., New York, 1922, p. 339.

sault, a riot, an arrest, a denunciation, the *introduction of a bill*, a *speech*, a *vote*, a *meeting*, the *expressed opinion of a well-known citizen*, an editorial in a newspaper, a sale, a wage schedule, a price change, the proposal to build a bridge. . . . There must be a manifestation. The course of events must assume a certain definable shape, and until it is in a phase where some aspect is an accomplished fact, news does not separate itself from the ocean of possible truth.

Naturally there is room for wide difference of opinion as to when events have a shape that can be reported. A good journalist will find news oftener than a hack. If he sees a building with a dangerous list, he does not have to wait until it falls into the street in order to recognize news.[1]

Among the list of happenings to which Mr. Lippmann ascribes news shape, we have italicized those common to social welfare work. There are, of course, many others.

A legislative hearing gives news shape to information about social conditions leading up to the hearing. Almost any announcement is "something definite" with "unmistakable form." The following paragraph from the New York Times is an example:

Announcement that no specific cure for consumption exists was made yesterday after a meeting of the Board of Directors of the New York Tuberculosis Association, because information had reached the organization of an increase in the number of so-called "cures" placed upon the market.

News Value. While a great many happenings and announcements may be said to have a news shape, comparatively few of them fulfil a more important requirement of the newspaper editor, which is that they shall have news value. The following is one of many definitions of the nature of news to be found in books and articles on the newspaper:

News is the immediate record of the most interesting, important, and accurate information obtainable about the things man thinks and says, sees and describes, plans and does.[2]

According to this definition news should have much the same qualities as a talk, a motion picture, printed matter, or any other

[1] *Ibid.* p. 340.
[2] Bastian, George C., Editing the Day's News. Macmillan Co., New York, 1923, p. 20.

form of publicity, with the added specific requirement that it should be recent or timely, which is to say that it should tell about something which happened yesterday or today or which is definitely scheduled to happen.

Since in good reporting the most interesting fact is always stated first[1] we may illustrate news values in social work by noting the contents of the opening paragraphs of news releases and articles from that field.

Value of Uniqueness. Whatever is the largest or smallest, the youngest or oldest of its kind, whatever, indeed, is in any way out of the ordinary has inherent news value. The headline given by the New York Evening World to the item quoted below was "Nation's Biggest Law Office Takes Record Day's Fees; $18.75."

A New York law office, handling more than 30,000 cases annually, had the most prosperous day in the forty-seven years of its history last Tuesday when its total retaining fees for the day amounted to $18.75. In addition, it was the busiest day in this law office's history, its thirteen attorneys and their assistants working from early morning until late in the evening. The law office referred to is "the Poor Man's Lawyer," as the Legal Aid Society, No. 239 Broadway, has been known for many years. Had this been a law office devoted to private practice which charged its clients even moderate fees, its annual profits would amount to several million dollars.

This paragraph may contain a more striking piece of news than most social agencies can produce. Yet many circumstances and events may reveal some unusual aspects if we look them over in search of unique features.

The presence of eight governors made the meeting announced in the paragraph below not only important but also unusual.

One of the most important health conferences in the history of the United States will take place in Chattanooga, Tennessee, on November 29th, when eight Governors of as many southern states will meet with tuberculosis experts from the National Tuberculosis Association in an effort to cut the tuberculosis death rate in the south and to endorse the Christmas Seal Sale. . . .[2]

[1] See "Writing the Lead," p. 78.
[2] This quotation contains a poor arrangement of material for the "lead." The eight governors should have been mentioned at the beginning of the sentence.

That the first health club for mothers of underweight children had been organized in Detroit was an announcement of sufficient interest to be printed by a New York daily. A newspaper paragraph to the effect that an attractive young woman was teaching a "hobo's college" in an evening school in a middle western city was unusual enough to be copied widely by other newspapers.

A state tuberculosis association, recognizing news value in the apparent incongruity of establishing fresh air camps for rural children, played up this fact in a news story of its children's camps.

While the publicity worker should make the most of whatever significance or uniqueness his information contains, he should not merely assert its importance without supporting evidence. Inexperienced news writers frequently strive for rhetorical effect by the use of superlatives. The paragraph below introduced an article which told of nothing far reaching but only that a group of local organizations expected to display some health charts in a department store and later on in other stores.

> An educational campaign more far reaching in its scope than any that has thus far characterized the useful work of even that active organization has been launched by the Child Hygiene Department of the Council of Mothers and Parent-Teacher Associations.

Relation to Current Topics of General Interest. Information, in itself only mildly interesting, sometimes takes on news value because it has some bearing on what is already important news or of great current interest. Thus, at a time when immigration problems were being discussed in Congress and when housing shortage was attracting attention, a statement by the Charity Organization Society of New York based on its annual report began as follows:

> "The decrease in immigration is the only factor that has made the housing shortage in any degree bearable," said Lawson Purdy yesterday, in commenting on the fortieth annual report of the Charity Organization Society, of which he is Secretary and General Director.

When the state of Minnesota appropriated a million dollars for the enlargement of its state tuberculosis sanatorium this fact was reported in a news release of the tuberculosis association of another state in order to bring into the news columns a statement showing the small amount available for sanatorium care in that state.

The discovery or even the supposed discovery of a cure for a baffling disease is always front-page news. An announcement that English specialists had established certain facts about the cause of cancer gave importance to the statement that the managing director of the American Society for the Control of Cancer was on his way to England to study at first hand the results of British research, and also to an interview given out by him in which the purposes of the Society were briefly described.

While it is appropriate to present as news information that has a real bearing on an event of the hour, it should be borne in mind that forcing facts into a fictitious relationship with news when no real connection exists is resented by editors as an attempt to obtain space not deserved.

Activities particularly associated with the current season, with holiday customs, or with extremes of heat and cold have news value because we are all affected by seasonal events and by unusual weather. Summer, as the vacation season, provides opportunity for announcing the publication of pamphlets giving advice about drinking water, first aid, and summer camps. When extremes of temperature increase the hardships of the poor, the comments of social agencies on the experiences of their clients are news. Autumn brings the opening of school and one health department takes account of it with the following:

> "Now that the 'ole' swimming hole and carefree vacation days have performed a fadeaway and the merciless and exacting school bell ushers in a season of parted hair and clean hands, every school child in Michigan should be examined," declares Dr. . . . .[1]

Prohibition, the modern woman, the behavior of the younger generation, and themes of the current "best sellers" are matters of perennial interest, and any information or ideas which are linked with these topics gain news value from the connection.

Interesting People. Social agencies are usually alert to recognize the news value of names of people. What is said or done by the president, governor, or mayor; by the man whose personality interests the public, whether he is a minister, writer, politician, or baseball player; by the women who are active in social or club life;

[1] News release from the Michigan State Department of Health.

or, indeed, by anyone at all distinguished becomes more or less important news.

Intensive campaign publicity makes generous use of the names and pictures of prominent people. Often they are brought into a campaign or other event for the purpose of supplying news. A story of a national contest among playground children in making models of airplanes was thus announced in the New York Sun shortly after Charles A. Lindbergh had made his famous flight across the Atlantic Ocean in May, 1927:

> Col. Charles A. Lindbergh has accepted the associate chairmanship of a national contest in the construction and flying of miniature airplanes to be conducted on public playgrounds this summer, it was announced yesterday by the Playground and Recreation Association of America, which will conduct the contest. Orville Wright is the general chairman.

Human Interest. Brief accounts of minor happenings which are humorous, pathetic, or dramatic, or which contain intimate revelations of character or experience, find place in all newspapers and in some, form a large proportion of the contents. Human interest stories about children always have high news value.

> That a charitable society took a hundred children to the circus is the kind of social welfare news which has a high mortality rate as it passes the city editor's desk. But when a stowaway in the party was discovered by an inexorable ticket taker, and each kid of the hundred chipped in a penny to get the culprit through the gate—there you have a story that any city editor would snap at.[1]

The following is an excellent account of a child's wanderings:

> It will take a great deal of happiness to wipe off John's mental slate the bitterness that has been written there during the past few days, since he has been peddled from door to door among his relatives, just looking for a place to stay till his mother comes home from the hospital. Late Saturday, word came from St. Vincent's Charity Hospital that there was a bed vacant which John's mother could have if she would come that night. She had been waiting for some time to get it for a much needed operation.
>
> The Associated Charities visitor who brought the message helped to get the mother ready, though there was little to do. The house was

[1] "Cultivating Newspaper Publicity." *In* Better Times, New York, vol. 4, Oct. 1, 1923, p. 10.

slicked up and two clean little bundles of clothing were wrapped up for John and his 10-year-old sister Agnes.

"I wanted to see my mother before I went to the hospital myself, and ask her to keep the children, but I know it will be all right, if you can take them there," the mother said, as the ambulance came to take her away.

Winking back the tears that would come, John watched them drive away with his mama, then picked up his little bundle of clothes and trudged out of his home with the Associated Charities worker and his sister. John could just remember how his father had been taken away, and they had told him that he was dead and would never come back, and now his mother. . . .

The story goes on to tell of a round of visits to relatives who refused to take him in:

Yesterday, the Associated Charities found another uncle whom John didn't know so well, and an aunt whom John had never seen. Here his quest for a "room in the inn" ended.

"Bless his heart, of course we'll take care of him, and he can play with our new baby!" said John's new-found aunt.

On top of the joy of being wanted, John found at the end of his four-day quest last night, the message that his mama wasn't going to die as he feared, at all, but that she was getting better and he could visit her in the hospital some day this week. But it's going to take a lot of joy to wipe out the bitterness of those banging doors which seemed to shut him out of every heart and home in Cleveland.[1]

The human interest story is often only a paragraph in length, but may be given a prominent position. Some newspapers "box" stories of this kind and run them on the front page.

Local News. An editor of a newspaper in a city of over 200,000 population in a letter explaining why he refused to give space to a great deal of material received from outside social and civic organizations, thus states his policy:

All local material received from social agencies is used either as a whole as received, added to, cut down, or rewritten in such manner as to make it acceptable—which sometimes is difficult.

Very little social material received from out-of-town is used unless it has a distinctive local angle.

[1] News release from Cleveland Welfare Federation.

Local news ranks high in value according to Willard Grosvenor Bleyer:

> Local events interest readers because they know the places and often the persons concerned. Local news, accordingly, takes precedence over news from elsewhere of equal or greater importance as measured by the general standards of news value. . . . We read more eagerly the account of a small fire in a building that we pass every day than the dispatch telling of a fire miles away. . . . Local phases, or "local ends," as they are called, of events that take place some distance away quite overshadow in interest more important phases of the event itself. Every effort is made in the newspapers to bring events, ideas, and activities elsewhere into some local relation.[1]

The fact that local people will attend a state or national convention lends interest to the event at home. A national Recreation Congress arranged by the Playground and Recreation Association of America gained in local news value by a competition among cities for the largest representation at the Congress. In several cities whose playground workers entered the race news stories announcing the local participation told at length of the program of the Congress. In reporting a meeting held by the New York State Charities Aid Association, about 20 papers of the state used the same story, introduced by a paragraph containing the name of a local worker who had attended. Here is one example showing the local headlines and first paragraph used:

CHARITIES AID DISCUSSES
THE CHILDREN'S COURT
Says Judges Should Be
Especially Suited for Big Task
Miss Adeline Daly, Herkimer
County Agent, Attends Meeting

Miss Daly has returned from New York where she attended the twelfth annual conference of the county children agents of the State Charities Aid Association on Monday and Tuesday. Miss Daly is children's agent for this county. . . .

When the legislature appropriates funds for work in child hygiene, the share of the appropriation that will be spent locally or the bene-

[1] Newspaper Writing and Editing. Houghton Mifflin Co., Boston, Revised 1923, p. 32.

fit the local community will receive from it is the element of the news most interesting to the newspaper readers in the towns throughout the state.

Names of readers or references to their affairs increase the news value of the article in which they occur. In a number of cities newspapers publish from day to day during money-raising campaigns the names of contributors.

A Pennsylvania county in which the sale of Christmas seals was very successful reported that both morning and evening newspapers printed daily lists of purchasers of large quantities of seals.

The report of the meeting of the finance committee for a social organization in a small city gave interest to what otherwise would have been a dull article by summarizing what each person of prominence had said in the discussion. The article quoted in full on pages 110–111 illustrates the use of many names in an intensive campaign story.

A Special Department of Social Welfare News. The same principle which accounts for the high value of local news applies to that about the activities of certain organized groups, like the American Red Cross, the Young Men's Christian Association, or a community chest. No small part of the news published about such organizations as these is read chiefly by members or supporters for whom it has personal significance. The Boy Scouts in some cities have a column of their own once a week, in one of the local newspapers. In Hartford, Connecticut, the Council of Social Agencies was given a department for a while on the editorial page, where the work of each agency was described in turn. A playground school of journalism in Auburn, New York, under the guidance of Mrs. Frederick M. Hosmer, superintendent of playgrounds and recreation, conducts a department of news appearing on Saturdays in the Auburn Advertiser-Journal and Auburn Citizen. Every week a child is appointed city editor for each playground and gives out assignments to his reporters; copy is prepared in correct form and delivered on time to each newspaper's city editor. Here are a few characteristic items:

> Tuesday Erney Baier received word from Syracuse that we could play Frazer Park Thursday, so the fellows got together and elected Bus Corkery captain. He was given a good run by Mickey Noonan. . .

The best small swimmers are Jean Irving and Ruby Murdock. They can do a great many tricks for their size. Helen Begley and Marion Higgs are the best middle-sized girl swimmers. Dorothy Jemison is the champion girl swimmer of the playgrounds.

There were 135 children here Wednesday afternoon. There was hardly room for the children on the bar, shute, and swings. One girl from Bradford Street said that our playground was better than the others.

By having its own column an organization is assured of the publication of news which sometimes might be crowded out by other items if space were not reserved for it. On the other hand, an important piece of organization news published only in the agency's own space loses the advantage which a more prominent position would give it.

Evaluation of News by Individual Papers. News values, then, appear to be found chiefly in the unusual occurrences; in the outstanding topic of the day; in activities or conditions affected by the season or the weather; in prominent and interesting people; in what is local and familiar; and in special group interests. Newspapers vary widely in their preferences among these types of news, as all of us know. Some give a great deal of space to human interest stories, which may be found in any or all of the sources mentioned above, while others use a minimum of this material. An editor may evaluate a certain individual as important according to whether or not his politics agree with the policy of the newspaper. The differences between the large city and the small town paper in the selection of news are very great. But the principle involved in all selections is the same; namely, that what is printed shall touch as closely as possible the individual interests of a large proportion of the readers and that it shall relate to a recent happening.

Good Reporting Impersonal

The opinions or point of view of the reporter are not supposed to be included in news stories. As we shall show later, there are sections of the newspaper in which a writer may appropriately express his opinion, give advice, or make an appeal, but he should not do so in news stories, even though the editor is willing to print this kind of writing, as he may be in small cities or towns. A mild illustration of too personal writing is contained in the following lead from a news release sent out by a state department of health:

We were gratified to see many health officers, physicians, and nurses at the New England Health Institute last week.

Probably newspaper readers, though indifferent, were at least not annoyed by the personal feeling expressed in "We were gratified." Nevertheless, that sort of information is not what people look for in the news columns and the habitual intrusion of personal expression, especially appeals or advice, into the news from a social agency may cause readers to avoid items in which the agency is concerned. But even more important is the fact that many newspaper editors will not publish such an editorial form of statement in a news release.

WRITING THE LEAD

The introductory sentence or group of sentences in a news story is called the "lead." It usually summarizes the facts of greatest interest or importance in the form of answers to the questions why, what, who and where, how, and when.

Most of the paragraphs quoted from newspapers in the preceding pages fulfil the requirement that the lead shall tell the substance of the story. A second principle, namely, that the lead shall begin with the most interesting fact seems to present greater difficulties to the average amateur writer. The attempt to put into the first six or eight words something that will attract the reader's notice helps the writer to test his whole story since it calls his attention to whether or not he has in it an idea or fact that deserves to be given prominence.

Seldom is time or place the chief interest, yet it seems to be a favorite beginning of writers of news about social work. For instance, there is nothing to hold one's attention in this beginning:

Last week Miss . . ., representative of the state board of children's guardians in this district, was called to Warren county to investigate a case which had been brought to the attention of her department.

If, however, the time of the occurrence is unusual, it may deserve to come at the beginning of the statement. In the following paragraph the lead is not only well chosen but effectively expressed.

Long before the milkmen had made their rounds yesterday morning, Miss . . ., Associated Charities visitor, hurried to a little frame house

78

out in the "East Seventies." She was answering a call from the police-
man on the beat. Death had come to the little house in the night,
leaving a grief-numbed bewildered woman and three frightened children. . . .

In the lead below the sentence in italics, which ought to have
opened the story, is placed near the end of the paragraph, and the
average reader would have lost interest before he reached it:

"The expectation of life at birth has increased in the registration area
of the United States between 1900-1920, for whites only, from about
49.5 years to over 55 years, or more than five years. For negroes the
increase has been greater over seven years, it is now about 41 years.
The highest expectation of life in 24 states of the United States in 1920
was in Kansas, where it is 59.7 for males and 60.9 for females. *In the
next 20 years we may hope to add another five years to the expectation
of life in the United States.*" This was the prediction made by Dr. . .
Health Commissioner of . . . .

The following well-written and well-organized lead appeared in
the New York Times:

The average New Yorker, entering a local hospital at 9 o'clock next
Monday morning as a sick man, will be discharged at 6:27 p.m. on the
second following Wednesday, according to a survey just completed by
officials of the United Hospital Fund. . . .

If the same information had been reported as the average untrained writer would express it, it would have read about as follows:

A survey of the services rendered by New York hospitals has been
completed by the officials of the United Hospital Fund. It shows that
the average length of time which a patient remains in the hospital is
one week, forty-five hours and thirty-three minutes.

The following announcement of recreation plans for a local
Young Women's Christian Association might logically have opened
"All girls and women are welcomed at the Wednesday evening
meetings," but a good news writer for a Boston daily put it this
way:

Moonlight hikes, star gazing, roller-skating, and folk dancing are all
on the program planned by Miss . . ., recreation director of the
Y. W. C. A., for the participants in the open recreation hour held
every Wednesday night from 7:30 to 9 o'clock at the Blue **Triangle**

7   79

Building, 97 Huntington Avenue. The Wednesday evening meetings are open to all girls and women of the city.

Newspaper Style

Simple words, short sentences, and short paragraphs are more desirable in news writing than in any other form of publicity. Broad, general statements and technical words that creep into the news writing of social and health workers as they do into their talks and printed matter should be avoided. How much more readable the following would have been if more concrete terms had been substituted for those in italics:

> The aim of introducing better *physical standards* among the *infant population* of . . . by better education of mothers in *child hygiene* is headed toward realization, the state board of health *avers* following last week's successful start of its rolling clinic, the Child Welfare "Special." Beginning at Evansville, the car spent the week in Rock County towns, averaging forty examinations a day. These *facilities* are intended to reach principally *rural populations* not usually in touch with *modern health resources*.

Editors differ in policy regarding the treatment of news, one permitting a lively, informal style which adds zest to a story; another preferring literal statement of fact. The following headlines of the same story as given in two New York morning newspapers illustrate this difference:

THREE-YEAR-OLD GOES SUBWAY RIDING - - LOST? NOT MUCH, HE SAYS

Parks Kiddie Car at Tube Entrance, Lands at Times Square, Struts About Rialto Until Man Takes Him to Children's Society Rooms

CHILD LOST OVERNIGHT

Leaves Mother Shopping and Sees City Sights on Pushmobile

When a story is prepared by a publicity worker and submitted to an editor for publication, it is usually best to make it a direct and simple statement of facts.

Syndicated and Local Features

An increasing proportion of space in both morning and evening papers is being given to special features consisting of departments of advice or information, humorous columns, cartoons, comic strips, and other material which is not news.

The Editor and Publishers' Annual Directory of Newspaper Syndicate Features lists hundreds of "general features" sold by syndicates, among them being many columns of advice about health and child training, short sermons and editorials touching upon a wide range of topics, paragraphs about interesting people, odd bits of information, human interest stories, and so on.

Some of these features offer an appropriate and advantageous place for social information and comment. The special department, section, or column has its regular readers, usually a large body of them, who turn to it every day, while the general news item is likely to be read only by those already interested in the particular subject indicated in its heading.

The social agency's material sometimes receives distinctive treatment from the popular and skilled special writers for these departments. Angelo Patri, in his daily feature called "Children," wrote under the title of "Chasing Butterflies" a moving plea against child labor, from which we quote the last two paragraphs:

"The children *like* to work!" Do they? Perhaps they do. We'll test it this way. Let the butterflies flit about them and leave the children free to decide whether they care to chase them or to ignore them and go on with their work.

If they turn their backs to the butterflies and turn to their tasks with shining eyes and eager greedy hands such as butterfly chasers show, they may go on with their chosen work and welcome. But if they chase the butterflies? Then they must be set free![1]

Since the syndicated material is distributed nationally, the opportunity to obtain the co-operation of their writers is open only to organizations having something to offer that is of interest to people in all parts of the country.

Editors of syndicated columns are sometimes willing to devote space to the topic of any important national intensive campaign. Some of the department editors announce and distribute to their readers pamphlets containing practical suggestions supplied by social organizations.

Local Features. Each of the newspapers whose columns we have

[1] Bell Syndicate, Inc., New York.

searched for items supplied by social agencies contained various departments of local news or features. An account of a talk by a recreation leader before the Chamber of Commerce was found in the "Club News" of one of the newspapers. In another, a department called "One Minute Interviews" contained an interview with a member of the local League of Women Voters about the juvenile court. "Republicanograms," a column on the editorial page of the Springfield Republican, carries brief comments, either serious or humorous, relating to news of the hour and provides a space for short paragraphs or "fillers." Humorous columns conducted by local writers were found in these papers under such titles as "The Merry-Go-Round" and "Sidelines." The columnist might occasionally print a few lines about an amusing incident reported by the visiting nurse or the probation officer. Columns called "Ten Years Ago Today" or "Reminders," in which events of ten or twenty or even fifty years ago are recalled, offer opportunity for a paragraph contrasting, favorably or unfavorably, some social condition of the past with a similar situation today.

A column in the New York Evening World, called "What Did You See Today?" published this story of tactfully given health advice:

> The man who sat two seats to my left at the piano recital by Shattuck in the Town Hall attracted much attention by his cough. It particularly distressed the woman in front of him. He coughed. She shuddered. He coughed again. She pulled her fur scarf closely about her neck. He was oblivious to everything except the music. . . . When he coughed again I saw the woman tear a page from her program and hand it to him. Thereafter whenever he coughed he used a handkerchief. . . . I turned my program and read: "Throwing Stones at Glass Houses," by Dr. B. S. Herben, New York Tuberculosis Association. Our bodies—the houses we live in are not so fragile as glass. Stones could not demolish them, and yet soft, microscopic bits of living material called "germs" can bring them to utter ruin. On one day, Feb. 5, 17 persons died of the "flu"; 375 new cases were reported; 67 died of pneumonia. These deaths were needless. They are caused by careless people who throw germs by coughing, sneezing, and expectorating into the air which people must inhale. Healthy people may unwittingly carry and spread these germs. . . . Don't

Throw Germs at People. It is worse than throwing stones at glass houses.—A. Greene, Brooklyn.

FILLERS

In various parts of the newspaper "fillers," which are, as the name implies, brief items used to fill in a column, may be welcomed. Sometimes a small box gives distinction to the news item, epigram, or brief comment sent in as a filler. A page of short items suitable for such use is occasionally mailed by the United States Public Health Service, under the title, "Healthgrams."

> Procrastination is the thief of more things than time. Many a child has departed this life because somebody waited a day or two to see if his illness was really diphtheria.

> For sleeplessness few things equal a warm bath and an easy conscience. A bath every day or two is a good thing anyway, whether you need it or not.

The Safety Service Bureau of the Elliott Service Company, New York City, sends out "Spark Plugs for Motorists."

> Will Rogers says: "If you can't lay eggs, don't cackle." We say: "If you can't be careful, don't drive."

> The only difference between an accident and a near accident is half an inch or half a second. Don't take chances.

> Fools used to blow out the gas; now they step on it.

> You never know what's around the corner. Go Slow!

THE EDITORIAL PAGE

Editorials. Editorial comment is barred from the news columns. On his own page the editor may approve or criticize, argue either side in a controversy, and recommend support of this or that cause or policy. Here also news of the day is interpreted or enlarged upon as it is in the special feature article, but more briefly and usually with a greater dignity of style than in the news columns.

Editorials grow out of the news. Those who are influenced by them believe in the soundness of the editor's judgment and opinions. The publicity writer, then, should gain access to the editorial page by way of the news columns. That is to say, he is concerned with supplying news which he hopes will inspire favorable editorial com-

ment. He may call his news to the editor's attention, or supply
the editor with facts and figures in convenient form for editorial use,
or take up with him errors that have appeared in the news or editorials. He may and sometimes does, after consultation with the
editor, write material to include in editorials which are printed, for
editors are sometimes glad to receive authoritative comment on
subjects of which they know little.

Letters to the Editor. On the editorial page of some city newspapers a definite section is devoted to letters from readers. Important communications from well-known people are occasionally
given considerable space, but ordinarily, short letters of from 100
to 200 words stand a better chance of obtaining publication. If
the writer wishes to have his name and address withheld from publication, he should be careful to say so. The editor takes no responsibility for opinions or statements in letters.

Here is the opportunity to which we referred earlier for appeals,
announcements, comment, protest, or anything else that the social
worker may have to say which does not belong in the news columns
or special departments.

Letters expressing appreciation of the newspaper's editorials or
accurate reporting are likely to be welcomed. Such letters will be
more significant to the editors if they include references to distinctive services of the respective papers in place of being a form letter
sent to all the papers. In a money-raising campaign a letter thanking the editor for his co-operation in bringing the services of the
particular organization to the attention of people is usually written
by the executive secretary or the president of the board. This
acknowledgment is the editor's due, but is too often forgotten.
Letters containing arguments for the support of measures or de-
nouncing some public nuisance are often printed. Corrections of
errors in news and editorial columns are likely to be printed here.

Clare M. Tousley, of the Charity Organization Society of New
York, which frequently obtains the publication of letters to the
press, tells how it is done:

Doing this sort of publicity means watching the papers very closely
each day, perhaps having some one clip them for you, and then answering anything that possibly has a bearing on your work. For instance in the "Letters to the Editor" column of the New York Sun ap-

peared one letter entitled "Find World Cruel to the Sick," from a man who said he had tuberculosis and nobody would help him. Our Society answered this in an open letter to the Editor telling just what we are here for and asking the man to come in. Our letter was then answered by two or three other open letters from readers complimenting the city on having a society that showed such interest in people in trouble. Perhaps a letter appears from a citizen on the subject of public begging. Answer it and get some constructive ideas across. Sometimes the public criticizes the methods of charitable organizations. Don't pass up such a challenge. Meet it. . . .

If weeks go by and no fitting chance comes to answer some article, then throw out something to the public on your own hook by submitting a letter on some subject close to the interests of your organization. You may get a four line nibble or even a thirty line bite in response to your literary casting.[1]

Special Campaigns Conducted by the Newspaper

A newspaper sometimes undertakes a campaign of its own to promote or to combat some project and for a few weeks or months devotes to it the time of members of its staff, space in its news columns, photographs, cartoons, and editorials. Money is raised for causes in this way. Fresh air funds, ice funds, and contributions for Christmas giving are a few examples. The New York Times, in co-operation with six charitable societies, conducts an annual Christmas season campaign of appeal for "New York's 100 Neediest Cases." This is one of the most successful of its kind, the total contributions having increased from $3,600 in 1912, the year the campaign was begun, to $280,000 in 1926 when nearly 400 cases were given aid. The Daily News, New York City, undertook to find homes among its readers for children under the care of a child-placing agency, all the social work in connection with selecting the homes, and placing and supervising the children being done by the agency. Baby contests have been run by newspapers. At the time of a New York health exposition some of the local papers took space to call attention to health campaigns of their own.[2] "Summer Opportunities for Volunteers" is the title of a campaign conducted annually by the Cleveland Plain Dealer in

[1] "Roots." *In* The Family, New York, vol. 3, July, 1922, pp. 126–127.
[2] See p. 308.

co-operation with the Associated Charities and also adopted in other cities. Each day the opportunity to give pleasure to a "shut in" person or to perform some other small service is described along with a story of what was done the day before.

The social organization which co-operates with a single newspaper in some special campaign or project usually finds it well to offer some other form of co-operation to rival newspapers in the same community.

FEATURE ARTICLES

Feature articles are published in magazine sections of Saturday or Sunday newspapers, and from day to day on editorial or other pages.

The special feature article is defined thus by Willard Grosvenor Bleyer:

> It usually deals with (1) recent news that is of sufficient importance to warrant elaboration; (2) timely or seasonal topics not directly connected with news; or (3) subjects of general interest that have no immediate connection with current events. . . .
>
> It aims to supplement the bare facts of the news report by giving more detailed information regarding the persons, places, and circumstances that appear in the news columns. News must be published as fast as it develops, with only enough explanatory material to make it intelligible. The special article, written with the perspective afforded by an interval of a few days or weeks, fills in the bare outlines of the hurried news sketch with the life and color that make the picture complete.
>
> The special feature article must not be confused with the type of news story called the "feature," or "human interest," story. The latter undertakes to present minor incidents of the day's news in an entertaining form. Like the important news story, it is published immediately after the incident occurs.[1]

Feature Articles Related to the News. An article giving the history of the Christmas seal of the National Tuberculosis Association was used in many Sunday papers during one of the annual sales. It told how a friend of the tuberculosis movement had heard of the use of the seal in Denmark; how the idea was tried in America;

---

[1] How to Write Special Feature Articles. Houghton Mifflin Co., Boston, 1920, p. 4.

A NEWSPAPER'S PHILANTHROPIC ENTERPRISE

A page from the New York Times during the period covered by its fourteenth annual appeal for "New York's 100 Neediest Cases."

Fifty Old Men and Women Make Christmas Toys

The Crawford Shop Is Celebrating Tenth Birthday—Gives Aged Work

Only three weeks till Christmas
And all through the shop
No hum has ceased to
The hum never stops
Of busy old fingers that fashion
Forth wonderful toys
For Santa Claus's children—
Little girls and boys.
There are ducks that can waddle,
And horses, and wagons,
And camels, and all
The wonderful things
That Santa Claus brings—
(Comes any old night)
Another that stops,
He's sending them, stacking them
To tuck in your stocking
On Christmas Day.

Can you imagine a Santa Claus workshop right here in New York City? Well, there is one—and it's just around the corner at No. 105 East 13th Street. Such a busy shop it is, with its patter and clatter! Why, it fairly hums at Christmas. But, instead of one old Santa, there are fifty of them, and just as shaggy old half-Santas. And fast as their gnarled fingers can fly they are making the toys, wonderful wonderful toys you ever saw for boys and girls.

Take a peek into the carpenter shop; look through the window in the old Jim Grayson. Grayson of the once-white hair and the merry twinkling eye, putting the last artistic flourish on his Noah's Ark. He'll delight in showing you this ark, with its broad procession of animals and he'll say with pride and a roughish look: "There's every animal that went into the ark—and more besides."

A little further along is old John Thompson, but nobody calls him that. He's "Reindeer John" to the old folks in the shop because—well, there's no one in New York can make a better reindeer than old John Thompson. He's good at making horses, too. Now he's making a hobby horse—the kind that small boys dream about, with a flying mane and lively eyes and a genuine leather saddle.

Grandad Parker is making a wonderful doll house and is sticking it together, bit by bit. Look in. There are tables and chairs and little beds and a tiny cradle. And there is a real kitchen with a stove and a place and windows that open and shut. Oh, it is too good to be true.

Any little girl would dance at the very thought of it.

So it goes. Everywhere you look some miracle of toyism is being performed—to the happy hum of hammer and saw—and by these men, all of whom are at least seventy-five or eighty years old.

Is the women's workroom it is different, but every bit as busy. There thirty grandmothers stitch away at the dolls' clothes. There is many a little old Mother Hubbard that's making her twenty-fifth pair of small boy's overalls, and they are applauded with "Grandma Parker—well, she's

colors! Did you ever see such funny little figures of cats and dogs, frocks as they are making. And even elephants and a real-looking bean bag! Some things make toys, and other fantastic toys.

SOME of the HEADS of SANTA CLAUS'S CABINET

(Left) JIM GRAYSON

(Right) THOMPSON

prim doll dresses, and there are baby dolls, baby dolls and even old black mammy dolls.

Far over in the northeast corner of the workroom is a group of ten or more busy women playing and starting great big piles of red. Would you believe it—they all can be made of it. "Reindeer John" was asked the name stockings. Each one has on it the name and address of some boy or the happiest-looking man in all the New York boys and girls. In many a heart each of them will go full of good things to some boy or girl.

Children of the Poor to Have Day Brightened by Articles Formed by Aged Hands

You, these fifty people made them all, and they will be sent to poor children everywhere—some will go to the hospitals, some to the orphanages and others to the scattered schools in the cities. Who fills them? Hundreds of schools, clubs and even busy mothers and women. You can fill one if you'd like.

"The Crawford Shop is celebrating its tenth birthday," Mr. Mathews said. "Mr. Mathews was the founder and still is the director of this old people's workshop.

"There have been all old people who have worked at the toy shop since the beginning," he continued. "Four of those of this early days still are with us—real patriarchs just past their eightieth three-score-years-and-ten when they first applied at the shop. 'Courageous old boys they were, hardly ever missing from their benches, no matter how bad the weather.

"Take old Jim Grayson. It was ten years ago that he came into my office after having worked several trades in search of some kind of a lighter job. 'I guess it ain't no use to look no more,' he said. 'I've tried all the places I can think of and they all say the same thing to me—you're too old to be of any use.'

"It was not a new story to me," Mr. Mathews said. "Scores of times I have heard practically the same words spoken in hopeless, discouraged fashion by old men and women as they came to realize that the doors leading to work are closed to them for all time. But we put Jim Grayson to work in the carpenter shop and when he first started making camels and giraffes for the Noah's Ark he remarked: 'You won't be sorry.' And all through it, He managed to make it adept at making the whole ark doors."

All through the shop one is conscious of the great contribution the old folks are making the toys and in the fact that through the aged of the handiwork they get the real joy they are self-supporting.

When they first come on to the New York boys and girls. Here's the basket which holds all them: "Merry Christmas. Here's a real old friend calling. And each of these will go full of good things to some boy or girl." And good wishes to some boy or girl.

and how, from modest beginnings, it grew until 650,000,000 seals costing one cent each were being issued in the campaign of that year. The fact that the double-barred cross, the emblem of the campaign, was widely displayed in advertising and posters, and frequently mentioned in the news, opened the way for a feature story beginning "The double-barred cross is seventeen years old today." How Oliver Wendell Holmes came to name tuberculosis "The White Plague" was another timely Sunday story. A sketch about the artist who designed the seal sale poster was widely published during one annual campaign.

While the Sheppard-Towner bill for the protection of maternity was before Congress and many news items were appearing about it, an article was sent out by the Maternity Association of New York describing current superstitions concerning childbirth. One of these was that the mother "marks" the baby through an unsatisfied craving; another, that if an expectant mother passes a man chopping wood the baby will have a harelip; and a third, that a complimentary remark about the new baby wards off bad luck. Accounts of these and other strange beliefs handed down from older generations paved the way for explaining how the appropriation called for in the maternity bill would be used to educate expectant mothers.

Timeliness is not essential to the feature article. "A Child's Day in Court," "Red Tape to the Rescue," and "Germ-Proofing a City" are titles of feature articles about social work which have appeared in magazine sections of Sunday newspapers. All these articles tell of routine experience with a liberal use of human interest material.

Interviews. The interview is a kind of article which may or may not be related to current news, but which will find its way into the newspaper if the subject material is fresh and the treatment skilful, or the person interviewed well known. During a campaign for funds, the National Girl Scouts gave to the press a story containing an interview with Mary Roberts Rinehart in which she is quoted as saying:

> There comes a critical time in a girl's mental and spiritual life when she is waiting impatiently for young womanhood. The things of her childhood have lost their interest, she has abandoned her dolls and she is

peculiarly isolated. At the same time, with no increased outlet for her activities, her imagination is being stimulated as never before by books, magazines, automobiles, moving pictures, all revealing this strange thing we call life, on which she is a yearning onlooker.

It is time to realize that hundreds of thousands of young girls in this country, doubly important now that they are future citizens as well as potential mothers of future citizens, must have occupation, a feeling of responsibility, a practical idea to which they can bring their loyalty and enthusiasm. They need organized play, they need to be taught that which is the "gang spirit" among boys, they need to learn that their young bodies are to be used, not decorated. Until they can learn that we shall have sickly mothers and puny babies.

The interviewer may collect opinions from a number of prominent people in support of or in opposition to some assertion which has appeared in print.

Style in Special Articles. Unlike the news article, the special article may begin in any way that attracts attention without regard to the why, what, who and where, how, and when of the matter. In the following paragraphs from the New York Evening World the jocular, apparently irrelevant, opening slips easily into an interesting account of a partnership plan which was one of the subjects in a series of industrial studies.

New Yorkers, when they get tired of making jokes at the expense of Yonkers, Hoboken, and Brooklyn, go sixty-five miles up the Hudson River and pick on Wappingers Falls. It is the original horse laugh for the residents of Poughkeepsie, five miles away.

Take your laugh now, and then settle down for a little serious enlightenment as to Wappingers Falls.

In that hidden village of 3,000, back of the Hudson banks and not yet dignified by a railroad station, is the Dutchess Bleachery, one of the largest establishments in this line of the textile industry. The Bleachery employs some 600 men and women, principally unskilled labor, and the families of the workers comprise the bulk of the town's population. Some years ago a new concern took hold. It inherited the traditions and the bad blood engendered by nearly a century of feudal domineering by the old management over its underpaid, ill-housed employees.

On the new Board of Directors was a man who had a new idea of the relationship of capital to labor, and he presented a partnership plan which has completely changed the old order of things. That plan has been at work now since 1919. It has had an opportunity to show its

88

usefulness or its futility, and the Department of Industrial Studies of the Russell Sage Foundation today makes public a 150-page report which declares the plan to be a wonderful success and a long step in the direction of a new industrial relationship.

Any readable style which the writer can handle with sureness and which fits his material is appropriate to the special article. It is, perhaps, for this reason, together with the less rigid requirements regarding news value in it, that many of the untrained or partly trained persons who write about social work for newspapers succeed better in writing special articles than in writing news articles. It is also true that social work provides much more and better material for special articles, as will be brought out in the next chapter.

Photographs in Newspapers

The increasing popularity of photographs is evidenced by the fact that a newspaper made up chiefly of pictures with brief captions and short paragraphs of news very rapidly acquired the largest circulation of any morning newspaper in the country.

In the daily newspaper photographs appear in connection with news articles and as illustrations in various departments. A number of newspapers now use once or twice a week or even daily a page of photographs with some such title as "Camera News" and "News of the Day Told in Pictures." In both daily and Sunday newspapers, groups of photographs and sketches illustrate many of the feature articles.

The best opportunity for graphic publicity, however, is in rotogravure sections of Sunday newspapers which have wider circulation than many of the daily issues and in which the photographs appear to much better advantage because of the better quality of paper on which they are printed. National organizations carrying on intensive campaigns devote a great deal of effort to getting pictures taken by the various photographic services which make a business of selling pictures chiefly to the Sunday graphic sheets.

The same principles apply to the selection of subjects for pictures as for news and feature stories. The news value of a photograph depends on timeliness, if an event is pictured; prominence, if the photograph is of some person; on human interest; on some

startling contrast; or on the unusual nature of the object illustrated. Children are very desirable as subjects of photographs,
partly because everyone enjoys seeing them, and partly because they
are not self-conscious and photograph much better than adults.
Underwood and Underwood, one of the newspaper photographic
services, at one time reported as their second most popular picture
that of a dozen children seated on a bench in a public playground.
It was taken by a photographer who, with one unexposed plate in
his holder, "stopped to 'shoot' these ragamuffins because their contagious good humor caught his fancy."[1]

Photographs of women are preferable to those of men. The child
shown with his pet dog or with some other animal is especially interesting because animals, too, make good pictures. The smaller
the number of persons in a picture the better as a general rule.[2]

Since pictures are likely to be seen by a much larger number of
newspaper readers than an article relating to the same subject,
it follows that captions have great importance from the publicity
standpoint. The first line usually suggests the significance or
sentiment of the picture and gives the name of any well-known
person or place that is to be featured. The caption accompanying the picture of a popular young film star holding up for view a
large sack evidently stuffed with supplies reads as follows:

> Bundle Day in Filmdom: Jackie Coogan Helps Pack the Million-
> Dollar Cargo for Near East Relief Which He Assembled in a Tour of the
> Country.

A photograph of an automobile struck by an engine to which cling
parts of the wrecked car has below it this caption:

> An Object Lesson for the Careless Motorist: Just what happens
> when a railroad train strikes an automobile was demonstrated thus
> by the Southern Pacific at Florence, Cal., while movie cameramen
> ground out films to be used in a safety campaign.

It is possible, indeed, to tell a story in some detail through a
page of pictures such as is sometimes secured in connection with
a money-raising drive or other intensive campaign.

[1] Cushing, C. P., "A Cat May Look at a Kaiser in the Camera's Best Sellers."
In Collier's, New York, Oct. 18, 1924.
[2] See discussion of photographs, p. 185.

*(Photographs by Underwood & Underwood
and A. Tennyson Beals)*

PHOTOGRAPHS THAT HAVE NEWS VALUE

NEWSPAPER ADVERTISEMENTS

By buying space in the advertising columns, the social agencies may say to newspaper readers whatever they please and also choose their own time for saying it. They may appeal, advise, persuade, announce, or present their side of a controversy. They may also have the advantages of display arrangement of type and pictures which makes their message stand out from the rest of the reading matter on the page. Nevertheless, as compared with other forms of publicity, paid advertising is very little used by social organizations. We find it most often in intensive campaigns in which half-page, full-page, or even double-page advertisements may appear, such as are shown on page 92. Appeal advertising has been used occasionally by groups of social agencies which obtain space at special rates on a page devoted chiefly to such material.

Advertisements of an educational nature, which are much used by commercial advertisers interested in health, as, for example, insurance companies, milk dealers, and organizations like the Life Extension Institute, suggest the possibilities of this medium of public information. Some health departments have used advertising in connection with special campaigns, such as vaccination against typhoid or the announcement of special clinics.

The Haverhill, Massachusetts, Tuberculosis Association for several years has bought space on the front page of the evening newspaper for a small box in which there appears a daily "Healthgram" over the signature of the association. These brief paragraphs give practical advice, simple physiological or psychological information, or, sometimes, notices of association events or other activities affecting the welfare of the public. Each insertion is preceded by

(Read yesterday's healthgram.)

and followed by

(Read tomorrow's healthgram.)

An idea of their range of subject and informality of style may be gained from the following samples:

Feet properly considered tend to keep their owners in good health. It is wise to buy good shoes, with plenty of room, wide at the toes, broad soles, low flat heels preferably of rubber. Do not continue to wear shoes that are out of shape and with the heels badly worn.

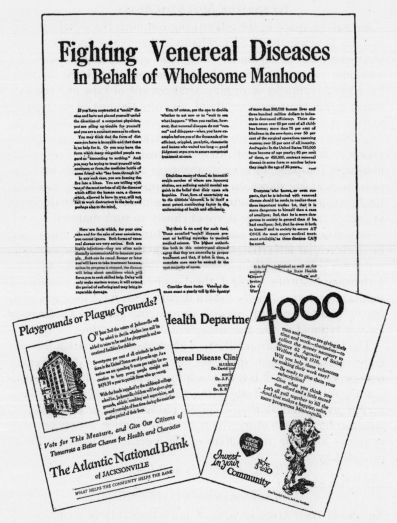

EXAMPLES OF SOCIAL WORK ADVERTISEMENTS

The full-page advertisement in the center was used by the West Virginia Department of Health in an educational campaign. The smaller advertisements below appeal for votes and money.

An underweight child is from six to twelve times more liable to have tuberculosis and from three to six times more susceptible to contagious diseases.

We know you will be interested in the proposed Curfew Ordinance. Watch the Gazette for an article explaining its much needed advantages.

Dr. I. J. Clarke, president of the Association, says of healthgrams:

They keep the name of our association before the public daily and help materially in raising a substantial sum each year with which to carry on our work. My reason for publishing them was primarily educational, to impress upon the mind of the public the importance of preventive medicine.

Mass meetings, exhibitions, and other events to which the public is invited, are often announced in paid space, where it is possible to state prominently the time, place, and admission price, which do not have an important place in the news article.

Newspaper space for non-commercial advertising is sometimes obtainable at reduced rates. Often the space used by the social agency is a contribution from some large commercial advertiser or an interested individual. In general, when it comes to buying advertising space, however, there seems to be a widespread feeling that this is an unnecessary expense and one which lays the social agency open to criticism.

A discussion as to whether social agencies should or should not advertise is fruitless. Whereas generalizations on this question are impracticable, a few considerations may be helpful in deciding any given case. Certainly one would not expect to pay for space in which to present anything which rightfully belongs in the news columns. The decision to be made is not between free space, or paid space, but between spending money for newspaper advertising or spending it for some other form of publicity, such as pamphlets or folders to be distributed by mail to smaller, selected audiences. Through display advertising one can reach a much larger audience at less cost than through mail distribution and certainly with considerable saving of time and trouble. On the other hand, a group of readers selected for a given purpose can generally be reached better by direct distribution. Again, it may be desirable to distribute one's appeal or information in a more personal way than through an advertisement.

CHAPTER VI

SOCIAL WORK AS A SOURCE OF NEWS

HOW much of what happens in the course of a month or a year in a given social movement is worth reporting? How does the publicity worker get at this news, or for that matter, how does he recognize it when he sees it? How can he develop what is known as "a news sense"?

Walter Lippmann[1] tells of a reporter who "guessed the name of the next Indian viceroy when he heard that Lord So-and-So was inquiring about climates." Here we have illustrated that ability for scenting a story which is commonly called "a nose for news." It is a gift worthy to be cultivated not only by the one who writes the social agency news but by the workers whose daily tasks may develop something of interest to the public, and the executives who decide what should be given to the press. With everybody on the lookout for news, whoever is in charge of giving it out may depend upon having it brought to his attention promptly.

Often the social worker's professional relation to his facts and experiences so overshadows all other aspects of them that he has difficulty in recognizing what is suitable for newspaper publication. If he regards himself for the time being as a reporter, and tries to look at his work from the angle of its interest to newspaper readers, he may more easily acquire a sense of news values and learn, when necessary, to subordinate his "inside" point of view.

ACCESS TO NEWS SOURCES

Much social welfare news which we see in print runs along a fairly dead level of unexciting, commonplace happenings. A meeting has been held; an annual report is out; or an appeal for funds is about to be made. These are the obvious things to publish; they are easy to get and may be written in stereotyped fashion with very little effort. But the best news material does not always lie on the surface. A good story may be buried in the files

[1] Public Opinion. Harcourt, Brace and Co., New York, 1922, p. 340.

because it happens to be contained in a letter; or it may be in a report where human interest has been effectively concealed under a mass of technical terms.

The publicity worker who gives out the news should be permitted every opportunity to tap fully the resources of his field. Given a complete understanding of what information is confidential and what is not, he should have free access to the office records and should attend not only more general gatherings but board and committee meetings as well, so that he will be able to select his material with discrimination and write his copy intelligently. He should know in advance what plans are afoot, for news is sometimes in the making long before it is ready to be reported, and preparing information for publication may require as long a period as carrying out the project. He may need to adjust his schedule for releasing the news to the demands of other events competing for public attention. He may even take a hand in making news by suggesting revision of some details of the plan itself so that it will interest more people. At the very least he should be consulted before dates, places, and participants are selected for any event for which newspaper mention will be sought.

It is very important that only someone who has the confidence of those responsible for the policies of the organization should be entrusted to give out the news.

For convenience in analyzing the resources of social work for newspaper copy we may divide the customary work of social agencies into five main types: that with individuals, usually called case work, with groups, social research, publicity, and administration.

Case Work

The unusual experiences of everyday people make good newspaper stories. Since a large part of social case work has to do with just such experiences, one would suppose that any social agency that serves individuals would be a mine of newspaper copy. But the relations of the nurse, the probation officer, and the family visitor with their clients are necessarily confidential.

Social agencies therefore find it necessary and proper to use extreme caution in protecting clients from having their affairs published. Even though the facts may not reflect unfavorably on the

8   95

person involved and the story may be given out with his permission, its publication may raise suspicion as to the general policy of social organizations in the matter of respect for privacy. Both those who support and those who use the services of the agency should be given every reason to feel that private affairs may be entrusted safely to the knowledge of its workers.

Occasionally something happens to clients of social agencies which may properly be reported. A lost child is brought to the office of a child-caring society and the newspaper report of the incident helps to locate parents or friends. Accounts of hardships endured by immigrant families separated through the operation of the immigration law are not likely to cause any embarrassment to the persons concerned, and they bring vividly before the public problems raised by legislation of this kind. Pictures and stories of children who win honors in spite of great handicaps may be published if no humiliation to the pride of their parents is involved in the circumstances reported. Street begging becomes less profitable and therefore less common when stories of beggars who refuse to accept suitable aid are given to the press. A letter, visit, or gift from a former client, now well and prosperous, contains the elements of a news story which may occasionally be used with the permission of the persons concerned. Sometimes they themselves are glad to spread the news of their better fortune.

There are ways to use case stories in newspapers without reporting names and identifying circumstances. When the news is contained in the fact that an annual report is just out, or an investigation has been completed, stories about individuals may be brought in as part of the report and only such facts told as are not likely to cause the persons concerned to be recognized. Feature articles, especially when they appear in newspapers of large cities or in a place other than that in which the persons written about live, provide the best opportunity for using without names material taken from case records.

The experience of a rural nurse is told in an article about the work of the department nurses released by a state department of health without identifying either the district or the family involved.

A public health nurse was called one night last week to assist with a surgical operation. Reporting it she said:

96

"The patient was in a farmhouse several miles from town and a half mile from the road across a swamp through which we had to walk. The house, barn and chicken-coop are all under one roof. We had a small kitchen table, a dripping pan, a wash basin, a teakettle, and two small dishpans to work with. We brought our own towels and sterile sheets. There were two beds in the room, in one of which there were five children, three at the head and two at the foot, and a baby slept in a cradle which was wound up like a clock and rocked itself.

"We got to the place about 10:30 p.m. We had one lamp and two lanterns for light. The patient is doing very nicely."

When several unusual incidents of similar nature have occurred within a comparatively short time, they may be brought together in a feature article. Data supplied by the Travelers Aid Society of New York City gave material to a newspaper for an amusing and at the same time sympathetic story about runaway grandmothers. Under the title " Knowing the Ropes," a charity organization society described a number of its experiences in which the real service was in directing its clients to sources of help which they might have obtained for themselves if they had "known the ropes." A state health department sent out a story containing an account of a dairy owner found to be a typhoid carrier. In the first of these articles the interest centers in the plight of old age which feels itself restricted or not useful; the second directs attention to an organization and its uses; the third, to a public danger. In each the individuals involved are only incidental and illustrative.

An account of a day at a health center or of the round of visits of a school nurse may be filled with stories which do not, to be sure, literally relate all the facts of any given case, but which do present a typical picture of such a day.

Work with Groups

Playgrounds, settlements, social or health centers, boys' and girls' clubs, and other groups develop much routine news from week to week because something reportable is always happening. There are debates, athletic and other contests, entertainments, festivals, demonstrations, exhibits of manual and art work, participation in public celebrations or special weeks, parties coming and going from the summer camp, and a host of other events. These

97

affairs take a news shape and rank with other current local doings in furnishing minor news stories or material for departments like "What the Clubs Are Doing," as is shown by this excerpt from a West Virginia paper:

> Plans are now practically complete for the Boy Scout camp at Beech Bottom on the Hughes river, July 28 to August 25. Physical examinations are being taken this week and the outlook for the general welfare of the camp is very good, this year promising to be the best ever. The advance party leaves next Monday morning at 6 a.m. and the boys going up for the first period leave one week later.

Bringing out the news value of occurrences like these is sometimes only a problem of good writing. While the mere announcement of an event is sufficient to obtain space in certain newspapers, there are often more interesting things to tell than are contained in stories like the following, which is typical of much dull reporting of group work:

> A series of community meetings is being arranged for next week at the following places: Monday at Van Zandt, Tuesday at Harmony school house, Wednesday at Ferndale, Thursday at Meridian, and Friday at Nooksack.
>
> The object of the meetings will be to arouse the interest of the communities in the vital problems of education.
>
> Afternoon and evening meetings will be held and a basket luncheon will be brought for the noon hour at each of these places. O. J. Brown, of the Normal School extension department, will speak at all the meetings, both afternoon and evening, and other addresses will be arranged to supplement the program at various places.

This bit about a boys' camp suggests the possibilities of camp life as a source of human interest material.

> A sentence to hard labor for ten minutes, anyway, is pronounced on every boy every Wednesday at Camp Carey. A letter or a postal home positively has to be written, or you can't get in to dinner. This keeps mother's mind easy. The big crowd that you see above congregates outside of the dining hall every Wednesday at noon. Literary efforts are taken as tickets at the door. Some of the postals are very funny. Gentlemen's disagreements are sometimes reported with stark realism. For example:
>
> "Dear Mother: You know why I hit Meyer because he hit me with

(*Permission of American Museum of Natural History*)

(*Permission of Tuberculosis Society of St. Louis*)

GROUP WORK WITH CHILDREN A FERTILE SOURCE OF PICTORIAL PUBLICITY

Above: Boy Scouts at the American Museum of Natural History working at taxidermy under the direction of the educational department of the Museum.

Below: The Health Gypsy of the Tuberculosis Society of St. Louis telling stories to a group of children.

a cup and a book over the head. They are giving us good eats. Will close until next week. Your truly son Joseph."

The excellent news value of the enterprise described below taken from the Brooklyn Standard-Union is obvious.

Pupils of P. S. 83 and children of the neighborhood now have a playground of their own as the result of a few hours of concentrated work on their part, yesterday afternoon, to the tune of music provided by the St. John's Home Band, and the clicking of a battalion of movie cameras.

The new playground, which, until yesterday, was a factory yard located on Schenectady Avenue, between Prospect and Park places, was speedily cleared of rubbish and vegetation and the transformation was so complete that it is with difficulty one is able to realize that school children so effectually provided their own playground. . . .

After forming at the school at 1 o'clock, the children marched in a body to the designated spot, and with spades, rakes, hoes, trowels, and even a plow, they speedily set to work to clear the lot.

Though the lot was cleaned up by the children of Public School 83, children from a wide area surrounding the school will undoubtedly congregate each afternoon at the new playground.

As one woman remarked: "The kids now have a place where they can play ball, run around and get in all the innocent mischief they want to without the fear of breaking a window or of having the cops chase them, as they do in the congested streets."

Group work, especially with children, is also a source of pictorial publicity which may sometimes be better than stories. The examples of news pictures shown on page 98 indicate some of the subjects which an alert photographer can obtain.

Social Research

Social surveys and other types of investigation with a social aspect carried on by private agencies or government bureaus supply the most important sources of news in the field of social work; editors are glad to receive news of this kind, and social programs are advanced through its publication.

The news interest in such surveys moreover lies chiefly in the social information itself and not in an irrelevant or incidental factor like the personality or prominence of persons connected with the undertaking. Hence publication of the results of the survey helps much more in spreading knowledge about social problems than does the usual social news item. In the following excerpts we find facts obtained in a survey used as leads in news stories.

> Thirty thousand women employed in the confectionery, paper box, tobacco, collar and shirt industries and in mercantile establishments in New York state are receiving less than sixteen dollars a week.[1]
>
> Corn bread and sorghum, dried beans, fat salt "middlings," and, as a redeeming feature, usually milk—for a large part of the year this is the diet of the Southern mountain children in a district where the Children's Bureau of the U. S. Department of Labor has made a survey of child care and nutrition.[2]

An announcement that a public institution or department will be investigated or that a study will be made of the causes of juvenile delinquency or of the extent of a disease, promises that facts will be uncovered which are certain to interest the public. The editor who gets wind of the proposed project immediately sends a reporter to find out everything he can about it.

When the investigation is begun, news value may be found in information about the committees which will sponsor it, the specialists who will gather the facts, and the motives for making the study.

> Dr. Haven Emerson, formerly commissioner of public health of New York City, arrived in San Francisco yesterday to begin a survey of hospital and health conditions under the auspices of the Community Chest and the Council of Social and Health Agencies. He will be here two weeks.
>
> Dr. Emerson is already familiar with the hospitals of San Francisco, having spent several months here last year when he lectured on preventive medicine at the Teachers' College and the University of California summer school.
>
> "The hospitals of San Francisco," he said yesterday, "are wonderfully well organized and equipped, but there may be lacking in this city provisions for the care of convalescents. We shall make a special study of the needs of convalescents and what provision may be made for their care so that they may be discharged from hospitals, and more quickly restored to health and strength. . . ."

[1] Brooklyn Citizen.   [2] Hoboken (N. J.) Observer.

At three o'clock Tuesday afternoon there will be a meeting of super-intendents of hospitals and clinics and delegates to the Council of Social and Health Agencies at the Sharon building, when Dr. Emerson will address them on the work of the survey.[1]

When a survey is completed, its findings may have news interest because they gratify local pride and stimulate continued good effort. "City Praised for Economy of Operation" runs the head-line of a story reporting the results of a health and hospital survey in Louisville, Kentucky. If conditions that need to be remedied are discovered, the newspapers are particularly interested in re-porting them:

Fire traps, conditions of overcrowding so bad that the children have to take turns standing and sitting, sanitation unspeakably filthy and water unfit to drink, gas escaping from obsolete lighting fixtures, gar-bage dumps beneath the windows—these are some of the things found by the Joint Committee on Education, composed of civic bodies, in its fourth annual survey of . . . schools, just completed.

An editorial writer is sometimes aroused to vigorous comment by the issue of a report on the conditions disclosed, as is shown by the following editorial:

Unfortunately, the recent demand for a survey of the elementary schools with a view of ascertaining to what extent the children are af-fected by ear trouble has proved to be only too well justified. In fact, the results of the survey may be legitimately described as astounding. In the 105 schools examined, there were found to be 191 cases of gen-uine deafness and 1,221 of defective hearing. It is no exaggeration to say that the average person, if told of these figures in advance of the test, would scarcely have thought them credible.

News value is added to the announcement of survey results if they are given out at a meeting of representative people:

Probably the most representative audience ever assembled in Roch-ester gathered in the ballroom of the Powers Hotel today to lunch and hear the report of the Rochester Juvenile Survey, a work which those who have directly interested themselves in it believe to be the biggest constructive bit of social service ever undertaken here. Out of it they expect a clearing of the vexatious problems of the delinquent boy and

[1] San Francisco Journal.

the delinquent girl, by overcoming certain impedimenta which they believe have too long obstructed the way.

This gathering today was composed of representatives from every social
and philanthropic organization in the community, of every church de-
nomination and creed—Protestants, Catholics and Jews having worked
together on the survey, or backed it up with all the strength that was in
them. Present were representatives of the courts, the various proba-
tional agencies, and the professions—medicine, law, teaching, newspapers and all the others. There were merchants, industrial heads and
many others—all come together to try to discover means for the prevention of what is called juvenile delinquency.[1]

From the standpoint of its value for immediate educational
effect, the best survey method is that in which a series of units
are completed consecutively, the findings of each being made public as it is finished. The Cleveland Education Survey in 1915,
conducted in this way, was continuously in the news for more than
a year. Following the report of each unit, the newspapers published cartoons, editorials, stories about the surveyors, and comments on the findings by educators and school board members as
well as the main results of the study.

The news value of an investigation may be greatly increased if
the information secured is assembled with an eye to interesting
the public. In the Cleveland Survey wide publicity was obtained
for the results of an investigation of the ability of school children
to spell, by circulating to the newspapers a record of the spelling
of one simple word. The fact that "seven out of every hundred
third-grade children cannot spell 'has'" figured in headlines in all
parts of the country.

Expressing figures in terms of comparisons increases the news
value of a survey report. Comparisons between neighborhoods,
nationalities, seasons, age groups, or sexes may contain the making
of news stories:

> That section of Detroit that lies west and northwest of Highland
> Park is the healthiest part of the entire city, it was said Monday by Dr.
> George T. Palmer, board of health epidemiologist. The death rate of
> this neighborhood is only 7.6 per thousand, while the average of the city
> as a whole is 10.3.

[1] Rochester Post Express.

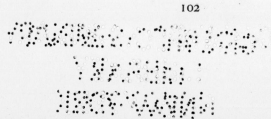

The neighborhood lying between Woodward avenue and Dequindre street, Rowena avenue and the river, has the highest death rate of any, 14.1 per thousand, and the district lying to the east of it, and extending to Mt. Elliot avenue, comes next with a death rate of 12.6.

Some years ago, by the device of ranking the educational systems of the 48 states according to their efficiency as measured by expenditures, school attendance, and other items, a tremendous amount of newspaper discussion of local school conditions was stirred up throughout the country.[1] Leading newspapers in nearly every state gave a prominent place to news and editorial comment about the standing of the state. In Missouri cartoons, editorials, photographs of educators and interviews with them expressed the chagrin or indignation of the citizens over the very low rank the state received, while headlines of Washington state dailies proclaimed that "Washington Leads the Country in Good Public Schools." In Alabama discussion based on the report continued for six months to hold a place in the news.

More recently in a study of municipal health departments,[2] the same method of comparative rating was used and added greatly to local interest in the returns. An editorial in a Pittsburgh newspaper, from which we quote, and editorial comment in many other newspapers showed that the rank attained by each city was an important element in the local news value of the report.

> Pittsburgh may well feel proud of the showing that it makes in a survey which has just been made of the health budgets of cities in the United States. It is well known by students of municipal matters that Pittsburgh is a notably healthy community. We at one time had a bad record in the matter of typhoid fever, in the prevalence of which we came close to leading the large cities of the country. But that was many years ago, and now, with a filtration plant which is regarded as a model for other cities to go by, and a water supply second in quality to none, we have one of the lowest typhoid percentages in the country.
>
> Public health, however, is not gained without liberal and even lavish expenditure of money.

[1] Ayres, Leonard P., A Comparative Study of Public School Systems in the Forty-Eight States. Russell Sage Foundation, New York, 1912 (Out of print).

[2] Report of the Committee on Municipal Health Department Practice of the American Public Health Association. Public Health Bulletin No. 136, Superintendent of Documents, Washington, July, 1923.

The World's Unemployed—A Study

Russell Sage Foundation announces the results of a five-year analysis, declaring that those out of work in all nations range from one million to six million, thousands exploited by agencies

YEAR 'ROUND IDLENESS FOR THOUSANDS SHOWN IN FOUNDATION REPORT

Big Percentage of American Workers Idle 12 Months of Year Regardless of Business Conditions, Sage Foundation Finds Through Study

FINDS JOBLESS MEN EXPLOITED

Sage Foundation Reports 10 Per Cent Always Are Idle; Urges Free Bureaus

Look in Man's Eye No Index to His Worth, Survey Shows

Nor Is Condition of Hands or Color of Collar, Says Sage Foundation; Free Employment Agencies Urged.

LARGE AMOUNT OF UNEMPLOYMENT IN UNITED STATES AT ALL TIMES IS THE DECLARATION OF EXPERTS AFTER STUDY

Report Which Shows that Unemployment Figures While Representing the Average During the Past Two Decades Is Not an Indication

Unemployment Costing Billions Annually

A Study of Employment Methods, Needs and Agencies Shows That Several Millions of Men and Women Are Constantly Unemployed Due to a Large Extent to Lack of an Adequate System of Helping the Worker to Find the Job. Result—Tremendous Losses to Industry and Poverty and Want in Many Families.

NATION-WIDE HELP FOR LABOR IS URGED

Defects Found in Federal Employment Service in Report of Five-Year Study

EMPLOYERS ARE OPPOSED

Federal "Help" Bureau Scored By Employers

Control by Labor Department Held to Render Service Partisan, Sage Foundation

NEWS GROWING OUT OF A SURVEY

Striking facts brought out in a study of public employment bureaus appear in the headlines of this group of clippings from newspapers and trade papers.

One reason (there are of course others, but this is an important one) why Pittsburgh is a healthy city is that it spends more money per capita on its health budget than any other city in America with the exception of the three small towns of Bridgeport, Conn.; Yonkers, N. Y.; and Flint, Mich. Pittsburgh devotes 81.3 cents per capita annually to its health budget.[1]

In discussing the news value of an investigation we have emphasized public interest in its local aspects. That social research on subjects of general concern may also be regarded as important news is indicated by the large amount of space given in newspapers throughout the country to reporting and commenting upon several studies which were national in scope. For example, nearly 2,000 news clippings and 1,000 editorials and signed articles were received by the Russell Sage Foundation from over 900 cities in the United States and 22 cities in foreign countries relating to a study of child marriages written by two members of its staff. The title of the book, Child Marriages,[2] contains the promise of human interest, and the facts brought out by the study were surprising, two elements which help to account for its high rating as news. Yet another study issued at about the same time on the much less dramatic subject of public employment offices[3] was also given wide attention from the press; approximately 1,000 news stories and 500 editorials were received from clipping bureaus.

Workers in medical research find newspapers eager to report experiments bearing upon the prevention or cure of disease, and the review of mortality statistics for a given area together with a health officer's comments on their significance is recognized as important news.

PUBLICITY AS A SOURCE OF NEWS

Social publicity, such as meetings, dramatic methods, intensive campaigns, and printed matter, described in other chapters of this book, offers abundant material for news, for photographs, and, in fact, for a number of the departments of the newspaper. Many

[1] Pittsburgh Press.

[2] Richmond, Mary E., and Hall, Fred S., Child Marriages. Russell Sage Foundation, New York, 1925.

[3] Harrison, Shelby M., and Associates, Public Employment Offices. Russell Sage Foundation, New York, 1924.

meetings and other events are planned with newspaper readers in view who furnish a much larger audience than the one directly addressed.

Meetings. A considerable part of all social welfare news is based on meetings of one kind or another. It does not always follow, however, that a successful meeting supplies good news. If newspaper publicity is in part the object of the meeting, a special effort should be made to see that the program promises something lively or distinctive enough to make an interesting lead.

> Just why "pure corn liquor" or "moonshine" has a more vicious kick than aged-in-the-wood whiskey was explained to the American Public Health Association meeting here today by. . . .

The news interest in this speech delivered in Cleveland secured the publication of half a column about other features of the convention in a New York newspaper.

In preparation for an address in a certain southern city, Hastings H. Hart, an authority on jails and prisons, visited the local police station. When he came before his audience of well-to-do men and women he said:

> To any woman in this audience who will go to the police station, enter the white women's cell, pick up the blanket and shake it, I will give $2, and to any woman who will lie down on the blankets and put her head on the pillow, I will give $5.

It takes only one such vigorous utterance as this in the course of a meeting to provide a lead good enough to carry with it a report of the meeting as a whole. In the paragraphs below taken from the Toronto Globe, the striking statement of the speaker of the evening carried with it into prominence the two news items accompanying it.

> "If a man steals he may be sent down for years, but if he is a brute and beats his wife to within an inch of her life he gets about 30 days," said Mr. Justice Riddell, the speaker of the evening, who addressed a dinner held at the Carls-Rite Hotel last night by the workers in the campaign for membership launched this week by the Toronto Social Hygiene Council. "Hogs, horses, and cows get all kinds of attention from stockbreeders and governments," said the judge, "but humanity gets very little attention as a Government industry or asset of the nation.

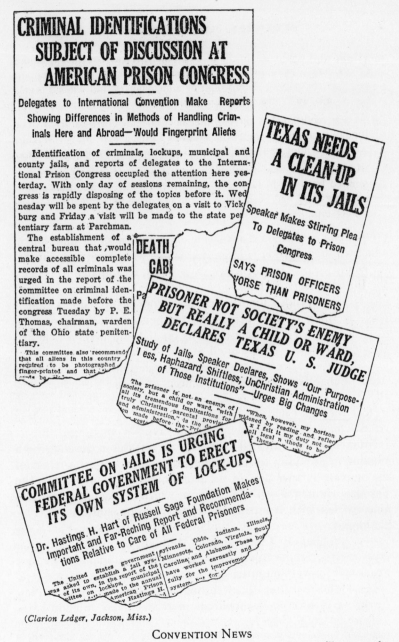

CRIMINAL IDENTIFICATIONS SUBJECT OF DISCUSSION AT AMERICAN PRISON CONGRESS

Delegates to International Convention Make Reports Showing Differences in Methods of Handling Criminals Here and Abroad—Would Fingerprint Aliens

Identification of criminals, lockups, municipal and county jails, and reports of delegates to the International Prison Congress occupied the attention here yesterday. With only day of sessions remaining, the congress is rapidly disposing of the topics before it. Wednesday will be spent by the delegates on a visit to Vicksburg and Friday a visit will be made to the state penitentiary farm at Parchman.

The establishment of a central bureau that would make accessible complete records of all criminals was urged in the report of the committee on criminal identification made before the congress Tuesday by P. E. Thomas, chairman, warden of the Ohio state penitentiary.

This committee also recommends that all aliens in this country required to be photographed finger-printed and that . . .

DEATH CAB

Pa . . .

TEXAS NEEDS A CLEAN-UP IN ITS JAILS

Speaker Makes Stirring Plea To Delegates to Prison Congress

SAYS PRISON OFFICERS WORSE THAN PRISONERS

PRISONER NOT SOCIETY'S ENEMY BUT REALLY A CHILD OR WARD, DECLARES TEXAS U. S. JUDGE

Study of Jails, Speaker Declares, Shows "Our Purpose-less, Haphazard, Shiftless, UnChristian Administration of Those Institutions"—Urges Big Changes

The prisoner is not an enemy of society, but a child or ward, with all its tremendous implications for truly Christian parental provisions and administration," is the . . . on made before the Pri . . . rest . . .

"When, however, my horizon widened by reading and reflex I felt it my duty not of all legal methods to be . . . those . . . where . . .

COMMITTEE ON JAILS IS URGING FEDERAL GOVERNMENT TO ERECT ITS OWN SYSTEM OF LOCK-UPS

Dr. Hastings H. Hart of Russell Sage Foundation Makes Important and Far-Reaching Report and Recommendations Relative to Care of All Federal Prisoners

The United States government was asked to establish a jail system of its own, in the report of the . . . ittee on lockups, municipal . . . made to the annual American Prison . . . by Hastings H. . . .

sylvania, Ohio, Indiana, Illinois, Minnesota, Colorado, Virginia, South Carolina, and Alabama. These boa . . . have worked earnestly and . . . fully for the improveme . . . system but for . . .

(Clarion Ledger, Jackson, Miss.)

CONVENTION NEWS

These clippings from a single issue of a morning newspaper illustrate the importance of convention speeches as a source of news in the city where the gathering is held.

107

If there were one-tenth of the disease among cattle that there is among our citizenry, disease of a highly dangerous character, which is sapping the life of the nation, there would be a huge outcry, but when it is only men, women and children, little is known about it and no fuss is made."

It was reported that the two first honorary members gathered in on Monday morning for the Social Hygiene Council were Mayor Maguire and R. J. Fleming, both of whom paid into the treasury of the club $100.

A 25 per cent new membership in the Social Hygiene Council was promised from the Rotary Club and other reports showed that a most promising start had been made in the big drive for a greatly enlarged membership.

Opinions as News. Canvassing opinions on some question in which an organization is interested is one way of getting material for news stories. In Rochester, New York, a campaign to remedy the throat defects of thousands of school children during one demonstration depended for its success on convincing parents that it was the thing to do. Principals, teachers, and physicians were visited, and their favorable opinions quoted in a news article had the desired effect. The United States Public Health Service sent out a questionnaire to several thousand persons, including presidents of chambers of commerce, officers of women's organizations, the mayors, and chiefs of police, asking for opinions on the question "Shall the Red Light District Go?" The 1707 returns from 572 cities which were overwhelmingly in favor of abolishing the restricted district, provided material[1] for articles containing both tabulations of replies and individual expressions of opinion. Gathering opinions on any controversial or timely question is a favorite device of the newspaper itself and one which is frequently available to social agencies, especially in legislative campaigns.

Dramatic Methods. The stunts, contests, parades, and plays described in Chapter XV, Dramatic Methods, are often planned to create news. Stunts especially are good news material because they are usually novel and often humorous or startling. The daily reports of the reducing squad during a health exposition in New York[2] were followed by hundreds of readers who, in addition to

[1] An Open Forum on the "Open House." U. S. Public Health Service, Washington, 1921.
[2] See p. 308.

being entertained, gathered also much useful information about diet and exercise.

The parade is participated in and seen by a great many people and the account of it in the press is likely to be widely read, since most people enjoy reading chiefly those things in which they have developed some interest. A local contest is another excellent source of news and is good for a story not only when it starts, and when it ends, but probably in between. In a community where contests have not been overdone the newspapers are quite likely to publish a photograph of the winner and an interview with him, as well as a story about the subject matter and purpose of the contest.

Exhibits. An exhibit may be a source of newspaper publicity at every stage in its career from its first announcement, through the first display, at the times of the visits of special delegations, and even on the occasion of its finally going into the scrap heap to be replaced by something else. The models, pictures, or whatever else make up the content of the exhibit may be photographed; the comments of visitors supply human interest stories; the facts and figures presented in exhibit form are retold in news and feature articles; the purposes of the exhibit are commented upon in editorials; and persons connected with its preparation are photographed and interviewed.

The exhibit is, as a matter of fact, sometimes more successful as a source of news than as a direct means of education because frequently the reporter, to whom the displays are carefully explained, makes clear to readers information contained in obscure charts or complicated models which confuse visitors. Again, if an exhibit has life and picturesqueness, a reporter describing it in vivid language may carry its lessons to a much larger audience than is included in the total attendance at the exhibit. At a health exposition a number of games for children were devised to combine instruction with entertainment. Here is part of the lively story one reporter wrote about them:

> Of course, there is an idea behind the games. If you bowl over a doll with a well-aimed baseball, and your name is Sammy, the conductor of the booth as he hands you your prize, also hands you a bit of a lecture, somewhat like this:

"Well, Sammy, you knocked out diphtheria that time. Now diphtheria. . . ."

And then follows a terse, illuminating lecture on diphtheria.

Measles, scarlet fever, mumps, in fact all the diseases from which children suffer, are grinning on the doll rack, and every time one is bowled over the lecture follows. The other games operate similarly. . . .

Campaigns. The exhibit is usually a part of a larger event, an exposition, a caravan, a healthmobile traveling through rural districts, or an intensive campaign. In Chapter XVIII, Elements of the Campaign, something is told of the great volume of publicity often secured by an affair of this kind where many people take part and varied and unusual things happen. In the article below from the Rochester Herald, announcing Milk Week, there are suggestions for no less than a dozen good news stories and twice as many excellent subjects for photographs. The article promises interviews with visiting speakers, stories of the health clown and health fairy, and authoritative information about milk. The subjects for additional news stories are italicized.

While the *pastors* of Rochester churches *will make announcements from their pulpits today,* Milk Week will be formally ushered in at 10 o'clock tomorrow morning, when one of the five traveling milk bars on trucks will visit the City Hall and *Mayor Clarence D. Van Zandt will drink the first glass of milk* to be sold from the bar.

Mrs. Benjamin Thompson, president of the Parent-Teachers' Association of Rochester and chairman of the milk bars committee, will serve the Mayor herself. Following the ceremony, the truck will begin the schedule to be followed by the *five traveling bars,* visiting factories during the noon hour, Baseball Park, schools after the sessions, and the factories at the closing hour.

Milk will be served at cost all this week from the traveling bars, as follows: Milk, four cents a glass; buttermilk, three cents a glass; Guernsey highballs and Holstein fizzes, three cents a glass. Use of the trucks has been donated by . . . .

Three hundred and fifty Rochester women will act as barmaids during the week, working in three shifts. Chairmen in charge of the trucks for tomorrow are . . . .

Cho-Cho, health clown, will be in Rochester for two weeks, talking before children in the schools in his unique way. *Professor Lucile Brewer, food specialist* from the School of Home Economics at the State College of Agriculture, *will conduct demonstrations* during the week, as well as Miss Elizabeth Holcombe; *Miss Anne Raymond, the Health Fairy*, will also arrive tomorrow morning to help in the campaign.

Numerous exhibits will carry the milk message all the week, among them being fifteen big milk bottles, which will be placed on the street corners where pedestrian traffic is busiest. Then there will be the mechanical cow in the window of the Sibley, Lindsay & Curr store, three exhibits showing milk as the sources of energy, lime and tissue building in the windows of the Duffy-Powers store, and other exhibits in . . . .

Slogans are already *being submitted* to the Milk Week Committee at headquarters at the Chamber of Commerce by children in the public and parochial schools. *Six prizes* are offered. High school pupils are busy after school hours competing for the *$25 and $15 prizes offered for the best milk fairy story* or children's story.

The Milk Week *activities will end with a big public mass meeting* at Convention Hall at 2 o'clock next Saturday afternoon, when prizes will be awarded to the nutrition class pupils for those showing the greatest gain during the year. Eight hundred seats will be reserved for members of these classes and their mothers.

Representatives of the organization cooperating in Milk Week will be on the platform. Cho-Cho will give a performance, Jefferson Junior High School pupils will give a health play, under the direction of Miss Gertrude Ermatinger, and a public school orchestra will play.

Agencies cooperating toward the success of Milk Week are as follows: Board of Education, Health Bureau, Business Woman's Club, Chamber of Commerce, ...

Printed Matter. Written publicity whether it takes the form of letters, circulars, an annual report, or a monthly bulletin, may appear in its original form or be summarized in the newspaper. The North Carolina Health Department built up a large mailing list for its monthly health bulletin by announcing in the newspapers each month the contents of the current issue and inviting requests for copies. When a folder on vacation advice is ready for circulation, or any other new piece of literature is received from the press, it may be reproduced in part in some department of the newspaper, it may be made the basis of an editorial, or, if it is impressive enough, it may be described in the book review section. Here are two examples in which the mailing of a circular letter was made the basis of news stories:

9 III

The County Tuberculosis Association is sending out today 40,000 letters to its friends and liberal-hearted citizens. In these letters will be found a number of Christmas seals which are offered for sale. It hopes that everyone will accept the enclosures and remit the amount asked. . . .

The State Board of Health has just issued a letter to the division superintendents of schools in Virginia thanking them for their co-operation in the conduct of physical examinations of pupils in the public schools. During the year 127,187 children were examined for defective vision, defective teeth, defective tonsils, and poor nutrition. . . .

ADMINISTRATIVE WORK

Meetings of boards of directors or committees, the making of budgets and financial reports, elections of officers, appointments or resignations of staff members, the purchase of new equipment, the launching of new projects, the redistricting of the field work, and many other matters having to do with making the wheels go round are routine sources which yield brief news items and occasionally important articles.

In the smaller places such minor happenings may be reported as that a new car has been purchased to increase the efficiency of the work of the rural nurse; that 100 telephone calls and 75 letters went out of the office during April, or that a former board member who has moved out of town dropped into the office to find out how things were going.

Such news undoubtedly deserves to be reported, especially when it is local and brings in prominent people, but it should not be overlooked that much of it is colorless and requires good writing to make it at all interesting.

When a member of a local staff attends a state or national meeting, the event may furnish a peg on which to hang news of the local organization. A story in the Johnstown Tribune, reporting the return of the secretary of the Municipal Recreation Committee from a conference of the Playground and Recreation Association of America reads in part as follows:

"Johnstown may well be proud of its playground work, the exhibit of dolls made and dressed, yarn rugs, bead work, wax work, cork and wooden toys, and handkerchiefs being highly commented upon by the delegates," Mr. Buettner stated. He declared the exhibit was one of the very best there, and as a result many applications have been received from various playground directors requesting that the exhibit might be loaned them to show to the people in their communities, with an idea of branching out along these lines. The exhibit was arranged under the direction of Miss Regina Maloy and Miss Frieda R. Fleck, instructors at the local playgrounds. Permission has been granted Mr. Buettner to send the exhibit around the country to those who apply for it. . . .

The Cochran Junior High School of this city was complimented by the Congress for the excellent artists' program it has arranged for this winter for the people of the municipality, a resolution being passed commending the authorities for their activity in arranging such an excellent program.

Personality. Resolutions passed at board meetings probably make dull reading, but the persons who proposed them and their relation to the organization may be of genuine interest. Many readers are more interested in people than in ideas, plans, elections, and budgets. Whenever administrative activities may be connected with notable people, they may be considered fairly good material for articles. That Mrs. S., who is a pioneer in the work of child placing, has been re-elected vice-president after fifty years of service is an occasion for an interesting interview giving some glimpse of her fine spirit of service. When a business man is elected a director of a health organization and talks about himself in relation to his new responsibilities, the interview will probably be read by other business men:

Firmly convinced that Health Work pays, M. J. Cleary of Milwaukee, vice-president of the Northwestern Mutual Life Insurance Company and a newly elected director of the Wisconsin Anti-Tuberculosis Association, has accepted the responsibilities of membership on the association's executive committee. This committee is composed of representative business and professional men who serve without pay, who meet together at least once a month throughout the year to transact association affairs, and to whom all questions of policy are referred.

"For years, as a business man, as an insurance man and as a citizen interested in community progress and in protection of the home, I have been keenly interested in the work which has been done by the Wisconsin Anti-Tuberculosis Association and if I can contribute something to the success of that work I shall be both proud and happy," said Mr. Cleary, when asked if he could find it possible to serve. . . .

"Naturally, insurance men are in a position to realize the danger and costliness of tuberculosis more than the average business man. As a rule, deaths from tuberculosis occur in the prime of life and while the loss in the case of insured men is heavy on the insurance companies, yet it is a mere trifle when compared with the losses that are inflicted on community and state and on the nation at large by the untimely cutting off of the producing power of these men, who should be in the very height of vigor and power, by the widowing of their wives and by the orphaning of young children."[1]

The services offered by day nurseries are generally of a routine nature, so a description of them has little news value. Yet this story of one nursery was retold during a campaign because of the interest in the personality of its superintendent:

"Where do you want to go when you die?" was the question put to Miss Newell just offhand, the other day by one of the babies at the old Adams Street Mission Day Nursery.

Miss Newell smiled. "I don't care much where," she said, "as long as there are a lot of babies there."

And from this intended bit of humor came the story of her work with children who come to the Day Nursery and bits of things about herself. . . . Miss Newell takes her work seriously. She says of all the things this big earth has to offer, there is nothing which to her seems so delightful and so gratifying as the handling of children—anybody's children—and "no children are bad," says Miss Newell emphatically.

The story of the individual worker need not always play up personality. "The Singular Story of the Mosquito Man" and "The Job Lady" are titles of articles[2] in which the unusual nature of the occupation supplied the human interest.

An editorial writer in commenting adversely on the type of health officer who is an "indefatigable limelighter" points out that we cannot ignore the value of personality as a good and legitimate news source:

In all fairness though, it should be interpolated, that there are some personalities which in themselves are news and a health worker should not be classified as an autogenous advertiser merely because his name

[1] News release from Wisconsin Anti-Tuberculosis Association.

[2] Bleyer, Willard Grosvenor, How to Write Special Feature Articles. Houghton Mifflin Co., Boston, 1920, pp. 242, 293.

adorns the public prints at frequent intervals. Some people are always a good story. Their simplest act contains that intangible dramatic, histrionic, arresting quality which always excites interest. . . . This type of man . . . is frequently a great asset in a health publicity campaign since he can always attract immediate attention through the press. . . .[1]

House Organs. Indirectly, the house organ, which is the logical place for much of the administrative news and which has a circulation only among those especially concerned with the activities of the agency publishing it, may be an influence in securing space in the daily newspapers. If well written, it arouses the interest of its readers not only in itself but in other news of the agency, wherever published. As an organization becomes widely enough known to justify editors in using some of its material, copies of the house organs should be sent to the newspapers in advance of the general distribution.

LIMITATIONS IN THE USE OF NEWS SOURCES

Not every item of social welfare news which the editor might accept is suitable from the social worker's point of view. Whereas a reporter appraises material for his paper on the basis of its possible interest to readers, the publicity worker must take into account also what the effect of its publication will be on the public attitude toward his organization, its policies, and the work it is aiming to do.

As a part of its educational work, a health center in New York City conducted a contest to find the healthiest child among those living in the neighborhood of the center. A reporter wrote up the results of the contest as follows:

The New York Herald reporter interviewed Mrs. La Faso regarding the system she employed to fetch her Frank to such a point of perfection as to let him walk away with the first prize offered by the Association for Improving the Condition of the Poor for the healthiest kid of less than six in the twenty-nine city blocks to form the Mulberry Health Center.

"What does he eat?" Mrs. La Faso was asked.

[1] "Personality in Public Health Publicity." *In* The Nation's Health, Chicago, vol. 4, Oct. 15, 1922, p. 604.

"Evr't'in. Francisco, taal heem what you like."

"Peekle," said Frank.

"W'at else," pursued Mrs. La Faso.

"Cocoanut, peekle, watermelon, lickerish, spaghetti, ravioli, pork, ice-cream, peekle, soda water," enumerated Frank.

"W'at you like heem best?"

"Peekle."

Frank has a Tom Sharkey chest and the lungs of a Joe Humphreys. Also he has six or eight brothers and sisters. He looks as though large quantities of fresh air were wont to percolate through his system. But inasmuch as the La Faso flat at 293 Elizabeth Street is no hanging garden, Mrs. La Faso was asked how she managed to keep Frank supplied with plenty of air.

"Planty air?" she repeated. "Sure. And planty brother and seester and coosin. Planty company for heem in hees bed all night. Planty, maybee three or four in hees bed wit' heem. Good for heem. Planty air. Sure!"

From the newspaper standpoint this story would be hard to beat. As publicity it is decidedly not a success. It seems to prove to readers, some of them only too willing to have this opinion corroborated, that the poor thrive excellently on poverty, bad diet, and overcrowding, and that such enterprises as health centers are a waste of money.

Unfair Reporting. A deliberate intention to report only what is favorable to a cause is without doubt the kind of propaganda condemned by those who claim that information given in the newspapers can no longer be depended upon because so much of it is not unbiased reporting of facts but prejudiced statements given out to serve a special purpose. This criticism applies also to news writing in which the motives and often the sources of information are concealed.

A social agency that is sound in purpose, ethical in its methods, and frank in its dealings with the press does not come within the scope of these criticisms which are for the most part directed either toward commercial advertising disguised as news, or toward insidious propaganda given out by one party to a controversy.

There are none of the elements of sinister intention, concealment, or unfairness which most of the critics of propaganda probably have in mind in the various movements for protection of the public against disease, accidents, and public nuisances or in the work of providing resources for education, play, family welfare, better housing, and the like.

TESTING THE PUBLICITY VALUE OF THE NEWS PUBLISHED

The customary method of evaluating newspaper publicity is to subscribe to clipping bureaus or to do one's own clipping of the newspapers to which publicity material has been supplied. The actual amount of space obtained is then counted and reported as evidence of achievement.

Quantity of publication, however, is only a small part of the goal of the publicity writer. An analysis of the clipping book containing the newspaper publicity during a given year should take account of other factors than amount of space obtained. Why not, as far as it is possible to do so, check up the content of the clippings with the purposes for which the information was sent out? How many times has the same name, idea, or fact, been published? How often and in what way has it been mentioned in the headlines? Has it appeared frequently enough and conspicuously enough to justify a belief that it is now familiar to readers? Has it appeared only in stories of the kind likely to be read by "socially minded" people or has it now and then been given sufficient human interest to attract the attention of general readers?

Such a critical analysis of the newspaper stories published would undoubtedly call attention to many omissions of facts and ideas which ought to appear in the news, as well as to overemphasis of publicity which merely brings the name of the agency before the public as against that which carries with it worth-while information.

CHAPTER VII

GETTING INTO PRINT

HOW does the social agency's newspaper story reach the editor's desk? In what form should copy be sent? What chance has it of being printed? How are duplicate copies distributed? The answers to these questions are aligned with current practice in making up and issuing a newspaper. They also depend not a little on the relationship established between those who offer news and individual editors or groups of editors, press associations, and syndicates.

Since the methods of getting news into print differ in many particulars according to whether it is distributed in a city, in a state, or throughout the nation, we will discuss the subject under these three divisions.

LOCAL RELATIONS WITH NEWSPAPERS

In a local community with the exception of the very large cities, the relation between editor and social worker is normally somewhat personal. News from local health authorities, for instance, is often written by a reporter after his routine visit to the department. Some private social organizations are also on the regular beat of a reporter.

Philip P. Jacobs quotes the following advice, part of a list of suggestions prepared by a group of newspaper and publicity men for the Federal Council of the Churches of Christ in America on the relationship to be sought with reporters:

They resent being used, but enjoy being consulted.

Newspaper criticism, however unpleasant, performs a great public service. Do not shut reporters out because you think something foolish may be said in the meeting. Let them in and you will be much less likely to say anything foolish.

. Reporters are glad to do nice things for people who are taking trouble to do nice things for them. Pass along any news items which may come your way, whether they be church news or not.[1]

[1] The Tuberculosis Worker. Williams and Wilkins Co., Baltimore, 1923, p. 42.

When the social agency's news is important, the publicity worker's share in the task of getting it into print may be to call the attention of reporters to it and to help them shape the material to their own purposes.

If, for instance [the agency], is giving a dinner, a publicity agent will have prepared a list of the important guests, a list of the speakers, a digest of the speeches, and a clear, brief statement of the purpose of the occasion and its significance. This will be supplied to each reporter so that he has, without effort, all the essential data, properly arranged—and correctly spelled—and can give his mind to watching for the amusing points brought out by the speakers and for incidents which may lend color to the story. That dinner will inevitably be better reported than the one where the reporters hang about the door trying to buttonhole someone who looks intelligent and to ascertain the reason why the dinner is being held and, if possible, the names of one or two speakers.[1]

It is also important to inform an editor well in advance of meetings, conventions and exhibitions to which reporters should be sent, to provide cards of admission for them, and to supply in advance copies of important speeches marked with release dates, that is, the earliest days on which the copy may be published. At a dinner the press table should be so placed that reporters can hear easily all that is said by the chairman and the speakers.

In controversial situations or circumstances in which accuracy is difficult to achieve, it is usually more satisfactory, both to the persons supplying the news and to the reporter, to have statements of facts or expressions of opinion made in writing.

Preparing News for Publication. Many local workers prepare much of their own copy, having it ready for the reporter when he calls or sending it direct to the newspaper office.

Social service copy is, of course, subject to inquiries from reporter or editor and to changes made by the rewrite man in the newspaper office. As suggested in Chapter I, Attracting Attention, Monday may be a desirable day for releasing social welfare stories, as it is the one day in the week when general news is likely to be lighter than usual.

Copy should be typewritten. Other requirements are that it

[1] Wilder, R. H., and Buell, K. L., Publicity. Ronald Press Co., New York, 1923, p. 87.

119

should be double or triple spaced, with wide margins, and written on only one side of the sheet. The release date should be put at the top of the first page; the copy should begin at least two or three inches below.[1] Punctuation, the use of abbreviations, numerical figures, capitals, and so forth should conform as closely as possible to the typographical style of newspapers generally. Simplified spelling should be avoided. Everyone who has to prepare copy should own or have access to a good style book. A local newspaper may issue a style book or style sheet which naturally would be the first choice. A school of journalism, one or more of which is located in nearly every state, probably has either a style sheet or book.[2]

Headlines on News Releases. Headlines are not usually included in copy, although they may be written in order to give the editor the writer's idea of what is important. Country papers are often glad of suggested headlines. Headlines to be most useful are written with some knowledge of the style and make-up of the paper to be served. They should fit the space commonly given to heads in that particular paper.[3] No main word should be used twice in the same head and no period should be used.

Delivering Copy on Time. The latest hour at which newspaper editors will accept copy for any given issue depends upon the nature and importance of the material, and also upon the schedule of each particular newspaper. The publicity worker who has established personal relations with the city editors in his community is likely to know when and how they prefer to have copy delivered.

Ordinarily, a story for the morning newspaper should be delivered at about 3 p. m. of the day before. If important news is likely to develop late in the day, the city editor should be notified in advance that the story is coming and asked what is the latest hour at which it may be delivered to him.

[1] For detailed instructions about form of copy, et cetera, see Hyde, Grant Milnor, Handbook for Newspaper Workers. D. Appleton and Co., New York, 1921, pp. 135–139.

[2] *Ibid.* Chap. VI, "The Office Style Sheet" and Appendix II, "Sample Style Sheet." pp. 105–117, 211–218.

[3] For discussion of type limitations of heads, see Bleyer, Willard Grosvenor, Newspaper Writing and Editing. Houghton Mifflin Co., Boston, Revised 1923, p. 321.

As a rule news for the afternoon paper should be turned in not later than 9 a. m. Human interest stories and photographs ought to be delivered a day early. Feature articles for Sunday newspapers are arranged for well in advance and delivered at least a week, and in some cases two or three weeks before the expected date of publication.

Recognizing Requirements of the Different Newspapers. When the same information is to be sent to several newspapers the publicity writer oftens varies the form of the story to meet the preferences of the different papers for certain kinds of news, for a particular style of writing, and for long 'or short articles. In fact, an understanding of the point of view of editors and reporters, especially if it has been gained from the inside, is one of the assets of a number of publicity workers. It is a matter of professional pride with the best of these writers that they "always pay their way with news," never offering copy that they would not themselves be glad to get if they were city editors.

RELATIONS OF NATIONAL ORGANIZATIONS WITH NEWSPAPERS

The problem of national social organizations is to get material published by many editors of newspapers in all sections of the country. This brings us to the question of when, where, and how copy shall be sent out.

The way in which newspaper copy is distributed depends partly on the particular audience to be reached. News of special timeliness and general interest is given to the three or four large press associations, each of which serves a group of newspapers running into the hundreds. Each of these news agencies may then send out a story of such length and style as it thinks its clients will use. Press associations have both wire and mail service. Social work news stories, however, are commonly distributed by mail since their timeliness is seldom so immediate as to demand transmission by wire. They should not exceed 500 or 600 words in length and they should be sent to the press association from two to three weeks in advance of their release dates.

Syndicates that supply features, as we have already seen, sell to local newspapers ready-to-print material in the form of editorials, signed articles on special subjects, humor, cartoons, feature stories, children's columns, and in fact every type of material that goes into the newspaper except news and advertisements. In national social organizations one of the principal tasks is the placing of material or ideas with editors of the various syndicates and with news bureaus. Sometimes, as a result of a suggestion of the social organization, the syndicate may request or have prepared a series of articles.

As a rule, if a national organization distributes press material direct to individual newspapers, it sends any given story to a selected list in accordance with the policy about exclusive press releases described on page 127. The social agency's newspaper list[1] is frequently divided into morning and evening dailies, Sunday papers, rural weeklies, and the foreign language press, and these may be again divided into groups by locality, by size of circulation, and according to whether plate matter or mats[2] are used. When an agency supplies several newspapers in the same city it sometimes assures exclusiveness of material by dividing the lists so that each paper receives a story not sent to its rivals.

National organizations with branches or affiliations often send their releases to the state or local office to be distributed, for in every newspaper office whatever comes from a local source is sorted out first from the mass of unsolicited copy; and is likely to be regarded as having greater news value than contributions that come from a distance. As already mentioned, the addition of a local angle or tie-up to the lead of the national organization's story will further increase its chances for favorable consideration.

National organizations sometimes send copy direct to newspapers of a single state, county, or city where its facts have a local significance. The National Society for the Prevention of Blindness, for example, while its field representative was conduct-

---

[1] For the most complete lists of all types of periodicals grouped by states, cities, and special interests, see American Newspaper Annual, published annually in January. N. W. Ayer and Co., Philadelphia.

Less detailed and less expensive is Lord and Thomas Pocket Directory of the American Press, published annually in April. Lord and Thomas, Chicago.

For detailed information about daily and Sunday newspapers only, see International Year Book issue of Editor and Publisher, published annually in January. New York.

[2] Plate matter is type already cast into plate form ready for the press. A matrix, or mat, is a paper mold of a piece of type matter.

ing a legislative campaign in Pennsylvania, sent stories about local conditions direct to the newspapers of that state after consulting local committees. The American Social Hygiene Association often prepares special material for certain newspapers that have shown an interest in its work. When a western paper commented editorially upon the attack made by a congressman upon the venereal disease program the Association advocated, it mailed the editor an article replying in detail to the attack.

Distribution of Duplicate Releases. The bulk of press material sent out is mimeographed or multigraphed. A variety of explanatory statements or notes to editors are used by agencies that distribute a great deal of publicity. Some of these notes aim only to identify or make conspicuous the source of the material; others seek to impress upon editors the importance, reliability, or exclusiveness of the news. As a rule, the less said in explanation of the news, the better. Clip sheets—that is, material printed in newspaper column width—are sometimes used with the idea that this form is convenient for the editor since he can tell at a glance how much space the material will require. The advantage is a doubtful one, however, since the editor is accustomed to estimating the space on the basis of typewritten copy. Plates and mats are sometimes used for national distribution of feature material.

Relations of State Organizations with Newspapers

State organizations in getting material to newspapers use methods similar to those of both local and national agencies. In the largest city or the capital city of a state, there is published usually one newspaper, sometimes several, with a state-wide circulation. With such newspapers and with representatives of state-wide press services the publicity worker of a state agency will seek the same personal relationship that the local worker maintains with editors in his community. The state organization that carries on field work or receives reports from local branches is in a position to send out a considerable amount of localized publicity to a single neighborhood, or to have it given directly to the newspapers by a local representative.

A common practice is to supply field organizers with stories which can be worked over to meet particular local conditions.

This is done partly for the purpose of simplifying the publicity job of the local or field worker, who often looks upon the preparation of newspaper copy as an irksome and difficult task.

In conducting its demonstration clinics the Wisconsin Anti-Tuberculosis Association has used a systematized and flexible scheme of localized publicity adapted to clinics of any size. A series of preliminary stories is prepared as well as the outlines of day-by-day articles about the clinic itself and the events which follow it. The actual order and content of these stories may be of interest.

Advance story No. 1. Date, place, and auspices of clinic announced. In form of interview with organizer. Its purpose and need explained. Clinics in other places described.

Advance story No. 2. Necessity for reaching contact cases explained. Date and place of clinic incidentally announced. Schedule of factory talks given.

Advance story No. 3. Clinic program of the Association briefly outlined. Purposes of publicity explained.

Advance story No. 4. Arrival of another field worker gave opportunity for interview explaining need for early examination, conditions revealed by the draft in the World War, and danger signals in tuberculosis.

Advance story No. 5. Special qualifications and experience of some of the physicians conducting clinic described. Emphasis put upon fact that children should be given special attention.

Advance story No. 6. Wide tuberculosis experience of other physicians described. Fact that they had had sanatorium experience stressed. Photographs of some used.

Current story No. 1. Picture of busy scene at City Hall during clinic given. By describing posters used, the tuberculosis danger signals were again repeated. In reply to often asked question, interview explained that clinic is paid for by Christmas seals. The names of local people cooperating were given.

Current story No. 2. Results of clinic described. Credit given to those who bought Christmas seals in previous year. Cheerful and hospitable attitude of workers described and illustrated by case story. Proper methods of diagnosis explained. City given credit for co-operation.

Follow-up story. Summarized results of clinic. Cases already sent to sanatoriums reported. Methods of follow-up and sanatorium facilities described.

The state organization, like the national, sends out prepared copy in the various forms already mentioned, and also uses plate matter, as it can in this way reach rural weekly papers. Unlike the national organization, however, it is better able to cover its entire field, since the number of newspapers published in a state runs into scores or hundreds instead of into thousands. The state organization, in most instances, is more justified in such intensive cultivation than is the national.

Plate matter is much used by agencies which seek publicity in as many rural weekly papers as possible. The publishers of these newspapers can set only a very limited amount of any news not strictly local. The company which supplies plates to the local newspapers charges for distributing the material. Philip P. Jacobs in his book, The Tuberculosis Worker, gives helpful information on the subject:

> The use of mats or plates will be found of particular value to state, county or district organizations where a number of publications—say more than 50—are to be covered, at periodic intervals. In using mats care should be exercised in the choice of papers to which they are sent. It is a sheer waste of money to send a mat to a paper that cannot cast or stereotype a plate from it. There are some papers that do not use plate. . . . It is usually wise to circularize a list of newspapers in advance, sending them either a synopsis of the story or an actual proof of the stereotyped material to be used and asking them if they will use the mat or plate, indicating which, and promising to send it to them free of charge on request. A return post card or form should be enclosed. This involves composition and the making of original plates and proofs as a speculation, but even thus, the use of ready-to-print material becomes a comparatively cheap method of keeping one's message before the newspaper press, especially where the attention of rural readers is desired and the list is large enough. The average cost of a page of newspaper plate from the Western Newspaper Union is $2.50. The average cost of mats is somewhat less, usually not more than one third that amount, depending upon the type of material used and the cost of composition. The reduction in cost of mats, moreover, is not only in the mat itself, but also in the mailing—the mat being comparatively light material while the plate is heavy metal.
>
> For the tuberculosis worker the use of mats and plates is of particular value in syndicate feature stories, general information regarding tuber-

culosis and public health, or such material as does not have immediate and timely news value, as for example, Christmas seal propaganda. Generally speaking, plates and mats are of little value in syndicating "spot" news.

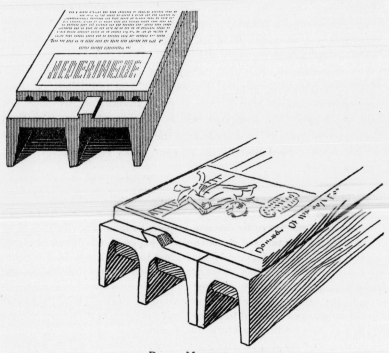

PLATE MATTER

These two cuts, pictured from slightly different angles, show the metal plate matter that is supplied to newspapers. Since the plate is a thin shell of metal, a base is necessary to raise it to the right height for printing. In the cuts the bases are pulled out to show how the plates are mounted.

Plate matter is one or more columns wide up to page width, and may be a full column in length or less.

The bases are lent by the Western Newspaper Union to publishers who retain them for continuous use. The plate matter, after it has been printed from, is shipped back to the sender to be melted down and used again.

Exclusive Press Releases. To supply exclusive material for local use a state agency may go even farther than do some of the national agencies. The Wisconsin Anti-Tuberculosis Association has systematized both its list of newspapers and the material it distributes. The address stencils for these papers, 458 in all, are filed in three major divisions. In the first division are the names of the most important newspapers in places where there are more than one. The second division contains the second most important newspaper in towns with two or more. The third division contains all those outside the first and second group. Each of these major divisions is in turn subdivided by counties. All dailies are indicated by a red signal. These devices make it possible to draw out the stencils of any group or type of journal desired. Each stencil is numbered serially to make its replacement easy.[1]

When a news story of general interest is released, it is sent to the whole list, but the story is changed somewhat for each of the three groups. This simply means that the story is written up in the usual way, but that for the second and third lists, the arrangement of material is varied. For the first and second lists, the story is mimeographed, while for the third list, enough copies are made by manifolding. Each of these releases tells the editor that it is "Not duplicated in your city." When an exclusive story is furnished to the papers on any one list it is marked "Exclusive in your city." In addition to the newspaper lists there is a list of house organs and other publications which receive press material from time to time.

Regular versus Irregular Releases. The established and seldom questioned custom of some agencies is to send out a regular periodical release. A story is mailed once a week, once a month, or at any period that tradition has set, without much relation to its importance or timeliness. Some state boards of health hold strongly to this practice, although experience with it has been on the whole unsatisfactory. One state board of health, for instance, which sent out a weekly résumé of news and activities, found that out of 600 papers receiving the copy, only 30 or 40 were making use of it with any regularity. In another instance the chief of the division of health instruction, who for many years was the editor of a small newspaper, sends out a story of never more than 300

---

[1] A type of stencil and addressing machine now on the market automatically selects for addressing any particular group of stencils desired without removing them or changing their order.

words, which is on the editor's desk every Monday morning with absolute punctuality. It is his belief that material should always reach the newspapers in the same form and at the same time. In this case there are no figures or returns by which to test results. Another state publicity worker, who has also had practical newspaper experience, sends out a general release only once ôr twice in two months or more. By refraining from sending material except when it is a live story, he feels that he is building up a reserve of goodwill for future use.

In most cases those agencies which have given the subject consideration have found it more effective to send out only such stories as have distinct news value. With a regular release of indifferent news arriving in the same style of envelope every Monday morning, for instance, there may develop a tendency to throw it into the waste paper basket without reading it. On the other hand, if the release always has some news value, the editor is likely to look at it and grows to respect the intelligence of the agency sending it out.

COMPETITION FOR NEWSPAPER SPACE

Getting into print is not merely a matter of conforming to the current standards of news value, knowing when and how to release news, and otherwise playing the game according to the rules. It is a matter of intense competition for space in which the social agency takes its place along with political, business, religious, industrial, and every other type of organization that has something to tell. Expressions of alarm and protest are voiced over the extent to which publicity bureaus are taking over, or seeking to take over, the reporting of news and editorial writing. But no more concrete picture of the chaos of undirected competition has appeared, to our knowledge, than the following enumeration of a single week's accumulation of publicity matter on the desk of the librarian of the Cincinnati Enquirer to whom all this material was referred:

From a desk full I select at random:

The National Research Council's permanent secretary wants to know what science is going to do about the passing of the sirloin steak. Cheaper food must be procured for livestock and we ought to have a National Institute of Nutrition.

The Chinese Famine Fund Committee sends copy and matrices.

The National Board of the Y. W. C. A. sends a clip sheet for "immediate release."

Matrix and portrait from the American and French Children's League.

Publicity for National Foreign Trade Convention, with return stamped post card, offering elaborate two column to full page illustrated features.

The American Social Hygiene Association tells of the alarming prevalence of venereal diseases and urges remedial measures.

The University of Virginia proclaims its historic surroundings.

The Federal Council of the Churches of Christ in America asks if we are not to look to Europe for our spiritual strength.

The League for Industrial Rights sends its monthly publication, "Law and Labor."

The American Farm Bureau Federation informs us of the intent and purpose of a new fruit marketing committee and other live topics in its weekly news letter No. 14.

The Joint Distribution Committee of the American Funds for Jewish War Sufferers submits a human interest story of Shimmie Schecter, war orphan, who wants to find his brother.

American Red Cross News Service announces meeting of one of its many national committees.

Ohio Committee on Public Utilities Information gives data gleaned from proceedings of State Public Utilities Commission.

An elaborate document purports to be "An Answer to the Attacks Made upon the American Smelting and Refining Company."

University of North Carolina Extension Leaflets, Vol. IV, No. 6, tells about "Music in the Public Schools."

A private citizen submits a sheet, evidently printed at his own expense, giving six suggestions for an improved taxation system for the state.

A New York bank gives a semi-monthly review of the export business of the country.

A building company honors us with a handsome volume giving pictures of the factories and residences it has erected.

The State Division of the Near East Relief wants slates—like the kind we took to school—thousands of them.

Red Cross News Service again.

Mississippi Valley Association news letter, "for immediate release."

Press Bulletin of the American Museum of Natural History tells about "Jazz in Prehistoric Peru."

Advance copies of addresses before National Civil Service Reform League convention.

Tired, eh? Why, I haven't really begun. There are 100 more on my desk.[1]

The above sample suggests the great volume of publicity that poured into newspaper offices in 1922, and since that time competition for space has steadily increased. The professional journals in the newspaper field frequently protest vigorously against the overwhelming amount of such material mailed to editors. Their objection is mainly to commercial advertising and propaganda on controversial subjects disguised as news. Unsolicited copy from social agencies, although it does not come within these categories, is often unwelcome because it lacks news value and yet claims an editor's consideration which he gives because of the source. In distributing to the press unsuitable material on the chance that it may obtain publication, social agencies not only strain the editor's patience, but also help to lower his valuation of social work as a source of news.

Co-operation among the agencies themselves can accomplish something toward reducing competition for space and also help to raise standards of work. In Cleveland, for example, news from a majority of the member agencies of the Welfare Federation reaches the newspapers by way of the Federation's publicity department. Material collected by the publicity department or submitted voluntarily by the organizations is reviewed and what is suitable is rewritten by the trained publicity staff. In New York City the various branches of the Young Men's Christian Association clear their publicity and advertising through a central bureau.

It may be observed that most of the publicity matter listed by the librarian of the Cincinnati Enquirer came from national and state organizations. The amount of material mailed direct from these sources to individual newspapers may be reduced as better co-operation is developed between the local and general offices of a given movement.

[1] Pence, Harry, "Why Not a Propaganda Editor for the Newspaper?" *In* Editor and Publisher, New York, July 8, 1922, p. 18.

PART III: PRINTED MATTER

INTRODUCTION TO PART III

IN ONE year more than 10,000,000 pieces of educational printed matter[1] issued by the Division of Venereal Diseases of the United States Public Health Service were distributed by state departments of health or reprinted by them. The total volume of health literature distributed by the Metropolitan Life Insurance Company, at the time of writing, considerably exceeds 486,000,000 pieces. The American Social Hygiene Association states that during one ten-year period it distributed 2,000,000 copies of its folders and pamphlets. As many as 450,000 copies of a single folder of instruction prepared by the National Tuberculosis Association have been distributed. In one year 2,757,000 pamphlets prepared in co-operation with the American Child Health Association were given out by the United States Bureau of Education, and in a similar period 1,345,000 pamphlets and circulars by the United States Children's Bureau. During one Cancer Week conducted by the American Society for the Control of Cancer, it was estimated that 6,000,000 pieces were spread throughout the country. But far outweighing in aggregate bulk the material issued for national use is the printed matter prepared and distributed by the state agencies and the large local ones. All this matter contains health information alone. If we should attempt to estimate the quantity of printed matter put out in any given year in all branches of social work, the figures would soar beyond the grasp of imagination.

Merely to prepare a piece of printed matter is a task which anybody with the help of a printer can carry out quickly and with little thought. One may put in writing any sort of ideas and instruct the printer as to the number of copies desired. Distribution may be equally simple, merely a matter of standing on a crowded corner and handing a copy to each passerby, or of placing it where it may be picked up.

But preparing and distributing printed matter so that it will

---

[1] Printed matter is used in this volume in the sense of pamphlets, leaflets, circulars, handbills, and so forth, as distinguished from periodical bulletins, books, and the various other means of using the printed word.

serve a useful purpose is far less simple. A booklet may be intended to persuade people to do unusual and even unheard of things, like being examined by a physician when they are well, or taking steps to avoid a disease with which they are not aware of being threatened. It may exhort them to revise their habits of eating, sleeping, and exercise; or, if parents, to go to a lot of trouble to give their children care which they themselves never had and never missed; or to turn their attention from their absorbing personal affairs to consider their civic duties, perhaps to vote to tax themselves or to restrict their personal liberty; or to give money for one more of the many causes presented to them.

Printed matter is seldom expected to accomplish any one of these difficult tasks by itself. It usually accompanies letters, or personal appeals, and is used at meetings, exhibits, and so forth. Nevertheless, it carries its fair share of the responsibility for getting results only when its form, content, and distribution are skilfully planned.

Take, for example, the appearance of the message. The color and quality of the paper, the kind of type, spacing and margins, the illustrations, all have an important bearing on whether or not the leaflet or folder is looked at, whether it will get itself read and be easily understood and favorably received. The attention it receives is influenced by what is put on the cover and what is left off. The ease with which it is read may depend very much on the way in which the information it contains is arranged and the extent to which it is broken up. As to its composition, the phrasing of titles, the content of the opening sentence, the use of familiar or unfamiliar words, and again, of vivid or lifeless words, the choice of an appeal, all these call for the application of skill and imagination. Even the way in which the message gets into the hands of the person for whom it is intended, assuming, of course, that it does get into the right hands, may help or hinder it in making a good impression.

As a basis for a practical discussion of the factors entering into the preparation and use of this kind of publicity, we have gathered and examined thousands of samples of printed matter which are as varied as possible in purpose, copy, form, cost, and method of distribution.

The bulk of this material was found to be of mediocre quality. Cheapness and speed in production were frequently placed above pleasing appearance and readability in planning the printing. Only in rare instances did the writers of folders or booklets show skill in composition. No doubt, some examples which would not stand up under criticism based on accepted standards of good printing and good writing, nevertheless, satisfied the organizations using them. However, those who issue printed matter seldom obtain reliable evidence as to its effectiveness, and even less frequently can they be sure that it would not have been more successful if the cover-page had been designed differently, the text written more interestingly, or the lines of type made easier to read.

The discussion of printed matter in the chapters which follow aims to place before the readers standards of excellence within the reach of those who have a modest budget for printing and ordinary ability as writers. Recognition of a few simple principles, and time and thought given to planning and to revisions are, after all, the main requirements for preparing good publicity literature.

CHAPTER VIII

TYPES OF PRINTED MATTER

THERE appears to be no uniform and well-established set of names in common use to describe the different kinds of printed matter. Various writers have found it necessary to make arbitrary classifications, which they have based partly on form and partly on use or content. Robert E. Ramsay[1] has made a list of these names including among others the following: (1) the folder, referring to the form or make-up; (2) the envelope enclosure, referring to method of distribution; and (3) the catalog, referring to the content.

Following the example of other writers, we have made our own classification of the kinds of printing commonly used by social agencies. The types discussed in this section include handbills, leaflets, cards, folders, letterheads, booklets, and odd and unusual forms. Posters, placards, and car cards are also classed as printed matter but are not considered here since they require different technique from that applied to literature for distribution to individuals.

HANDBILLS

The handbill or dodger is a single sheet printed on one side which is handed to people on the street, dropped into house mail boxes, thrown on doorsteps, or posted in public places. In some communities the distribution of handbills is controlled by legislation, so that it will be well to see if there is any law on the subject before giving them out. Cheapness and quick preparation are the reasons for using them. With paper of a better grade and good type composition, effective handbills have been prepared for enclosures in envelopes for mailing.

The handbill is usually small enough (about 6 by 9 or 8½ by 11 inches) to be carried in the hand and large enough to be posted on a wall or bulletin board. Generally printed on the cheapest news-

---

[1] Effective Direct Advertising. D. Appleton and Co., New York, 1921, pp. 39–112.

print paper, it clamors for attention through large black letters on a white or colored background.

Even so simple and cheap a thing as a handbill may be planned and used either well or badly. In make-up it calls for brief emphatic text, good display arrangement, and strong contrast between paper and type, for no matter how it is distributed it is likely to be glanced at hastily.

In rural districts where comparatively little printed matter is received or displayed, the handbill may be quite as satisfactory as a more expensive form of printing, but nowhere should it be used for a long message or for text which deserves more dignified treatment. When a traveling clinic or educational show is coming to town, a handbill announcing the time, place, and chief attractions meets a distinct need for widespread and cheap advertising. On the other hand, instruction about how to feed the baby, or a list of the social agencies in a given city together with directions about how to use them would require a more substantial form and one more likely to be kept and consulted.

One very cheap and informal looking handbill carried an appeal for contributions addressed to "a select list of old friends and members of the society." The use of so unattractive a form in addressing a presumably discriminating audience would seem to be poor economy.

LEAFLETS

Any small unfolded piece of printing may be called a leaflet to distinguish it from a piece that is folded. It is also frequently referred to as a circular, a term which is too inclusive, however, for our use in distinguishing it from other forms. Still another name for it is envelope stuffer, given when it is enclosed with other material in an envelope. Both leaflets and handbills are used as package enclosures by stores and laundries. One practical and not very common use of the leaflet is to have it contain a brief list of addresses to be carried in a pocketbook. It may also be used appropriately to make an announcement or to supplement a letter of appeal.

Like the handbill, it has the advantage of comparative cheapness, especially when printed on only one side, and so one may allow for a large percentage of waste in the effort to get copies

MALARIA

CAUSE

Malaria is not contracted by drinking bad water, nor by breathing bad air, nor by eating vegetables or watermelons. Malaria is transmitted from person to person in no other way than by a certain species of mosquito. This mosquito first must bite a person who has malaria organisms in the blood and in so doing, the mosquito receives this organism into its stomach, then incidentally in biting a well person, the organisms are injected into that person's blood, who soon becomes sick from malaria.

PREVENTION

We know, therefore, that if we prevent the reproduction of mosquitoes, we ultimately control the spread of malaria. Hence the war on this species of mosquito, and incidentally a war on this species includes a war on the others. In reducing efforts to an attack on the breeding areas, it is found that mosquitoes do not breed in weeds, tall grass, vines or bushes. They must have water to pass through the process of development. This process consists of four distinct stages, covering a period of from one week to ten days, depending upon the temperature. First the egg, then the wiggler, then the pupa and last the adult mosquito. Being familiar with these important points, we are in position to intelligently apply some of the simple measures that have been found practical in destroying mosquito breeding, viz.:

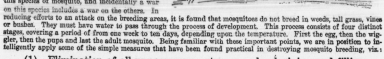

(1) Elimination of all unnecessary water areas by draining and filling.

(2) Covering all other standing water where possible.

(3) Destroying breeding by the application of a thin film of oil on the surface where mosquito wigglers are present.

(4) Destroying wigglers by the employment of natural enemies, such as a certain species of "top-water minnow" commonly know as the "pot-belly," in such areas where it is impractical to oil or drain.

(5) Other protective measures include preventing mosquitoes from becoming infected as well as transmitting infection. All houses s h o u l d be properly screened with No. 16 mesh wire.

(6) Where mosquitoes and malaria are abundant, additional precaution should be taken by using mosquito-bars and immunizing by the use of quinine.

Any town or community desiring to introduce a systematic Anti-malaria Campaign, can avail themselves of the assistance of this Department. This includes the privilege of sending a local representative for field training to one of the several Demonstration Units in the State. This training is free of charge, the only expense to the town being that incurred by actual substistence and transportation of the representative.

For Additional Information Communicate with

THE STATE BOARD OF HEALTH

BUREAU OF SANITARY ENGINEERING

Austin, Texas.

AN OVERCROWDED HANDBILL

This handbill is less compelling than the one on the opposite page. The detailed advice given might better have been put into a folder.

NO MOSQUITOES!
NO MALARIA!!

NO WATER!
NO MOSQUITOES!!

DRAIN! OIL! SCREEN!

DRAIN all standing water where feasible. Oil
or stock with minnows such areas where
drainage is impracticable. Screen
thoroughly all houses, adjacent
cisterns and containers

TEXAS STATE BOARD OF HEALTH
Bureau of Sanitary Engineering
Austin

A GOOD HANDBILL
The striking make-up of this handbill compels attention, and a single
reading is enough to fix its contents in one's mind.

into the right hands. Convenient sizes are 3¼ or 3½ by 6 inches, and 4 by 9 inches.

The examples shown opposite illustrate the possibility of attractive and effective make-up of leaflets intended to serve a single purpose in keeping with their small size.

CARDS

Mailing cards and small placards are other examples of one or two-page pieces of printing.

The postal card is economical because the government gives the paper. When used for a brief message told in an interesting way, it may get attention from persons who will not take the time to read a letter or a larger piece of printed matter. Brief statements of fact or incidents reported in this form to ministers, teachers, and other busy persons may be more welcome than if embodied in a letter.

A dental association has used postal cards effectively for a series of messages on the care of the teeth, which were sent to persons whose names were provided by the members of the association. Announcements of new publications may be very satisfactorily presented on postal cards.

When the issue of a single card, or of a group which can be printed at the same time, is large enough there is a saving in press work through buying the government postal cards in sheets.[1]

In most cases privately issued cards,[2] approximating government postal cards in size and quality, are more expensive to use than the official issue. These cards may bear the words "Post Card" or "Private Mailing Card" on the face side. Either these, or larger cards which may not bear the words noted above, offer an opportunity for variety in stock and color not possible with government cards.

Distinction can be given to the government card by printing

[1] The government postal card No. 5 (3 by 5 inches) is made up in sheets of 18 which can be run through the press at one time and then cut to the regulation size. Card No. 8 (3¼ by 5½ inches) is available in sheets of 40 and 48; the latter only until stocks on hand are used. Either of these sheets can be cut to run a smaller group at a time.

[2] Consult the postmaster or the Official Postal Guide for latest rulings as to size and postage rates on these cards.

LEAFLETS TO BE ENCLOSED IN PACKAGES, LETTERS, AND PAY ENVELOPES

Number 1, a package enclosure, is an invitation. Number 2 is a breezy reminder for general use in an open window campaign. The panel on number 3 reproduces in bright orange the poster that the leaflet advertises. Number 4 is a reminder of a coming convention.

the back, or the third of the face of the card which the sender is privileged to use, with a tint block. By this means the message is printed on a ground of yellow, buff, green, or other color.

Fairly heavy cards, attractively printed and enclosed in envelopes, are appropriate for invitations to meetings or announcements which require something more dignified than a leaflet or postal card.

Small placards may take the place of the handbill for information that should be kept for reference. Diet cards for children of different age groups are punched so that they may be hung conveniently on a nail in the kitchen. Small maps showing the locations of clinics, recreation centers, or hospitals are convenient for the office or home if put up in placard form.

FOLDERS

Any piece of paper with printing on it which has been folded one or more times to increase the number of pages is, according to our definition, a folder. For distribution in large quantities at comparatively small expense, the folder appears to be the most widely used form of printed matter. Health organizations have given away millions of folders of advice about disease prevention. The letter of appeal is very likely to carry a folder as an envelope enclosure. Even annual reports, surprisingly enough, have on occasion been reduced to this simple form.

The folder has the advantage over the leaflet of allowing a page for cover design and a back page on which to print names and addresses or other copy that seems desirable, in addition to several pages for the text.

Much used sizes for folders are 3½ by 6 or 6¼ inches and 4 by 9 inches. When the size is increased to 6 by 9 inches or 8 by 11 inches, as is occasionally done, unless printed on heavy paper the folder seems rather flimsy.

The four-page folder in a size convenient for envelope enclosure is the kind most generally useful. Evidently, however, social agencies find it difficult to keep their messages down to four pages, for we receive many six-page folders and indeed some, quite inexcusably, folded into 16 pages. When the reading matter increases beyond the limits of the six-page folder the booklet is usually to be preferred for several reasons. Chief among the objections to the use of several folds is that the reader does not receive the message in the proper sequence. As he opens an eight-page folder, his eye may fall on pages six and seven, or two and seven. Although both the arrangement of the text and the method of folding are supposedly carefully planned to make the intended sequence unmistakable, it more often happens that the series of folds are a source of confusion to the reader.

Another objection to much folding is that when the folder is opened, the spread of several pages of type interferes with concentration of attention on a page at a time. Occasionally, this factor is turned to good account when one side of the sheet is used for display of several related panels of pictures and text, as is well illustrated on the opposite page.

Folding is sometimes done in some other fashion than conventionally in the center as is shown in this illustration.

The Broadside. The greatest opportunity for obtaining display space in a folded piece of printed matter is in the broadside, which Robert E. Ramsay defines as a "printed sheet 25 by 38, or down to half that size, folded down for mailing purposes to about 5 by 10½, 9 by 12, or 10 by 6, mailed either under its own cover or in a special envelope. . . . The folding is always simple, no 'stunt' or 'trick' folds being used in broadsides."[1] To obtain the full advantage of the broadside, the copy is sometimes planned so that a question or an incomplete sentence is displayed on an outside cover and the suspense is kept up by continuing the same sentence or idea as the folds are opened until one reaches the climax, when the whole sheet is spread out before one. Here copy and pictures have generous display space such as is obtained in a double page spread in a magazine or newspaper. The broadside seems to be little used by social agencies and very widely used in commercial advertising. Occasionally social agencies greatly misuse it by covering the large sheet with closely typed material which might much better have gone into the smaller pages of a folder or booklet.

LETTERHEADS WITH PRINTED MESSAGE

A letterhead designed for a particular use rather than for general correspondence may carry a printed message. One of many

[1] Effective Direct Advertising. pp. 97–98.

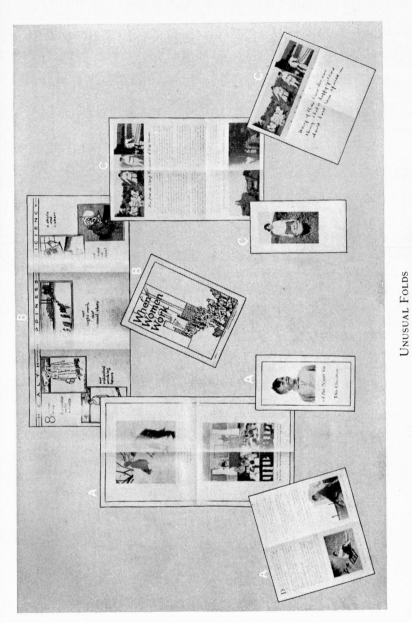

Unusual Folds

Groups A, B, and C show three different folders, each creased in such a way that in opening the folds one receives the message in the order intended. When completely unfolded, the large page size allows for interesting arrangements of text and pictures.

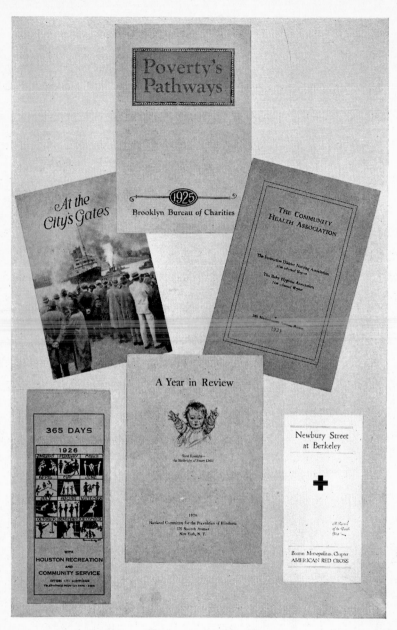

VARIED TYPES OF ANNUAL REPORTS

A group of annual reports, one a formal business record, the others more
unconventional and popular in appearance and titles.

varieties is the single sheet with a few printed lines and a symbol, or a picture illustrative of the organization's activities. A slogan or an appeal, usually only one line, may be printed across the bottom of the sheet.

Folds or flaps which may be on either side or at the top or foot of the sheet are used for a printed or pictured message. The fold may carry both text and illustrations, taking the place of an enclosure. New forms are frequently devised and may get attention for the letter because of their novelty. However, if the letter itself is intended to be the real center of interest, the less there is of distracting pictures, type, and folds, the safer.

In the four-page letterhead the first page is used generally for the letter itself and the two inside pages for printed text and illustrations. This arrangement may be, and frequently is, varied, but it has the advantage of giving the letter the most prominent position. Business firms make considerable use of such letterheads. They are used also to some extent in appeals of social agencies. One health agency sent a letter to parents of school children found to be undernourished. The letter on page one was typed and personal in tone, while the inside pages contained printed health information and pictures.

An advantage of the four-page letterhead is that one may thus reduce the number of enclosures. Many letters of appeal enclose a leaflet, a subscription blank, and a reply envelope. Not a few add a second leaflet telling more about the types of membership a society offers or listing reasons for giving it support. The use of a four-page letterhead makes a return card and reply envelope the only necessary enclosures.

Advertising specialists seem on the whole to agree that the back page of a letterhead should be left blank. One of them, Homer J. Buckley of Chicago, wrote in a letter in answer to our question on this point:

> On definite tests we have made, we have found that the printed matter on the fourth page, when it is enclosed in a regulation envelope has the psychological effect of giving the recipient the impression that it is a printed circular. This danger is somewhat lessened if the window envelope is used, and page four is folded inside, leaving only the typewritten page exposed, but even then there is a danger of its failing in its

purpose. In a great many large business houses the mail addressed to the firm is opened in the Mail Receiving Department, and printed matter on the fourth page in such instances has a bad effect, and does not always get personal attention as it would if the communication were a typical typewritten letter, with the back page free from any printed matter.

BOOKLETS

The booklet, as its name implies, is anything in book form, that is, with a series of pages held together by wire, glue, or stitching, which is less than a book. It ranges from the small eight-page envelope enclosure to the larger pamphlet bound in stiff covers. Booklets used for enclosure may, like folders, be of any size with good proportions that will fit into a standard envelope. As a rule, odd shapes and unusual sizes involve increased expense because of the waste in cutting paper to the special size. Pamphlets intended for reference use have a fairly well-standardized size of 6 by 9 inches.

Whereas the leaflet or folder may carry only a reminder, a simple suggestion, or a few tersely stated facts, a booklet allows room for giving detailed information. In a booklet one may tell about as much as in a speech, or a newspaper article of a column or more in length, with the advantage of a more permanent form and the opportunity to select each individual who is to receive the information. This advantage is, of course, obtained at much greater expense than the newspaper article or speech entails.

In an intensive money-raising campaign, a booklet generously illustrated and explaining in some detail the object of the campaign is usually distributed to a selected list of probable givers. Booklets are also much used for health advice. Attractively prepared handbooks for mothers on the care of babies are issued by many health departments and are likely to be kept and valued more highly than a series of folders covering the same subjects. Government and private health agencies are prolific publishers of booklets large and small.

The almanac is an example of a booklet that is valued and generally preserved. For generations it has served the purposes of the patent medicine maker and by years of use its place in the kitchen corner has been established. It seems time that the bona fide health almanac should step into its place. The Louisiana State Health Department is one of several health organizations that issues each year an almanac patterned after the one made popular by patent medicine companies containing the usual astronomical facts, birthdays of well-known persons, jokes, and pictures, but with practical health advice replacing the advertisements of nostrums. It has even that prime requisite, a loop by which it may be hung on a nail.

Reports. Annual reports, formerly the only means of informing the public used by some organizations, still have an important place in the program of publicity. As yet there are wide differences of opinion as to the functions of an annual report. Some organizations continue to publish under the title "49th Annual Report of the . . . Society" a formal statement accompanied by tables of figures and bound and printed in a form that suggests utility only. Such reports are evidently chiefly useful as records.

Again, organizations that publish house organs include in these weekly or monthly publications much of the information which would otherwise go into the report. One number of a bulletin may be an annual report number. On the other hand, special gifts contributed for the purpose have made possible the publication of some beautifully printed and illustrated reports, telling the story of the year's work in a style that invites persons not as yet interested in the organization to read it. The illustration on page 143 shows some of the efforts of social agencies to escape from stereotyped forms in designing and arranging the contents of booklets of this sort.

Reports of investigations and surveys are usually published in pamphlet form, even though the findings and recommendations may have already been afforded space in local newspapers. Usually these reports should be given a page of book size and a dignified and substantial form which will encourage preservation during their period of usefulness.

The pamphlet form permits of much greater amplification than is likely to be possible in presenting the report through the newspapers, meetings, or exhibitions.

Tables of supporting figures, diagrams showing comparisons in detail, and examples to illustrate recommendations are possible in the pamphlet report, making it useful to committees and to all citizens who wish to understand the details of the survey or investigation and the proposals it offers.

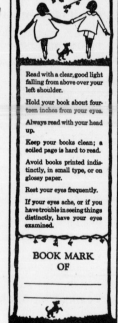

EXAMPLES OF USEFUL NOVELTIES

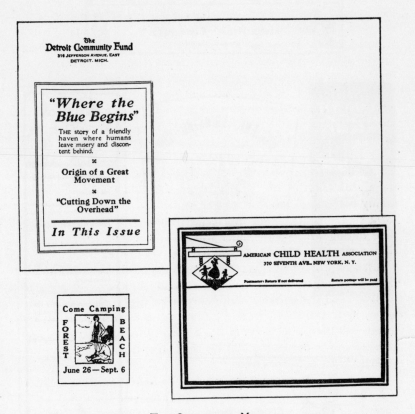

THE OUTSIDE OF MAIL

The large envelope with its printed message is intended to arouse interest in the house organ which it contains; the small poster stamp advertises a coming event; the package label effectively displays the emblem of an association.

Odd and Unusual Forms

Small and unusual forms of printed matter sometimes known as "novelties" have a limited usefulness. They may get attention in competition with many other pieces and are often prized sufficiently to be kept and shown to other persons. They may be distributed at expositions and fairs, given as prizes to school children, sent as season's greetings to contributors or friends, or as announcements of special services, such as clinics or libraries.

They include a variety of articles made of cardboard or paper which may carry a printed message. Of these, blotters are the most familiar and the most widely used by social agencies as well as by commercial advertisers. In the Christmas Seal Sale, check book blotters have been used with the slogan "Use This to Blot Your Check and Help to Blot Out Tuberculosis." Blotters carrying a health slogan and a calendar are distributed each month to family hotels and clubs by one city health association. A calendar for a single month offers an excellent method of lengthening the time during which a reminder will be kept before the recipient, since a month is about the expected life of a blotter.

A health worker who has made much use of blotters calls attention to the importance of having both sides absorbent. If one side is glazed and the business man in his hurry uses it and smears the letter, he is naturally irritated. Plate finish blotting paper is absorbent on both sides and yet has a good surface for half-tone engravings. The better the blotter, the longer it will remain on the desk before it is thrown away.

Bookmarks are another inexpensive and effective form of publicity for the single slogan or fact. They are especially useful when libraries or schools will co-operate in distributing them. Calendars, writing pads, rulers, drinking cups, and book jackets are also used.

Puzzles; trick cards in which motion is secured by some simple device, such as a figure with arms that move; devices which cause one picture to be replaced by another; cut-outs[1] in the shape of human figures or buildings or other objects are souvenirs for the

---

[1] Cut-outs are known technically as die-cuts. In considering their use, it is well to remember that the United States Post Office Department has sometimes refused to carry them unless they were enclosed in envelopes so that they would not be injured in the mails.

CUT-OUTS

The walking doll was sent out with a membership appeal from the Child Adoption League of the New York State Charities Aid Association. When moved lightly along a level surface she walks very nicely. A cut-out of Cho-Cho, the health clown, showing a bright yellow carrot, was given at fairs and expositions as a souvenir with health examinations. Health rules are printed on the back. The Tenement Times, a tiny newspaper folded and slipped under the boy's arm, is an appeal from the United Charities of Chicago for funds for their summer outing work.

children to carry home from an industrial exposition or fair. The walking doll, a cardboard cut-out that calls attention to the right kinds of shoes, or leads the way to the health center, is an example of what may be done with printed matter of this sort.

At expositions and fairs each person weighed and measured may be given an attractive card or tag on which is recorded his name together with the data obtained from the examination—height, weight, and so forth.

The warning in an earlier chapter[1] against novelty which attracts attention to itself rather than to the idea to be presented is especially applicable to these bizarre forms of printing. If the form is an appropriate one for the text printed on it, as in the case of the bookmark shown on page 146 with its directions to readers about the care of their eyes, this objection does not hold. Calendars printed by boys in a training school might well be sent as greetings to friends of the institution. A blotter on which the telephone number of a service bureau is printed is a convenient thing to have about.

Hangers and labels for outdoor display, the sticker for windshields of automobiles, tags for milk bottles, cards for windows, rotogravure sheets, and portfolios of pictures are a few examples of printed matter used during safety, health, or clean-up weeks, or money-raising campaigns.

The Outside of Mail

Poster stamps in attractive colors and designs, used as seals on the backs of envelopes, may carry the date of a convention, a slogan, or an announcement. The printing on the envelope itself may serve the same purpose. On occasions when packages are to be sent out, the label or tag may be utilized to carry a reminder or a message of goodwill.

[1] See p. 16.

CHAPTER IX

THE PHYSICAL MAKE-UP OF PRINTED MATTER

I S GOOD printing merely a luxury, something on which a social agency should not spend the money given by contributors, or on which government departments should not spend public funds? If the appearance of printing, which is dependent on the type, arrangement, paper, color, and illustrations, has anything to do with getting the text read, then there should be no question as to whether or not money should be spent to make it inviting and readable. The question might better be asked: "Can an organization afford to call upon specialists to gather facts for the public, or busy executives to prepare reports on their work for their supporters, only to have the information given out in a form which definitely lessens the probability that it will be read?"

Some social agencies think that the information or advice they publish is so greatly desired or so useful to those who receive it that attractive appearance is not necessary to get it read. It is also argued that a bad impression is created when contributed funds are spent on expensive printing. But there is a wide difference between printing which looks and is costly, and that on which only enough is spent to make it inviting and easy to read.

It is supremely important to remember that a large percentage of publicity material is offered to people more or less reluctant to read it. This reluctance may be accounted for in many ways: preoccupation with routine activities which absorb the attention of busy people; competition with the mass of other free literature received by professional and business persons; resentment at having unwanted things thrust upon one; the arduous work that reading means to persons unaccustomed to it; the poor eyesight of a considerable number of persons; and many other causes.

In view of this widespread tendency not to read any information for which a desire does not already exist, the person who plans printing needs to test his output by two simple questions: "Does it invite the eye?" and "Is it easy to read?"

THE PHYSICAL MAKE-UP OF PRINTED MATTER

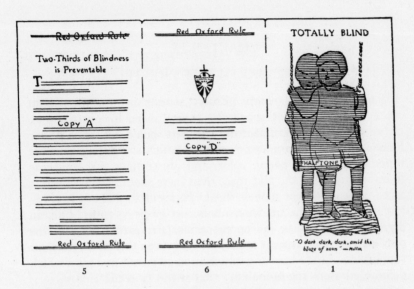

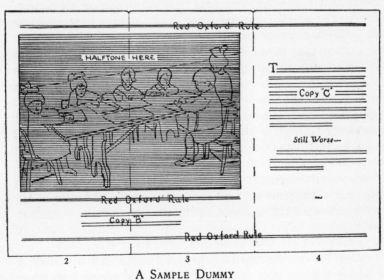

A SAMPLE DUMMY

151

Benjamin Sherbow[1] expresses briefly and in easily understood language the chief things which anyone who uses printing should know in order to answer these two tests. His insistence on the common-sense point of view that printing should not show off or attempt any frills makes his work especially useful to social agencies. We have drawn liberally from his book and from those of other writers on the same subject in selecting for this chapter such suggestions as may serve the needs of social workers who plan occasional printing with the help of an ordinary printer. The factors are considered from the standpoint of the person who orders the work done.

The Layout or Dummy

The person who prepares manuscript for printing will be better able to visualize the finished piece if after writing the first draft of his text he arranges a layout or dummy. This is paper cut and folded to the size to be used for the finished piece of printing, on which illustrations are roughly sketched and the allotted space for headings and text indicated. A simple device for approximating the number of words that can be used is to select from a magazine a block of printing in which the spacing and size and face of type are the same as that desired. As many square inches as will fit into your allotted space may be cut out and pasted into place and the words counted. With this guide the text may be revised to fit the space. Certain manufacturers of paper provide sample books containing a variety of printed material which can be cut out and pasted on the dummy pages. The assortment usually includes text, illustrations, borders, and headings in various sizes. A sample dummy is shown on page 151.

If the printed matter is to be sent through the mails, a dummy made up of the same kind of paper as that proposed for the finished product is useful in determining the amount of postage required.

Design of the Cover-Page

When Mr. Brown, running through the pile of mail waiting for him every morning, finds publicity matter along with his letters,

[1] Effective Type-Use for Advertising. Benjamin Sherbow, New York, 1922. (Now published by Marcus Sherbow, Brookhaven, N. Y.)

COVER-PAGES OF FOLDERS AND BOOKLETS

1. Instead of making this cover-page pleasing to the eye the writer assumed that it would be noticed and so filled the space with text (regardless of its appearance).

2. This catches the eye because of its simplicity.

3. The picture of a familiar scene and the caption arouse interest in the contents of this folder.

4. The title, picture and text are crowded, making it less inviting than the more open page below.

he is quite likely to shove it aside or drop it into the waste basket unless the outside page is sufficiently attractive or striking to hold his attention. Mrs. Brown, busy with household tasks, subconsciously applies the same test when Johnnie, coming home from school, thrusts into her hand the folder or booklet he has been told to give her.

The make-up of outside pages shows marked differences. Of those illustrated on page 152, one is almost solid with reading matter; another has a title in attractive lettering; the third combines title, illustration, and reading matter; and the fourth shows a picture with a brief, appropriate caption. If the cover-page does not invite attention, the inside text may not be read by the persons receiving it unless they happen to be particularly interested in the subject it discusses. A brief, artistically lettered title may be as effective as a picture and is even better for subjects which do not suggest appropriate and pleasing illustrations. A combination of title and reading matter is likely to be spotty and uninviting. A good illustration with an informing or provocative caption almost always arrests attention and secures interest. Titles and captions are discussed in Chapter XI, Copy.[1] The good quality and the color of the paper used are important factors in the pleasing appearance of the cover.

DESIGNING PAGES OF TEXT

Whereas attractive appearance is a more important consideration in designing the cover, readability comes first in planning the text. Incidentally, many of the same factors that make a page easy to read add to its good looks. This is especially true of the distribution of "white space."

White space is the term in common use for blank space. It has in itself an important function. That required for margins and for separation between lines and between paragraphs may not be encroached upon without definitely reducing the readability of the page. Generous margins provide strong contrast to the block of type and make the page look more interesting. Space between lines, which is called "leading" because it is obtained by placing thin strips of lead between the lines of type, opens up a page so that

[1] See p. 191.

WHAT IS CONSUMPTION

Consumption is tuberculosis of the lungs, and is caused by a very small germ which is taken into the body through the nose or mouth in dust or in food.

It is never caused by anything else but this germ.

It is a preventable disease.

It is often cured if taken in time.

It kills one person out of every ten who die.

SUSPICIOUS SYMPTOMS

Continued coughing or spitting in the morning, even if only a little.

Weakness and loss of weight, very suspicious, especially if there is slight cough.

Blood Spitting. If blood is coughed up the cause is almost always tuberculosis.

A little fever in the afternoon points to this disease.

Pains in the chest (pleurisy), night sweats, are very suspicious.

If any of these symptoms are present, no matter how well you look or feel, go to your physi-

of sleep from whatever cause is an important element in lowering resistance to tuberculosis. The weakened condition of the body which usually follows or accompanies convalescence from pneumonia, influenza (grippe), whooping cough, measles and typhoid fever permits of a lowered resistance to the development of tuberculosis, whether in children or grown people.

Bad Shop Conditions

Bad shop conditions may cause a lowered resistance. The exposure of the workers to dust in their shops or factories, the presence of dampness, darkness, stagnant or impure air, intensive heat or cold, are all unfavorable for the maintenance of vigorous health and good bodily resistance, upon which protection most tuberculosis is usually dependent. Sedentary work and work which from any cause develops unusual or persistent fatigue generally lowers the worker's resistance by interfering with his rest and nourishment, as is commonly the case in the "speeding up" process and over-time work. Where dirty conditions of the factory or shop prevail there is more likely to be neglect of precautions as to spitting and other forms of spreading infectious germs from the nose and throat, by which means fresh and active tubercular germs are spread from those suffering from disease. Combined with bad home conditions and careless personal habits, which interfere with regular sleep, meals and exercise, the insanitary conditions of the shop and persistent bodily fatigue give the tubercular germs, commonly

TYPE SIZE AND SPACING

The effort required to follow the fine type and long, solid paragraphs of the page at the left would discourage any but the most interested reader.

Short paragraphs and generous spacing make easy reading of the page at the right, even though the type is of the same size as that of the other page.

154

the eye follows the text with greater ease than it could if the lines were close together. If the printer receives too much copy for the size and number of pages allowed, he has no choice but to narrow the margins and close up the lines, although by doing so he jeopardizes the usefulness of the material.

Breaking Up the Copy. The breaking of text into paragraphs provides additional white space, which may be increased by making the space between the paragraphs twice as wide as that between the lines. Still greater openness results from the use of short paragraph titles, printed on separate lines or as cut-in heads at the side. There is a striking difference in the openness and ease in reading between the two pages illustrated on page 154, although the size of type used in both is the same.

Sometimes when page-proof comes back from the printer, a blank half-page is discovered at the end. This space should be considered as an asset in setting off the text and adding to its attractive appearance rather than as an opportunity to add something more. In a folder among our examples such a space has been filled with an intricate diagram which apparently happened to be on hand, and which, without making the text any easier to understand, detracts from the inviting appearance of the folder.

Massing of Space and Type. Usually, as we have said, the problems arising in connection with white space have to do with finding room for a given amount of text, but occasionally the opposite is true and a small amount of text needs to be displayed to advantage on a broad background. The commonest example is in the arrangement of cover-pages. The make-up of any page with considerable white space demands a good sense of design.

Without attempting to go into detail, we may call attention to the most important and most frequently violated principle of design in printing, namely, that there shall be solid areas of type in contrast to solid areas of white space.

One of the most difficult kinds of text to compose into a pleasing page is a series of short sentences, phrases, or words. The illustrations on pages 156 and 157 show both poor and effective arrangements of such material. The problem is to make the separate items distinct and at the same time to avoid, as far as possible, uneven

WHEN YOU ARE WALKING

Use the street crossings.
Keep your eyes open.
Wait for the traffic signals.
Make haste slowly.

NEVER TAKE A CHANCE!

WHEN DRIVING AN AUTOMOBILE

Drive carefully—Do not speed.
Examine your brakes frequently.
Do not trust the other fellow.
Give trains right-of-way.

LOSE A MINUTE AND SAVE A LIFE!

SCATTERED LINES NOT EFFECTIVE
Uneven lines and a slanting arrangement give this page a spotty effect
which is not pleasing.

When You Are Walking

Use the street crossings.
Keep your eyes open.
Wait for traffic signals.
Make haste slowly.

When Driving An Automobile

Drive carefully—don't speed.
Examine your brakes often.
Don't trust the other fellow.
Give trains the right-of-way.

Never take a chance!

LOSE A MINUTE AND SAVE A LIFE!

TYPE SYMMETRICALLY BLOCKED

The illustration above shows how by a few slight changes the different blocks of type can be balanced and the whole page made more attractive than the one at the left.

lines and the scattering of words or phrases so that the eye is distracted and the page looks uninviting.

A skilful printer will find many ways to deal with this problem and still hold to principles of composition already pointed out. Good display advertisements in daily newspapers show how it can be done.

SIZE OF TYPE

Type large enough to be read with comfort is worth having even at the cost of reducing the amount of copy, if a choice must be made. The following paragraphs composed by Benjamin Sherbow give an excellent demonstration of the increasing comfort and pleasure in reading as you move up from six-point to twelve-point type:

You are having a rather hard time reading this, aren't you? The letters are so small and thin, they strain your eyes so much, that you are having considerable of a job to make out what I am saying. Well, nobody likes to read this kind of type any better than you do, so if you want to get your advertising read, don't use type so small as this. It is six point.

This eight point type is a little easier on your eyes. It does not require quite so much effort to read. You read it faster and with less strain. But you would not get much fun out of reading a book set like this, would you? Then don't set your booklets and catalogs and circulars and house organs in type so small as this. Not enough of the people you want to reach with your advertising message will read it.

This ten point type begins to warm you up to your job a bit. Now at last you've struck something that you can read with a little more comfort. You are reading it about twice as fast as the two preceding paragraphs—getting over the ground with more speed and less strain—taking in what I am saying with more ease. It is a good rule never to set any part of your advertising message in type smaller than this. Sometimes you can't help it. But do as little of it as possible. Just think how fine it would be if our newspapers and magazines were set in ten point!

Some folks think they have reached the height of readability when they set their advertising in ten point. Far from it. The eleven point type in which this paragraph is set is a good deal easier to read. You could read a pretty fat booklet in this type without tiring your eyes. You would get more pleasure out of reading it than if it were set in smaller type.

Remember, the easier you make reading the more people you will get to read your advertising. There is a limit, however, to the size of body type which can be read easily. That limit is almost reached in the twelve point type you are now reading. This size is plenty large enough for most things. Occasionally it is desirable to go beyond this, for advertisements with short copy in big space, for large booklets, catalogs or broadsides. But for the average piece of advertising print, twelve point type is a joy to behold and invites reading beyond any other size.

This is fourteen point type. A very useful size indeed for big forms of printed matter and large space in publications. But it reads rather more slowly than the twelve point and is therefore not so generally useful for long stretches of reading.

Reading is slowed up considerably when we come to eighteen point type, of which this is a specimen. It will take more effort to read a given number of words in this size than in fourteen or twelve point. For a few introductory paragraphs in big space this size is useful, but to read a large quantity of it at one time would quickly tire the eyes.[1]

[1] Effective Type-Use for Advertising. pp. 115–117.

We find type as small as eight-point much used in publicity literature, even in instructions sent to persons unaccustomed to read, and in appeals for support, which must be easily legible if they are to be read by any considerable proportion of those receiving them. Many persons who contribute to social agencies have reached middle age, when their sight is likely to be less keen, while the appeals to their benevolence are constantly multiplying.

TYPE FACES

The printer usually has specimen books containing paragraphs printed in different sizes of various styles of type. From these a selection may be made of the type best suited to the purpose for which the printing is intended.

D. B. Updike, an authority on the printer's art, says:

> In the class of types which appear to be beyond criticism from the point of view of beauty and utility, the original Caslon type stands first.[1]

Caslon Old Style is generally recognized as a standard type for English and American printing. Scotch, sometimes called Scotch Roman, comes second on Updike's list of dependable types. These types are easy to read, pleasing, and do not call attention to themselves. They are well adapted to use in booklets, house organs, and bulletins.

For announcements, advertisements, or other forms of printing which contain a small amount of reading matter and seek to catch the eye by their artistic appearance, a more ornamental type such as Garamont, Cloister, Kennerley, or Bodoni may be appropriate. It is well to avoid altogether the fancy types in which flourishes and the irregular lines of the letters interfere considerably with readability. When anyone unfamiliar with typography departs from the familiar styles, he needs to be guided by the skill and experience of someone well trained in printing design. One pitfall especially to be avoided is that of using many different styles, or "families" as the printer calls them, and sizes of type on the same page or in the same folder.

Hand lettering is sometimes used for titles or headlines. The title of the folder "When Women Work" shown on page 142 is

[1] Printing Types. Harvard University Press, Cambridge, 1923, vol. 2, p. 228.

It *is* NOT NATURAL *for babies*
TO HAVE SORE EYES!
If the Eyes BECOME RED AND MATTERY, *send for*
A DOCTOR—AT ONCE!

HE HAD THE SORE EYES OF INFANCY; PROMPT ACTION SAVED
HIM FROM BLINDNESS

It was WORTH WHILE to save the sight of
THIS LITTLE FUTURE CITIZEN!
HE THINKS SO!

IT IS not natural for babies to have
sore eyes! If the eyes become red and
mattery, send for a doctor at once!

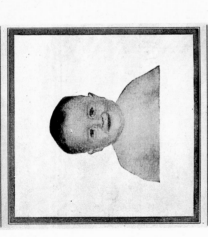

Prompt action saved the sight of
this little future citizen! He thinks
it was worth while.

TWO DESIGNS FOR A PAGE COMPARED

Lines of uneven length and a mixture of capital letters, lower case, and italics give a poor distribution of white space and a ragged effect in the grouping of type on the page shown at the left.

The pleasing effect of the page shown at the right is due largely to the symmetrical proportions of the blocks of type, the generous spaces between them and the illustration, and the brevity of the text.

hand-lettered. Needless to say the letters should be well drawn and the style in harmony with the thought expressed.

LENGTH OF LINE

Among other factors that affect readability is the length of the line. "The one thing that makes the atrociously small type used by newspapers at all bearable is that it is set in short columns," said Mr. Sherbow.[1] Without the help of a short line it would be almost unreadable.

When the length of line is increased beyond the four inches customary in book pages, the eye must travel back and forth across the page and reading is slowed down. The use of a wide illustration sometimes makes necessary a long type line to correspond. In most instances, it would be better to omit or cut down the size of the picture than to throw the page out of balance.

EMPHASIS

For purposes of emphasis in printed matter—the equivalent to gestures, raising the voice, or changing the tone in speech—there is a wide choice of methods. There is bold-face type in contrast to light-face; there are italics, capital letters, color, underlining, or isolated position. It is obvious, however, that any device must be used sparingly or lose its advantage, since not size, color nor position, but contrast to its surroundings makes an object stand out.

Again, the use of too many different devices results in a distracting and disorderly page without gain in significance for any one idea. This is shown in the example on page 162, which contains practically all the means of emphasis listed above.

Another reason for using the emphatic forms sparingly is that their overuse makes reading more difficult. Capital letters, especially, are less easily read than small letters.[2]

[1] Effective Type-Use for Advertising, p. 124. See also p. 127 of Mr. Sherbow's book for table for length of lines in relation to type size.

[2] "We have already seen that we tend to find meaning in the tops rather than in the bases of things. This is particularly true in reading printed matter. The eye tends to follow the upper part of the line of letters and the upper parts of the type faces are the parts which show variety and differentiation as between the different letters. Partly for this reason the 'lower case' letters are more easily perceived and read than are capital letters." (Hollingworth, Harry L., Advertising and Selling. D. Appleton and Co., New York, 1913, pp. 182–184.)

DON'T NEGLECT YOUR OPPORTUNITY

Whether well or sick, young or old, rich or poor, get the habit of a regular medical examination. Made **by appointment,** free of charge, at the Health Center.

1. *Everybody!* Consult first your **own physician,** if you can possibly do so.

2. *Future mothers!* If you have made no other arrangement use the **Health Center Prenatal Service.** Open every afternoon.

3. *Babies!* Bring babies to your nearest **Well Baby Conference.** Lowell House, 198 Hamilton St., Neighborhood House, 221 Wooster St., Health Center, 578 Grand Avenue or to Seamen's Bethel, 61 Water St.

4. *School Children!* Go to your School Nurse. She is your **Health Teacher** and will help keep you well.

5. *Examination of Lungs!* Consult **at any time** the Municipal Tuberculosis Clinic No. 2 at the Health Center.

6. *Everybody Else!* The Health Center is always at your service from 8:30 to 5:00 o'clock and Tuesday evenings to give you

   Helpful Advice

   Hygienic Instruction

   Medical Consultation

   Physical Examination

AN ATTEMPT AT OVEREMPHASIS THAT DEFEATS ITSELF

In the original the heading and the last four lines of the page above were printed in red ink. By means of bold-face and italic type, exclamation marks, capital letters and the use of the red ink at top and bottom, this page strove for emphasis, but succeeded only in looking spotty.

ONE NEEDS ONLY TO OBSERVE THE CONTRAST IN
READABILITY BETWEEN THIS PASSAGE PRINTED IN
CAPITAL LETTERS AND THE LOWER CASE LETTERS
ON THE REMAINDER OF THE PAGE TO RECOGNIZE
THIS FACT.

Underlining makes reading more difficult because it diminishes
the space between the lines. Colored or heavy-face types which
are in strong contrast to the surrounding type have such great
attention value that they have a tendency to minimize the rest
of the text.

The despair of the person who has many important facts to impress strongly on people's minds is that there is no possible way
to make them all stand out prominently if they are in close prox-
imity to one another. He succeeds only in creating confusion if all
his ideas clamor for special attention at the same time.

Color

The greater attention value of color over black and white hardly
needs demonstration since we know so well that people almost uni-
versally like color. Advertisers are using it increasingly although
the cost is greater for color printing than for black and white.

Color in printed matter may be in the paper, the pictures, the
decorations, or the text. Studies have been made and much information compiled in regard to harmonious and pleasing combinations and in regard to the psychology of colors.[1]

The least expensive way to secure color in leaflets or folders is
by using colored ink or colored paper, or both. Paper of a light
color is generally preferable to dark, for there must be a decided
contrast between paper and text in order to make the latter readable. It is well to remember that the strength of the color has
most value in attaining the desired contrast. We find in our collection of printed matter several examples printed in a very weak
or light shade of blue or green which compare unfavorably in
readability with others printed in deeper tones. Intensely dark
green, brown, or blue inks are good. A surprising number of

[1] For color chart and psychological appeal of colors, see Ramsay, Robert E.,
Effective Direct Advertising. D. Appleton and Co., New York, 1921, pp. 354, 356.

folders are printed in blue type on dark gray paper or black type on a blue background, making reading so difficult as to discourage any but the most zealous seeker for information. Buff paper with dark brown ink is a popular and pleasing combination.

William Feather,[1] in criticizing a group of examples of health literature, notes especially the tendency to use gray as a background. Gray is a sober, quiet color lacking the suggestion of vitality which is appropriate for the subject of health. In light tones it may be used where dignity and restfulness are to be desired.

A second color may be added to printed matter in borders, small ornaments, or symbols; in initial letters or the first word of the text, or in illustrations. Red is most often used because it readily attracts attention. A single spot or line of it is usually sufficient to give life to the page. Too much of it draws attention away from the text. Color can seldom be used to advantage for a single word or a phrase in the text. No color equals black for intensity so that larger type must be used where part of a line is printed in orange or red to secure the desired emphasis.

Paper

To select the right paper for a particular piece of printing it is necessary to take into account what will go on the paper and what sort of impression will be conveyed by its appearance and texture.

The best paper for printing text is one that has no gloss and therefore will not reflect light. Another important factor in the relation of paper to the readability of the text printed on it is color. The paper on which the Atlantic Monthly is printed illustrates an excellent choice for text, the paper being toned from white and so roughened in its surface that no light at all is reflected. Buff, cream, or India tints are good.

For half-tone engraving, the process by which photographs, paintings, and some drawings are reproduced for the printed page,[2] a paper with a smooth surface known as supercalendered or coated, is best. The finer the engraving, the higher the finish needed. The reason for this is clear if we understand some-

[1] "Health Education and Publicity." *In* American Journal of Public Health, New York, vol. 13, March, 1923, p. 248.
[2] See "Reproducing Illustrations," p. 188.

ADAPTING THE HALF-TONE TO THE PAPER

The picture above is clear because the screen for the engraving was coarse enough to suit the paper. In the lower picture the use of too fine a screen has obliterated the details, which are in the shadows, and has darkened the high lights.

thing of the process of making the plate. To make a half-tone plate it is necessary first to photograph the original sketch or painting through a fine screen. This screen consists of two pieces of glass ruled with parallel lines and joined together in such a manner that the lines run at right angles. The light passing through the spaces produces minute dots which form the picture. The number of lines varies from 55 to 200 to the linear inch. The more lines there are, the finer will be the half-tone, and the smoother must be the paper upon which it is printed. The illustrations on pages 98 and 165 show the contrast in reproductions of the same half-tone on coated and uncoated paper.[1] When a fine half-tone and text are to be printed on the same page, the requirements of both can be met by the use of dull coated papers. Half-tone engravings in coarse screens may be printed on some uncoated papers as is done regularly in the newspapers, but satisfactory results are not easily obtained with the inexpensive and quick process which is so frequently demanded in the production of publicity material. It is especially important in ordering half-tone illustrations that the engraver should be given a sample of the paper on which these are to be printed and that he should submit proofs on paper of this kind. The difference in effectiveness between the two half-tones shown on page 165 illustrates this point.

Line drawings can be reproduced successfully on the rough finish papers which are most suitable for text as may be observed from some illustrations in this book.[2]

The appearance and quality of the paper used undoubtedly have much to do with the impression made by a publication, and the importance conceded to it by persons to whom it is distributed. One manufacturer has made familiar the phrase "paper is part of the picture." Handbills which are expected to be thrown away quickly may properly be printed on paper of the cheapest grade. For most folders and booklets used in publicity, the suitable paper is one which takes print well and yet does not suggest expenditure beyond what is regarded as reasonable for contributed or public funds. The quality of the paper selected may convey any one of a

[1] For a table showing different screens suitable for half-tones used on different grades of paper, see Ramsay, Robert E., Effective Direct Advertising. p. 365.
[2] See pp. 173, 175, and others.

number of desired impressions, such as dignity, distinction, liveliness, coolness, or richness. These are perhaps elements that do not often come up for consideration in the comparatively inexpensive printing used by social agencies. It is well to know, however, that there are many varieties of attractive papers from which to select one which lends the right atmosphere to the text and pictures. Paper manufacturers and dealers are interested in reaching the users of paper directly and will, on request, furnish sets of paper samples for office files.

When printed matter is to be mailed, the weight and strength of paper are factors to consider in making a selection. At times, one may, by using a heavier grade of paper, take advantage of the full weight allowed under a given postage rate. On the other hand, it may be desirable to reduce the cost of mailing by choosing a paper of lighter weight, especially for bulkier pieces, such as pamphlets. In doing this, it is important to avoid the use of paper so thin that the type shows through. Text printed on both sides of a sheet of thin non-opaque paper is not readable.

The weight and grain of the paper are considerations if the piece is to be folded. Paper weighing from 60 to 80 pounds per ream of 25 by 38 inch sheets is best for folding.[1] It is less likely to crack or tear when *folded with the grain* than when folded across it.[2]

The relation of bulk to strength and stiffness affects the condition under which the folder or booklet will arrive at its destination. Light weight printed matter will carry just as successfully as heavy weight if firm and strong.

Paper is sold in sheets of standard sizes.[3] It is highly desirable that the page size selected for a leaflet, folder, or booklet should be one that can be cut without waste from these sheets. Suitable sizes both from the standpoint of economy and use were suggested in the previous chapter.

The publicity worker, in dealing with a printer, may plan type,

[1] On January 1, 1927, the standard for marking and selling paper officially adopted by paper and printing trade associations was changed from the ream (500 sheets) to 1,000 sheets. This would double the weight quoted above.

[2] The direction of the grain of paper can be learned by tearing off a small sample and wetting one side thoroughly. The resulting curl will be with the grain.

[3] See Ramsay, Robert E., Effective Direct Advertising, Appendix C, "Standard Weights, Sizes and Names of Papers." pp. 575–577.

paper, and other elements in a printing job in much detail, but he will do well to take it to the printer with an open mind toward suggestions. The size he has chosen may not be advantageous for the paper selected, so that either paper or size should be changed. Again, the paper selected may not be easy to obtain or another equally suitable kind may be obtainable at a saving sufficient to warrant its use.

The Visiting
Nurse will teach
you how to prepare
wholesome food for
your sick husband or child.

Are you living away from home? When
you are sick, let the Metropolitan Nurse
take the place of the home folks.

(Permission of Metropolitan Life Insurance Co.)

PICTURES HELP TO CONVEY THE DESIRED IMPRESSION

These sketches for a folder, "Your Friend the Nurse," help to bring out the idea that the service is intended for persons who do not need charity.

CHAPTER X

DECORATION AND ILLUSTRATION OF PRINTED MATTER

DECORATION, illustration, feeling—one or all of these are the ends to be attained by using ornaments or pictures in printed matter. The artistically designed initial letter is a decoration only. A picture of laboratory equipment may illustrate or interpret the text of a booklet about a hospital but can hardly be called decorative. The laughing face of a child makes an appeal to our liking or sympathy and may also decorate the page on which it appears, but it may not increase our understanding of the thought expressed in the text.

If the same picture can be made to serve all three purposes, so much the better. But the designer should know which is most important in the printing under consideration. If the theme needs accurate illustration, his picture should accomplish this regardless of beauty. The absurdly inappropriate decorations or sketches sometimes used distract attention and add nothing to the forcefulness of the message.

DECORATION

Borders, initial letters, and head or tail pieces are the chief forms of decoration in printing.

Not only the selection of a suitable decoration but the question of using any at all is a matter calling for good taste and good judgment.

Decoration exists never for itself, but always for the thing before which it goes. When it becomes aggressive, impertinent, or ostentatious, and shows off before the main idea, it is in bad taste and is no longer decoration. On the other hand, ornamentation exists to show itself and uses the thing upon which it is applied as a vehicle for exposing itself. . . .

Decoration, then, must never appear more prominent than the copy or the other necessary material out of which the display is made. The intensely bad taste of elaborate borders, over-ornamented initials,

169

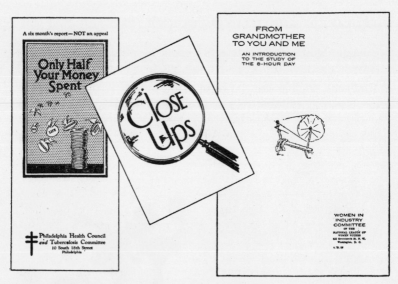

SIMPLE, FAMILIAR OBJECTS MAKE PLEASING ILLUSTRATIONS

WHIMSICAL LITTLE FIGURES MAY CALL ATTENTION TO SERIOUS FACTS

grotesque head and tail pieces, is a result of misconception as to the difference between the decorative idea and the ornamental one.[1]

Emblems, such as are shown on page 36, are decorative. They are, of course, suitable to practically any publication issued by the organization using them and serve to identify it. Many emblems have come to stand for certain ideas as clearly as do words.

SILHOUETTES THAT DECORATED AND ILLUSTRATED A HEALTH ALMANAC

DECORATIVE SKETCHES

An endless variety of simple designs which decorate or animate the page may be obtained without calling upon the skill of the high-grade artist. Objects symbolic of the spirit or theme of the subject are often used with remarkable success in increasing the attractiveness of the cover-page. One of the illustrations on page 170

[1] Tipper, Hotchkiss, Hollingworth and Parsons, Advertising—Its Principles and Practice. Ronald Press Co., New York, 1919, pp. 307–308.

shows a cover design of a pile of winged dollars with several of
them in flight across the page accompanying the title, "Only
Half Your Money Spent." The spinning wheel, loom, or a part of
a machine suggests some type of industry.

Figures of people in outline or silhouette are decorative and lend
more animation to the page than objects. A health almanac,
sections of which are shown on page 171, is illustrated throughout
with silhouettes, chiefly of animals and children. Emblems made
in silhouette form are striking and artistic and make an inexpensive decoration. Because of the absence of detail the silhouette
centers attention on the significant feature of the picture. It has
also a value in arresting attention because of the strong contrast
between the solid masses of black and white.

Grotesque figures, such as we find occasionally in books for
children, are pleasing to older persons also and may be used effectively to decorate printed matter. The boy on the card shown on
page 170 is obviously there to tempt you to read the words. In the
original the deep orange of his upstanding hair and long leggings
added to his elfish appearance. One receiving the card would respond willingly to his request to "Turn this slip about."

Thumbnail Sketches. The amusing sketches shown on page 175
are appropriate to the text. In spite of the great economy in the
number of lines used these small figures engage in a surprising
variety of activities. Rows of little thumbnail figures sometimes
replace the usual lines or dots in diagrams and charts in order to
express comparisons between sets of figures. They are, of course,
often ludicrous and, if so, it would not do to use them where it
seems important to maintain dignity or seriousness.

PICTURES TO CONVEY INFORMATION

A picture which is in itself informing serves an important purpose in publications intended for the instruction of the readers.

Especially in pieces addressed to those who dislike reading, or
perhaps read with difficulty, pictures of this kind are preferable
to those which serve only to enliven and to beautify the page.
If these illustrations are good to look at as well, so much the
better, but it is of chief importance that they give the intended
information.

THE AIR LINE TO HEALTH

Learning to Walk. The average child begins to want to stand at about the tenth month and to walk from the twelfth to the fourteenth. Earlier efforts at standing and walking should not be encouraged. A child never should be urged to stand and walk, especially if he is heavy. He will want to stand and walk of his own accord as soon as the little legs are strong enough to bear his weight.

Learning to Talk. A child learns to talk by hearing older people and other children speaking. At first, speech to him is but a jumble of sounds as a foreign language is to us. Later, he begins to learn that certain sounds means certain people or things or movements.

It is very necessary that he should hear these words and sounds correctly spoken and that when he begins to talk he should hear correct

SIMPLE OUTLINE DRAWINGS THAT MAKE SATISFACTORY ILLUSTRATIONS

The picture on page 173 of the child learning to walk is excellent in that it shows the process accurately without the addition of a line to distract attention from the main idea. The sketches of the visiting nurse which illustrate a folder offering her services do exactly what they are intended to do; that is, they prepare those on whom she may call to recognize her, and welcome her because they already know how she looks and how she will go about her work. Persons reading the leaflet illustrated on page 173 urging support of open-air schools receive a remarkably clear picture of what an open-air school is like. All these sketches are simple outline drawings without any pretense to artistic merit, but they do their work satisfactorily. They have an advantage over photographs in the omission of distracting and needless detail. Not infrequently the true-to-lifeness of a photograph has less teaching value because it tells too much.

THE APPEAL OF THE PICTURE

In contrast to the instructive sketch, we may use one which appeals to the reader's sympathy or arouses pleasurable associations with the ideas presented in the text. A picture showing two children happily bathing in the ocean, which illustrates a health folder, shows that splashing in the water is fun, and so encourages cleanliness. The series of pen and ink sketches on page 169, entitled "Your Friend the Nurse," suggests a friendly service to persons in comfortable surroundings. The intention is to convey to those who would object to being classed as objects of charity that this nursing service is meant for them. The impression is created through the skilful work of the artist, particularly through his finely etched lines.

A sketch intended to arouse sympathy or compassion requires better drawing and more imagination on the part of the artist than one which attempts accurate representation. A striking example of a picture in which the appeal is weakened through the crudeness of the conception and work is found on a health department publication intended to arouse public sentiment with a view to reducing a needlessly high infant death-rate. The picture shows a mother sitting by her baby's coffin. The woman's figure is almost a caricature and the absurdity of the composition—a mother ap-

174

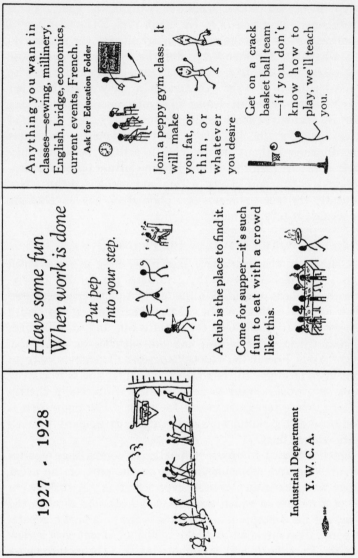

1927 · 1928

Industrial Department
Y. W. C. A.

Have some fun
When work is done

Put pep
Into your step.

A club is the place to find it.

Come for supper—it's such fun to eat with a crowd like this.

Anything you want in classes—sewing, millinery, English, bridge, economics, current events, French.

Ask for Education Folder

Join a peppy gym class. It will make you fat, or thin, or whatever you desire

Get on a crack basket ball team —if you don't know how to play, we'll teach you.

THUMBNAIL SKETCHES

The antics of these absurd little figures help to convey the idea that it is fun to go to the Y.W.C.A.

parently about to bury her baby herself, a tombstone near by and a skull and cross-bones suggestive of some secret society—turns sympathy into amusement.

Sketches out of Harmony with the Subject. Some of the sketches found in booklets and folders do not fit the text they are intended to illustrate. For example, a page of text about the baby's first tooth is accompanied by the picture of a child of six brushing his teeth. The cover design for "The Traveling Health Clinic Is Coming" shows only children entering the health truck for examination, although the message inside the folder is chiefly an invitation to adults to be examined.

Occasionally, not the picture as a whole, but some of its details are inappropriate. By introducing some object, an expensive looking lamp, perhaps, to give balance to the picture of a room, an artist may transform what is intended to be a very unpretentious setting into one that suggests luxury. Beautifully tiled bathrooms are frequently pictured in booklets about personal hygiene sent to people who have never seen such luxury except in show windows. The very fact that pictures engage the attention of more readers, and are remembered more vividly than the text, is the reason for making sure that they present accurately the thought intended.

Standards and tastes in art vary too widely for anyone to be able to say positively whether or not a given picture will please or fail to please those who are to receive it. It is worth while to test a picture before it is used by obtaining opinions about it from some of the persons to whom it is expected to appeal. If they find it amusing when it is intended to arouse sympathy or if it is merely acceptable when it should give genuine pleasure, it is probably not done well enough for your purpose.

CARTOONS

The cartoon may present any mood or any kind of information, telling its story through a single picture or a series, as the material requires. Its emphasis or exaggeration of significant features helps to get an idea over quickly. Readers of newspapers are accustomed to cartoons and so are fairly quick to grasp the points made even though somewhat involved, if the subject matter itself is familiar.

LOOK OUT! HERE COME THE NATURE LOVERS.

(Permission of J. N. Darling)

A GOOD CARTOON

The lesson contained in this series of four pictures is unescapable, yet only a dozen words are used.

Advice given repeatedly begins to be tiresome long before readers have reached a stage where it ceases to be needed. When the unsought advice is in humorous vein, it is often accepted good-naturedly by those who would be bored or irritated by serious commands and warnings. The cartoon, therefore, offers an excellent form of illustration for folders and booklets of instruction which deal with safety, personal hygiene, and keeping yards and streets clean.

Cartoon characters created to lighten advice on health topics have been used not only to illustrate printed matter, but also in graphic material and have even been personified by entertainers who go about giving talks. The famous clown Cho Cho of the American Child Health Association started out as an illustration for a book. The adventures of comic characters are frequently described in a strip or series of pictures. Two persons may be pictured at successive stages in a conversation, one character convincing the other in favor of some action. Most people follow conversation more easily and with greater interest than they do impersonal argument or discourse. Even the soliloquy of a person or an object shown in a series of sketches is probably enjoyed much more than the same information would be if presented directly by the writer to the reader.

Opportunities, dangers, noble sentiments, traits of character, and other abstractions are personified in the allegorical cartoon which makes a serious appeal. Cartoons of this sort were among the most telling forms of war-time propaganda. Those newspapers which best understand the popular imagination use generously cartoons of sentiment, always taking care to represent their ideas through familiar objects and situations, and holding to a single easily understood theme.

Some of the cartoons which appear in the bulletins or house organs published by social agencies attempt to portray situations that are too intricate to express in cartoon form. One example attempts to show in a single picture the sources from which "little victims of neglect" are referred to a child welfare society, how field workers lead them away from "rivers of delinquency, criminality and vagrancy over the bridge of supervision and care, and into good homes to be trained for good citizenship." The elabor-

THE BEGINNING AND END OF CHILD LABOR

Courtesy THE NEW YORK WORLD

"Shine, mister?"

A CARTOON THAT MAKES ITS POINT WITH FORCE

179

ateness of the resulting cartoon with its involved groupings of buildings, streets, rivers, bridges, and human figures may well be imagined.

Again, in health cartoons, the menace of disease is sometimes presented with such exaggeration that it seems more likely to inspire scepticism or revulsion than caution. The fact that most people naturally draw away from what is repulsive or gruesome makes it likely that they will give less attention to the message presented through pictures of this kind than through those that suggest pleasure, happiness, and achievement.

As in other types of sketches which aim to make a serious appeal, absurdities in the picture due to crude work on the part of the artist are likely to arouse amusement or contempt, which is decidedly detrimental to the publicity.

Newspaper and magazine cartoonists interpret effectively current situations in which social agencies are interested. Usually their cartoons may be reprinted, by permission, on posters, mailing cards, and in house organs; but their use in booklets and folders is somewhat limited by the desire for dignified appearance. They are well suited to illustrate printed matter, urging new laws or amendments, in which arguments and situations are presented satirically.

Ordering Art Work

The sketches used by social organizations are obtained in some instances from the drawing departments of schools. Others are done by illustrators who work chiefly for magazines or for advertisers. A clever young woman who occasionally sketches and writes for her own amusement has illustrated several booklets very well. A staff artist of a city department store or advertising agency occasionally contributes a drawing. The cover design of a folder, used first as a poster, was obtained through a competition in which a prize was offered. Any of these sources are satisfactory for the purposes of social publicity if the artist is instructed regarding what is desired.

It should not be taken for granted, however, that the person who draws delightful whimsical sketches can also interpret certain definite facts or ideas, nor can one who draws pretty girls for advertisements necessarily be depended upon to portray sympatheti-

A POSED GROUP AND ONE IN ACTION

Contrast the formally posed picture of a group of children about to go on an outing, with the eager and impatient children entering the motor bus to start on their adventure.

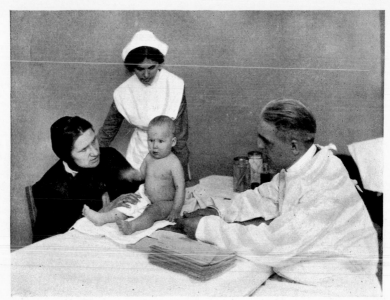

(Permission of Infant Welfare Society of Chicago)

ADVANTAGES OF POSING A SMALL GROUP

The small group above which shows a mother receiving sympathetic advice from a physician makes a more appealing picture of clinic service than the crowded waiting room below.

cally a neglected child or an overworked mother. It will be necessary first to learn whether the artist selected is accustomed to doing the type of work needed and whether he uses a medium that is practicable for reproduction. Charcoal work, for instance, is expensive to reproduce. The second requirement is that the person giving the order should himself know and be able to explain just what he wishes portrayed and what are the limitations of size, shape, and method of reproduction. Before the order is concluded he should receive from the artist a rough draft that will give a fairly clear idea of the final picture. There may be a slight charge for this preliminary sketch but even so it is usually an economy.

With these precautions it is safe and wise to allow a competent illustrator to develop his own ideas of interpretation. He is likely to do better work when he has some latitude for originality.

One more consideration especially important if the artist is inexperienced is to encourage him to revise his sketch until he has produced the best work of which he is capable. Many of the crude drawings which appear in publicity material of social agencies could have been better if they had been done over again a second or even a third time.

Borrowing Pictures. Pictures of attractive children playing happily out of doors or eating the kinds of food which public health agencies recommend; young women with beautiful teeth and with faces and figures which show radiant health; vigorous looking mechanics working at various kinds of machinery; these and many other types of pictures used in advertisements are sometimes borrowed by health organizations and other social agencies for use in their publicity work. Cartoons published in the daily papers depict emotions and situations which often fit into the needs of social publicity. Social agencies have used Briggs's "grand and glorious feelin'" to illustrate a variety of subjects.

Many well-known paintings deal with themes which relate to certain phases of social problems and it is frequently possible to secure the privilege of reproducing them.

A serious objection to the use of a picture not drawn for the particular purpose for which it is used is that often the text has to be adapted to the picture rather than the picture to the text, and in the process, the real message is lost. It may also happen that undesirable changes must be made in the size and shape of the publication,[1] and perhaps in the paper to be used, in order to meet the requirements of reproducing the borrowed illustrations.

Still another factor to guard against in borrowing pictures is the tendency to become interested in the picture itself and to lose sight of its relation to the copy. The picture of the popular "Skin-nay," shown at the left, would be appropriate for information or advice given on a subject that could be treated humorously, but in the present instance it misleads the reader, for the folder is about the ravages of tuberculosis and the toll of unnecessary deaths.

A PICTURE UNSUITED TO ITS PURPOSE

The gleeful "Skin-nay" is used here as a cover illustration for a serious talk about tuberculosis.

Combining for Better Pictures. Agencies in different cities working upon the same problem may unite in obtaining sketches which will be of much higher grade than one agency alone could afford. This has been done to some extent by tuberculosis associations, community funds, and other groups; but it has been a more or less casual and incidental procedure, and has been limited almost entirely to posters. Probably the best results will be obtained when some central agency studies the publicity material of a group of organizations and arranges for pictures to meet definitely recognized needs of them all.

MAPS, DIAGRAMS, AND CHARTS

Maps are interesting to many people. They are generally understood because their use has long been common in elementary education. Spot maps show the distribution of population, the location of parks, schools, or hospitals, or comparisons of the extent of disease in different parts of a given area. Maps of this sort

[1] See p. 161.

gain in attention value if pictorial symbols[1] replace the dots which indicate the locations of buildings, playgrounds, or other items. Different parts of the territory included in a map may be ranked by means of shading and cross hatching, black areas usually indicating the most backward sections and white those that have advanced most in the matter of social legislation or some other social progress.

It is better to use a series of maps than to crowd a single map with too great an assortment of information. For example, to show the social resources of a city, one map of its playgrounds and parks, another of its hospitals, and so on, is preferable to a map on which symbols indicating all of these are combined.

Statistical diagrams are less widely understood than maps because they were very little used in education when the present generation of adults went to school. However, the growing practice of charting business information is adding to the number of persons who do not find bars, curves, and sectors formidable. For non-technical publications diagrams should be made exceedingly simple. Probably the vertical or horizontal bars which require of the reader only a comparison of lengths or heights are the easiest diagrams to understand. If one wishes to give a quick impression of the changes taking place over a given period of years, a curve may be better than bars. A circle is a familiar form, and a comparison of the size of its sectors is quickly grasped. Showing the divisions of a budget in terms of the parts of a dollar spent for different purposes is a common use of the circle. One disadvantage of the circle is that as the number of sectors increases it becomes more difficult to place reading matter or figures horizontally on each one.

Color adds greatly to the attractiveness of maps and diagrams and it may be used ingeniously to make important facts stand out sharply. It is especially important that diagrams used as illustrations should be large enough so that all printing on them can be read, a point too often overlooked.

Rows of pictures of objects or silhouettes may replace bars or

[1] A system of 103 different symbols for identifying social and economic institutions and facilities on maps has been developed by the Russell Sage Foundation. They are supplied by the Publication Department for a nominal sum, and come in three sizes, gummed ready for use.

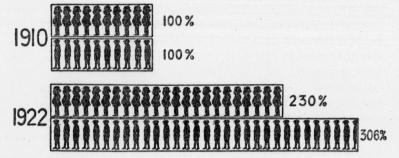

On the top line, the adult figure represents the city in 1910 and the child figure, the schools. Below is shown the relative growth in both city and schools.

(*Permission of Detroit Educational Bulletin*)

In a study of 80 cities, 2.1 out of every 10 children were retarded in school.

Among Toledo school children as a whole, 2.9 out of every 10 are retarded in school.

4.8 out of every 10 newsboys in Toledo are retarded in school.

4.1 out of every 10 of the route carriers in Toledo are retarded in school.

(*Permission of Toledo Consumers' League*)

DIAGRAMS ENLIVENED BY CONVENTIONALIZED FIGURES

be enclosed in bars, and so increase the popular appeal of the diagram. On the other hand, when a comparison between two amounts is presented by placing side by side two objects or persons of contrasting size, the difference appears greater than is actually intended since two dimensions of each object are brought into the comparison.

Sometimes liveliness is obtained by introducing a picture without making it an integral part of the map or diagram. Thus by the simple device of drawing an enlarged figure of a mosquito on a technical map which showed the distribution of malaria cases in Louisiana, dramatic interest was added. The mosquito addresses his readers as follows:

> I am the anopheles mosquito. I cause these deaths. I killed many more in previous years and expect to kill more in years to come. I also cause many thousand cases of sickness and cost Louisiana about $4,000,-000 a year. What are you going to do about it?[1]

PHOTOGRAPHS

When we look at a picture, we read into it what our personal interest or memory contributes. Photographs as well as sketches for publication use should be tested for what they convey to the reader. We fail, not unnaturally, to realize to what extent our own interest in the activities carried on inside a building accounts for our enjoyment in a photograph of its exterior. The reader of an illustrated bulletin on health may supply from his own experience associations which lead his thoughts quite away from the direction we intended them to take. He may associate the picture of the equipment of a dispensary with a painful experience and instinctively draw away from it, while those who worked hard to secure the new equipment will naturally take pride in a photograph of it.

Pictures without animation are ineffective unless the purpose is merely to give readers the pleasure of recognizing familiar faces. Some 25 children stiffly posed with heads erect are grouped in a photograph reproduced on page 180. They are a group of children from some nutrition classes. They are supposed to be starting for camp but the reader receives no impression of an excited crowd

[1] The Rockefeller Foundation: A Review for 1921. New York, 1922, p. 44.

of youngsters starting out on a happy visit. We see only that they are having their pictures taken. Again, the waiting room of a health center is shown with as many visitors as possible crowded on its rows of benches. The intention may have been to show how many people come to the center. The reader, however, sees chiefly the depressing spectacle of the people herded together on hard benches with no occupation or entertainment to make their waiting less weary.

A photograph lends animation to a piece of printing when it shows people in action or things in use. For example, a doorway is pictured on the cover of an annual report of a boys' club not merely as an architectural detail but as an entrance crowded with eager boys who are impatient to get in. "Let's Follow the Line Inside" says the caption, and turning the page we see the boys on their way up a flight of stairs to the various clubrooms pictured in the remaining pages of the book.

The photograph of a group of nurses as they are starting out from headquarters on their daily round of visits interests us much more deeply in their work than does a group picture of the same nurses stiffly posed.

Individuals in Preference to Groups. A single individual or a group of three or four persons can be posed much more effectively than a large group. The greater appeal of the photograph on page 181, showing a friendly interview between patient and doctor, over that below it, of the women waiting for consultation, is a striking demonstration of this. The first picture suggests an intimate and kindly service and all we need is the caption stating that "Two Hundred Mothers Receive This Service Every Month" to be impressed with its extent as well as its value. The second picture suggests cold, impersonal, and machine-like methods of handling crowds of applicants. Again, the individual is more interesting to most of us than is the crowd. Another advantage is that an uncrowded picture can bring out action and facial expression. The picture of blind children playing with their toys, shown opposite, contains so many figures that we do not fully realize the significance of the original caption, "With Only Their Busy Fingers Can They See the Forms They Build." In a smaller group, it would have been possible to show the "busy fingers"

186

IMPORTANT DETAILS EMPHASIZED BY SELECTION AND ENLARGEMENT

The picture above, which has been trimmed and enlarged, gives a clearer idea of how blind children see with their fingers than can be obtained from the one below in which the same boy appears in too large a group for so small a space.

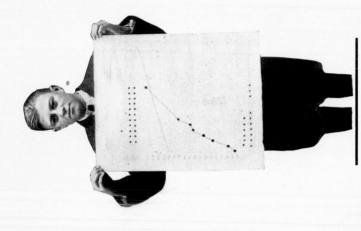

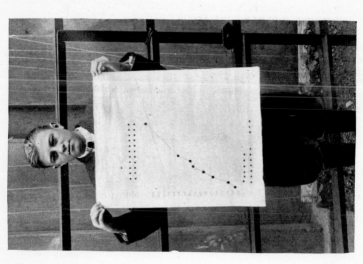

OMITTING A USELESS BACKGROUND

The background in the picture at the left distracts attention from the chart displayed.
It would have been much better to have omitted it, as shown in picture at the right.

much more distinctly in the same space. More and more, the social agency sending out an appeal is selecting as a subject for a photograph a single child, like the one who comes smiling toward you from the cover of the booklet on page 55.

Playing Up Significant Details. A second point of interest about the boy who walks toward us out of the cover-page is that we see only the boy himself, and not the meaningless wall against which he may have leaned, or the sidewalk and strip of curbing where he happened to stand because the light there was good for getting the photograph. Sometimes the background is an integral part of the story and needs to be retained, but often it is unessential. In the latter case it is well to outline the picture or trim or "crop" it, so that the significant objects receive our whole attention. A good illustration of the gain in taking out the background is shown in the two cuts opposite, in one of which the background is retained while in the other it is cut away. The additional objects are not only distracting, but also unsightly. From the cover of a "keep well" pamphlet, the figure of "a young man grown old too soon," stares hopelessly. A pillar against which he is posed and a meaningless chair in the background divert our attention, which should be centered wholly on the drooping figure and drawn face of the man himself.

Combining Two Pictures. The boy and girl looking out over the city in the picture on page 18 would appear as tiny specks if they had been photographed as a part of the picture. By superimposing a photograph of the boy and girl upon a view of the city we obtain the interesting result shown on the folder. This is one of a great variety of ingenious effects obtained from combining, or "stripping," two different photographs or a photograph and a sketch. A background may be sketched in, so that while our attention is centered on the people in the picture, the significant features of the setting are merely suggested. Thus the mother at her washtub with her two children is the real subject of the story in the mailing folder on page 188. The bit of broken plaster suggesting poverty, and the bed close to the washtub revealing congestion are all the background needed. In another picture a row of children seated on a fence are photographed, and a background of shadowy factories and tenements is sketched in. Other examples are the smiling baby's face breaking through a map of Ohio to go with the caption "The State of Ohio Is Interested in Your Baby," and the grim reaper with his scythe, hovering over the busy street of tenements "where the poor fight the scourge of filth, disease, and death, all the year round."

Reproducing Illustrations

Before the illustrations are selected for a given publication, as already stated, one must consider whether or not they can be reproduced successfully and at no greater cost than is permissible.[1] Roughly, the art work may be divided into pen and ink sketches, crayon or pencil sketches, wash drawings, oil paintings, and photographs. Of these the pen and ink sketches are on the whole the most practical form for reproduction since they require only line engraving, which is the least expensive process. Also the sharp distinct black lines can be reproduced well by the engraver of average ability and there are no special requirements as to the kind of paper to be used. Pencil, crayon, or charcoal drawings, on the other hand, require expert handling. Photographs, oil paintings, wash drawings, and some sketches require half-tones.[2]

We have already pointed out in the discussion of paper the fact that half-tones print well only on smooth finished paper. It is well to remember also in planning illustrations that a good half-tone generally cannot be made by photographing another half-tone print. If this has to be done, the half-tone to be reproduced must go through a retouching process, but the final result is likely to be unsatisfactory and in most cases it would be better to get a new picture.

[1] For discussion of illustrations and their reproduction, see Ramsay, Robert E., Effective Direct Advertising. D. Appleton and Co., New York, 1921, pp. 339–370.

[2] See "Pictures Help to Convey the Desired Impression," p. 169, and "Advantages of Posing a Small Group," p. 181.

COMBINATION OF SKETCH AND PHOTOGRAPH

To provide appropriate background for this photograph of a tenement mother and her children, an artist sketches in a window, a bit of plaster, and part of a bed.

CHAPTER XI

COPY

COPY is manuscript in the form in which it is ready to go to the printer. The manuscript may be an historical study, a medical treatise, an appeal for charitable funds, instructions on some health topic, or an advertisement of goods to be sold. The term "copy" includes all that which is to be printed—titles, headings, illustrations, and decorations.[1]

TITLES AND HEADLINES

For the person who runs his eye over a list or a display of reading matter in search of a particular topic, it is sufficient that the title shall identify the subject of the publication. "Malnutrition," "Prenatal Care," "Health Rules," and "Prevention of Cancer" are titles which serve this purpose admirably. Publicity literature, however, aims to reach many readers who are not seeking the information it contains, and a descriptive phrase which provokes attention is better publicity than one which merely names the subject matter.

"Measles, a Wolf in Sheep's Clothing," "Bright Eyes, How to Keep Them Shining," and the "Air Line to Health" are titles which attract the reader and also tell something about the contents. "The Red Trail of the Automobile," and "When It's Sizzling Hot" take hold of the imagination. It is possible, then, for a title to identify the subject of the publication and at the same time capture attention by its vivid suggestion.

Such a title as "A Worker's Message to Workers" identifies the audience to which the message is directed. "To the Mothers of Shorewood" and "Mr. Indoor Worker, Do You Want to Keep Well?" are captions likely to get the attention at once of the persons so addressed. "You—and the Six Million" addresses each reader as a distinct personality. "A Message to Humanity" fails in its attempt to address the reader because humanity is such an

---

[1] Illustration and decoration as related to copy have been discussed in Chap. X, Decoration and Illustration of Printed Matter, p. 169.

indiscriminate group that the title arouses no response from any one person.

Some titles fail to reveal the subject of the message at once, but endeavor to excite curiosity about what is to follow. A single word, a blind phrase, or a curt question piques us into turning the page to solve the mystery. For example, "Shut Your Eyes Tight and Imagine" and "The Password Is," use the device of continuing a sentence on successive pages so that in order to finish it the reader is led on to the body of the text. A question, "Who Is Knocking at the Door?" or a mystifying phrase like "A Touch of Heather" may arouse a desire to learn more.

An example of a title which fails in its purpose is "Our First Thought." Readers are not likely to be curious regarding the thoughts of some unknown person. Such titles as "Some of Our Problems," "Is It Worth While?" and "Do You Know?" which are often used on the covers of folders also fail, since ordinarily people are not interested in "our problems" or in the worth of something they are ignorant of, while merely asking "Do You Know?" gives them no reason to wish to be informed.

A question may have more life than a descriptive phrase, but the mere asking of a question is not enough to get attention. The question itself must be arresting. "Why Must I Judge These People?" is the excellent title of a popular article on the causes of crime.

Action in titles or headlines helps to carry the thought forward to the text. "The Traveling Clinic Is Coming" arouses a sense of anticipation. Contrast "Vital Facts about Cancer" with "A Message of Hope—Cancer Can Be Cured," as a means of arousing interest. "When an Epidemic Strikes New York" suggests greater possibility of something happening than does "Epidemics in New York."

A rhetorical device which may sometimes be used effectively in titles is alliteration. The repetition of letters or syllables makes a phrase easy to catch and remember. "Sanitation and Sanity," "The Lady with the Lamp," and "How to Live Long" are good examples. Alliteration becomes so easy once one gets in the way of it that an inexperienced writer is likely to overuse it, turning out insipid phrases in which sense is sacrificed to sound.

Section and Paragraph Headings

The same purposes served by cover titles—to identify, to describe, to provoke curiosity, to associate the reader with the text, or to suggest action—are to be considered in writing section and paragraph headings. Whereas the attractive title helps to get attention in the beginning, headings conspicuously placed throughout the text invite the reader who glances over the pages and help to carry forward the one who reads carefully. The very fact that these headings stand out boldly in the physical appearance of printed matter is a reason for making them as interesting as possible. Such trite and obvious headings as "Some Facts," "Things to Remember," "What We Do" and "Rules" are more likely to repel interest than to arouse it.

A booklet on typhoid fever intended for the ordinary reader contains these paragraph headings: "Name," "History," "Cause," "Incubation," "Complications," "Prevention," "Treatment." The composition of the following, taken from another discussion of the same subject, is better: "What It Cost Smith," "Typhoid Is a Filth Disease," "No Germs, No Fever," "A Story about a Dug Well," "Flies Carry Typhoid Germs Sometimes," "When Typhoid Visits Your Home." The titles in this group have life and are stated in terms of the reader's experience.

Organization of Subject Matter

The inexperienced writer is likely, in arranging his text, to follow the logic of the material itself. A general report or history will begin with the inception of the movement and following its development through five, ten, or twenty-five years, as the case may be, come down through many pages to the present time. The annual report often follows the customary "order of business" of an annual meeting, beginning with the report of the president, continuing with reports of other officers and concluding with acknowledgments of contributions.

The logical arrangement of an explanation or treatise on disease is first a definition of it or an explanation of its nature; next, a brief history of its discovery and prevalence; then, information about the methods of prevention and treatment; and finally, specific advice to the reader to "act at once." The appeal for funds is less stereotyped in form since it is directed as much to the sympathy of the public as to its intelligence. Nevertheless, logic may still be a strong influence. The writer of a hospital appeal divides his text under these headings: "The Claim," "The Proof," "The Conclusion," and "Action," believing apparently that he can reason his way into the reader's sympathy.

Advice about conduct and arguments for a proposed course of action are likely to take the dogmatic form of a numbered series of statements or phrases: a list of six rules for keeping well, 10 reasons why births should be registered, or 12 questions and answers explaining "What We Do."

A logical or categorical arrangement may be acceptable, perhaps even desirable, if one can safely assume that a reader will bring to the subject an inquiring mind and close attention. Although readers are as a rule uninformed about what writers of annual reports, or booklets on disease prevention have to tell them, they seldom are curious or eager to know it. Therefore, the start must be made at the point of greatest probable interest to the reader, then having got him interested, he can be informed, advised, exhorted, or solicited.

From Particular to General. One of the simplest and soundest rules for the inexperienced writer is to go from the particular instance to the general application of it. If you will glance through the articles published in popular magazines, you will find that most of them proceed from the particular to the general.

The writer of an article about tax reduction begins by describing in lighter vein the state of mind of an individual taxpayer, thus leading the wary reader by easy stages to a consideration of tax problems which he might have avoided if his attention had not been caught by the personal note in the introduction:

> Ever since last October John Smith has been in a state of anxiety over what Congress is going to do to his income tax and his automobile taxes. Up and down the aisles of suburban trains, along midday lunch counters, and from the driver's seat of the family car his voice has been heard, raised in argument, invective, and hope. . . .
>
> On the whole it is well that John Smith should behave in this nervous and uneasy fashion when his taxes are under consideration, for it is

through such anxiety that a common sense of responsibility for government expenditures, too feeble at best in such an immense and scattered country as this, is seeded down. The next time that a good roads subsidy or an increased allowance for the navy is proposed, he will look upon it with a sterner eye, for he will have had a recent reminder that he is paying for it, just as surely as he is paying for his children's winter coats.[1]

Another arrangement which follows the natural development of the reader's interest leads him from the point of his own experiences to matters which he has not as yet realized are his concern. Here, for example, is a beginning addressed to fathers and mothers:

> Some day your daughter will marry. He'll be a nice young man, apparently. Perhaps truly. *But how do you know?* He may ask you for her hand or just brazenly take it as seems to be the custom these modern days. What will you say?"

This mental picture of a situation all parents of daughters anticipate is followed by urgent advice to insist that the prospective son-in-law present a clean bill of health. Then follow several pages of discussion and illustration of the evil effects and widespread prevalence of venereal diseases, and finally a description of the work of the Illinois Social Hygiene League.

Almost any theme which concerns welfare or pleasure, health, recreation, housing, and so on, may begin naturally with a paragraph about the reader himself and the similarity or contrast of his experience with that of others, proceeding thence to the general situation to be described and leading at the end to the suggestion or request for the reader to act.

The Text Made Up of Units. Some very effective booklets are put together in the form of a series of independent units. "Building Happy Childhood," published by the Connecticut Children's Aid Society, is composed almost entirely of separate stories about children interspersed with short descriptions of various distinctive features of the Society's work.

If the material is organized in this way, however, each unit although complete in itself should be related to a central theme. All the threads should be gathered up at the end in a specific appli-

[1] Comstock, Alzada, "Smith's Taxes." *In* The Survey, New York, vol. 55, Jan. 1, 1926, p. 425.

cation of these apparently independent items to a single purpose or idea. "Close Ups," a booklet issued by the Charity Organization Society of New York to enlist the interest of its contributors, is a good example of composition in which variety and unity are combined. A series of entertaining anecdotes, entirely disconnected with one another, gives glimpses of the work of various departments. Following these are brief descriptions of the departments, the staff, and the membership, and a paragraph summarizing the activities of the Society and crystallizing the impression made by the stories. The appeal for support is contained in two forcible italicized lines. The whole booklet can be read in ten minutes, yet through its excellent plan and vivid, concise writing it provides a clear, many-sided view of a large, complex organization.

Extraneous Material Inserted. It frequently happens that after copy is written and before it goes to the printer, the writer or someone else breaks up the well-thought-out relationship of title and text by putting in unrelated material. Perhaps some quotation, a creed, or a motto is placed where it disturbs the continuity of the thought; or a curiosity-provoking title which ought to lead directly to a good opening paragraph and carry forward the interest is followed by an explanation of why the booklet was written. Half of one cover-page shown on page 152 is devoted to information addressed to a few persons rather than to the general reader. In another publication a foreword explaining something the reader is not yet prepared to consider is introduced at a point where its only effect is to slow down the interest.

Sometimes several pages of names delay the reader in reaching the opening pages of the text. Printing the names on a back page should serve the purpose of acknowledgment as well as that of adding authority to the message, without running the risk of breaking in between an attractive title and a good opening paragraph. The cover-page of the booklet, "A Worker's Message to Workers," is followed by a page of acknowledgments of assistance in the preparation of the booklet, explanation of the use to be made of it, and lists of individuals, many of them of no particular interest to the intended readers.

Unnecessary admonitions to read the text are sometimes printed
194

on the cover or on the first page. The title of a booklet on patent medicines is "A Chapter from the Life of a Quack." This title catches our interest but immediately it is dampened by this solemn sentence: "An important lesson is to be learned from this story and all should read and profit thereby." Space that should have been left blank on the outside of a small envelope enclosure is covered with these words: "It takes only a minute to read this but it may save a life or years of suffering." As it happens, the text on the following pages does not in the least satisfy the expectations aroused by the title; consequently the words merely introduce an anticlimax.

STYLE OF WRITING

A reviewer of a pamphlet of advice to mothers praises it because it is "thoroughly non-technical, friendly and conversational in tone, practical, and quite within the comprehension of the average mother." Here we have summed up pretty much all we need to attain in a style of writing advice and information—directness, a good non-technical vocabulary, and an informal, or at least not a pompous and heavy, manner of expression.

Technical Terms. The average writer on social topics fails to realize that certain terms and phrases are a part of his technical equipment and have a content for him made up from an experience entirely lacking to the reader. For example, in a certain recent appeal to voters for a tuberculosis hospital, such terms as "latent infection," "incipient cases," "segregation," and "equitable distribution" are freely used. Terms which are merely working tools, like "case load," "the pre-school child," "well baby conferences," find their way into popular literature.

The use of phrases of this kind is sometimes defended on the ground that "our people" have become familiar with them. One may question whether even the members of volunteer committees or board members feel very much at home with "case loads," or that women who bring their children to "well baby conferences" know what they really are. And even so, publicity literature seldom goes only to the limited group who have these personal contacts.

Advice about colds might easily be given in the terms of medicine and personal hygiene, but how much more quickly grasped is the following:

> Colds are spread . . . by the hands, and really more by the hands than in any other way. "Oh ridiculous! Catching cold through your hands!" . . .
>
> Well—think. You have a cold; you sneeze; to prevent your mouth-spray from flying, you cover your nose and mouth with your hand; so far, so good. Then you shake hands with your friend—and the mouth-spray which you saved him from getting through the air you give him on your hand! "But it won't hurt him on his hand?" No, not while it stays there but watch him; in a minute he has his fingers in his mouth or on his lips or he pulls out some chewing gum with his fingers or picks up his pipe by the stem and puts the stem in his mouth.
>
> "But I don't sneeze on my bare hand—I use a handkerchief to keep my sneezes to myself!" Good—then you put your handkerchief in your pocket—presently you pull it out again; and where do your fingers go this time? Right on the very place on the handkerchief where you sneezed the first time.[1] . . .

Thick-shelled Words. "Thick-shelled words make a prison— they are something that the human mind cannot penetrate," said James J. Davis[2] in writing of the need for simpler forms of expression. A reader who is really seeking information about a subject may have the patience and perseverance to master even a dry, heavy article about it, but the wise writer, trying to get the attention of an unspecialized, unliterary audience, will avoid words that are barriers to ready understanding and use only simple and vivid ones easy to grasp. Writers on health are especially fond of words like "preventable," "purchasable," and "negligible," which to the average reader seem decidedly thick shelled. Dr. W. W. Peter, who is notably successful in popularizing information, summed up the futility of this style in the sentence "China egg publicity won't hatch." The title on the cover of a folder, "Dangers of Migration," is a sample of what Dr. Peter would call a "China egg." As one critic said of it "Does anyone ever migrate? Most of us move from one place to another."

The difference between a stiff and an easy style is strikingly

[1] Hill, H. W., "Catching Colds by Hand." A radio health talk by the New York State Department of Health.

[2] The Iron Puddler. Grosset and Dunlap, Inc., New York, 1922.

illustrated in these two paragraphs taken from two folders describing kindergarten methods. Says the first:

> The educational material used in the kindergarten, known technically as the "kindergarten gifts," was developed according to a mathematical plan. Through the use of this material and the sets of larger floor blocks more recently invented, the child learns to count, to deal with simple combinations of numbers, and becomes familiar with such mathematical forms as sphere, cube, triangle, brick.
>
> In the best kindergartens such training is incidental to the use of this material for play purposes.

The other, circulated by the National Kindergarten Association, talks to the readers, thus:

> The kindergarten child does not have lessons in numbers, but he uses numbers in a practical, concrete way. He and his companions are told to march today in two's and that if this is well done they may march tomorrow in two's and two's, thus making four's. He is told to choose six children to play a game and that the next time he may choose nine, if he can count the number correctly. And so by using numbers and their combinations he learns numbers. He applies what he learns, too. A little boy who had played with a set of blocks containing eight cubes was given a new set containing eight blocks of another shape, whereupon he announced almost at first glance, "Same much as cubes."

Vagueness. Often the words used are familiar enough, but they lack force and are put together into vague, lifeless sentences which do not drive home. The exhortation "Do all you can not to get hurt during Safety Week" is simple but it is also weak and indefinite. Mere assertions that "everyone should be interested," that "every family is in danger," or that the subject "concerns the entire community" are not convincing. Readers want to know the cause of this common danger or concern and why they should be interested. In the report of a hospital the assurance is given that "Progress has been our watchword during the four years" and "Co-operation of many charitably inclined persons has made the work possible," which is probably true of a thousand other institutions. Turning the pages of reports and appeal literature we come upon a number of such phrases as "adjusting herself to local conditions," "an investment in community goodwill," "our purpose is to create a social unity" and "in each community visited, an impetus to civic pride resulted." These leave no impression behind them. Such dullness results from vague thinking on the part of the writers or even, perhaps, from an effort to cover up with fine phrases the lack of a tangible program or definite accomplishment to tell about. The attempt to summarize a great deal of information in a few words is responsible for such expressions as "creating social unity," which may mean something specific but certainly does not reveal what it may be.

The search for concrete and vigorous words and ideas is worth all the time it takes because it is likely to make the difference between having your message drive home and having it merely read and forgotten. Here is a fine example of writing that gets hold of the reader and carries him along into the heart of a problem:

She leaned forward eagerly, her great dark eyes looking out beseechingly from the pale Slavic face, framed in dark curls.

"Oh, I would *love* to be some-kind-of-educated!" she breathed.

That was long ago, in 1918. Today Rebekah is a mature, capable, young woman, a bookkeeper in a small concern which places upon her shoulders a real responsibility. Today she looks out upon the world with calm assurance, knowing that she has in her hands the means of her success.

Often since that day the scholarship counselor of the White-Williams Foundation of Philadelphia, sitting in her little office and receiving the shy expressions of secret desires from the boys and girls that come to her, has thought of Rebekah. "Some-kind-of-educated" is what they all want to become; and more or less blindly, along the path that opens most naturally, their young souls are reaching out to attain that Mecca, an education, the gates whereof open out upon that dimly conceived but radiantly dreamed-of land—wider opportunity.[1]

GOOD WRITING

Ineffectual appeals may be accounted for by the writer's failure to address himself to people of the kind who will receive them. A help to good writing is to keep before one in imagination a real person or family, a "Babbitt," or the "Potters," and as one chooses words or phrases to test them by trying them out mentally on these people. Often it is in the second draft rather than in the first that the

[1] Shipley, Elizabeth Taylor, "Some-Kind-of-Educated." *In* The Survey, New York, vol. 49, Jan. 15, 1923, p. 519.

copy becomes popular in form and pleasing in style. The first writing sets down the ideas to be expressed without much regard to such factors as organization and vocabulary. The second writing aims to adapt the copy to the particular uses for which it is intended, perhaps by reducing the length or enlivening the style, by finding a good story for the first paragraph, and writing a strong, impressive sentence or paragraph for the close.

Some of the best results have been obtained when the facts were set down first by a person well acquainted with them, then given to an experienced and able writer to put into popular form and reviewed later by an authority on the subject matter. A striking example of successful collaboration of this sort is the pamphlet, Conquering an Old Enemy, which was written by Will Irwin for the American Social Hygiene Association.

James Harvey Robinson sums up the attitude of mind in which the writer of social or scientific information should approach his task:

> We need in short, a new form of literary ambition if scientific knowledge is to reach a fair proportion of the population and the scientific mood is to be widely cultivated. This ambition should be to bring home to the greatest possible number of readers as much knowledge as possible, in the most pleasing, effective, and least misleading manner. . . .
>
> A book or article for the general reader—a being, we may safely assume, with no great surplus of time, preparation, attention or initial interest—must do three things. And these three things it should do whether it be a sermonette by Dr. Crane in four or five hundred words, or a popular treatise on plant fertilization, the labor problem, or the history of architecture, running through four or five hundred pages. First, it should enlist the reader's attention. This must not be assumed, but must be wooed or conquered by graciousness or by force. There are many ways of doing this, but still more ways of failing. I suspect that success comes when the writer manages forthwith to identify the reader with the enterprise and make him feel that it concerns him personally and individually. . . .
>
> The second duty of the writer is to present his facts and information in terms and in an order which will be understood by the reader and will fit into his ways of looking at things. Lastly, the significance of the information in its bearing on the reader's thought and conduct and his judgments of others should be wisely suggested.[1]

[1] The Humanizing of Knowledge. George H. Doran Co., New York, 1923, pp. 104–105.

INDICATING DATE AND SOURCE

Two important details often overlooked in issuing pamphlets or reports are the name of the organization and date of the publication. Now and then an organization fails to name itself even on a report of its own work. A larger number give their names, but not the city. Many more give the city but omit the state, even though there are cities of the same name in several states. This happens more often than anyone who does not have occasion to look over a great deal of printed matter on social work would suppose.

There are numerous possibilities of confusion or uncertainty growing out of the practice of omitting this information. Printed matter from all over the country gathers on the desk of a business or professional man. Leaflets may be carried from city to city in pockets or bags. Many agencies exchange literature with kindred organizations in other states, but the value of such exchange is lessened if the source cannot be identified. Libraries often file social welfare publications when they can be sure of the source; otherwise, they are less likely to be kept and their usefulness is curtailed.

The name and address of an organization need not be the most conspicuous feature but they should be placed on all printed matter in order to identify it.

Of even greater importance sometimes is the date. Much educational material gets out of date. Many statements are valuable chiefly in relation to the time of issue. Librarians dislike to file undated material. The year alone is usually enough, and it may be quite inconspicuous, yet available to the one who needs it.

CHAPTER XII

DISTRIBUTION OF PRINTED MATTER

A N AIRPLANE dropping quantities of propaganda leaflets became a familiar spectacle in many cities during the World War. The same device has since been used occasionally as a feature of intensive publicity campaigns. As a method of creating news or a flurry of excitement, this may be a successful stunt, but as a means of getting one's message into the right hands, it represents the extreme of inefficiency. Yet many of the methods of distribution in common use represent almost as great a volume of waste.

The chart on page 202 names most of the avenues of distribution available for publicity literature. We may test the effectiveness of any one of these methods by asking:

1. Is the literature actually delivered into the hands of individuals?
2. Does it get into the hands of the persons for whom it is intended?
3. Is it received under conditions favorable to getting it read?

Is Printed Matter Delivered to Individuals?

Between the agency that prepares printed matter and the individuals expected to read it, there may be as many intermediaries as there are between the manufacturer and the consumer of goods. A national organization issuing a booklet supplies it in quantity lots to its state branches or to other agents who correspond to the wholesalers or jobbers in business. The state organization in turn supplies quantities to local groups, who may be the retailers or who may in turn deliver packages to clubs, committees, employers, schools, and home visitors, the final distributors responsible for getting the material into the hands of individuals. At every stage along this route a large or small amount fails to be delivered to the next point. A certain amount of waste is to be expected. There is no way of estimating how much material can actually be put

METHODS OF DISTRIBUTION OF PUBLICITY LITERATURE

BROADCAST DELIVERY	PERSONAL DELIVERY	MAIL DELIVERY	DISPLAY DELIVERY
Scattering from an airplane or other moving vehicle	By inspectors insurance agents nurses school children social workers	Mailed direct to selected lists	Cashiers' desks
			Counters of exhibits
Package enclosure		Enclosed with bills of public utilities	Racks in offices and public buildings
Leaving on seats of parked cars	House to house	Requests for copies invited	Store counters
	At exits of	through	Tables or racks in waiting rooms
	factories	advertisements	
	schools	car cards	
	offices	circular letters	
	stores	conventions	
	theaters	expositions	
	other gathering places	letters to editors	
	Distributed at church services	news articles	
	conventions	posters	
	exhibitions	radio	
	fairs	return postal cards	
	lectures	order lists enclosed with current correspondence	
	traveling shows		
	entertainments		

into the hands of readers; but some of the loss is unnecessary and could be eliminated by better planning.

Sources of Waste. Printers have told us that they receive many orders for printing from persons who evidently have no plan of use in mind. In a conversation with the director of a state health association about several clever and interesting folders, it was brought out that he wrote and published one whenever he happened to have a good idea to express. The size of the order was a more or less routine matter, the custom being to print in lots of 10,000. After they were in stock, the folders were "moved off the shelves" by sending them out in any convenient way.

Producing printed matter with no plan for its use is a cause of waste which occurs not infrequently. Sometimes, as in the instance cited, a folder is issued because someone feels moved to write it. In other cases, waste occurs from failure to plan the material in a form that may easily be distributed. A state health department printed several thousand copies of a small placard on dangers from dust, to be posted in factories. The copy was written without taking account of the fact that manufacturers would not care to display information which criticized conditions in their own plants. Naturally, there was little demand for the placards, although the same information might have been distributed usefully in a less public way to both manufacturers and employes.

The way to avoid waste in production is to plan the method of distribution before the copy is prepared and the form decided. The more experienced national and state organizations get out most of their printed matter for some specific cause or campaign for which they know it will be needed. The Massachusetts State Health Department, in connection with a babies' rights campaign in which local health organizations were invited to participate, planned literature to suit the type of campaign. Since department stores were to take an active part, leaflets which could easily be enclosed with packages or displayed on counters were printed in large quantities.

Ordinary everyday inefficiency is in part responsible for the quantities of literature which gather dust on the shelves of some state and local offices. Perhaps through someone's carelessness the whole supply arrives too late to be used in the particular campaign for which it is intended. Perhaps a local society ordered or requested a supply of folders or pamphlets from a national organization without having seen copies and found, when the material was received, it was not what was expected. We have no remedy to offer for average human carelessness. But we believe that one factor responsible for it in the present instance is that so little value is placed on printed matter. The easier it is to get, the more casually is it handled. When agencies make a charge to cover, perhaps, the cost of production, distributors are likely to value printed matter more highly. Very often requests come from people who think that giving away printed matter may bolster up their confused or weak programs of publicity. These requests may be recognized by the vague way in which they call for "something to give away" or "something to distribute at a meeting" on some such general topic as health or child welfare, for instance, and one may be fairly certain that such indefiniteness about what is wanted indicates just as hazy an idea of how to make the best use of the material when obtained.

Efficient Distribution. Those who prepare printed matter can do a great deal to help those who receive quantity lots to distribute it to advantage. Many advertisers maintain office and field staffs whose chief responsibility is to see that advertising material is well used. As a step in this direction, some state health departments have arranged to have their district supervisors or their field staff go over the supplies on the shelves of local health officers to suggest ways in which they can be put to use. When the literature is used in a planned campaign the method of distribution probably takes care of itself, since the supplies are ordered specifically to fit into some part of the program.

Delivery of folders or booklets into the hands of individuals can be accomplished thoroughly enough through most of the methods listed on the distribution chart.

The most wasteful method on this list, as already stated, is tossing leaflets or handbills from an airplane or truck. Placing printed matter on store counters, cashiers' desks, in waiting rooms, and other public places has the advantage that those who take it do so because they wish to read it; but as frequently practiced the quantities so placed are too large for the demand. The left-overs in some instances mean a considerable percentage of waste.

Social agencies frequently look to school children as the most convenient messengers for getting printed matter into the homes. In many cases, they undoubtedly do obtain through this means as many actual deliveries as they could by any other method. If the school itself is genuinely interested in the distribution, the children are more likely to take the material home to their parents. Something in the nature of a message from the school to the homes has importance to the children and also to their parents. If, on the other hand, the school agrees to ask the children to take home material unrelated to the school or to what is discussed in the classroom, too often it will fail to reach its destination. In one city grammar school the principal made a study of the children's response to the many requests to deliver educational folders to their parents. He found that a direct message from the school to the parents was carried home, but that other kinds of material were likely to be thrown away at or near the school.

Is Printed Matter Delivered to the Right Persons?

On the whole, it appears that getting one's supply of literature into the hands of individuals is chiefly a matter of ordinary care and common sense. Getting it into the right hands, that is, to the persons who can or should act on its suggestions, is less simple.

In the early campaigns against cancer an important problem during Cancer Week was to get the information on prevention to men and women over forty. How could members of this age group be found and given the folders of advice addressed to them? In this case the device used was to give them away by so many methods and in such large quantities that through sheer volume of distribution it seemed likely that the right persons would get copies.

In intensive campaigns material is sometimes distributed from house to house so that all homes and business places in the community are reached. Again, in a campaign for a bond issue, a folder may be sent to each registered voter and there are other circumstances in which every individual for whom the information is intended receives it in printed form.

More often, however, a social agency issues so small a quantity of copies in proportion to the population of its territory, perhaps

10,000 copies being printed for a possible audience of 100,000 or five times that number, that some way must be found to send them to those only who are likely to profit by them. Among accepted methods used to this end are inviting requests for printed matter, mailing it to selected lists, and delivering it personally to groups or individuals most likely to act on the suggestions it contains.

Inviting Requests for Literature. One of the simplest means of getting booklets or folders of useful information into the right hands is to let it be known generally that this material is available for free distribution. Some of the health agencies distribute much printed matter through inviting requests for it.

When a state or city department issues a booklet containing new information, the fact has news value, especially in the smaller communities; and newspapers will, as a rule, carry an article about the publication announcing that it will be mailed on request. Syndicated columns on health, home economics, child training, and so on, are appropriate channels for announcements of free booklets on their respective subjects. If the announcement does not deserve space in the news columns, it may appear in the form of a letter to the editor.[1]

In some instances health organizations have followed the custom of advertisers and used paid space in magazines or newspapers to offer free booklets and folders. The Health Service of the New York County Chapter of the Red Cross tried the experiment of advertising its health material in several daily newspapers. Each advertisement described a single publication. The American Social Hygiene Association once advertised some of its booklets for sale at a nominal price in six leading magazines of national circulation. Records kept in these instances showed that the cost of distributing the printed matter through paid insertions was high, varying from 25 cents to $2.50 for each request received. In both these instances, however, the offer of instructive literature carried with it publicity for the organization and its message; therefore it would not be fair to charge the whole cost to distribution. The United States Public Health Service has obtained free advertising space in newspapers and farm journals in which to announce new publications.

Posters and car cards, also used to announce literature, are likely

[1] See p. 84.

to be less effective than advertisements in periodicals, because the names and addresses given must be jotted down or memorized, whereas the newspaper or magazine advertisement may carry a coupon or check list which can easily be filled in and mailed.

Lists of their publications are made a regular feature of many state and city health department bulletins. Some organizations enclose such lists in outgoing mail. Radio audiences are invited to send for pamphlets on the topic covered by the speaker.

In the social hygiene movement circular letters have been relied upon largely as a method of finding prospective readers for pamphlets and books. Both the American Social Hygiene Association and the United States Public Health Service have circularized such professional groups as ministers, physicians, teachers, and others whose names and addresses are easily obtained. With the letters were enclosed postal cards or blank forms bearing lists of publications which could be ordered. This method, however, like paid advertising in periodicals, is usually too expensive a means for getting free printed matter into circulation, but part of the purpose of the letters is to build up a mailing list to circularize further or to solicit some form of co-operation in the program of the organization. It is also an excellent method for both national and local organizations to use in sounding out the demand for literature on special topics.

Preparation of Mailing Lists. Only material already wanted, or for which a demand can be stimulated, may obtain wide distribution through securing requests for it. For literature of appeal or propaganda, lists of prospective readers to whom it will be mailed should be carefully prepared.

To the social agency engaged in raising money or spreading propaganda by mail, a good list of names of persons likely to be interested in the work or the subject in hand is essential. This may be secured by careful search through the sources of lists,[1] and by testing and continually revising those in use.

Many original sources of lists of names are shown on page 208. Some of these lists give reliable indications of the interests or

[1] Firms compile and sell classified lists of many types. The names of many inexpensive or free lists may be found in, Morley, Linda H., and Knight, Adelaide C., Mailing List Directory. McGraw-Hill Book Co., New York, 1924.

SOURCES OF MAILING LISTS

DIRECTORIES

LOCAL			NATIONAL	
City	Telephone	Blue Book	Rating books	Trade directories

NOTE: The sources given are suggestive only, as the nature and number of directories differ with each locality.

NOTE: Each line of trade has its own quota of directories. The publishers of trade journals devoted to the lines of trade you wish to reach will willingly supply you with a complete list of directories available for your use.

GOVERNMENTAL RECORDS

MUNICIPAL	COUNTY AND STATE	NATIONAL
City tax lists	Registration lists	Income tax lists
Permit records	County tax lists	Labor records
License records	Secretary of state records	
Marriage records	Labor reports	
Building permits		

NOTE: These sources are suggestive only. Inquiry of local, state and national governmental offices will uncover many valuable lists available for use. In some cases printed lists may be purchased. In others, permission can be obtained to copy the permanent official records.

ORGANIZATIONS

BUSINESS		GENERAL		
Commercial Club	Advertising Club	Fraternal	Labor	Social
Civic Organization				

NOTE: As organizations differ with each locality, any attempt to list them all is futile. Inquiry among prominent local, business, society, technical and professional men and women will yield many names of clubs. Lists of members can usually be obtained from the secretaries.

PRESS CLIPPINGS

Names of advertisers	Removals	New incorporations
Society notes	Real estate	Notices in general that relate
Fires	Business changes	to your proposition

ADVERTISING

Magazines	Newspapers	Trade journals

MISCELLANEOUS

Employes of local concerns	Salesmen's reports	Delivery men
Exchanging lists with other concerns	Investigators	Bank cashiers
	RFD carriers	Justices of the peace
Addressing companies	Customers	Country editors
		Dealers

(*Copyright by Addressograph Company*)

characteristics of the persons whose names appear in them. It is possible through the use of such lists to limit appeals for money to persons whose income is known to be large enough to make the request reasonable; to invite support for neighborhood improvement from the taxpayers of that neighborhood; to circularize members of almost any profession in regard to their particular interest in a cause; and in many other ways to take advantage of what membership in a certain group reveals of the individual's interests. An argument in favor of a bond issue for a county hospital would naturally be mailed to voters in the county. To enlist the co-operation of the medical profession in the work it was doing, the American Social Hygiene Association once circularized physicians whom the medical directory showed had been out of college for ten years. The organization sent literature to them and an invitation to participate in the social hygiene movement, the theory being that at this stage in their careers they would be most active in the health and social welfare activities of their communities and at the same time young enough to be more interested in new ideas than would some of their older associates. Requests for funds for summer outings for tenement children have been sent to city automobile owners, who, being in a position to get out into the open country, were expected to feel more sympathy for those deprived of the privilege.

One obvious limitation to the successful use of ready-made lists is that they are equally available to all agencies, both social and commercial, and are likely to be too much used. Persons known to have large incomes receive hundreds of letters of appeal. Ministers are much circularized with requests to bring all sorts of messages to their congregations.

The best lists are made up name by name, sometimes through years of slow accumulation and frequent revisions, sometimes by study of the interests of individuals. News items sometimes yield names accompanied by information which gives a clue to the sort of social service most likely to appeal to persons mentioned.

Care of Mailing Lists. A list does not stay alive indefinitely. One state health department mailed its monthly bulletin regularly to all persons who had at any time asked for a single issue in order to read a particular article. The mailing list built up in this way grew until it contained 50,000 names. Except that the names were crossed off when the post office was unable to deliver the mail, the list was used for several years without any effort to find out whether or not the bulletin was going to actual readers.

If a list is to be used more than once, it requires continuous revision, not only in the selection of names, but in the correction of names and addresses. Some of the factors in the preparation and use of mailing lists are that the spelling should be checked up with the utmost care; that no duplication should occur through using the same people's names obtained from several sources; and that addresses should be complete and up to date. A misspelled name suggests lack of knowledge of the identity of the person to whom the mail is directed as well as inefficiency. A form letter appears even more impersonal and less compelling than it should when a person receives several duplicate copies. These precautions are important to show a proper regard for the persons addressed, as well as to avoid waste.

This whole subject of the making and care of lists[1] relates more directly to the mailing of letters than to that of printed matter which oftener goes out as an enclosure with a letter than by itself. In studying problems of lists, however, one comes closer than in any other way to a realization of what can be done in selecting the right audience for publicity, whatever form this may take.

Personal Delivery. Literature entrusted to persons who can distribute it in the course of their regular work may get into the right hands more easily than that which is mailed. The literature intended for clients of social and health agencies may reach their homes by using as messengers the nurses, family visitors, probation officers, inspectors for city departments, and other workers who visit homes as part of their routine work. When these visitors are given reading matter to deliver which has to do with their own business in relation to the home, they usually are glad to distribute it and perhaps to give a word of suggestion about its use. It should not be taken for granted, however, that merely because they are going into the homes they may as well hand out any sort

[1] For much practical information about preparing and using lists, see Ramsay, Robert E., *Effective Direct Advertising.* D. Appleton and Co., New York, 1921, pp. 113-144.

of educational literature regardless of whether they themselves are concerned with it. These workers are, as a rule, already overtaxed and hurried and they should not be called upon when some other method of distribution equally good for the purpose is available. Nevertheless, it is worth while to seek their co-operation if the printed matter concerns the subjects in which they are interested.

A folder called "Summer Time Is Health Building Time," issued by the Toledo District Nurse Association was distributed to all families in the city through ice stations, called in Toledo "jitney stations," where purchasers go for small quantities of ice. Because of the reference in the circular to the importance of using ice to keep food fresh, the manager of the chief local ice company very willingly agreed to have the circulars distributed and also paid for envelopes in which the folders were enclosed.

The General Audience. Much literature is addressed to "a general audience"; so one person seems as likely as another to read it. It is natural to distribute it to persons who happen to be easy to reach, to enclose it in miscellaneous outgoing mail, or to give it away at any gathering where it can be handed out to those who enter a hall or pass a booth.

Material given out at random should be inexpensive because for each copy that gets into the right hands, a large number of copies are wasted. It should also be recognized that indiscriminate distribution of printed matter can be but a supplementary part in any well-planned program.

Is the Method Favorable to Getting It Read?

Even though folders or booklets reach the right people, the chance that many of them will not be read brings in a third element to increase the gap between the number issued and the number serving their purpose. While the appearance and content of a publication are chiefly important in getting it read, the manner in which it comes into the hands of the recipient is also of consequence.

Whether appeal or sales literature should be mailed under third or first class postage has been the subject of much discussion and experiment. How many enclosures should be sent in one envelope? What sort of envelope should be used? These and other questions should receive careful thought from those who are seeking returns by mail. Distribution should be planned so that the person receiving the material will value it more at the time of receipt than he would if it should come to him at another.

Factors of timeliness in the delivery of printed matter are that it shall be sent out at the right season of the year if it has any seasonal significance, and that it shall go out promptly when its topic happens to have a relation to the news of the day. Some health officers send a handbook on the care of infants to each mother immediately upon receiving the birth registration of her child, thus making sure that it will reach her at a time when it is needed.

Distribution at Meetings. As people leave a meeting it is appropriate to hand them literature on the subject of the talk they have heard. Especially if the speaker succeeds in creating a desire for more information, the time is favorable for giving the audience a folder containing ideas, facts, or names which they can recognize as connected with the subject discussed. People may desire to have for reference certain information given in the talk, the address of the place to send for further information, or directions for carrying out the speaker's advice.

Printed matter given out at a meeting may be well received if the chairman of the meeting calls attention to it. In any case, it should not be something merely thrust upon the audience, having no relationship with the meeting they are attending. Social agencies frequently think of meetings as suitable occasions for getting into circulation any literature they happen to have on hand and sometimes place a number of leaflets or folders in the seats. It seems likely that the chances of getting any of them read are lessened by giving out too many or by including topics in which no interest has been created by the speakers.

A Personal Message Sent with the Literature. Ordinarily, what we see in print does not touch us very closely, unless we are already interested in it. Part of the problem of distribution is to do it in a way that makes the material seem more personal or otherwise increases its value to those receiving it. If a folder goes out in the mail, it is the accompanying letter which makes the message personal. If it is distributed at a meeting or exhibit, a spoken reference to it or a little explanation may give it added importance. If school children deliver it to their parents, it is the message sent by the teacher which distinguishes it from a dodger picked up from a counter or handed to them on the street.

A report of work accomplished is sometimes sent with a personal card of the writer or of some sponsor for its contents, known to the recipients. One organization sent out several hundred copies of an annual report on each of which was written in ink a line of greeting from its well-known president. Another sent this note with a report to a selected list of persons whose interest it was important to secure:

DEAR MR. SMITH:

Our annual report has just come from the printer. I take pleasure in sending you a copy because I should like to have you look it over and see just what we have been doing.

A folder entitled "Your Friend the Nurse," addressed to the policy holders of the Metropolitan Life Insurance Company, was delivered to them personally by the company's agents. The instructions sent to the agents in regard to distributing it are well worth noting:

One of the most important things for an agent to do is to make sure that a copy of "Your Friend the Nurse" is in the home of every policy holder entitled to the service, and that it is understood.

It might be well to go over it with them, explaining just what the Metropolitan nurse will do in case of sickness, what policy holders are entitled to the nursing service, the nature of the visits of the nurse and how to call the nurse.

Be sure there is a copy attached to each industrial policy and group certificate that you deliver in a district covered by a nurse. Enter the nurse's telephone number in the space provided.

Competition with Other Literature. A big factor in favorable distribution is to lessen competition with other literature. Handing out leaflets and folders in wholesale fashion to visitors at fairs and expositions is a common practice of social agencies. At a health booth in an industrial exposition, an attendant handed indiscriminately to each visitor four pieces including a folder addressed to employers describing a health service, another about a charitable organization, a card announcing a meeting, and a leaflet giving addresses of clinics. It would be hard to find an occasion when

printed matter is so little valued and when it encounters so much
competition as at these places where each of a number of exhibitors
adds one or even a half-dozen pieces to the collection gathered up
by visitors.

The same is true of whatever is sent by mail. When four or five
enclosures are found in an envelope, especially those which must be
unfolded, the prospective reader is discouraged at the start.

NEED FOR MORE DISCRIMINATING DISTRIBUTION

Much matter is hastily written and cheaply printed because of
the expectation of waste and then, in turn, since its money cost has
been slight, agencies do not think it necessary to spend time and
money on careful and thorough distribution. Some agencies are
satisfied if most of what they print leaves their hands no matter
what becomes of it. The driver of a healthmobile carrying motion
pictures on tuberculosis into various city neighborhoods handed
quantities of leaflets to children who were standing about, telling
them to give them to the grown persons in the crowd. The children
were delighted, but after a time, having tired of passing the leaflets,
they devised the game of tossing them into the air and letting them
come down in a colored shower to litter the ground. Probably the
secretary of the health organization having cleared so many thousand copies off his shelves by sending them out with the truck
supposed that he had actually delivered these leaflets to thousands
of individuals.

There would seem to be no hope of better returns being received
from printed matter until those who issue it value it more highly
because of the time and skill devoted to good writing, the money
and care spent on its good looks, and the recognition that it has
a definite task to perform which can be accomplished only by its
being read by the right persons.

PART IV: MEETINGS

INTRODUCTION TO PART IV

VOICE, manner, and personality have a power of appeal not to be obtained through the resources of printing—whether italics, bold-face type, large headlines, or any other form of typographical emphasis. Good public speaking reaps the additional advantage of the interest felt by an audience in the speaker as an individual. If he is well known, people are attracted to a meeting in order to see and hear him. Moreover, the speaker may adapt himself to his audience. He may quickly note their responsiveness or their lapses from attention, and revise his planned speech accordingly. He may vary his manner of presentation to suit the degree of education or the special interests of each group addressed. Again, if obtaining united action is the speaker's objective, a meeting offers the best means of approach to his goal. Many persons who would fail to respond to a letter, because they feel powerless as individuals to make their opinions or services count toward getting results, realize their strength as members of a group.

A further advantage of a meeting is that it may be a peg on which to hang other forms of publicity. Graphic material may illustrate or supplement the speaking. Leaflets may be distributed to the audience. What is said by the speakers may be reported in the newspapers next day.

Scientific inventions opening up new opportunities for spreading information seem to increase the use of public speaking rather than to replace it. Through an amplifier a speech may be heard by enormous audiences in great buildings or in amphitheaters. The radio makes it possible for a talk to be heard in a million homes at once or in halls far away from the place where it is delivered.

It is hardly necessary to urge upon social workers the desirability of public speaking as an avenue of publicity. Perhaps no other method is so generally used, whether by the rural public health nurse who now and then tells the church societies about her work, or at the other extreme, by the large city council of social agencies, which, through its speakers' bureau, arranges in the course of the year hundreds of talks to reach thousands of persons. Meetings of all sorts furnish the mainstay of the campaign in which votes are to be won or opinions changed. Popular health education is extensively carried on through talks in schools, factories, settlements, churches, and clubs, as well as by radio.

What needs to be urged is not more meetings, but a better use of them. An enormous amount of wasted effort goes into the hundreds and thousands of talks on social topics given every year. Considered as a tool for education and for propaganda, a speech must be something more than a flow of words, and the planning of meetings more than bringing a speaker and an audience together. A report that a certain society "arranged 155 lectures last year which were heard by 20,000 people" is impressive, but the significance of these lectures as an educational achievement depends on what use each speaker made of his opportunity, what people were in the audience, and what they thought about the things they were told.

The problems of the speaker which include proper use of the voice, wise selection and arrangement of subject matter, and interesting presentation, are discussed in the chapter on Public Speaking, which follows.

There is room for skill and good judgment in providing conditions under which the speaker has the best possible opportunity to get results. Problems of securing suitable audiences and of arranging and conducting meetings are discussed in Chapter XIV, Arranging and Conducting Meetings.

CHAPTER XIII

PUBLIC SPEAKING

THERE will always be a demand for talks by persons who are engaged in interesting and important work. Furthermore, it is particularly desirable that persons active in social betterment should be known in the community, and one of the most effective ways of accomplishing this is through occasional speaking.

Social workers may chance to be naturally good speakers, but the ability to address an audience has never been demanded as part of their professional equipment. Those who attend conferences and conventions frequently express keen disappointment because specialists whom they have traveled long distances to hear speak inaudibly or do not make their subjects interesting or intelligible.

Engineers and architects are learning that ability to present their plans well is frequently a necessary factor to getting them adopted. Business and professional men and women in ever increasing numbers are studying public speaking. Social workers might well follow their example and seek training and practice in both the preparation and the delivery of talks.

LEARNING THE ART OF SPEAKING

To learn the theories of public speaking and to practice them step by step, one should seek a competent instructor. Courses are now given at many colleges and universities, Young Men's and Young Women's Christian Associations, and advertising clubs. For those who wish to study the subject by themselves, there are excellent textbooks.[1] In this chapter we shall attempt to point out a few factors which our observation suggests as important in delivering an address and outlining talking points for the purpose of social publicity.

The Voice. The voice is to public speaking what type is to

[1] James A. Winans in his book entitled Public Speaking (Century Co., New York, Revised 1917) discusses in a thorough and practical way both the preparation and delivery of speeches. Other good textbooks are referred to in the following pages.

219

printing; the proper use of type makes the printed word easy and pleasant to read, while the correct use of the voice causes the spoken word to be heard without effort and makes listening a pleasure.

When we stop to realize how important an instrument the voice is in all human relations, it is amazing that so many of us allow faulty habits of speech to go uncorrected. If what we say is lost on those addressed or misunderstood by them, all sorts of complications arise and much effort is wasted. Failure to be heard is often due to insufficient volume or strength of tones caused by improper breathing. Indistinctness is caused by speaking too rapidly so that words are run together, or by not articulating properly. These are faults that can in most cases be corrected by exercises such as are described in various textbooks.

On the modulation of the voice depends the right placing of emphasis and the avoidance of that monotony of tone which lulls an audience into drowsiness. Joseph A. Mosher suggests as the standard for effectiveness, "a normal, unaffected voice . . . modulated substantially as in animated conversation."[1]

When a speaker with a voice of ordinary volume cannot be heard by all in an average audience, it may be due to his failure consciously to speak to the last row of seats or to a habit of addressing one side of the room. If his inability to be heard is more deepseated, a competent teacher should be consulted.

Mannerisms. Many otherwise good speakers are burdened with unfortunate habits or mannerisms. The frequent repetition of some word, too many gestures or monotonous repetition of a single gesture, an incorrectly pronounced word, fingering papers on the desk, certain facial tricks, a habit of rhythmic emphasis of words without regard to their importance are likely to distract attention from his speech and center it on himself. Almost any speaker may drift into such disturbing habits. In many cases calling them to his attention is all that is needed.

Practice. As in everything else, nothing will take the place of practice to secure facility in doing. The beginner, especially, needs to make the same speech a number of times. The worker with something to say to women's organizations, for instance, should start with several of the small church societies and neighborhood

[1] The Essentials of Extempore Speaking. Macmillan Co., New York, 1917, p. 189.

groups in outlying districts. With these he will not feel the strain of reaching a large audience. But he must seek to win these small audiences. Then when he reaches the larger groups, he will have gained facility and confidence in handling his ideas. John Dolman, Jr., suggests a more easily available way to practice speaking:

> . . . the best way to work out his thoughts for effective public speaking is by talking them over with somebody else. . . . If the student is timid and afraid to meet people, his first task is to overcome that feeling in everyday life. To communicate effectively with other men he must know other men, and he must get used to the feeling of having them know him. To develop a thought most effectively for sharing with others he must seek the reactions of others to that thought. And to perfect himself in the useful art that is expanded conversation, he must expand himself through conversation.[1]

Getting into Touch with One's Audience

A well-known speaker with a reputation for being entertaining generally finds his audience ready to listen. He gets their attention quickly and even if circumstances require that he make some preliminary explanation or apology he does so gracefully with but little delay in getting at his theme. With an audience wholly uninformed about the subject, perhaps indifferent or even antagonistic to the meeting, as is sometimes the case with meetings called to consider social service matters, the speaker must create friendliness and win attention.

A speaker on tuberculosis will be likely to approach his audience at the point of their own concern with the subject. If he is to address printers, for example, he looks up in advance the death-rate from tuberculosis in the printing trade and the hazards of the occupation. A nurse about to talk to a group of Italian mothers concerning the care of infants drew her chair into the circle and began by questioning the women about their own babies. Experienced speakers aim never to permit vacant space to separate them from their audiences; they either move down among their listeners or gather them closer to the platform. A woman lecturer on the importance of correct posture sent out to address groups of men

[1] A Handbook of Public Speaking. Harcourt, Brace and Co., New York, 1922, pp. 126–127.

workers broke through their reserve by getting some of them to help her set up her stereopticon machine, adjust the lighting, and demonstrate positions of sitting or standing. A health speaker about to give an illustrated lecture established friendly footing with the crowd of giggling factory girls he was to address by joking with them about the smock he put on before setting up his apparatus. An organizer for the Camp Fire Girls says she has frequently startled a lifeless group into alertness by asking: "How many of you can fry an egg on a stone without a frying pan?"

If the speaking for an organization must necessarily be done largely by one person who will be obliged to meet audiences of all ages, degrees of education, and varied interests, obviously he or she must have broad experience and a natural liking for people.

> One reason for Mr. Roosevelt's success with audiences lies in his varied career, as son of an old New York family, Harvard student, politician, cowboy, historian, naturalist, hunter, traveler, rough rider, police commissioner, president and one forgets what else,—all giving him intimate knowledge of many kinds of people, of how they think, what their associations are, and what allusions and illustrations will appeal to them.[1]

BEGINNING OF A SPEECH

Roy S. Durstine tells the story of a young copywriter who had been told to prepare material for a booklet.

> His boss read the first page and then carefully drew his pencil through the first paragraph.
>
> "But you've cut out my whole introduction," the young man protested.
>
> "Exactly," said the boss, "you are like an acrobat who comes out, wipes off his hands, tosses away his handkerchief, puts rosin on his feet and then starts to work. We haven't room for the preliminaries in advertising."[2]

There is perhaps no more familiar and difficult problem in short speeches than that of getting launched without delay on the subject itself. At a conference of public health workers, nine speakers were assigned ten minutes each to cover a phase of the problem of

[1] Winans, James A., Public Speaking. p. 115.
[2] Making Advertisements and Making Them Pay. Charles Scribner's Sons, New York, 1920, pp. 98–99.

how to reach boys and girls in industry. Nearly every speaker spent five minutes or more getting under way and was then disconcerted to find only a few minutes left in which to rush through his whole topic.

The following rambling introduction to a twenty-minute talk on personal hygiene which the writer heard given before factory workers well illustrates the difficulty:

> Physicians are now devoting a great deal of time to preventive medicine. An ounce of prevention is worth a pound of cure. We read a lot about health in newspapers and magazines but seldom pay attention to it. During the war, in England, out of every four young men examined, one was disqualified on account of physical defects. One third of the men in this country were disqualified for the same reason. The first time they learned anything was the matter with them was when they came for examination. Over half of this was preventable if taken care of at the right time. What are we going to do to maintain our health so as to be efficient? The matter of personal hygiene is a long subject. We cannot go into it in detail in the time allowed.

The preventive for such a situation lies in careful preparation. In the first draft of either a speech or a written composition, the opening paragraph is quite likely to be a groping around to get a good start, and nine times out of ten the best thing to do with it is to cut the paragraph out entirely. It serves a purpose as mental exercise but it does not belong in the finished product.

CONTENT OF A SPEECH

From full knowledge and a varied experience, it is often hard for a speaker to choose just those few facts and illustrations which fit the time limit, the audience, and the occasion. A common weakness of social workers as speakers is their tendency to try to cover too much ground.

The speaker on hygiene, after telling his audience that lack of time made it impossible for him to go into detail about his subject, proceeded to attempt that very thing. He told how necessary air is to the body and how little we get; he gave an explanation of the physiology of the lungs, showing how decay follows the lack of use; a suggestion about ten deep breaths a day; a reassurance about drafts not being dangerous. Then he spoke of food, of the habit of eating too much; he emphasized the importance of elimination. He was just beginning to explain the value of medical examinations when he was interrupted in the middle of a sentence by the clanging of the bell which sent the workers back to their machines. It seems quite unlikely that his audience remembered any of this health lesson well enough to make a practical application of it. Laying out a talk is as much a matter of balance as laying out a page of advertising. We cannot imagine an advertiser devoting practically all his space to introductory generalizations and crowding his real message into a line of small type at the bottom of the page. Yet that is in effect what a speaker does when he is caught at the end of his time with the important part of his speech still undelivered.

The British Trade Union Congress, we are told, enforces rigidly the five-minute limit on the speaking time of each delegate. A man comes from his local union instructed to put over or to defeat some measure and his standing at home depends on what he can accomplish in that precious five-minute period. Needless to say, the ability to speak forcefully, tersely, and to the point is developed to a high degree by these labor leaders.

The speaker's problem is always one of selection in relation to the returns he seeks. If the health lecturer instanced above had started out with the definite intention of inspiring his audience to put health information into practice, he would have selected as his theme fresh air, or diet, or some other aspect of the subject not too broad in scope to allow of specific advice.

If, instead of attempting to bring in many different points, the speaker holds himself to a carefully selected few, he will have time to emphasize these by restatement, amplification, and illustration.

Repeating and amplifying one's main points are much more important in spoken than in written publicity. Mr. Dolman gives a graphic and easily recognizable picture of the mood and circumstances which make it important to the listener that statements shall be repeated or reinforced.

In a large audience the room will be too hot for some and too cold for others; the lights will be bad for some; some will be too near the doors, others too far from the speaker; some will be in one mood and others in another; some near-sighted, others far-sighted; some in good health, others in bad; some fresh, others tired. If the speaker talks rapidly he will confuse some of his hearers; if he talks slowly he will bore others; and except on the most informal occasions the listener who has failed to understand a point, or has been interrupted or distracted, will allow his attention to lapse permanently rather than ask the speaker to repeat a passage.

Obviously the speaker cannot forestall all of these sources of inattention. Momentary distractions are bound to occur. He cannot prevent them; therefore he must fight them.

Whole-hearted attention on his part will help; so also will directness and sense of communication; and so will the concreteness which makes so strongly for primary attention. But most important in this connection is the simple device of *reinforcement of ideas*.

Audiences, though passive, are generally well disposed and rather anxious to listen. Given a fair chance they will recover from their distractions and renew their attention. But frequently the speaker does not give them a fair chance; he says everything just once, and leaves it to the listener to catch it if he can. . . .

A really effective speaker . . . realizes that there is a constant leakage in his speech: some of his ideas are escaping some of his listeners all of the time. To counteract it he resorts to a piling up of effect, to a constant reinforcement of ideas, by more repetition and more illustration than a writer ever has need for. His motto is, "Hit them again in the same place."[1]

In the following paragraph a phrase unfamiliar to many is repeated and amplified in a way to make it clear to practically any type of person who might happen to hear or read it.

The "health of the community" is a phrase that slips out very easily and is, I am afraid, a bit unreal to most people until they realize that it only means the health of the maid that serves your breakfast, the health of the tram conductor who takes you to work, of the man who sells you cigarettes, of the newspaper boy, of the janitor and scrubwoman in your office building, of the people who work beside you, of the teacher in the school to which your brother goes, of the children he plays with, of your neighbors and the women your wife meets at your neighbor's house, and so on. The health of the community is just the health of the people you see about you and of many more that you do not see. If an epidemic of influenza strikes "the community" you quickly see what the health of the community means, because the tram conductor, the scrubwoman, one of the men at the shop, the neighbor's little girl, and

---

[1] A Handbook of Public Speaking. pp. 48–50.

one out of fifty or one hundred other people in the town will be missing from his place for a couple of weeks, and some will go to make up that other vague abstraction called the "Mortality Statistics."[1]

The amplification in the paragraph above has been done by the introduction of concreteness. How much more vivid the images of men, women, and children become through being designated not only by their occupations but, still more specifically, by their relationship to the reader: *the conductor who takes you to work, the scrubwoman in your office building, the man who sells you cigarettes.*

In his book of sound advice on this subject, James A. Winans has an excellent discussion of the relation of the concrete and the specific to the attention of audiences as well as to clearness of thinking on the part of the speaker himself.[2] Glancing through the volumes of Proceedings of the National Conference of Social Work, one finds that the speeches at general sessions, to which lay audiences as well as social workers are invited, teem with generalizations and abstractions. Many of these are acceptable to the social worker because, as Mr. Winans points out, concreteness is relative. An abstraction becomes concrete when we see its particular application to our own affairs. The speaker may talk of "maladjustment" and social workers in the audience quickly supply actual instances from their own experience. The "disadvantaged child" is a term coined for convenient use among a limited group whose members can no doubt call to mind readily actual children whose situation is described by the term. On the other hand, members of the audience not in frequent contact with social problems, even though they understand these terms, cannot fill in the concrete examples which give them significance. This the speaker must do for them.

This habit of talking in general and abstract terms often tends to loose thinking. Speakers, as was found true of writers, obtain such facility in the use of phrases common to their fields of work that they do not actually put any meaning into them. Seeking for a specific illustration to accompany a general statement, or for the

[1] Clark, Walter, "The Partnership for Health." *In* The World's Health, Paris, vol. 4, Sept., 1923, p. 25.

[2] Public Speaking. pp. 62–70, 135–139.

too large for objects to be seen across it, they are again a source of distraction rather than of help. Nor should we fail to remember that any form of illustrative material is but an added tool for use by the fairly skilled speaker; it cannot be successfully used as a crutch by a poor one. But assuming that illustrations are appropriate and can be well and conveniently displayed, and that the speaker knows how to use them to advantage, they are a desirable addition to the program.

Charts and Maps. The simplest, most familiar form of illustrative material used by speakers is the statistical chart, in which curves or bars bring out contrasts or similarities of various kinds. Its size must be so adapted to the dimensions of the room that the details can be seen from the back rows and, if possible, it should be displayed in such a way that the speaker need not turn his back to the audience in pointing to it.

The chart shown on page 230 was tested in a room 60 feet long. It was found that the words on the chart below the title line could not be read comfortably at a greater distance than 40 feet and not at all at the back of the room except by those with exceptionally good eyesight.

The figures at the bottom of the chart presented the greatest difficulty. These evidently needed to be heavier and with more space between the two figures in a given number. The broad and heavy lines of the curve could be seen from all parts of the hall. The chart seems to illustrate the smallest dimensions practicable in a chart for platform use to be seen by an audience any of whose members are more than 50 feet away.

If the facts explained by charts are interesting, and the charts are not obscure or technical, people usually like them and give closer attention because of their use. A chart so constructed that the bars are moved into place as the speaker explains them is especially good for holding interest.

Maps, as a rule, need to be shown on slides in order to be large enough for details to be seen. A map for platform use before a large audience needs to meet the same conditions set forth above for charts. For a small audience a speaker may sometimes use a map mounted on corrugated board, and holding it in front of him, push colored pins into locations he wishes to indicate.

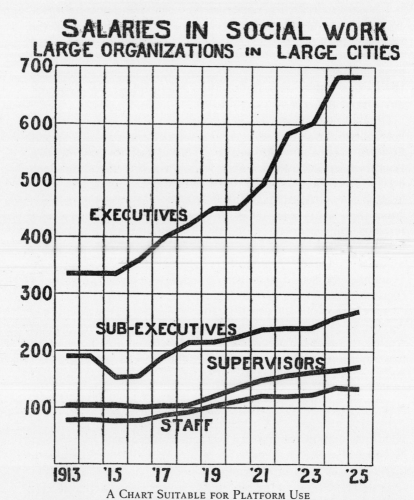

SALARIES IN SOCIAL WORK
LARGE ORGANIZATIONS in LARGE CITIES

A CHART SUITABLE FOR PLATFORM USE

The dimensions of the original of this chart are 36 by 45 inches. The letters of the top title line are 1½ inches in height, the second title line 1¼ inches high, and those on the chart itself about one inch in height, and nearly ¼ of an inch in thickness. The figures are 1¼ inches in height, the lines of the curves are ⅜ of an inch thick. It would have been better not to have used any letters or figures less than 1¼ inches high.

The Use of Properties. Speeches in which the points are made with the help of objects, most conveniently designated by the theatrical term "properties," have been used in talks before college students, business and professional men, and manual workers quite as successfully as before school children. If the properties illustrate the speaker's ideas successfully, they do not offend the dignity of any sort of audience.

Dr. Eugene C. Howe, of the Department of Hygiene at Wellesley College, developed several mechanical devices to supplement his lectures on community health. To illustrate the progress of a typical epidemic, he made a map of the town of Wellesley on which every case of German measles reported in an epidemic, 270 cases in all, was represented by a small electric light. By a simple manipulation these lights came on in the order in which the cases were reported, thus showing graphically how the disease traveled the length of the town. The mechanism was so arranged that 20 lights were always shining. As number 21 came on, number 1 disappeared, as number 22 flashed, number 2 disappeared, giving an effect of continuous movement across the map.

Some of the topics on which social workers speak lend themselves very easily to the use of such devices. A health lecturer demonstrated the need for periodical physical examinations by showing two watches, one cleaned each year and useful, the other neglected and worthless. Point by point, the facts that he wished to impress on the audience, were illustrated by some such simple device or object lesson.

Dr. Graham Lusk, of Cornell University Medical College, made vivid for an audience of social workers the idea that food should be bought for its calory value instead of its bulk, by the use of a market basket filled with packages of foods. As he talked, he arranged the packages on the table in the order of their actual prices. He then placed on each package a label showing the cost per 100 calories of each food, demonstrating that the foods of highest price in money had in several cases the lowest actual food values. The American Museum of Natural History in New York City has made up compact suit-case exhibits, each containing models of individual portions of food for three well-balanced meals for one person.

The speaker explaining food values may arrange on a table before him in succession the portions for each of the three meals for a day.

Here and there a health teacher or speaker has made effective use of the "chalk talk," a method which should lend itself to wider use for the interpretation of social facts. Diagrams and simple outline sketches can be made before an audience, even by those who lack a technical knowledge of drawing. Some cartoonists have developed a method for outlining in light colors the pictures to be drawn in the course of a chalk talk. These outlines, invisible to the audience, can be traced with crayon by the speaker, thus producing effective illustrations.

Lantern Slide Lectures. Lantern slides still have untried possibilities of development for illustrating a talk. Sets of slides are made up by state and national organizations and government bureaus to illustrate a great variety of topics. Especially in the health field, one can obtain them on almost any subject desired— flies, milk, nutrition, prenatal care, and so on through the list. Unfortunately, however, many of these slides would handicap rather than help the speaker in presenting the topic they are supposed to illustrate. Having been prepared in response to a vague demand for "something to use in an educational campaign," all too frequently they are merely reproductions in the form of slides of whatever photographs, exhibit panels, sketches, maps, or charts happened to be obtainable. In one instance a speaker had literally cut up an annual report and reproduced its statistical tables, graphs, and copies of letters on slides. Such material as this is seldom interesting and often does not fit the points the speaker wishes to emphasize.

A speaker engaged in telling the public of the work of his organization in placing dependent children asked a staff member to supply him with slides. He was given pictures of institutional buildings, rows of white beds, playgrounds, and classes of children at work. Institutions were the smallest part of the work of this child-placing agency, and the speaker, wishing to show what is done for the individual child, discarded this material and went to a great deal of pains to obtain pictures which would tell the story of a child placed in a family home. A village street, the exterior and interior of a real home, the country school, the swimming hole, and other places and situations which entered into the experience of a child being adjusted to the home of his foster parents were photographed and used. In his talk, he filled in the actual story of the child so that as the audience looked at the pictures they saw the settings of related incidents.

Lantern slide talks can be made humorous, dramatic, or lively by the use of a little imagination.

A misconception which has brought many a meeting to grief is the idea that a stereopticon machine, a set of slides, and an operator furnish everything needed for a successful stereopticon talk. It is safe to say that in most cases when the showing of the pictures works smoothly, the machine itself has been gone over to see that it is in good condition; the slides have been cleaned so that they are not blurred on the screen, and are properly thumbmarked and arranged so that the operator need make no mistake in taking them out of the box; and a method of signaling and other forms of co-operation have been worked out between the speaker and the operator. Indeed, even so minor a detail as arranging with someone to turn the lights off and on at the proper moments has been attended to in order to prevent interest from being diverted from the illustrated talk to the mechanical difficulties of presenting it.

The speaker also needs to remember to talk to the audience and not to the pictures if he wishes to be heard. He should be familiar with what his slides contain and know what he intends to say regarding each one. Indeed, he should know his slides so well that a quick glance will assure him that the right slide is on the screen, or allow him to point to a particular part of the slide. In the case of "ready-made lectures" he will give this fleeting glance to assure himself that he is reading the text about the slide then being shown. The writers attended one slide talk in which the speaker, reading his lecture, went ahead of the slides so that his text and his pictures never agreed. The successful use of lantern slides at a meeting calls for a trained speaker, and does not, as is sometimes supposed, take the place of one. Even when a prepared lecture accompanies slides the person who delivers it should be a capable speaker and should familiarize himself with both lecture and slides beforehand. He should avoid the amateur's fashion of introducing every slide with "this slide" or some similar phrase.

Several types of portable projection machines in which a roll of film takes the place of a set of glass slides are now on the market. Thus the problem of giving illustrated talks is greatly simplified, since a speaker may carry a roll of film containing 30 or 40 pictures in his pocket and the machine may be attached to any electric light socket in the hall. The one advantage of the slides over the film is that they may be rearranged in any order that the speaker desires for use on a given occasion, whereas the film is made up as a unit.

RADIO TALKS AND AUDIENCES

The National Broadcasting Company of America, New York City, in its printed instructions to those who broadcast from its stations says:

> The radio audience is larger than that which can be assembled in all the theaters in New York City combined. At each radio set receiving your program, there are from one to two hundred or more listeners. The average is four persons—a small and intimate group, much better adapted to giving close attention to you than a large and distracting crowd. . . .

> Your radio audience is composite and cosmopolitan. It is made up of people in cities and country districts, in homes and clubs. It includes the rich and the poor, the cultured and the uncultured, representing as many interests as all kinds of theater audiences combined.

While this picture of the character of radio listeners necessarily based in part on estimates may be over-optimistic, anyone who has the opportunity to broadcast a talk has reason to be greatly impressed by the large number of persons he can reach in this way. Departments of the government and the more important unofficial social agencies are being given many opportunities to broadcast. The United States Public Health Service, which has been serving 48 co-operating stations in addition to the Naval Station at Arlington, states that nearly every portion of the country is within range of a station releasing its health talks. Several state health departments are broadcasting weekly, and many community funds and other social agencies conducting intensive campaigns have had the opportunity to speak to radio audiences. Many important meetings are also reported by radio.

While broadcasting lacks the advantage of the direct personal contact a speaker has with his visible audience, many who listen get something of the feeling of being personally addressed. Probably no form of communication involves so little effort on the part of those who are to receive the information. They do not have to leave their homes to attend a meeting; they do not need to spend a whole afternoon or evening listening to a program of which they may be interested in only one or two numbers. They may make themselves as comfortable as they please while listening.

For these reasons it seems likely that radio audiences contain many people whom it is most difficult to reach in other ways. One would suppose that those who read the least "listen in" most regularly. Those who go out of the home the least are also more likely to have a radio set and to use it. Many housewives who have perhaps a half-hour to spare when their morning work is finished are said to be among the regular audiences for morning programs. Night workers with little opportunity for recreation listen in on late morning or afternoon programs.

Broadcasting stations encourage listeners to send their comments, ask questions, or request literature. These communications not only indicate whether or not the talk was enjoyed, but they also bring to light individuals whom the social agency may wish to find: those in the early stages of disease, or those who have a little leisure to devote to volunteer service, for instance.

The radio talks of which we have read manuscripts contain the same proportion of over-technical, impersonal, and uninspiring material that is often found in other kinds of social publicity.

The advantages of radio broadcasting are indeed many; yet, we doubt very much whether they are to be had regardless of the merits of the speech. There are competing programs at all hours when people are likely to have leisure. It is as easy and as natural to "tune out" when one is bored as to throw a dull booklet into the waste basket or to skim the headlines of the newspaper, skipping everything but what invites interest.

A well-trained voice and suitable selection of material and the use of repetition and illustration are even more needed in talking to a radio audience than to a gathering of people whose interest or lack of it can be observed.

235

CHAPTER XIV

ARRANGING AND CONDUCTING MEETINGS

EACH of the many kinds of meetings held for social publicity has its distinct characteristics. The dignified annual meeting consists chiefly of officers' reports followed by a formal address and occasionally enlivened by a play or motion picture. In contrast to this is the campaign rally, which is always lively, sometimes boisterous, and purposely worked up to a high pitch of excitement. The anniversary dinner brings together friends and members of an organization in an atmosphere of reminiscence, sociability, and good feeling, without the tenseness of the rally. The more serious and practical meetings of social work conferences offer a crowded program of speeches and discussion packed with information slightly popularized for the benefit of the lay members of the audience. Of gatherings where the social worker in his official capacity meets the outside public, perhaps the most familiar are club meetings and church services or school assemblies which are turned over wholly or in part to the social agency that has a request to make or instruction to give. Less common and strikingly different from all other types is the mass meeting with its objective of arousing indignation against some injustice, either by impassioned speeches or the convincing recital of shocking facts.

Not only the kind of meeting but the size and type of audience to be desired varies with the nature of the objective.

The plea of the eloquent speaker who urges every voter to get behind a proposed measure is futile if only a dozen persons instead of expected hundreds hear him or if his audience is not made up of voters. Again, if he needs the support of organized group opinion, it is a waste of time for him to address a miscellaneous assemblage. Nor should he expect to capture the interest of people already absorbed in some other subject, for instance, a group of striking union men anxiously waiting to discuss their next move.

It is necessary, then, to consider what types of audiences are

236

appropriate to certain purposes; what conditions are favorable to attention and response; and how people of the right sort may be induced to attend meetings in large numbers. The discussion of publicity meetings takes up first what is done when a place is sought on the program of a meeting already arranged, and later the steps taken in arranging and conducting one's own meeting.

READY-MADE AUDIENCES

The variety and number of societies and clubs in which persons from all walks of life come together for meetings is truly amazing. When Edward Bok sought an expression of opinion on the American Peace Award from the voters of the country he gathered at a dinner in New York City some 80 or more people from organizations with branches in every part of the country and with a total membership of approximately 10,000,000. Represented at the gathering were professional, commercial, and trade organizations; societies for self-improvement, or esthetic enjoyment; religious bodies and social and civic groups. Yet, these represented only a small proportion of the total number which hold regular or occasional meetings in every community.

Social workers seem to have little difficulty in obtaining opportunities to speak in the meetings of these groups. Annual reports of those organizations which make a point of this kind of publicity show impressive records of the numbers of churches, schools, and clubs addressed.

The health officer of a town of 15,000 describes as follows his futile efforts to get people voluntarily to attend health meetings and, on the other hand, the ease with which he secured ready-made audiences:

I planned a series of public health meetings, ten in number, one to be held every two to four weeks. My subjects were garbage and odors, communicable diseases, milk, education of children in public health, industrial hygiene, public health nursing and venereal diseases. I was determined to make these meetings a success and, after repeatedly calling the attention of the public to them through the press, I spoke personally in several of the churches before their Sunday morning services, announcing the purpose and plans and giving subjects and dates of the various proposed meetings. Nevertheless, in spite of my being able to

237

secure the services of state speakers at every meeting and in spite of the wide publicity, our meetings were not a success, at least not in numbers. At the first meeting we had an attendance of about sixteen including members of our own Department; at the second about twenty-two; at the third about six; and at the fourth only one man showed up and he was half an hour late. . . .

After being confronted with my failure to get the people to come to our series of meetings, I tried another method of reaching them. . . . I secured enough interest among two young men's organizations to arrange for an evening when I might give them an illustrated lecture on venereal diseases. . . . I addressed some seventy-five or more men on this important subject.

Later I was asked to address a young ladies' society and, after that, two short addresses on the city's milk supply and the garbage question were arranged for at the close of a musicale given by one of the young men's organizations to some one hundred and fifty or more people.

I next arranged with the State Department for the loan of a few films on milk, flies and mosquitoes, and for over one week I spent most of my time at the four movie theaters of the city speaking on milk and garbage, making two and three addresses in each theater. During the week I reached over 2,000 people.[1]

As the health officer discovered, the expense and effort of arranging a meeting are avoided when a social worker can find a ready-made audience to address. Such an audience may include many persons whose attention can be secured only by presenting the information to them at meetings which they are accustomed to attend.

The largest use of ready-made audiences is found where permanent speakers' bureaus are maintained. Such bureaus are now regular departments of councils of social agencies and of some of the larger city and state health agencies. The object of some bureaus appears to be the booking of as many engagements as possible. Numbers alone, however, do not indicate that the meetings have been successful. As has already been stated, to accomplish the purpose of the organization, the nature of the audience is quite as important as the size.

During an intensive campaign every available ready-made audi-

[1] Van Auken, W. B. D., "Does Public Health Educational Work Pay?" *In* Health News, New York State Department of Health, Albany, vol. 17, Sept., 1922, pp. 204–205.

ence is an appropriate one for campaign speakers. At other times, however, a policy of seizing any opportunity to speak without regard to the interests of the persons who will attend the meeting may be a waste of the speaker's time. In the main, audiences brought together primarily for a fairly serious purpose should be chosen.

Information about Audiences. An aid to the selection of desirable audiences is a card catalog[1] of organizations that gives enough information to guide the bureau in choosing suitable groups and in knowing what speaker to send. This catalog should be a classified list extending down to apparently the most insignificant organization in the community and should have data about the aims of each, its officers, its place and time of meeting, and, if possible, comments about the usual number of persons in attendance and the nature of the organization. For instance, the mere name of a club that is a branch of a well-known national organization does not tell the speakers' bureau whether or not this particular branch is typical of the organization as a whole. Nor do the names of local organizations always reveal their possible civic or social interests, or those of their members.

Before deciding to send a speaker whose time is valuable, it is worth while to find out also, in a general way at least, what the particular meeting to be addressed is likely to yield in the way of goodwill, service, subscriptions, or whatever else is desired. Will it be an appropriate occasion on which to present a request or a plan? Or has the same group been appealed to by so many other speakers that its sympathies are dulled? Will the speaker have the "main chance" or be crowded into a program that is already too long? Has he been invited primarily to entertain a gathering made up of people who come together for pleasure only?

The health officer, whose experiences were described earlier, demonstrated that he could reach many more people with less effort through addressing ready-made audiences than by arranging meetings of his own. But his account of his experiences leaves a doubt regarding the value of some of the meetings. One wonders,

---

[1] For a "Suggested Grouping of Organizations" see Routzahn, Evart G., and Routzahn, Mary Swain, The A B C of Exhibit Planning. Russell Sage Foundation, New York, 1918, p. 209.

1

NEW YORK TUBERCULOSIS and HEALTH ASSOCIATION Inc.,
244 MADISON AVENUE, NEW YORK, N.Y.
TELEPHONE CALEDONIA 1240

JAMES ALEX. MILLER, M.D.
PRESIDENT

HOMER FOLKS
VICE-PRESIDENT

THOMAS W. LAMONT
TREASURER

NATHAN E. BRILL, M.D.
SECRETARY

HARRY L. HOPKINS
DIRECTOR

IAGO GALDSTON, M.D.
SECRETARY

REBEKAH MONROMAN
ASSISTANT SECRETARY

HEALTH SPEAKERS SERVICE

INFORMATION FOR AUDIENCE

Name ------------------------------ Address ----------
Title of Lecture ----------------
Date ------------- Time ------------ Duration ----------
Speaker sent by ----------------
Name of Lecturer ----------------

REPORT OF LECTURE

Please fill in and return this report immediately after talk has been given

Title of Lecture -------------------- Duration ----------
Audience—Number ----------- Character ----------
In your opinion is the speaker able to address this type of group effectively?
Remarks ----------------
Was there a question period? ----------------
Specimen Question ----------------
Amount of interest shown ----------------
Were the following used? Chart? Slides? Film? (title)? Etc.
Signed ----------------

2

NEW YORK TUBERCULOSIS and HEALTH ASSOCIATION Inc.,
244 MADISON AVENUE, NEW YORK, N.Y.
TELEPHONE CALEDONIA 1240

JAMES ALEX. MILLER, M.D.
PRESIDENT

HOMER FOLKS
VICE-PRESIDENT

THOMAS W. LAMONT
TREASURER

NATHAN E. BRILL, M.D.
SECRETARY

HARRY L. HOPKINS
DIRECTOR

IAGO GALDSTON, M.D.
SECRETARY

REBEKAH MONROMAN
ASSISTANT SECRETARY

HEALTH SPEAKERS SERVICE

INFORMATION FOR SPEAKER

LECTURE HELD BEFORE

Organization ------------------ Person in Charge ----------
Address ----------------
Date ------------- Time ------------ Duration ----------
Subject ------------------ Language ----------
Audience—Number ----------- Character ----------
Lecturer ----------------
Sent by ----------------

SPEAKER'S REPORT

Please fill in and return this report immediately after talk has been given

Title of Lecture -------------------- Duration ----------
Audience—Number ----------- Character ----------
Were arrangements for speaking satisfactory?
Remarks ----------------
Questions: How many? ----- Specimen Questions ----------
Interest Shown ----------------
Were the following used? Chart? Slides? Film? (title)? Etc.
Signed ----------------

Request Referred To _____

1. _____
2. _____
3. _____

Speaker Assigned _____

Data to Group _____ Data to Speaker _____

Group Report Received _____ Speaker's Report Received _____

New York Tuberculosis & Health Association
Speakers Bureau - Form #1 - 2/27 - 1M

3

Date of Meeting _____ Hour _____

The attached literature is available for free distribution to your audience at this health talk. We will be glad to send you the quantity you desire. Please fill in and return this card.

Please send me _____ copies. I will assume responsibility for their distribution.

Signed _____

Send literature to _____

5

Date _____

Organization _____

Address _____

Foreign _____

Date _____ Time _____

Subject _____

Duration _____ Language _____

Type of Audience _____ Telephone _____ Number _____

Equipment _____

HEALTH EDUCATION SERVICE
Operated by the
NEW YORK TUBERCULOSIS AND HEALTH ASSOCIATION, Inc.
244 Madison Ave. Telephone Caledonia 2240
IAGO GALDSTON, M.D. REBEKAH HIRSCHMAN
Secretary, Health Education Service Assistant Secretary

ANNOUNCEMENT OF SPEAKER

Name of Lecturer _____
Sent by _____
Will talk on _____ will _____
The lecturer will not answer questions after the lecture _____
Further information may be had from _____
Name _____
Address _____

4

BLANKS USED BY A SPEAKERS' BUREAU IN ARRANGING AND REPORTING MEETINGS
1. Chairman's report; 2. speaker's report; 3. the front and reverse of an office record; 4. chairman's announcement; 5. postal card for requesting printed matter.

for example, whether the audience at the musicale were in a receptive mood for a talk on garbage disposal. Motion picture audiences gathered for entertainment sometimes resent the intrusion of addresses on civic matters into their programs.

As a speakers' bureau grows in experience, it adds to its record of organizations through reports made by speakers on meetings which they have addressed. A blank for speakers' reports is included in the set of forms devised by the Health Speakers' Service of the New York Tuberculosis and Health Association reproduced on pages 240–241.

Some well-planned speaking campaigns have been carried out through the systematic cultivation of a single type of organization during a period of six months or a year. Thus, speaking tours to reach the physicians of the state through their medical societies have been arranged by state tuberculosis organizations and by venereal disease bureaus. A state tuberculosis association planned a series of talks to business men's associations on economic reasons for preventing tuberculosis. An advantage in the systematic cultivation of a single element in a community is that a "made-to-order" talk suitable for its members can be used repeatedly with slight variation. Still another is that this concentration on a particular field offers a basis for follow-up work, which may result in securing the continued support of an organized group. Both of these considerations are especially applicable to shop meetings arranged to give instruction to workers in industrial plants, stores, and offices.

Noon-Hour Shop Meetings. The shop talk is usually given during the luncheon period. In rare instances far-seeing employers have been willing to arrange for instructive talks during working time. One organization was frequently successful in following a noon-hour talk with a second and sometimes a third given on the employer's time. Another arranged to use the last fifteen minutes of the workers' noon hour and the first fifteen of the afternoon work period.

Is it desirable to make use of the workers' rest and recreation period for talks? This question has brought both affirmative and negative answers. A mental hygiene lecturer reached the conclusion that the mental health of workers would be benefited more through recreation than through instruction. A speaker on fresh air and exercise felt it absurd to bring workers in from outdoor games to advise them about going out into the open air. Another speaker noted the restless glances of a group of girls toward the clock and the piano, and realized their dissatisfaction in losing the fifteen or twenty minutes they could have spent in dancing. It might be well for an organization arranging these talks to make it a rule to speak at noon only in shops where three-quarters of an hour or an hour is allowed for luncheon.

Perhaps the chief disadvantage of factory talks is the unsuitable room or space frequently allotted to such meetings. Examples of places where lectures have been given by health workers are a car barn opening on a noisy street, a cafeteria in which the clatter of dishes competed with the voice of the speaker, a room in which men stood about or sat under machinery on all sides so that the speaker could not face more than a small section of his audience at a time. In contrast to such places as these some plants possess excellent auditoriums.

Procedure in Making Engagements. The customary procedure of a speakers' bureau is to compile a directory of men and women qualified to present the subjects about which the social agencies maintaining the bureau wish to spread information. These lists of speakers, together with titles of their addresses are printed in attractive folders or booklets for distribution to clubs and churches. Some bureaus do not publish the names of speakers because when this has been done, the requests for the best known speakers have been excessive while others equally capable are not in demand. Many bureaus offer also motion pictures and other features for programs. When social organizations first began offering addresses, some of the subjects announced were "Social Hygiene," "Mental Hygiene," and "Prevention of Blindness." The wide-awake bureaus have become more specific and at the same time more imaginative. Among titles found in recent announcements are "Germs—Friendly and Otherwise," "Who Pays for Child Labor?" "Folks Close to the Poverty Line," and "Minds That Grope in Darkness."

The first step in obtaining engagements is to send a form letter to a group of organizations with which is enclosed the list of titles

243

or directory of speakers. The letter below was sent to women's clubs in St. Paul, Minnesota:

"Where can we get a good speaker for our club program?"

This is a question which club executives are forced to face frequently, and sometimes an answer is not easy. But a glance inside the enclosed folder will show that the problem need no longer be difficult.

The Community Chest Speakers' Bureau has just issued this new directory of 35 prominent speakers who are prepared to discuss such interesting social questions as Juvenile Delinquency, What Is the American Family to Be in 1950? The Men of Tomorrow, and Economic Aspects of the Negro Migration.

A study of the directory will reveal the important men and women of St. Paul who are at the service of your club through the Speakers' Bureau.

Call Community Chest Speakers' Bureau, Cedar 4810, for engagements.

It is desirable to enclose with the letter a return card requesting the bureau's representative to advise about the selection of speakers and titles. Through conferences arrangements can often be made for a series of intelligently planned meetings instead of a single engagement.

It was pointed out earlier that the speaker is sometimes provided with a form on which to report his impressions of the meeting which he has addressed. The chairman or other person in charge of the meeting also receives a blank form on which to send confidential information to the bureau about the speaker. The questions asked cover such points as, how the speaker was received, whether he read from his manuscript or overstepped his time, and what was the principal thought developed. On the basis of these reports, speakers may be given helpful suggestions and the bureau learns what types of audiences each one is best fitted to address.

When an engagement has been secured, making sure of a welcome for the speaker requires tactful planning. Perfunctory agreements frequently result in embarrassing experiences for those who volunteer to address meetings.

A health speaker, arriving at a factory where he was to give a noon-hour talk, found that the foreman in charge of arrangements had forgotten all about the engagement. Consequently, fifteen of the thirty minutes allotted to the talk had to be used in selecting a place to set up the motion picture machine and collecting workers from several floors of a large plant.

A physician, giving his services at great inconvenience to speak on health topics to clubs and church societies, withdrew his offer after several experiences with chairmen who had not expected him and who presented him lamely only after recalling that "someone was coming from some organization to speak about something or other." One of the disconcerting experiences for a speaker is to be introduced as "Mr. So-and-So who has asked for the privilege of addressing us for ten minutes."

The speakers' bureau may do much to prevent such awkward incidents. In negotiations for a series of health talks to a group of labor unions, not the least important step was to request that a vote be taken by each union to decide whether or not it should invite the speaker.

The bureau should make sure that the person in charge of the meeting receives a few days in advance a written confirmation of the engagement including the name of the speaker, the title of the speech, and a reminder of necessary arrangements such as providing a stereopticon machine or connections for a portable machine. It may be wise in some cases to telephone on the day of the meeting, to verify the place, hour, length of talk, and other details.

Assembling One's Own Audiences

Ready-made audiences, valuable as they are, by no means serve all the purposes of the social organization in presenting its cause at meetings.

At many of these assemblages the social worker's subject must share attention with other topics. When the message needs the main chance the audience must as a rule be gathered for the purpose and a suitable program arranged.

Working up an audience and planning a program, although apparently separate tasks, are very closely related since the nature of the program is the deciding factor with most people who are making up their minds whether or not they will go to a meeting.

Getting Attention for the Meeting. The forms of advance publicity generally used for meetings are articles and notices in newspapers, house organs, and bulletins; oral announcement in meetings; posters and placards displayed on bulletin boards; handbills personally distributed or posted; invitations and programs sent by mail; and personal invitations.

The first news story may well be timed to coincide with or to follow closely the invitations sent through the mail. It is intended to make people take notice of the event which they will be persuaded by a personal invitation to attend. The bulletin board posters, which incidentally should be done in bold colors or striking design, have a like purpose. Although to make the meeting widely known is only one part of the task, it is a very important one. The announcement of time and place should appear often and in several places to fix it in people's minds.

Publicity which brought a large attendance to the fifth annual dinner of the Indianapolis Community Fund was planned to keep the event before the public for a month in advance. Short items accompanied by photographs announced respectively on different days the chairman and members of the dinner committee, the reception committee, the hostesses, the small boy who would light the candles in honor of the Fund's fifth birthday, the girl who would sing. Each story repeated the date and place of the meeting and some information about its purpose. Several features of the program were reported at length in advance stories. One of these was the executive secretary's report, which, it was thought, might not be given such full notice in the news stories following the meeting in view of the more human news elements to be found in the event itself. Suspense was obtained by withholding until the day of the dinner the names of the winners and the text of the winning plans in a contest for a "progress plan" for the future development of social work in the city, and the name of the person awarded honorary membership for the year.

The speakers are as a rule given prominence in the announcement. Many persons will attend because they are curious to hear, or perhaps merely to see, someone who is engaging public attention at the moment, or who has a reputation as a humorous, brilliant, or dramatic speaker.

When the speakers are not well known, interest may be created by getting their pictures into the newspapers along with stories of

246

what they have done or anything unusual about them. Perhaps interest can be aroused about what they will tell. A bulletin of the Norfolk, Virginia, Council of Social Agencies announced:

> Mrs. Walter C. Fain, representative from Norfolk in the Virginia legislature, will speak on the subject: "The Life History of a Legislative Bill."
>
> Mrs. Fain will tell how and why most bills come to an untimely end; what the gauntlet is that they must run; how the surviving few win through.

A newspaper man told how he aroused public curiosity by playing up an unusual feature of a speech:

> I had an experience with a philologist . . . who asked me to get a notice in the paper regarding a philological society convention. He came to me later and complained that it was not printed. . . . I asked him what he looked for in the paper. As I suspected, he was looking for a headline stating "Washington Philological Society Will Meet on Thursday," or something of the kind, and I said, "If you will look on the back page of the Post-Intelligencer you will find 'Eggs Were Cheap Five Hundred Years Ago.'"
>
> The headline that he received was worth a thousand times more to him than the headline he conceived. Every member of the Washington State Philological Society knew a convention was going to occur and when, and where, and nobody else gave a whoop about it until I got hold of one of the members of the Society who was going to report on a cook book of the early fifteenth century. In it was a cake recipe that called for six dozen eggs, worth at that time about a penny a dozen, whereas we were paying about a dollar a dozen in Seattle. *There* was human interest; and probably 10,000 people read the story "Eggs Were Cheap Five Hundred Years Ago," though not two people would have read the notice that the Washington Philological Society was going to meet. What is more, many people came to hear the paper who never otherwise would have attended.[1]

Among other attractions which can be featured in advance publicity are motion pictures, a play, a debate, or music.

One method which seems to succeed in securing a good attendance is the serving of refreshments in connection with a meeting, even though the food is paid for by those who attend. A state

[1] White, Lee A., "Newspaper Publicity." *In* American Journal of Public Health, New York, vol. 15, April, 1925, p. 319.

department of health conducted a series of rural campaigns to improve sanitation in farm homes and found that the attendance increased to a surprising extent when a church supper preceded the meeting. In cities, luncheon or dinner meetings have succeeded over and over again in bringing people together to hear about a subject which would draw a mere handful if offered without the accompanying social feature.

The Invitation. The invitation received by mail usually brings the person receiving it to a point of deciding whether or not he will respond, whereas the more impersonal kinds of publicity may interest him but leave him without a feeling of responsibility in the matter of a decision. Many different forms of mail announcements are in use; the formal and dignified engraved invitation, the mailing card with its wide range of possibilities in the use of color and the effective display of the copy, the letter telling why the meeting is important, the attractively printed program, and so on.

An invitation issued by the Travelers Aid Society of Norfolk, Virginia, was typed on a single sheet of yellow paper about the size and color of a telegram, with a printed heading imitating a telegraph blank. It was called a "Dinnergram." The typed message read:

```
THE DIRECTORS OF THE TRAVELERS AID

SOCIETY WILL BE VERY GLAD TO HAVE

YOU WITH THEM AT THEIR LUNCHEON

WEDNESDAY FEBRUARY ELEVENTH AT ONE

FIFTEEN SOUTHLAND HOTEL MEZZANINE

FLOOR
```

Enclosing admission cards or tickets with an invitation or announcement may make attendance more of a privilege. A lecturer giving a series of talks to foreign-born workers on safety, after many failures to get them to come to evening meetings, greatly increased the attendance by distributing admission tickets to a limited number for each meeting.

A personal follow-up—by letter, card, telephone, or call—is the surest means of getting people to come to a gathering.

Telephone calls following the sending of a letter or printed invitation will often double the attendance. They bring out those who would otherwise forget about the meeting, those who take more interest in it because Mrs. Blank asked them to come, and others whose inertia about making the effort is overcome by this added personal suggestion.

In a small southern city, a meeting was planned for the purpose of creating interest in the building of a county sanatorium. The chairman of the committee sent a formal notice of the meeting to the members and a brief announcement to the newspaper. Only eight people came. A second attempt combining with notices a few personal visits and many telephone calls brought 75 people to the meeting on the hottest night of the year and they spent two hours in animated discussion.

Especially in the case of meetings at which the attendance of selected community leaders is desired in order to promote some civic or social measure, impersonal forms of publicity are not to be depended upon. A successful plan for bringing members of selected organizations to a dinner arranged by Better Times, a welfare magazine in New York City, was to follow the original invitation by a letter from the president of each of the various organizations urging the members to come.

Slipshod Advance Work. An amazingly casual attitude toward advance arrangements is sometimes found among those responsible for meetings. To illustrate: A state health department was conducting an educational campaign by sending to different towns for three-day periods a unit of lecturers, motion pictures, and literature. The plan in arranging these meetings was to send an agent of the department to each town three weeks in advance to meet the important people and to obtain their promise of co-operation. After these first steps were taken, however, the arrangements were left to a local representative who was entrusted to carry them out without further instruction or checking up.

Among the typically slipshod features of the work noted in one town where the local representative entirely failed in his task was the hiring of irresponsible boys to distribute at a mill gateway handbills announcing an evening meeting. The boys reached the mill after most of the men had left for the day. Also three separate afternoon meetings, one for young girls, one for young women, and the third for older women, were announced for the same time and place. The three meetings were, of course, completely wrecked. The only advertising done to promote a meeting for boys consisted in an oral announcement made to 40 persons present at a meeting the evening before. The results of this carelessness were that the speakers who had come a hundred miles were greeted by four persons. Aroused by these failures, the local representative made at last a genuine effort to have one good meeting, with the result that an audience of 300 people came, showing what could be done by intelligent work.

In contrast to this ineffectiveness was the energetic work of the North Carolina Health Department in preparation for a tour of two specialists who were to demonstrate diagnosis and treatment of gonorrhea to the medical men of the state. The steps taken to get the physicians to attend the meeting included:

A general letter to all members of the State Medical Society telling them about the plans and paving the way for a notice of a particular meeting in their town.

A letter to the county health officer, asking him to arrange a meeting with his county medical society and to supply a list of county physicians. If no response came to this first letter, it was followed up by letters or by telephone or telegraph until some action had been taken.

A personal advance visit to each county by the specialists to meet the leaders and enlist their co-operation.

Every doctor in each district was told personally about the planned meetings and their value to him. The state health department wrote to him telling him about the meetings. An advisory board composed of leading physicians of the state wrote assuring him that the films to be shown were well worth seeing. The United States Public Health Service wrote him that it had learned about the meeting and urged his attendance.

In response to these efforts, half of the 1,200 physicians invited appeared at the meetings, a good proportion in view of the fact that many had to come 20 or 30 miles over bad roads.

The Meeting

Planning the meeting itself includes obtaining the right physical conditions for the comfort of the audience, selecting the chairman, speakers, and special features appropriately, and arranging the program so as to hold interest and expectation until the purpose of the meeting has been accomplished.

Given a choice of meeting places, a hall small enough so that it will be filled or even crowded is to be preferred to one so large that many empty seats suggest failure to realize the expectations of attendance. Speakers have more inspiration and an audience is more responsive in a well-filled room.

Good ventilation, essential as it is to keeping the audience alert, seems to be difficult to secure. If it is not possible to combine a continuous current of fresh air in gentle motion with a comfortable degree of warmth, one usually can at least provide short recesses during which the windows are opened. Someone should be assigned to see that the temperature is kept at approximately 68 degrees Fahrenheit. Care should be taken to avoid having strong light shine in persons' eyes. Reasonably comfortable seats so placed that everyone can see and hear the speakers, and absence of distracting noises are other important factors in securing attention.

When the conditions for hearing speakers cannot be made altogether satisfactory, the chairman or ushers may bring the audience forward if seats are vacant in front, ask speakers to talk louder or to move nearer to the audience, and as far as possible suppress any distracting noises. One needs only to notice how easily the attention of an audience is diverted by a slight noise or movement or how restless they become when the room is close or warm or injudiciously lighted to realize the importance of providing the best possible conditions for listening.

The Chairman. The following excellent description of the functions and suitable characteristics of a presiding officer at a public dinner applies equally well to the chairman of any public meeting:

He must have many qualities, above all a warm, friendly personality. He must realize that his function is to link up the events of the evening, —to gather up wandering thoughts at the end of one speech and direct them with renewed interest to the next one. He must give the dinner pace, and supply the impression of quickening movement if by ill-fortune a speech be overlong.

Many public dinners have a presiding officer chosen for his fine presence and address and for his prominence in the community. Very frequently his conduct of the dinner is regulated by penciled directions carefully worked out for him by the person responsible for the program and arrangements. Better Times has found it expedient to eliminate this middle man, and to entrust the conduct of the program to the person who knows all its strength and weakness, who has the biggest stake in the success of the dinner and who is free to take liberties with prearranged plans if as the evening progresses this seems advisable.[1]

The Program. A program too often "just grows" instead of being made. The purpose for which the meeting was originally planned drops out of mind during the series of steps that are taken in securing speakers, a chairman, and special features. As a result, the program is loosely put together although unity is essential in order that the audience may carry away and retain an outstanding idea or sentiment.

An illustration of the way in which program planners lose their way in the intricacies of advance arrangements is found in a gathering held in a little country church as part of a program of health education for Negroes. The steps taken in getting ready for the meeting were about as follows:

1. A truck was equipped by a state health organization to carry a health lecturer and educational films to rural districts.

2. The lecturer prepared a talk on personal and household cleanliness, the lesson thought to be most needed by the people in the backward communities to be visited.

3. Motion pictures were believed to be a most effective aid to instruction, so films on the topic of the speech were sought but not found.

4. To show motion pictures had by this time come to seem more important than to teach health and many possible sources for obtaining pictures rent free were canvassed.

5. The program as finally presented included along with the talk on cleanliness, a two-reel film on poultry diseases lent by the United States Department of Agriculture; another film showing how a large city health department guarded the health of children from

---

[1] "Dinner Is Served." *In* Better Times, New York, vol. 7, March 1, 1926, p. 15.

infancy through school age; and as a final bit of entertainment, a war film accompanied by spirited comment from the lecturer who had himself seen service.

While audiences may not often be carried so far afield as this, it happens frequently that motion pictures inappropriate to the topic of the meeting are shown because after deciding to use pictures, those who arrange the program find themselves obliged to accept unsuitable films or go without them.

Program makers are similarly diverted from their original aims by the difficulties in securing good speakers. Thus, a meeting on boarding homes for girls is planned with one eye on its news possibilities. Since crime is the topic of the hour, a prominent judge is secured to speak on "Youth and Crime," a topic which, to be sure, is distinctly related to finding homes for girls, although it is doubtful whether the speaker will be prepared to discuss it from this angle. Attempts to secure still other speakers of note proving difficult, the task of planning a meeting soon resolves itself into one of finding speakers of power regardless of what they have to say. Finally, a specialist in recreation and a well-known psychiatrist are secured and given topics related to their own experience. Whether or not the audience learn anything about the housing problems of girls, they will at least find the program interesting; the newspapers also will probably report it. Having achieved this much, many a social organization regards its meetings as wholly successful.

On the other hand, closely knit meetings combining concentration on a central idea with the variety so essential to sustained attention are not uncommon. Many points of view on a single topic presented by persons with different backgrounds of interest and experience give strength and coherence to a program. An example is a conference on "Building Homes for Small Wage Earners" held recently in a large city. A research worker described a survey of present housing needs; two visitors from another part of the country gave illustrated talks about workers' housing projects in their city; a similar experiment was proposed; a lawyer presented the legal problems involved; and the mayor of the city gave his endorsement to the proposal.

Variety in the form of presentation may be combined with unity of theme by showing suitable pictures, conducting demonstrations, or using dramatic methods such as are described in the chapter that follows. Singing by the audience which helps to relax tension and break down reserve has an appropriate place in some meetings.

Questions and Discussion. A period for discussion or for questions and answers also avoids the monotony of continued platform speaking. If questions are to be invited, however, the program should be so planned as to provoke a desire to ask them. Everyone is familiar with the perfunctory invitation from the chairman: "Has anyone any questions?" followed, after a brief silence by, "If not, the meeting is adjourned." The chairman or leader may use various devices to bring members of the audience to their feet. Sometimes questions written out and sent up to the platform are read and answered. Perhaps early in his talk the speaker may remind his hearers to have questions ready when he has finished. He may speak very briefly on a certain point suggesting that the audience ask him later about those aspects of it that interest them especially. Several persons may be asked beforehand to raise questions when the proper time comes.

Audiences sometimes lose their reluctance to participate in discussion if called upon to express joint opinions through a show of hands. Having thus expressed themselves as members of a group they are more inclined to explain their views individually. This is especially true of those who find themselves in a minority, or who find that the yes or no answer to a question required by voting is not a satisfactory expression of their ideas.

General discussion[1] following speeches is often of such a scattered nature that it confuses the issue. This danger will be lessened if the speaker or chairman has prepared a series of questions which provide for a logical development of the subject. The speaker may close the discussion by summarizing it briefly or by again placing emphasis upon the most important point made.

Bringing the Meeting to a Close. A strong close is an essential element in a good program. In an earlier chapter examples were given of the arrangement of a program to create suspense which held interest until the meeting reached its climax.[2] Many a meet-

---

[1] The pamphlet, Creative Discussion (The Inquiry, 129 East 52d St., New York, 1926), shows how any average group can carry on an orderly and searching discussion of an issue. [2] See p. 23.

ing trails off to a weak and confused ending in which the hurriedly condensed talks of the last speakers are flung after a disappearing audience or rushed through apologetically because of the obvious impatience of those who remain. Whether the situation is due to an overcrowded program or to the unwillingness of the chairman to interrupt earlier speakers who have overstepped their time allowance, it involves great discourtesy and unfairness toward the last speakers as well as toward the audience.

The unwillingness of people to remain at a meeting beyond a certain length of time is so generally known that it is rather amazing that so many meetings are allowed to drag along after the audience have begun to show restlessness. Perhaps those arranging the meeting do not estimate carefully enough the maximum time required for each item on the program. It is possible, after all, and well worth the trouble, to time the numbers on a program almost as exactly as is done in the motion picture or vaudeville theater. The time schedule should be given in advance to everyone who is to take part in the meeting. Once this has been done, it is the responsibility of the chairman to see that it is carried through.

PART V: SPECIAL OCCASIONS

CHAPTER XV

DRAMATIC METHODS

THE kinds of publicity grouped here under the title "Dramatic Methods" have in common a picturesque or spectacular element or the quality of unexpectedness. Any particular dramatic method is suitable chiefly for occasional use, since if frequently employed, it loses the advantage of surprise and ceases to be conspicuous or compelling. These "features," as they are frequently called, are not what may be called bread and butter methods of spreading information. Among a number of methods combined in some publicity project, the dramatic feature is the attention-getter. If well done it has unusual news value and so reaches through the newspaper many persons in addition to those who witness the performance.

The dramatic forms most frequently used by social agencies— plays, puppet and marionette shows, pageants, parades, contests, and stunts—appear in intensive campaigns, expositions, fair exhibits, and meetings. Some of these are used quite extensively in the health education of children. The descriptions in the following pages are drawn partly from the activities of children, but more especially from the smaller number of examples we have been able to find of features planned wholly for adult propaganda.

PLAYS

The power of dramatic performances to move people, and sometimes to make them think, is well known, and social workers often find that "the play's the thing to catch the conscience" of the people who need to feel a situation before they are moved to remedy it. To meet the requirements of social service publicity, it is not necessary for a play to be theatrical nor for it to conform to all the canons of dramatic art. Only such dramatic elements as suit the particular situation need be borrowed. The play may be fanciful or realistic. Generally it should be short.

Allegorical Plays. Writers of health plays have shown an over-

259

whelming preference for the allegorical form of drama, using a more or less standardized plot of which the following outline is a pretty fair sample:

> A boy (let us call him Clarence) is somewhere (in a room, or a garden, or a field). He doesn't feel well and after telling us about it, lies down and takes a nap. While he is asleep, a beautiful health fairy with silver wings and a moonbeam gown prances up, waves a wand and then conducts Clarence to the land of Good Health. Here, Imps, Goblins, Dragons, Demons or Witches of Bad Health beset him. His plight is dire, when in dash Knowledge, Doctor, Nurse, Fresh Air and their concomitants. The powers of evil are dispelled, good triumphs, Clarence emerges, pure and enriched by the experience. He immediately resolves to follow the six (or eight, or eleven) rules of health forever more. Curtain.[1]

It would probably be impossible to make any sound generalization as to whether plays like this induce good health habits, or whether they merely offer the pleasure of make believe and dressing up for the children who take part in them. As for grown-ups, one would not expect them to enjoy this sort of entertainment for itself. Parents like to see their children perform and possibly they assimilate the lessons of the play when these are not too heavily veneered with metaphor and simile. Such matters are deserving of test.

Rarely do we find an allegorical play which is really artistic and appeals to people of discriminating taste. The Narrow Door,[2] written in blank verse, illustrates with considerable imagination and beauty the symbolic treatment of the theme of saving child life.

> As the curtain rises two women, Vita and Hygeia, are discovered spinning thread from a distaff in the foreground of an outdoor scene, while in the background the grim, shrouded figure of Mors leans upon a great two-edged sword at the right of the Narrow Door. Groups of children are playing happily with colored balloons. Vita complains that the little threads are brittle and snap too easily. Hygeia tells her that this is so because of "plague bred in crowded alleys, ignorance and neglect that have made the slender threads so weak and delicate that they

[1] Tobey, James A, "A Review of Health Plays." *In* Public Health Nurse, New York, vol. 14, March, 1922, p. 133.

[2] The Narrow Door was written and produced by George M. P. Baird for Pittsburgh Baby Week, 1915.

are scarcely twilled before they break." As the spinners talk one of the children shows signs of weariness and drops out of the game. Soon Mors calls the name of the child, who slowly moves toward the Narrow Door and passes through. In the course of the play three of the children thus disappear and the others, puzzled because they cannot follow, ask the women to explain. The children are told that they must appeal to mankind to stop this criminal waste of young life. As the children pray the Narrow Door begins to close.

Plays of Real Life. The everyday experiences of social work abound in the materials of which plays are made. An example of what can be done merely by staging an occurrence from the day's work is found in a fifteen-minute sketch entitled From House to House, written by Paul B. Howland and Robert B. Jones for the Providence District Nursing Association. The action takes place in a home such as the district nurse visits daily.

> A tired mother with a sick baby is ashamed of the dirt and disorder of her house and worried about the baby. A well-intentioned neighbor, adding a touch of humor as the typical joy killer, offers comfort by assuring her "you look a heap sight worse than when I saw you last" and saying of the baby, "eight months old and so thin!" The nurse enters upon this situation quietly and sympathetically, and surprises the mother by taking for granted the condition of the house and reassuring her about the baby: "He is not nearly so thin as some I have seen today." What takes place shows the sort of service the district nurse would be expected to give under the circumstances. The "happy ending" does not attempt to give the impression that the woman's troubles are all over and that hereafter the house will always be bright and clean and the baby properly cared for. The action ends merely on a hopeful note. The mother has braced up just because she feels that someone is standing by her. "Do you know," she says to her neighbor, "I feel as though I could eat a boiled dinner."

This simple dramatization of nursing service was presented frankly as an appeal for support in connection with the annual fund raising. A local vaudeville theater gave it a place on its regular bill and paid for the act. In fact, it was so successful as entertainment, as well as in promoting interest in the Nursing Association, that the manager did not feel that he had made any sacrifice in giving it a place on the program.

Another play, At Ellis Island, presents routine situations that visualize the problems of immigrants detained for special inquiry.[1]

The first scene brings out the experiences and anxieties of a group undergoing examination. An Italian woman and her children arrive with no one to meet them and the authorities learn that the woman's husband, because of their failure to leave Italy on the date first set for their sailing, has become worried and impatient and has started over to get them. A Polish woman with her children has come to join her husband, who lives in Iowa. The quota from Poland is exhausted. Two orphans from Armenia, a boy and a girl, have come to live with their uncle. The Armenian quota, also, is exhausted. A pretty Czecho-Slovakian girl of twenty expects to join her sweetheart, but she has forgotten the name of the town where he lives; she tells his name and shows a photograph of him.

The second scene, which takes place three weeks later in the Women's Deferred Room, shows the services of social workers to the people waiting there. Besides their regular duties, it generally falls to the workers to break the news of decisions for admission or deportation. To the Polish woman with her family and to the Armenian girl comes the tragic message that they, with the girl's younger brother, are to be deported. The Italian woman and her family are taken out happily to join the husband, who has returned from Italy and has come to claim them. The Czecho-Slovakian sweetheart, also, has been found and the girl dons her native wedding costume to have the ceremony performed before she leaves the Island.

Simply presented and without exaggeration, these typical situations and the need for social service at Ellis Island are made much more vivid and understandable than they could be in any other form.

Few, but successful in stirring people to a desire to take action, are plays which dramatize social conditions but do not attempt to make any suggestions or to point any moral. The First of May[2] is such a play.

Four young girls, Nelly, Agnes, Emma and Marie, clerks in a five-and-ten-cent store, share a shabby room in a dingy lodging house kept by a

[1] Razovsky, Cecilia, Three Per Cent. Published in 1922 for the General Committee of Immigrant Aid at Ellis Island by the Home Mission Council, New York City (Out of print).

[2] By Eleanor Rowland Wembridge. Awarded the Walter May prize in 1924 in a contest conducted by the Committee on Publicity Methods in Social Work. For permission to produce, address author at 247 Arandel Road, Cleveland, Ohio.

not too respectable landlady. It is the first of May, and the smell and feel of spring are in the air. The girls are hot, tired and restless. The thought of staying indoors is unbearable. So when Emma's husband comes around with a car and another young man, Emma decides to drop the divorce suit she has started against him for brutality and she and Marie go off for a good time. Soon Agnes's beau comes for her and Nelly, a country girl who has been in the city only a few months, is left alone.

The landlady coming in on an errand, sees that Nelly is lonesome and presently she brings in a young man, introducing him by a false name. The man is Tom Mackie, whose people live in Nelly's home town. Nelly and Tom do not recognize each other, but Tom soon learns where Nelly comes from and he is entertained by getting the home news from her. A story he tells about a "Chink" identifies him as a boy of whom she has heard from the other girls—a boy who "steals cars and sells dope and has just got out of the Pen." She is horrified, but upon learning that he is Tom Mackie of East Fairville she forgets her horror in the pleasure of talking with someone who knows the same people she does, and she begs him to take her riding, as he had suggested when he first came in. Tom refuses. He tells her the girls she is with are about as tough as he is, and advises her to quit the city, where she cannot earn enough to live decently, and to go back to East Fairville. When she refuses, he thrusts some money into her hand to pay for her journey home and disregarding her protests, goes out.

Without a line of moralizing the play draws attention to serious needs which social service is trying to remedy: the need for better housing conditions, better wages, better recreational facilities, and more intelligent interest in youth.

Difficulties in Dramatizing Remedies. The tendency to overweight plays with propaganda and to exaggerate the efficacy of social service work should be avoided.

The temptation likely to beset the social worker who seeks to use the drama is that of attempting to dramatize his remedy rather than the wrong to which it applies. This tack is encouraged by the prevailing temper to be constructive rather than destructive. It is, however, for three reasons, exceedingly difficult to weave a new social program into a poignant plot: (1) the social playwright is generally so preoccupied with the multitudinous details of his remedy that he is unable to compress them into an ordinary recognizable human situation; (2) the remedy is hard to "put over" because of its novelty and strangeness;

and (3) it seldom yields moments as dramatic as the ill for which the remedy is prescribed. In a health play, for example, the dramatist can develop a tremendous emotional situation by simply making the destinies of several likable people converge upon the deathbed of the husband and breadwinner of the family. It would be difficult, however, to take the recovery of the same man in a modern sanitarium and condense it into a single dramatic crisis of equal poignancy. The reason is, of course, simple. The remedy here begins to operate—if it operates at all—long before the patient has reached a condition of obvious peril and it works gradually, under cover and without dramatic manifestations. So it is with most social remedies. They either prevent the ill from happening or they get busy long before the disease has become critical. Drama must deal with crises.[1]

While remedies, as Mr. Perry has said, are not as a rule dramatic, on the other hand, the drab realities of many social situations are too sordid and depressing for the average audience to endure. Audiences react to plays in which unrelieved misery is portrayed by refusing to believe that the conditions are true to life. If there is a way out, and the social agency usually believes that there is, the playwright can introduce a gleam of hope or some bright moments to offset the unbearable picture of suffering even though the play comes to an end before the remedy has been applied.

Securing Good Plays. Plays of the sort which social agencies can use to advantage are not easy to secure. Few have as yet been written. The way in which From House to House was secured by the Providence District Nursing Association, suggests one source of help in obtaining well-written plays, and in having them well acted. Both the authors and the actors of the play were members of the local players' club. Little theaters are springing up in towns and cities throughout the country, and many of them are doing excellent work. Their co-operation with social agencies in producing good plays should not be difficult to obtain.

The Narrow Door was written by a university instructor of dramatics. Classes in play-writing might welcome the material that social agencies can supply. Still another source for securing plays is the play contest. In two play contests conducted by the

[1] From "Dramatizing Social Information," a paper, by Clarence A. Perry, presented at a session of the Committee on Publicity Methods in Social Work in Toronto, 1924.

Committee on Publicity Methods in Social Work the offer of substantial prizes brought out serious efforts on the part of publicity workers and writers who found a way to utilize the dramatic quality of situations daily encountered in social work.

PAGEANTS

When "King Health" slays the "Dragon Disease" or "Queen Knowledge" rescues the children from the dark cave of "Ignorance," the performance is sometimes known as a pageant and sometimes as a play. There seems to be very little distinction in the minds of those who are writing and using allegorical material between the two terms. The genuine pageant, which is a series of episodes, presupposes a theme of some breadth and dignity as well as an occasion of importance. Its characteristics are nobility of thought, appeal to high emotions, beautiful imagery, interest, and suspense. The difficulty of finding something really good to fit the purpose makes the pageant impracticable for frequent use in educational or publicity campaigns. We find, however, a few examples of pageants that fulfil all the requirements and have been produced with marked success.

The Spirit of the Double Barred Cross. An interesting pageant in six episodes weaving together allegorical and actual happenings, written by Helena V. Williams and Elizabeth Cole, was first presented at a meeting of the National Tuberculosis Association. It was called the Spirit of the Double Barred Cross, its title being taken from Spirit who tells the story before the curtain, episode by episode. In simple, artistic setting, with spectacular lighting and many colored costumes, from 60 to 75 persons portrayed important incidents in the history of the world-wide tuberculosis movement.

Humanity, "of no age, of no class, and yet of all ages and all classes," beset on every side by the veiled writhing figures of Diseases, led by Tuberculosis, struggled in vain for Health. To help Humanity, brave leaders started out on a Crusade, with the Crimson Cross as their emblem. The episodes depict scenes from the lives of Laennec, inventor of the stethoscope in the 17th century; Koch, discoverer of the tubercle bacilli in the 19th century; and the beloved Trudeau of Saranac. Other events portrayed were the birth of the National Tuberculosis Association, the coming of the first Christmas seal, the organized campaign, and the Modern Health Crusade. Symbolic of the influence of the Crusade of the Double Barred Cross was King Arthur, with his knights, protector of Humanity. The death of Arthur and the breaking up of his Round Table were shown in the Prologue; his Spirit, summoned by Love, came in the end to aid mothers and their children in their quest for Health. Excalibur, the magic sword of Arthur was seen to change into the Cross with Double Bars, and the Spirit, displaying Excalibur as a symbol of victory, concluded the pageant with a plea "to all the people living, be you sick, rich, poor, good, bad—or big or little"—to work for blessed health.

This pageant was especially successful in its happy combination of history and allegory. In their book on the pageant, Mary Porter Beegle and J. R. Crawford point out the advantage of such a combination. They call attention to the tendency of the English pageant to use only historical material:

> The historical pageant itself had a tendency to become monotonous to audiences. There was a similarity common to all episodic representation of history that made variety, to say nothing of novelty, almost an impossibility. Pageantry limited to a single type soon threatened to exhaust itself.[1]

About the strictly allegorical pageant they say:

> Naturally, the artistic success of this type depends upon the poetic imagination of its creator. Nothing is more dull or dreary than a thin and uninspired allegory dragged out over two hours. Such a pageant is the most difficult of all to create, for it really demands a poet. If it is presented in a trite and unimaginative way it will not stir the emotions or minds of its spectators.[2]

One justification for undertaking this difficult and elaborate form of publicity is suggested by the same authors in the statement: "The essential basis of the pageant is its amateur and co-operative nature." Any form of publicity is quite worth while if it affords means of self-expression to large numbers of people and gives them a better understanding of the movement or the ideas which the publicity aims to promote.

[1] Community Drama and Pageantry. Yale University Press, New Haven, 1916, p. 18.
[2] *Ibid.* p. 27.

Puppets and Marionettes

Puppets and marionettes have amused and instructed people of every race and age. They were used in Greece and Rome, and we still find them in Egypt, India, China, and parts of Europe. They have served the purposes of religion as well as of simple entertainment.

In some continental countries, particularly in France, there are puppet or marionette companies which serve the same purpose as our stock companies do. They have their characters famous and beloved in all the region about. The well-known Guignol, the Punch of the French puppet world, is as real to the public as a living actor. During the World War, in one of these puppet companies drafted into service by the American Red Cross, Guignol, in a dramatic little story, took the part of a baby's nurse. After an amusing but alarming experience for the poor baby, a French poilu appeared and insisted that the mother nurse her child. Guignol as a nurse was greeted with howls of laughter, but the moral of the story, that a mother should nurse her own baby, went home to the French audience.

The English puppet, Punch, is derived from the same Italian ancestry as the French Guignol. There are infinite variations of the Punch and Judy shows but Punch always appears as a knavish, boastful, and cowardly person given to the reckless use of a club, which is often in play upon the back of his wife, Judy, and other characters. A clever version of the Punch and Judy story adapted to the purposes of health education was at one time produced for the Pacific Division of the American Red Cross.

Whereas puppets are manipulated from below, with the showman placing the thumb and second and third fingers inside of the sleeves and head of the figures, the marionettes, which Tony Sarg has made famous in this country, are moved by strings operated from above the stage. Such manipulation, however, requires great skill since for each figure there are a number of strings.

With their many possibilities for entertainment and propaganda, puppets and marionettes have one chief limitation, in that much practice is required to manipulate the characters effectively. Still another drawback is that an amateur performer is likely to experience difficulty in talking loudly and distinctly enough from his working position behind the scenery.

PORTABLE THEATERS

Several types of portable theaters have been devised in which these difficulties of voice and manipulation are not present. The characters have very few movements or none at all, and the operator appears before the audience.

One of these theaters, designed for the New York State League of Women Voters by Stella Boothe, was The Little Red School House made of painted muslin drawn over a wooden frame work put together with pin hinges. When the theater is taken apart and packed flat in its canvas case, the total weight is about 16 pounds. The figures are mounted on wooden rods. Their backs are painted the same color as the floor. When they are not in the scene, they lie face downward. Settings are changed by turning the cardboards that form the interior of the case. The front of the theater is an ordinary window shade painted to represent the front of a school building. The operation is simple and the demonstrator tells the story and operates at the same time.

The first scene shows a dark, dingy schoolroom with all the undesirable features often met with in rural schools. The second scene shows a clean, properly lighted room, well equipped as to health and convenience. Besides the teacher and pupils the characters are two taxpayers, Mr. Ordinary Taxpayer and Mr. Joseph Objector, and a member of the League of Women Voters. The dialogue aims to show the physical and economic advantages of good school conditions over poor. In the second scene, with the model room, the taxpayers are shown to be saving money, and the curtain drops upon the complete conversion of Mr. Joseph Objector.

Miniature theaters can be used over and over again in a number of ways and are easily portable. Any kind of theater which can be packed for easy carrying and operated by one or two persons would seem to be especially well adapted to the traveling educational campaign. Members of a traveling staff giving frequent performances can become expert in its use.

PARADES

Two types of parade are familiar. The first, like the pageant, is spectacular, consisting of floats with tableaux, costumed marchers, and decorated vehicles bearing notable persons. The second is the less colorful demonstration made up of long lines of marching citizens holding banners and slogans to express some protest or demand or to celebrate an event or achievement. Sometimes both these types, the spectacle and the demonstration, are combined in one parade.

Floats. The float is an exhibit on wheels and may be designed on much the same principles as the window display or the booth at a fair or exposition. A favorite but rather trite idea for floats is some sort of allegorical tableau; for instance, a figure in Grecian robes seated on a throne is Hygiene or Public Health or Nursing Service, with children gathered about her whom she has saved from some evil figure representing Disease. While they may be beautiful to look at, the meaning of these symbolic figures is usually obscure. The stark realism of floats which portray conditions needing correction may prove to be more effective propaganda. On such a float in a civic parade rode a scrub cow in insanitary surroundings, while on another was a sanitary stable in which was housed a clean and healthy cow.

In a safety week parade a grim, but telling float consisted of a small tombstone carrying the inscription "1,054 Children Killed in Accidents in New York City, 1921." The base of the stone was decorated with flowers and on its side was printed "Must This Sacrifice Continue?"

Of the photographs and descriptions of floats which we have been able to gather, few show originality. The impression they give as a whole is that social organizations have not yet displayed a great deal of imagination in planning this type of feature.

Marchers. The marchers, as well as the floats, may be grouped and costumed to express ideas or represent organizations. In many large parades we see marching groups in the uniforms of the Red Cross, the public health nurses, or the scouts; or without uniform they may be identified with some local group by sashes, badges, or banners. A large number of marchers are especially important in a demonstration parade.

269

The idea of a clean-up week parade held in a Minnesota town was expressed by a section of Boy Scouts in uniform carrying clean-up placards, hoes, and rakes. A squad of high school girls dressed in Dutch costume carried cans of washing powder; others in aprons and caps, carried brooms, mops, and dusters. In a boys' parade in New York City, the American Child Health Association was represented by a section carrying gaily colored balloons and dressed to illustrate various elements contributing to child health.

A health parade carried out by Dr. W. W. Peter in several cities of China had for its most striking feature Mr. Cholera Germ, a tall man on stilts in a long yellow robe with electrically lighted eyes. As he walked he would note some insanitary condition by the wayside and point it out calling "There is where Cholera lives." Preceding him were several units of young men with megaphones who shouted such messages as "Cholera is at your doors. If you will keep clean Cholera will be vanquished."

The Banners. A minor point of technique that should not be overlooked in arranging for parades is that the slogans and the titles should be well displayed. Every banner and transparency should have its slogan repeated on two sides or even four, so that the onlooker can see it as the parade approaches him, while it is passing, and as it disappears. It is also important that banners should be carried high enough to be seen by those at the back of the street crowds.

The weight of banners is an important consideration. They should not be so frail that the wind can destroy them before the parade is half finished nor too heavy for marchers to carry in a wind.

Advantages of Parades. As part of any community campaign, such as the special week or the annual drive, a parade has unique advantages. It is a feature not likely to be overdone, since the frequency of such events in any place is automatically limited by the demands of traffic. As a result, a parade continues to have the value of novelty, and the stirring music of the band and the rhythm of marching feet never fail to thrill. Many people who would not attend a meeting or exposition see a parade because they happen to be on the street when it passes. They tell others about it and accounts of it are also read in the newspapers, so that it makes an impression on many more people than could be gathered together

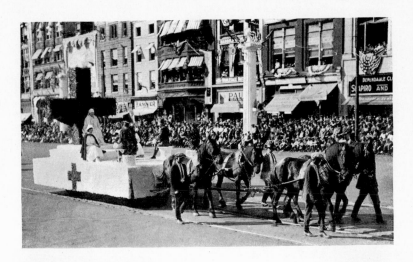

PARADES

Above: Red Cross Float in 175th anniversary celebration of Reading, Pa.
Below: The Vegetable Battalion of the Children's May Day Health
Parade, Syracuse, N. Y.

at one spot. Particularly novel or attractive floats and costumed marchers are likely to be shown in the picture pages of the newspaper and occasionally in the motion picture newsreels.

STREET STUNTS

Many types of street features are simpler and require less preparation than the organized parade. These "stunts," as they are usually called, are also suitable for fair grounds, amusement parks, or exposition buildings. Commercial advertisers have long since made us familiar with the sandwich man, the grotesquely costumed figure sauntering along a busy street, the man on stilts who appears to be about 12 feet tall, the mule driven cart, or the strikingly painted truck. During the period of war drives it seemed as if every conceivable device for attracting and holding street crowds was tried out, from the painting of gigantic posters in the public square by prominent artists to the installation of a giant telegraph sounder for announcing at a busy corner the sales of liberty bonds, or an airplane flight by Douglas Fairbanks.

A street stunt is sometimes offensive or undignified, but there is no inherent reason why it should be. Its effective and appropriate use has been demonstrated, and new and ingenious ideas are continually cropping out in money-raising drives and other publicity campaigns.

A street feature with wide possibilities is the town crier. A news item from the Red Cross Courier shows the town crier idea used for the simple purpose of working up a meeting:

Up and down the streets of the village of Barneveld, Wisconsin; containing less than 300 inhabitants, walked a youth bearing a homemade sign reading: "Mothers' Meeting: Health Talk at School Today: Four O'clock, Come!" By his side marched a "megaphone" in knee breeches, calling attention to the sign. "We counted all the people that came to the windows to see us go by," said one of the boys when they came back to the school, "and there were 54." Sure enough, 40 mothers appeared at four o'clock to attend the health meeting at the schoolhouse, which the principal and the Red Cross secretary, who was weighing and measuring the children, had arranged for this branch of the Iowa County Chapter.

A town crier dressed in picturesque costume may add a colorful note to a campaign. He may walk or ride through the streets.

19   271

PUBLICITY FOR SOCIAL WORK

An unusually vivid method of advertising homelessness in London in connection with the campaign to sell London housing bonds is described thus by Lawrence Veiller, secretary of the National Housing Association, New York:

> One of the methods employed has been to send a huge moving van through the streets loaded with furniture and carrying household pets, including a rabbit hutch and a couple of rabbits, with a bird-cage alongside. In the pouring rain on July 5 this moving van made its way along Regent Street, one of London's main shopping thoroughfares. On the tailboard disconsolately sat a woman and two children; they were evidently the outgoing tenants. As the spectators saw more clearly the side of the van they were able to read on it a huge notice, which read: "They have the furniture but nowhere to put it. Buy London County Council 6% Bonds and help them to build a home." It is stated that the van is to tour all parts of London with a view of emphasizing the importance of securing money for houses.[1]

Whatever calls attention to conditions on the street is a good subject for a street feature. The prevention of accidents, keeping the streets clean, walking to work, wearing the right kind of shoes, scarcity of homes for working men are among the subjects that may be appropriately called to people's attention while they are on the streets.

Other picturesque or spectacular devices, familiar chiefly as the exploits of press agents, are staged almost wholly for the purpose of securing space in the newspapers. They include using the services of well-known women as clerks in stores, bell hops in hotels, or in other forms of unaccustomed work; engaging the hero of the hour, whether aviator, prize fighter, motion picture actor, or politician, to auction off the first bond or an autographed picture or book or any other prize; having the governor or the mayor pose for motion pictures on the steps of the capitol or city hall, drinking a glass of milk during Milk Week; gathering together a number of people to make a pilgrimage on foot to present a petition or resolution to the President.

There is a narrow line between the stunt that will attract favorable attention and the one that may offend or displease.

[1] How England Is Meeting the Housing Shortage. Lawrence Veiller, London, 1920, p. 11.

272

A STREET STUNT

The Boy Scouts of Greater New York celebrated the One Hundred and Fifty-second Anniversary of Lexington Day by placing a wreath at the foot of the George Washington Statue at the Sub-Treasury Building. Two scouts represented Paul Revere and William Dawes.

Chalking sidewalks, accosting citizens, posting signs on poles may easily become public nuisances and are not tolerated in some cities.

Again, the more daring methods often arouse as much unfavorable comment as approval. The burning of the President's speeches in front of the White House by a group of women; the auction of the unemployed on Boston Common during the peak of unemployment in 1921; the display in the Wall Street district of New York of a group of repellent and disreputable men who advertised themselves through sandwich boards as victims of venereal diseases; these and many similarly spectacular features have been highly successful in securing newspaper space and widespread discussion but have at the same time aroused considerable antagonism. Their promoters believe that such drastic methods are justified by public indifference in the face of extreme situations. They claim that in spite of the protests, conservative people who would not otherwise pay attention to their cause do read and talk about it; that there seems to be no reason why important information should not be brought to the notice of an indifferent public in a vivid way. But if we do not want the information discredited in the minds of many people, we should avoid presenting it through means which are generally considered to be objectionable.

COME AND SEE TOURS

Excursions, sometimes called "know your city tours," are generally made in automobiles which have been lent for the purpose. Leaders in political, social, and business life, and in industry are taken to see various social work agencies in operation, as well as to unsightly dumps, crowded tenement districts, and dangerous streets where children play who have no public playground. In money-raising campaigns delegations of contributing citizens are sometimes taken to the organizations their funds are helping to support. Visiting days in schools and institutions are arranged to let the public see how and what the children are taught.

A series of tours planned and carried out with marked success by the Central Council of Newton, Massachusetts, is described as follows:

A letter of invitation to the tours was sent to a carefully selected list of about a thousand people, and these mail invitations were followed up by personal telephone invitations on the part of a committee of volunteers—one or more for each of the eleven "villages" of Newton. The result was two afternoon and two evening tours, with tour groups ranging from thirty to sixty-eight people (in all, 210 tourists). The mayor, the assistant superintendent of schools, and two well-known business men acted as tour leaders. . . .

The tours were restricted to those social agencies which had something of human interest to show at their buildings. Each tour included from three to five organizations representative of various types of social work. For example, one evening tour group assembled at the Young Men's Christian Association. A simple sixty-cent supper was served by the Women's Auxiliary of the Association. The tour leader spoke briefly, welcoming the guests, describing the route to be followed on the tour, and suggesting that the agencies to be visited carried on only a fraction of all the social and health work of the community. Because the "office agencies" were not included in the sights to be seen, a representative of one of them—the family welfare society—spoke briefly of the service of her organization.

The general secretary of the Young Men's Christian Association led the visitors through the Association building, where the ordinary evening program was in progress, plus a special exhibition in the swimming pool.

Leaving the Y.M.C.A., the group visited in turn a school center, a Swedish home for the aged, a neighborhood house, and a hospital. In each institution the executive or some board member told briefly of the kind of service given and then conducted the visitors through the building, or at least through enough of it to give a cross-section view of the work.

As an educational project, it is felt that the Come-and-See tours were distinctly successful. . . . One visitor was so much impressed by the work of a certain institution that he voluntarily sent them a check for a hundred dollars the next day. The same institution reported that several of the tour guests came back later, of their own accord, bringing with them friends whom they wished to interest. . . .

As a sequel to the tours the Council has been asked to arrange for another special tour for thirty high school boys and girls representing classes in community civics.[1]

[1] Dunham, Arthur, "Come-and-See." *In* The Survey, New York, vol. 53, Dec. 15, 1924, pp. 331–332.

Out of his experience in managing these tours Mr. Dunham mentions in a letter a few details which should not be overlooked:

Time is saved and confusion avoided if auto buses are used instead of private automobiles. Buses are expensive, however; private automobiles can be secured free.

Twenty-five or thirty is about the ideal size for a tour group. Fifty is close to a maximum.

Care should be taken to see that visitors get a fair cross-section of the work of each agency, but without any elaborate special program being staged.

It is desirable that the driver of the tour leader's car drive over the route in advance, in an automobile, so that he will know it when leading the tour and also estimate the time the trip will take.

Arrangements should be made to have a newspaper photographer take pictures of the tour groups.

Each aide ought to make a brief, written report, covering the number of persons present and noting any items of news interest.

CONTESTS

Contests to secure a trade name or a slogan for advertising copy have served to put many minds at work on the merits of the advertised product and to get the advertising material read by many people who do not themselves enter the contest but who are interested in seeing who wins the prize.

The contest as a feature of social publicity may serve the same purpose that it does as a form of commercial advertising. If made interesting and lively enough, observers, as well as contestants, will keep in touch with it and thus become acquainted with the information around which it centers.

The technique of a well-planned contest extends to such factors as the selection of suitable prizes; the framing of clear-cut and practical instructions,[1] which should be published and distributed in mimeographed or printed form to prospective contestants; the selection of judges competent to pass on the various kinds of merit involved; the apportionment of points for judging so that the task of the judges is simplified as much as possible and the contestants

---

[1] When a contest is conducted through the mails, it would be well to submit the conditions to the postmaster before sending them out, as there are certain postal regulations to be observed regarding material of this sort.

are assured of fair treatment. The awarding of prizes should be made an important and conspicuous occasion.

The Care of the Baby. The baby contest as conducted formerly was a beauty contest. Health organizations, seeing its possibilities, took over this popular idea and gave the prize to the baby in best physical condition without regard to beauty. They found, however, that even with this improvement, the contest attracted the parents of the best cared for babies and did not reach those in greatest need of help. In connection with the Illinois State Fair this objection was met by substituting a baby improvement contest. Children under six years of age were entered and given a thorough examination in the course of which the needs for improvement were pointed out to mothers. The next year at the fair these children were re-examined and rated according to the gains made over their previous records. Each year invitations were sent to mothers who had entered children in the previous year's conference, particularly urging those whose children showed remediable defects to enter and profit by correcting the defect. Additional propaganda value was obtained by making a condition of entry the possession of a birth registration certificate.

An interesting variation of the baby contest is a mother contest. As each mother with children enters the exhibit space she is asked to answer a few simple questions such as:

Are the windows in baby's sleeping room kept open or shut?
Do you give the baby anything to make him sleep? What?
Do you give the baby a pacifier?
How often is the baby bathed?

The answers are filled in on a card by an attendant, and as the mother leaves she is presented with a tag showing her grading as revealed by the information put down on the card, which has in the meantime been scored by a nurse. In presenting the award the nurse takes the opportunity to compliment the mother on the points in which she stood well and to explain those that she did not understand. At a contest of this kind held at Greenwich House, New York City, the prizes were an aluminum saucepan, measuring cup, nursing bottle, and other utensils useful in preparing babies' food.

A BETTER BABY CONTEST

Above: The Better Baby Building at an Indiana State Fair.

Below: Examination of children in the annual Better Baby Contest conducted by the Division of Infant and Child Hygiene of the Indiana State Board of Health.

Competition between Groups of People. Experience shows that members of any group will rally to the support of a project which introduces the element of friendly rivalry with other groups. A competition among organized units may accomplish more than one among individuals.

An ambitious campaign to enlist this spirit of team work was undertaken by a rotary club in Oklahoma. It was called a better cities contest. Each of 36 middle sized cities, after a year of intensive effort, presented its claim to be considered the most nearly ideal community in the state in which to rear children. Better cities contests have also been held in recent years in Wisconsin and other states.[1]

The Utah Public Health Association once invited each school district to conduct a contest among its own rural schools for the purpose of improving the appearance and conditions of buildings and grounds, cleanliness of rooms, proper adjustment of seats, ventilation, heating, lighting and sanitary arrangements. While not all the districts carried the contest through, the total result was to stimulate a considerable amount of activity. In studying the points on the score card, school boards and citizens became more conscious of local conditions in the matters under review.

Rivalry in Obtaining a Health Demonstration. When the former National Child Health Council decided to undertake a demonstration of methods to improve child health in a community of average size, representative organizations of such cities throughout the country were invited to submit requests for the demonstration, and in doing so to show why they believed their town a most suitable place for such a project. The zeal with which many localities entered into the competition was surprising.

In one city, seventy citizens each sent a cordial telegram requesting the Demonstration for their community. Another city submitted a large, loose leaf book containing endorsements of all city and county officials and all local organizations. A petition was submitted by one community signed by over eleven hundred mothers, each stating the number of children in their family, ranging from one to thirteen. An essay contest was conducted in the schools of one city on the subject of

[1] For description, see McKeever, W. A., "The Better Cities Contest in Oklahoma." *In* American City, New York, vol. 25, Dec., 1921, p. 472.

"Why We Want the Demonstration in Our Town." The prize essay, and many others were sent to the National Child Health Council. Where petitions were circulated, slides were shown in the movies advertising what the petition was for, and urging all to sign it. In one community, special days were set aside to arouse popular enthusiasm for this purpose. Child health literature was distributed and banners were displayed bearing such slogans as "Make (name of town) The Health Town." In some cities school children and the school nurse assembled and were photographed in front of one of the school buildings with placards prepared by the children expressing their desire to have the Demonstration in their city. Many cities offered to send delegations to present their cases to the Council or invited the Council to visit them as guests of the city. One town planned a "community dinner" and invited representatives of the National Child Health Council to attend. Governors, state health commissioners and other state officials wrote cordial letters inviting the Council to hold the Demonstration in their states and promising the utmost cooperation.[1]

Poster Contests. Poster contests have set many thousands of young people to work, while parents looked on or gave suggestions, trying to draw suitable pictures for such slogans as "Always Be Careful," "Help Others to Help Themselves," "Safety or Sorrow."

The school poster contest seems to fit very well into the routine work of the classroom. The art teacher welcomes it as offering a definite problem for students to solve. Civics, home economics, hygiene, and other departments find that it provides an opportunity to awaken a new interest on the part of children in information for which the contest gives them an immediate use. The social agency occasionally obtains posters suitable for educational purposes through these competitions, although to secure a good poster is seldom the primary object for which they are conducted.

APPROPRIATE USE OF DRAMATIC METHODS

The social agency sometimes slips into an unconscious preoccupation with a dramatic form of publicity for its own sake, forgetting about its educational purpose. In poster contests judges have become so delighted with the ingenuity of the children

[1] "Plans of National Child Health Council." *In* The American Child, New York, vol. 3, May, 1921, pp. 11–12.

in the use of color and design that they have failed to realize that the slogans and pictures have often presented no message at all or one that was not true. In money-raising drives it is easy to fall back on a novel scheme, such as having society women run a hotel for a day, which obtains generous space in the newspapers and may bring in considerable amounts of money, but gives very little if any information about the organization itself.

Most of the methods described in this chapter may easily be managed to dramatize social information or social objectives and not merely used as stage trappings designed to enhance uninteresting facts or ideas. Most people like action, suspense, color and picturesqueness but they do not like them as a sugar coating for material which in itself has none of these qualities. For example, when health precepts are set forth in a play by having the characters preach health, the dramatic form is employed in a very artificial way.

As stated in the beginning of the chapter, dramatic or spectacular methods are suitable for occasional use only, and they should never be the sole dependence of any agency in getting public attention. There seems to be a lack of solidity about the organization that is always theatrical in its methods; but almost any movement, however dignified, can afford to vary its customary news stories, speeches, and printed matter with an occasional use of more colorful or dramatic forms.

CHAPTER XVI

FAIRS

ORIGINALLY state and county fairs were exhibits of live-stock, garden and orchard products, and handiwork, enlivened by horse racing and a few wholesome amusements. Latterly in many places they have deteriorated until they are little more than an excuse for a midway of flashy diversions. Here and there over the country, however, movements have been started to eliminate the objectionable features and to enlarge the educational program and make it more attractive. In the Middle West many managers state that their fairs are both informing and prosperous. A writer describing the Kansas Free Fair, an annual affair which has had an attendance as high as 350,000 a week, quotes the secretary as saying:

Farmers come to our fair from all parts of the state and from beyond. . . . Thousands come in motor cars from as far as a hundred miles away, starting from home by early lamplight, staying on the fair grounds until ten o'clock at night, then making the long drive back home again. Farmers don't go to all that trouble these days for amusement alone, just to see the clowns, the circus acts, and shows. Farmers don't have to go that far for amusement. They don't come so far merely to see a fair, because the sixteen counties from which we draw most of our visitors each has a fair of its own. In our advertising we don't emphasize the amusement end of it so much as we do the educational features. . . . But a fair must not . . . try to cram education into people; it must mix a lot of fun and interest with its educational features.[1]

A social service executive whose organization has exhibited at many fairs divides the types of visitors into the rushing, pushing, jolly mobs of fairs held near cities and the slower-moving, slower-thinking, but more seriously interested groups at rural fairs. City dwellers can be reached in many ways, but rural fairs afford a

[1] Macdonald, A. B., "The Friendliest Fair." *In* The Country Gentleman, New York, vol. 87, Aug. 19, 1922, p. 7.

point of contact with country people different from any to be had by other means. Visitors come in a sociable, expansive mood which is favorable to publicity if it is made entertaining and comprehensible. They come for a good time, though not necessarily a hilarious time, and if education does not interfere with their pleasure, it will be quite likely to find them receptive. How social publicity may be presented at fairs through amusements, exhibits, and personal contact is the topic for consideration in this chapter.

METHODS OF THE MIDWAY

What is there about the midway, with its side-shows, fortune tellers, paddle wheels, and other chance-taking devices, its sales of nostrums, cheap jewelry, and ephemeral fountain pens, which lures and entertains people in spite of its tawdriness? Anyone may hazard an opinion. Ours is that probably the attracting quality is very little in the wares and very much in the manner in which they are offered. However important the sales may be to them, on the surface at least, the showmen and hawkers at the fair are in complete accord with the holiday spirit of the crowd. Their language and often their methods and costumes are picturesque, their wit is ready and their interest never flags until they have secured their audience or made their sale. Omitting the deceptions, the social worker does well to adopt a part of their technique for use in his own publicity, and to a certain extent he has done so.

As long ago as 1914, the Indiana State Department of Health borrowed from the side-show its flamboyant methods of attracting a crowd. Outside the Health Department's large tent were hung gaudy canvas banners carrying such announcements as "The Most Powerful Bug in the World Which Kills 4,000 Men, Women, and Children in Indiana Yearly," and "Disease, the World's Champion Always on the Job, to Be Seen Inside." A newsboys' band played in front of the show, and after a crowd had been attracted by the music, a barker or ballyhoo got up and told through a megaphone of the wonders within.

The old amusement park maze has been used by the Illinois Department of Health. In this case it was called the "Labyrinth of Life." One had to find one's way from "Infancy," at the entrance, to "Ripe Old Age," at the exit. Many obstacles and dead ends representing the preventable diseases were encountered.

"Your Health Is Your Fortune" is the legend blazoned across the top of the Health Fortune Teller's tent which has been a popular feature at many fairs. The ballyhoo, with rakish fez, bright sash, and stick, introduces "The Princess Whatshername of Whereisit," a nurse or health worker in gipsy costume. The barker not only draws the visitors into the tent but, in a casual way, throws out a few health hints:

Now ladies and gentlemen, all you need to do to have the Princess tell you the future of your health is for each of you to step on this little steel platform, commonly known as a scale. Then you walk further into the tent. Within a minute or two you will be given audience with the Princess. She will tell you according to your weight and your height whether or not you are fit for the work of life.

The Princess will tell you, ladies and gentlemen, whether you should eat much or little. She will reveal the secret of these marvelous objects upon the front of the tent (touching with wand or cane the cut-outs of vegetables and a huge milk bottle).

The food which comes to us from the clean and wholesome country-side; this, ladies and gentlemen, we know to be the true elixir of life. The eager Spaniard never discovered the fountain of youth, but the Princess will reveal to you the cow, the wondrous cow, as a veritable fountain of youth for youth, for middle age, and for old age.

A different device with a similar aim is the health ouija board which answers all questions on health. Painted on the board are the alphabet and a few words likely to be useful, while strings at the back connect with various charts. The operator is concealed.

The secret of success is having a fluent speaker as a demonstrator who stands by, guiding the questions and amplifying the answers. The ouija is not touched by the fingers but moves apparently of its own volition, and besides traveling over the board can whirl around in a circle and can leap up and down with its front leg at the will of the operator.[1]

A dramatic event at the fair in Cattaraugus County, New York, in 1925 was the visit of Willard J. Shannon and his dog team. Shannon was one of the heroic band of men who, with their teams

[1]Hennepin County Tuberculosis Association, Minneapolis.

of Alaskan dogs, had carried antitoxin 800 miles to diphtheria stricken Nome the previous winter. He appeared under the auspices of the Cattaraugus County Health Demonstration and described his hazardous drive.

After Shannon and his dogs had raced down the track, the crowd that gathered to witness this exciting performance listened to a speaker who urged parents to have their children protected from diphtheria by treatment with toxin-antitoxin.

The patent medicine hawker usually selects an open space on the grounds, his crowd forming a circle in the center of which he stands with an assistant in costume to hand him, as he needs them, his various properties—a human skull, a snake, whatever he can devise to fascinate and hold the crowd. His information is untrustworthy and his medicine may be harmful, but his exhibition technique is excellent. A few social exhibitors have tried it.

A one-man show devised by the Wisconsin Anti-Tuberculosis Association some years ago had for stage property a long piece of cloth on which two roads were painted, each beginning at the center and extending in opposite directions to the ends. At one end was "Bad Health," and at the other "Good Health," and along each road were crudely painted pictures representing those things which go to make health and sickness. With this simple paraphernalia a staff member would ride into a fair on a motorcycle, select a well-located fence or wall of some building, and begin to unroll his canvas. As people gathered around him he explained in a popular, familiar fashion what it was all about.

At a Michigan fair a cartoonist, sent out by the Detroit Tuberculosis Association, gave exhibitions from a platform throughout the day. His usual method of arresting attention was to draw an elaborate colored landscape. Then he turned the show into a health lesson by writing the caption "An Outdoor Life Is Nature's Tonic." Following this introduction, other objects were sketched. Common vegetables were transformed by swift strokes into healthy boys and girls and an animated milk bottle knocked out an animated coffee pot. After each picture had been shown he would tear it off and give it to someone in the crowd. During a ten-minute period he drew three or four cartoons and then closed his performance in order to gather a new audience.

Persons who can draw cartoons or do clown tricks and at the same time give a sound, lively talk are not easy to find. When there has been enough demand for them, professional entertainers have been trained by national or state organizations, and here and there home talent is discovered which is quite as good as any that can be imported. If the performer is known, and if he knows many of those in the crowd, he can give local color to his talk, which increases its popularity.

The community theater, which has sprung up in many states under the auspices of the dramatic departments of the universities, according to a writer in the New York Tribune, "plainly threatens Bosco, the celebrated snake-eater, the nautch dancers, the Wild Man of Borneo, the Hit-the-African-three-shots-for-a-dime, and other denizens of the rural midways and carnivals."

In both 1921 and 1922 at the state fair in Syracuse, New York, the little Country Theater, under the auspices of the Cornell Dramatic Club, played to 16,000 people, giving 43 performances in five and one-half days. Following this auspicious beginning, the movement spread throughout New York State until in 1925 little theaters were numbered among the important features at 15 county fairs. One-act plays lasting from thirty to forty-five minutes have been found to be most suitable. From four to six performances are given during the day, the most popular hours being those between 11 a.m. and 4 p.m.

The plays and especially the puppet shows described in Chapter XV, Dramatic Methods,[1] might, if entertaining enough, find a place in these little theaters, or may be given a show place of their own. The miniature theater, The Little Red School House,[2] and the play, The First of May,[3] are dramatic attractions which have a special bearing on the life of rural communities. Some exhibitors have offered plays or pageants in their own tents or other exhibit space. Many have given motion picture shows, using films which combine entertainment and education. Puppet shows and bands of strolling players might well be added to the list of attractions which the state or national organization offers for booking at rural fairs.

[1] See p. 267.   [2] See p. 268.   [3] See p. 262.

SHANNON AND HIS DOGS AT THE CATTARAUGUS COUNTY FAIR

A County Fair Theater

Community Players giving an outdoor performance at the Franklin County Fair in Pennsylvania.

Competitive Exhibits

Exhibits of livestock, fruit, vegetables, and handiwork, entered competitively, give the fair a personal element and a certain amount of community spirit. The custom generally is to award many small prizes and so distribute interest as widely as possible.

The Home Bureau of Cornell Agricultural College has encouraged exhibiting housewives to substitute for the old-time fair exhibits of handiwork, such as gaudily decorated china, crude water color and oil paintings, and colored embroidery in stiff and meaningless designs, such practical home products as clothing, labor saving devices, and menus for family meals and school lunches. For these displays, special score cards have been prepared on which the ratings are entered to be used in awarding the premiums.

Especially where children are concerned, there are varied opportunities for the social worker to take part in competitive exhibits. At some county fairs health organizations have offered a prize for every child whose teeth were found in good condition. Announcing a prize beforehand has brought a great rush of business to dentists. The examinations are made in a tent or booth on the grounds. Shiny silver quarters pasted on blue ribbons were awards in one case, a whole dollar in another. In an Iowa fair all children up to twelve years old found by the Red Cross nurse to come within a pound of their normal weight were given free rides on the merry-go-round.

Baby shows have always been a great attraction, even more popular than the side-shows, according to some fair managers. Contests under the auspices of health departments, such as those described on page 276, have made these affairs educational without detracting from their popularity.

Exhibiting Ideas for Everyday Use

A demonstration of something that has a place in the everyday life of the farm is practically sure to receive attention. It need not be actually new if it is something not widely known in the territory represented at the fair. Home-made fireless cookers and ice boxes have been introduced to many homes in this way. The display of equipment for the baby often contains something new—patterns, a bed made in a clothes basket, or a kiddie coop. Demonstrations of methods of fly trapping, making the bed for outdoor sleeping and collections of home-made toys are practical and welcome. "Would You Like to Learn to Make Something Out of Nothing?" read the sign over a Red Cross booth at one fair. Visitors who accepted this invitation saw garments being made out of old clothing and discarded scraps. Patterns were cut for those who asked for them.

The sometimes distasteful and always offensive tone of talking down to people contained in demands that the visitors eat this, or wear that, or avoid something else, is done away with when the keynote of the exhibit method is the more attractive idea: "Here is something new and practical. Would you like to try it?"

Demonstrating Methods of Social Work

The large amount of space available at some fairs makes possible the reproduction of actual conditions—always an effective method of exhibiting. A display giving an interesting but inadequate picture of case work reproduced a miserable, one-room home existing in the county. Possible causes of the family's wretched condition were listed on a placard and visitors were invited to call upon the Associated Charities for help in dealing with situations of a similar kind.

To show what a rural school building can and should be like was the object of the exhibit described below:

A full-sized one-teacher rural school building was the center of the Department's State Fair exhibit this year. The building . . . was complete in every detail, embodying the most satisfactory features of rural school construction and equipment. . . . It measured thirty-seven and a half by twenty-five and a half feet and contained accommodations for twenty-eight pupils. Included in the building were toilet rooms, coat rooms, a vestibule, a fuel room, and an alcove containing a heater. The most modern equipment was installed. Lighting, heating, and ventilating facilities, adjustable seats, blackboards, window shades, drinking fountain, toilets, and other features conformed to the recognized standards of proper schoolroom equipment. The tinting of the walls and the selection and hanging of wall pictures added to the attractiveness of the building.

Although the school was so complete and attractive as to make it a center of interest, visitors themselves remarked that there was in its construction and equipment nothing elaborate or prohibitive in cost. . . . Practically any rural community in the state could duplicate it. That it stirred in many rural residents a desire for such a building to replace an antiquated or dilapidated structure was evident from the comments of those who inspected it.[1]

On the grounds of the Eastern States Exposition held at Springfield, Massachusetts, 80 Girl Scouts at one time constructed a pioneer shack, working continuously on it throughout the week. The raw material had been collected from nearby woods, and crude tools had been made by the girls themselves. Model playgrounds at some fairs have served the double purpose of demonstrating playground work and providing a place where children can be entertained while their parents are visiting the fair.

SERVICE TO VISITORS

Another opportunity for social service publicity lies in providing the various conveniences which fair conditions demand. There is the matter of food, for example. Although many of the country people bring lunch with them, eating and drinking are part of the fun and booths where food is sold are patronized at all times of the day. Here is a chance for the organization that has anything to teach about the selection and care of food.

At a few fairs, milk bars have been conducted by one of the agencies interested in encouraging the greater use of milk, or in demonstrating the methods of keeping it clean and cool.

At the Louisiana State Fair, the state supervisor of home economics conducted a demonstration for the purpose of promoting and introducing hot lunches in the schools throughout the state. A well-screened, sanitary kitchen was fully equipped through the courtesy of local firms and agencies, and the various home economics departments carried on practical demonstrations in preparing hot lunches such as might be served in any high school. These lunches were served each day to many visitors attending the fair. The kitchen was open throughout the day.

[1] Bulletin to the Schools. University of the State of New York, Albany, vol. 11, Oct. 1, 1924, p. 20.

The control of the conditions under which food and drinks are served at fairs is usually a function of the state department of health, or the department of agriculture. While more or less strict supervision is attempted, the lack of running water and adequate means of heating it so that dishes and utensils can be properly washed, and the general custom of having the food in sight, make it hard to enforce rules for cleanliness.

The Department of Agriculture in Massachusetts has aimed to arouse concessionaires at fairs to live up to its standards by awarding a certificate of merit to approved establishments.

In Wisconsin the State Health Department has required that fair officials provide all food stands with covered containers for garbage and have them emptied at least once a day. Foodstuffs must be covered with cheese cloth, and owners of stands have been trained to appreciate the value of clean white oilcloth covering for the stand and of having neat attendants.

These practical regulations and demonstrations would seem to offer a far more effective method of instilling a desire for clean handling of food than the old system of displaying placards about clean food on the walls of a health booth while dirty food is being sold without protest in a booth across the way.

Various other services may be offered. They are well described in an exhibit manual[1] formerly issued by the American Red Cross for its local chapters:

The Red Cross County Fair Exhibit should first of all *give service to the visitor*. Even if there can be no regular exhibit, a service done for the Fair visitor will be an excellent exposition of Red Cross work. A chapter making an exhibit should be ready to give one, at least, of the following services:

1. First Aid Station. A First Aid Kit with a Red Cross nurse in constant attendance and arrangements made to get a doctor quickly. Such service is expected of the Red Cross and will mean much.

2. Rest Room. The smallest booth can have a few chairs for tired women to sit on.

3. Kiddie Koop. A place where small children will be taken care of. Admit only well children.

4. Information and Lost Articles. Very little booth space is needed to care for lost and found articles—a sign with a red cross on it and the

[1] Out of print.

words "Information—Red Cross Lost and Found Service," and a willing worker are all that are needed. Bundles could be checked also.

5. Weighing and Measuring Children. Arrangements made, if possible, to give the children their weight and height on a tag.

6. Free Ice Water for Thirsty People. Individual cups can be supplied by having squares of paper folded by the user.

The opportunity for education afforded by conducting a rest room for mothers with children lies in making the place really restful, unobtrusively caring for the baby in the right way, providing sanitary toys for the children, perhaps displaying a few attractive posters, not too "preachy," for the mothers to glance at, and in informally getting acquainted with the women. It has been the experience of some agencies that "teaching" in their rest tents made these places unpopular. Possibly it was not well done, or there may have been too much of it.

OVERCROWDED EXHIBITS

The principles of planning fair exhibits are the same as those for exhibits at expositions.[1] Many social work exhibitors make the mistake of attempting to show too much. A typical display is described below:

> The walls were covered with educational panels relative to the subjects of public health nursing, the state sanatorium, the Modern Health Crusade, the Open Air School, and some of the original health posters made by the school children last year in the state-wide health poster contest.
>
> The other features of the exhibit were a cot, a robe, and blanket from the Open Air School, crocheted articles made by the patients, a miniature of one of the pavilions at the Hospital, a large map showing the forces combating tuberculosis throughout the state, a case containing all the food substances found in one gallon of milk, a shadow box for reproducing X-Ray plates, and a microscope with slides showing the tubercle bacilli. . . .
>
> Samples of the various pamphlets to be obtained from the Association were displayed, and everyone interested in receiving these were asked to sign name and address.

The usual explanation offered in justification for displaying such a medley of ill-assorted objects is that they make an impressive

[1] See pp. 299–303.

showing, and that among so many objects there are sure to be some which will attract each one of a number of persons with varied tastes. This explanation overlooks the fact that people at fairs do not go to much trouble to find for themselves, or make known to attendants what interests them. Indeed, the bewildering effect of such an array of unrelated material without doubt deters many people who glance at the exhibit from giving it further attention.

PERSONAL CONTACT

Some exhibitors believe that it does not matter that streams of people pass the booth without stopping. They plan their exhibits purposely to appeal to the few rather than to the crowd. The booth is furnished comfortably as a conference room, with chairs, tables for the display of pamphlets, and a few posters decorating the walls. A trained attendant encourages those passersby who appear at all interested to take some of the printed matter or to talk over personal or community problems.

New acquaintances are made and old acquaintances are brought into friendlier relations with the exhibiting organization through chance contacts made at the fair. A farmer and his wife who had seemed unapproachable may be invited into the booth and given a better understanding of the organization's work.

Some of the county tuberculosis workers utilize the acquaintanceship made at the fair to secure new neighborhood leaders for the annual Christmas Seal Sale, which must be planned not many weeks after the close of the fair. One worker reported that a personal conversation with a school superintendent at a fair had interested him for the first time in the work of the organization.

County hospital appropriations have been advanced by representatives talking to influential people in the friendly atmosphere of the fair.

SOUVENIRS

Everyone expects to take something home from a fair. Souvenirs and free samples of foods or novel kinds of printed matter are distributed in great abundance, and trinkets of all kinds sold at small prices. The exhibitor who wants to be remembered will do well to provide a distinctive kind of souvenir which has inscribed on it, or in itself expresses, the idea he wants to impress on the minds of the visitors.

Printed matter in novel forms[1] is likely to be kept. A bright idea which combined an important lesson with a toy to take home was carried out by a county health department in Georgia a few years ago.

Birth registration was brought to the attention of parents by an exhibit which contained a small doll for each baby born in the county during the year. Each doll was marked with the name of the baby and exact date of birth. There were 400 dolls in the exhibit, one for each registered birth, and the parents who visited the booth were presented with the dolls. In case a notice of birth had not been filed for a baby and in consequence there was no doll for it, the nurse in attendance immediately made out a certificate and a doll was provided.

Preparation for Taking Part in a Fair

Exhibiting at the fair requires space, ideas, display material and personnel. What resources has the social agency for obtaining these things?

Some fairs have a group of spacious permanent buildings with numerous smaller structures and abundance of space for the erection of tents and for the movement of crowds. Other fairs have no more than a small group of tents. Some of the county or local fairs are as well equipped as some of the state fairs.

The space available to the social exhibitor ranges from a booth of 10 by 12 or 14 feet, to extensive space in a main building, a separate tent or building, or even a group of large tents. The Illinois State Department of Health has permanently assigned to it a long gallery. Here suitable rooms and booths for its baby contest and its graphic devices were erected. A group of health and welfare agencies in Minnesota use a large building for joint participation and are able to plan their display with some uniformity.

On the other hand, at some fairs, the exhibitors have been assigned an unsatisfactory place in a part of the grounds or a part of a building to which it is most difficult to attract visitors; sometimes they have neglected to secure booths until the desirable

[1] See pp. 146–147.

locations have been taken by others. If the social exhibitor makes a good exhibit plan and knows how much space it requires, he is in a better position to obtain suitable quarters than if he asks for space first and delays planning the exhibit until it is secured.

There is a great demand on the part of social agencies for actual ready-to-use exhibit material. Letters and telegrams pour into the national and state offices during the fair season asking for something to show at the fair. These requests are, for the most part, vague, partly because the applicant does not know what is to be had, and partly, also, because he does not know what he wants.

Very little material suitable for fairs is, as a rule, available. When the fair season sets in, such heterogeneous material as is on hand is lent to local people. The central agency is also called upon to furnish printed matter and here again whatever is on hand is sent along. Frequently the available stock of films and slides is drawn upon without regard to its fitness to the occasion or to its physical condition. Recently, however, several state health departments report that they have scrapped the old panels, charts, and models which they used to send out to fairs, as they consider them no longer suitable. One state tuberculosis association has met requests by preparing a special exhibit for each case, designing it to meet local conditions or to utilize local information.

The Health Fortune Teller, described on page 282, was arranged because of the many requests for new ideas, and it received a very cordial welcome. A detailed description of the plan was widely distributed, and a number of local fairs in New York and other states used the idea with some variations and, indeed, some improvements. Ideas are often more helpful than material since they can be adapted more easily to local needs.

Clowns and other entertainers who may be engaged for a day or a week were for a time supplied by several of the national and state organizations and were usually kept busy throughout the fair season. Punch and Judy shows and marionette theaters have also been lent or sold by a few states to local branches. As yet, however, very little has been done in orginating ideas which take account of fair conditions and of the limited resources of the local worker. It would seem that here is a wide field of usefulness for state and national organizations.

Summary

It appears then that if a social agency can enter into the spirit of the occasion, it will find in state and county fairs an excellent medium of publicity. We have seen that visitors are attracted by entertainment; instruction of a very practical nature, especially that which helps to solve everyday problems in the home; competitive displays or awards for participation in contests; conveniences that add to the pleasure and comfort of the day's outing; and something to take home as a souvenir of the occasion.

Many forms of social work do not lend themselves to exhibiting on these terms. Under such circumstances, it may be well for the social agency not to try to present its information at the fair. On the other hand, its leaders may content themselves with the attention of a few of the more thoughtful visitors. For the crowd, one must provide life and color.

CHAPTER XVII

EXPOSITIONS[1]

THE term "exposition" brings to mind the picture of a large hall, frequently an armory, with long rows of booths in which exhibits or demonstrations are presented, and with throngs of people moving up and down the aisles. Elaborate and sometimes very beautiful decorations give impressiveness to the scene. A band plays in a balcony. In a separate hall a program of motion pictures, talks, and special features is carried on throughout the afternoons and evenings of the week or ten days of the event.

The exposition is an affair of the city rather than of the country. There are three main types with which social agencies are concerned: first, the commercial exposition—often a food or an industrial show, in which some unsold space is offered to a few agencies. Second, the combined social welfare and commercial enterprise, in which the cost is covered by the proceeds derived from selling space to commercial exhibitors, the social agencies contributing as their part the asset of public confidence and goodwill. Many health expositions, milk shows, and some safety expositions are of this type. Third, the entirely non-commercial undertaking. This type includes among others child welfare exhibitions, and some civic and housing expositions.

Practically every city social agency is asked at some time either to exhibit in an exposition or to join in sponsoring one. When free space is offered, the invitation is especially alluring because it seems to promise the opportunity of reaching large numbers of persons at moderate expense. But the ultimate cost of an exhibit is not always low, planning and preparation take the time of staff members, and at least one worker should be present continuously during the exposition. Moreover, the particular exposition in which space is offered may or may not draw the kind of people

---

[1] For a more detailed discussion of expositions, or exhibitions, see Routzahn, Evart G., and Routzahn, Mary Swain, The A B C of Exhibit Planning. Russell Sage Foundation, New York, 1918.

the agency wishes to reach, and may or may not offer advantageous conditions for exhibiting.

The prospective exhibitor should know before taking space whether or not the exposition in question is a sound enterprise conducted under responsible management. He should consider whether or not the exhibit promises as good results as other forms of publicity into which he might put the same amount of time and money. Those who are asked to launch or to sponsor an exposition should know something of what an enterprise of this sort is worth educationally, how much of an undertaking it will be, whether it is timely, and how it should be promoted and managed. These questions are discussed in this chapter.

Competition among Exhibitors for Attention

In theory, and to some extent in fact, the hundred or more exhibitors in an exposition are working together to make the strongest possible impression in regard to a given subject within a certain limit of time. Actually, in most expositions, however, each is competing with all the others for attention for his particular exhibit, and all are competing with a band concert and a program of plays, speeches, and other forms of entertainment designed to attract as many people as possible. The success of each exhibitor depends on his ability to induce people not only to stop at his booth but to remain there long enough to understand his show and to carry away from it a definite and lasting impression. In this competition the advantage goes to those who have planned their exhibits with an understanding of the characteristic behavior of crowds at an affair of this kind.

What People Notice at Expositions

Visitors at an exposition generally move slowly along the aisles glancing at each booth as they pass, but stopping only when they are especially attracted by something, or when other people appear to be interested, and remaining only if what they find makes an immediate appeal. It is, therefore, of first importance to the exhibitor to know what methods of display are successful in attracting and holding attention.

At a visit to a large health exposition, the writers made several tours of the hall at different hours of the day and evening for the purpose of finding out through observation and inquiry what types of exhibits the visitors preferred. The attendance was good and the crowd represented most of the elements in the community, including parents of school children, members and supporters of all kinds of civic and welfare movements, and the varied types of people who respond to generous newspaper publicity and advertising. The impressions gathered there regarding the most successful kinds of exhibits agree very well with those formed at other expositions and with those of other observers.

In a first tour of the hall, stopping only where knots of a dozen or more people were gathered, eight exhibits were visited. The first stop was in front of a booth where members of the police force were engaged in a wrestling match as a demonstration of the physical work by means of which they kept fit. A bystander said this exhibit was "the best of the whole show." The next crowd was found before a pigpen containing on one side of a partition several fat and husky pigs and on the other some that were puny. The attendant explained that all were the same age, but the fat pigs had been fed milk while the thin ones had not. After passing a dozen sparsely attended booths, we came to one where a shifting but always large group were listening to a social hygiene talk. The talk continued much longer than any one visitor would remain, but the speaker never failed to attract and hold a part of the stream of passersby. Continuing one fourth of the way around the hall, we found few exhibits with more than one or two visitors, but in front of a small projection machine as many as could crowd into the space were looking at a motion picture. Exhibitors in neighboring booths said that people sometimes remained here fully ten minutes. Apparently the most popular booths of all were two sections of an extensive school exhibit. In one a child was playing a xylophone. In the other a circle of kindergarten children were listening to a story, and although the group around the railing could not hear the story-teller's words the absorption of the youngsters, who paid no attention to visitors, was in itself a matter of interest. An exhibit which drew many women was the dressmaking department of a trade school. Here girls were cutting out garments without a pattern and fitting them on a figure. The work was done so rapidly that it did not take long to see the material transformed into the roughly finished product, a dress or an apron. The final stopping point was with a group collected before a shoe manufacturer's exhibit, where a young woman wearing the advertised shoes walked about on a stage with a curtain lowered so as to reveal only her feet and ankles.

A second tour of the hall at another session showed that popularity was extended to other centers of interest. The guessing contest of a life insurance company was at this time a great attraction; a clever device called Healthland, which had had no visitors on the first trip, was now being explained by a guide to an attentive group; in a dental booth, although the displays were not distinctive, an interested audience listened to a dentist talking about the care of the teeth. At none of these exhibits had there been anything going on during our first visit. The exhibit material had been there, but by itself had failed to hold attention.

At other exhibits people paused a moment without remaining long enough so that more than three or four were gathered at the same time. One of these displays was a mechanical model of a child drinking milk, in which the milk was actually poured into a glass and to all appearances the doll figure drank it. It required but a few seconds to read the rhymed caption which told how much she liked to drink milk. An illuminated model of a children's cottage home, like a miniature city at night, was attractive to look at, and the simple message of the attendant—"These three buildings are already in use, the rest are the ones we hope to build"—required but a moment to grasp. A reproduction of two butcher shops—one dirty and rat-ridden, the other clean and sanitary—told its story at a glance, while a single sentence repeated by the attendant to each new group of visitors went straight to the point—"Think it over, folks; think it over. In which kind of shop do you want to buy meat?"

These and other displays receiving the greatest amount of attention had one point in common, activity or movement, and in most of them people were talking or doing something.

Ingenious mechanical devices had great value in catching the eye, but it was noticeable that their power to hold attention was weakened because they were so numerous. When mechanical movement was in competition with a fluent speaker or a demonstration, the larger crowd was always with the latter.

IMPORTANCE OF THE ATTENDANT

The preference for personal explanation is easily accounted for by the fact that exhibits are seldom self-explanatory, or if they are, understanding them requires greater mental effort than can be expected under the crowded and bewildering conditions of the exposition. One display showed a beautifully made model of a group of buildings surrounding a plot of real grass on which stood cleverly painted cut-out figures of people. There were no captions and the attendant seemed too shy to talk. Consequently most visitors saw only the attractiveness of the scene and after admiring it would move on no wiser than they were before. Those who were curious enough to ask questions, however, learned that the exhibit pictured the progress of a young man and a girl from high school, through the public health training course, and on to the field of public health work in a rural district.

A safety exhibit showed a room with an unguarded fireplace, matches, and bottles of dangerous fluids on tables and shelves too near the floor, and other conditions which made it easy for children to injure themselves. To those familiar with safety work or those who would stop to study the exhibit, it was a convincing warning against a familiar situation, but at none of our visits was there an attendant to explain and we did not see anyone looking at the exhibit more than casually. We were told, however, that at times an excellent talker was present and that on these occasions there was a good audience.

What seemed to count most as a qualification of the attendant was that he should be alert and enthusiastic, quick to catch the attention of passersby, and capable either of holding it himself by a short talk or of turning it to the objects displayed. Some of the exhibits required a three minute talk, dramatic or lightly humorous in character; for others a straightforward explanation seemed to serve. Where good captions were supplied, the attendant needed only to use a pointer and to read the captions aloud, thus helping visitors to follow the development of the subject in the order intended.

The importance of the attendant is frequently overlooked by exhibitors. Summing up his impressions of an exposition put on, as so many are, by agencies without previous experience, a social worker actively interested in the results made the following criticism:

> Our exhibitors practiced little of the art of explaining their material to visitors. They set it up and let it stand, which meant that the public drifted through the aisles, noticing large patches of color and devices in motion, and taking in about as much as a stranger gets from a glance through the spinning room of a cotton mill.

Often the failure of the attendant to explain the exhibit of which he has charge is due to diffidence in accosting strangers—a fear of rebuff, a lack of confidence. This can sometimes be overcome if attendants are carefully trained. As far as possible, persons who are naturally easy speakers should be chosen. But it is even more important that they should thoroughly understand the subject of the exhibit. Some qualified person in the organization to be represented should help attendants to prepare their talk, coach them in giving it, and if possible should be with them during the first day at the exposition. After that, they will find, as timid canvassers have found in their somewhat similar task, that disagreeable experiences are rare and that there may be a satisfying sense of accomplishment in presenting information in an interesting and intelligible fashion.

In the Healthland exhibit already referred to the guides were normal school students. They were instructed as part of their practice in teaching to work out a means of interesting visitors in the display, to keep a record of the relative amount of interest displayed by children and grown people, and to distribute no material unless it was asked for.

GETTING IDEAS ACROSS

If the purpose of an exposition were only to amuse the crowd, it would be enough to know what sort of displays held attention. But the intention of the school exhibit was not that visitors should enjoy hearing a child play a xylophone or the sole aim of the life insurance company to have people enter its guessing contest.

Presumably, each exhibitor has a definite reason for entering an exposition. The merchant, of course, would like to sell his goods. The social exhibitor wants to give out practical information which visitors will act upon in the future, or to create an understanding of the organization he represents and the ideas and ideals it stands for.

The exhibitor cannot expect visitors to get anything but a hazy impression from his display unless he himself has a clear purpose in mind. The contrasting clean and dirty shops definitely warned visitors to trade in sanitary shops. The mechanical doll drinking milk invited everyone to follow her example. An exhibit of equipment needed for home treatment of tuberculosis was of practical help to those who had that problem to face. On the other hand, the mere display of rugs, pottery, and other handiwork from a state prison must have caused visitors to wonder vaguely if the objects were for sale, or were to be admired for the skill displayed in their making, or to show the kind of training given.

The Connecticut State Hospital once exhibited examples of the handiwork of patients with a record card attached to each object. From the card visitors learned the mental condition of the patient, his special aptitude, previous occupation, and the results sought in having him do the work. Thus the display gained an educational significance entirely lacking in the collection from the state prison.

One exhibit excellently designed from the standpoint of attention value illustrates the failure of the exhibitor to make clear what he wished the visitors to think or do because of seeing the display. Prepared by the department of vital statistics of a state department of health, it included two high arches, one carrying birth figures for a given year, listed by counties, the other death figures for the same year similarly listed. A flashing light in the keystone of each arch indicated the frequency of births and deaths. On a table were some volumes giving the registration of all births within a certain number of years, and nearby stood a large machine used for punching and sorting record cards. The designer had used ingenuity and careful work in putting facts and methods into graphic form, but evidently had not considered their significance or lack of it for visitors. The punching machine, especially, must

(Designed and Photographed by Paul Parker)

SCENES REPRODUCED IN MINIATURE MODELS

Models made by enlarging and cutting out photographs and placing them in relief against a painted or photographed background.

Above: This scene shows the Pennsylvania Sanatorium for Tuberculosis.

Below: This model of an interior shows the work of the Visiting Nurse Service of the Henry Street Settlement.

have been mysterious and meaningless to most of them. The simple though novel scheme for interesting parents in birth registration described on page 291 was more appropriate.

Ideas are sometimes obscured in the intricacies of an analogy worked into the form of a mechanical model. An exhibit of this sort showed the unloading of two railway cars, one of gloomy black arriving from "Dark Valley," the other of hopeful green coming from "Sunny Mountain." The packages of freight labeled as good and bad health habits were supposed to make the suggestions the organization wished to convey. A miniature football game, set up by another exhibitor, called the players on the winning side by such names as "Clean Living," "Right Knowledge," and "Strong Patience," while among the losers were "Rough Surroundings," "Bud Worry," and "Bull Indifference." The score board showed statistics of death and disease. Such devices seem to be too elaborate and pedantic to have much teaching value. A simpler exhibit with a less complex analogy was a mechanical model, displayed by the Minnesota Public Health Association at a state fair exhibit, that showed figures of persons moving along two paths, one leading to "Health," the other to "Illness." The tales of their adventures, printed on milestones and guide posts, pointed out health lessons in an entertaining and understandable way.

In criticizing a lack of apparent and clear-cut purpose in some exhibits, due allowance must be made for the fact that agencies sometimes take space at expositions only because of the desire of some of their members to be represented or at the urgent request of the exposition leaders. Many organizations are concerned with matters too technical or too remote to be of interest to the miscellaneous crowd which gathers at expositions. This is especially true of national organizations which exist primarily to serve their local branches or constituent bodies and have little to say direct to the general public. The results of their attempts to exhibit are usually perfunctory, uninteresting displays which add nothing to the exposition and might better be omitted.

A motive not uncommon among exhibitors is to make the organization better known. With this end in view it is natural to try to present as complete a picture as possible of its aims, methods, and achievements. Thus a federation or council of social agencies, in an effort to express the concentration and economy that is effected by co-ordination, sets up a beneficent, symbolic figure from whose hands extend ribbons, each leading to a placard giving the name and purpose of a member agency. This device means little to anyone not acquainted with modern social service methods. Probably the casual visitor has a hazy impression that the central figure represents the spirit of charity pervading all the organizations named on the placards.

Indeed, it seems doubtful whether an exposition display can express any but the most easily understood forms of social work. A day nursery can be exhibited satisfactorily because its rooms and its activities can be reproduced. A boys' class in manual work or a department of food inspection can demonstrate methods or show results. Family welfare societies, on the other hand, have seldom succeeded in preparing successful exhibits because their most important services, the steps in helping a crippled father learn a new trade whereby he can support his family, for instance, are difficult to illustrate in concrete forms nor can they be put briefly into words. The best that can be done under these conditions is to exhibit some one phase of the work which has aspects familiar to visitors. A federation of social agencies perhaps has an information service and can explain its usefulness to the public; a family welfare society may tell visitors where to send people in need who apply to them for help.

A cleverly constructed model to demonstrate public health nursing service was shown at a health exposition in Newark, New Jersey:

> The Child Hygiene Division of the Department of Health displayed a painted street scene made from photographs taken in the districts where much of its work was done. This composite street, four feet high by twenty feet long, was placed on a table behind a rail so that the interiors showing the work of the child hygiene nurses in the home were about at eye-level. The painted interiors were concealed by the fronts of the houses.
>
> "This is the home of a little Italian bride," the explainer would say, opening the front of the upper story of a house. "She doesn't speak English and she wants someone who will understand her own language when she is confined. So the Italian midwife who is to care for her

(indicating the figure of the midwife in her gray uniform) belongs to the Midwives' Association and she co-operates with the Department of Health. She has asked the nurse of the Division of Child Hygiene (indicating a figure in blue serge uniform) to visit the home with her and they are arranging to go to the city's pre-natal clinic, where a specially trained doctor will make an examination. All New Jersey midwives are supervised and the careful ones are proud to belong to the Association."[1]

In the same way other interiors showed pre-natal clinics, baby keep-well stations, convalescent homes for nursing mothers, and so forth.

Displays excellently conceived and ingeniously designed often fail through some minor fault to bring out the intended idea. Perhaps an explanatory caption has been omitted, poorly placed or designed, or some slight defect in mechanism prevents a model from working effectively.

An example of defective mechanism was found in a ferris wheel in continuous motion. As the wheel revolved, a succession of baskets appeared, each containing an object above which was a label. Unfortunately, however, the wheel was geared so high that one could hardly read the quickly disappearing labels, and the contents of the baskets were indistinguishably blurred.

Giving Away Printed Matter

Printed matter, which exhibitors have on hand for free distribution, contributes little unless it is plainly connected with the exhibit idea and material. Yet many attendants make no attempt to form any association in the mind of a visitor between what he sees and hears, and the printed information he carries away with him. Literature is left lying around for visitors to take or leave, as they will, or it is handed out without comment and often in a manner which invites the recipient to move on. An enormous amount is wasted. At one exposition, without attempting either to collect or to escape from receiving printed matter, the writers obtained 40 pieces, nine of which, through the carelessness of distributors proved to be duplicates.

[1] Boothe, Stella, "The County Fair Health Exhibit." *In* Trained Nurse and Hospital Review, New York, vol. 73, Aug., 1924, pp. 134–135.

303

Some exhibitors, after experience in several expositions, have decided that it is wasteful to give out reading matter at all unless they can succeed in stimulating a desire for it. This is largely the concern of the attendant. Having done his duty as showman, he can call attention to the literature, giving any explanation that seems necessary or answering any questions that may be asked about it. The contents of the literature should repeat or supplement the information given at the exhibit and it is desirable that visitors should be influenced not only to take it but also to want to read it.

Influence of Conditions on Visitors' Impressions

Although the individual exhibitor may put into his display all that is needed to attract and hold attention and may supplement his carefully selected material and his good design and execution with a fluent, interesting explainer, he may still be handicapped in his effort to make a lasting impression on visitors by conditions at the exposition. The wealth and variety of ideas tend to confuse a visitor who is presented in rapid succession with a series of unrelated facts expressed in unfamiliar forms, and whose status in relation to these facts is continually shifting according to the purpose of each exhibit. At the booth where articles are sold, he is approached as a prospective buyer; a health display may seem to take for granted that he is uninformed or careless and needs to be taught or admonished; at the booth of some benevolent institution, the appeal is to his public spirit and generosity; a display which shows a condition to be remedied legally, recalls him to his duty as a voter. He has to be continually readjusting his mental attitude. Moreover, when the band is playing, the music will probably claim his attention to the exclusion of everything else, and in the afternoon and evening there is also the program of plays, lectures, motion pictures, or other entertainment to distract his thoughts from the exhibits.

Another source of confusion, especially in a partly social and partly commercial exposition, results from irrelevant and often contradictory appeals. Things interesting in themselves and appropriate elsewhere may be entirely out of keeping with the spirit of the occasion. At one health show, for instance, tombstones were exhibited! At another so-called health exposition where children were reported as "hanging on one another's shoulders in fascinated groups before the various exhibits," the bureau of police was represented by an assortment of ash cans and milk cans made into stills, and a display of guns and jimmies.

Soft drinks, evening gowns, and talking machines are among the things which have been displayed at health expositions. The xylophone music and the children's story group mentioned in the beginning of the chapter had no relation to health, and the dress-making exhibit only a remote connection. The claims of floor coverings, vacuum cleaners, bathroom fixtures, and washing machines to a relationship with health are not wholly unreasonable, although in many cases exhibitors of these wares made no effort to bring out the connection. Occasionally, unless exhibits are censored and supervised by fully qualified persons, participating agencies may find their teachings opposed by commercial concerns, whose trained salesmen acting as explainers are usually more persuasive than the representatives of the agencies.

Possibility of Co-operation among Exhibitors

Each exhibitor may get more out of the exposition than he individually puts into his own show if the whole project is made a co-operative effort instead of an aggregation of independent displays. It would seem entirely feasible for exhibitors, by uniting, to plan an exposition which will have unity of purpose and will avoid confusion. Let us take, for example, as an exposition theme or as one unit of it, the idea that health is promoted by outdoor exercise. To make this suggestion inviting, commercial exhibitors of garden tools, seeds, sporting goods, camping outfits, correct shoes, and other paraphernalia of outdoor life could unite with organizations interested in physical training, vacant lot gardens, walking clubs, playgrounds, Boy Scouts and Girl Scouts. The aim of each exhibit would be to show how persons in all walks of life could combine exercise with their present mode of living.

Similarly, in a food show exhibitors might join in demonstrating how different foods may be combined in wholesome, varied, and palatable diets adapted to different needs. The exhibitors would include dealers in such wholesome foods as dairy products, vegetables, fruits, and whole wheat products, also those interested in promoting better school lunches, home-making, nutrition classes, food inspection, and kindred projects. A competition might be organized offering a prize for the best group of menus made up from the exhibited products suitable to the needs of overweight or underweight persons, children of a given age, desk workers, or manual laborers.

The exposition with a central theme and unity, both in the selection of material and the forms of display used in separate exhibits, is not altogether new. America's Making, held in New York, had for its subject the contribution made to our civilization by many of the nationalities that have come to our shores. Each exhibit was prepared by a different national group, who displayed only such material as illustrated the contribution to our national life from its particular homeland. The Centenary Celebration Exposition of the Methodist Episcopal Church, held at the state fair grounds of Columbus, Ohio, in the summer of 1919, gained unity through a scheme of settings which reproduced typical scenes in the mission field, and through the common use by many of the exhibitors of the demonstration method which took the form of acting out incidents in the lives of the people.

Social agencies might with profit get away from the exposition which is an aggregation of competing exhibits, and by choosing a central theme work out a plan which will make it as easy as possible for visitors to grasp its significance.

DESIGNING THE EXPOSITION AND THE EXHIBITS

Many expositions, large and small, have had artistic settings, appropriately designed, which contributed much to the public interest in the event. The Panama Pacific Exposition at San Francisco, for example, is remembered for the beauty of the lighting of the buildings, and the grounds. Seldom, however, has any designer been called upon to make a plan that carried over into the actual exhibits. The artistic, dramatic, and educational elements of an exposition should be harmoniously combined. This can only be done when someone with imagination and a vivid conception of the possibilities of the theme prepares a plan which includes decoration, settings, and methods of interpreting

306

the ideas and facts to be presented. The Centenary Celebration
of the Methodist Episcopal Church and America's Making are
examples of expositions in which a central theme was developed
consistently throughout settings and exhibits.

When the exposition is an aggregation of independent units,
each exhibitor, within certain limitations, designs his own display. The manager is usually a good promoter or business executive, but not a designer or an educator. He may give exhibitors a
little advice but, as a rule, he appears to assume that they are
amply qualified to plan displays themselves. Practically all social
organizations, however, are inexperienced in this work. They
take part in expositions only at long intervals and usually some
staff member, whether he has any ability for it or not, is assigned to
do the work because he can spare the time better than anyone else.

A planner and designer with imagination to conceive attractive
and easily understood forms of display, and with enough knowledge
of the exposition topic to advise the exhibitors regarding what can
best be expressed in exhibit form, is the first requisite of a good exposition. There have been, here and there, a few persons who
have specialized in designing exhibits but the demand is not large
enough to encourage them to keep at it.

Until expert designers are available, a step in the right direction would be the addition to the directing staff of a consultant,
who would help the exhibitors to visualize their aims and their
audience and to see how their ideas can be expressed best in graphic
form. The management of the Cincinnati Health Exposition
provided this service to a degree through a special committee on
educational exhibits. The exhibitors were informed in advance
of the plan and the standards set for the exposition and were told
emphatically that exhibits consisting of posters alone would not
be accepted and that each exhibit must contain some unique and
interesting feature. Each exhibitor was asked to submit to the
committee first a preliminary plan, and later a final one, both of
which were fully discussed. Many plans originally lacking in interest were improved considerably after the exhibitors had discussed
them with the committee. Results showed, however, that a need
still remained for trained direction in design.

METHODS OF INCREASING ATTENDANCE

Gain from participation in the exposition depends on how many persons come, who they are, and how the attendance is distributed over the hours of the day and the days of the week. Overcrowding looks like success, but the individual exhibitor loses more than he gains by it. He wants as many to come as can see his exhibit to advantage, but a selected audience made up of persons who will be likely to buy his goods or to adopt his ideas is more important to him than a miscellaneous crowd. Visitors themselves are impressed by crowds and are eager to see what others are looking at; but, on the other hand, if too many are present at the same time, they are greatly hampered in moving along the aisles and in getting a view of the exhibits.

The methods used in advertising an exposition may be evaluated then not only by the number of persons drawn to the show, but also by their success in spreading the attendance over the week to avoid congestion, in bringing out those for whom the exposition is intended, and in extending the educational work through getting the theme of the exposition talked about before, during, and after the event.

The first newspaper publicity that an exposition receives is an item stating that such an affair is contemplated. This appears months, or perhaps a year, in advance of the opening. As the plans progress, everything that may be of interest to the public is supplied to the newspapers, including reports of the extent and progress of the scheme, the names of prominent people and organizations acting as sponsors or taking part, and stories of the purpose of the exposition and the character and aims of participating agencies. In Cincinnati stories of a large exposition held in October appeared in the local papers almost daily from the middle of the preceding June, and the week before the opening paid newspaper space was used generously. A New York health exposition furnished some lively advance news through contests which had their climax at the exposition. The most striking was a reducing competition entered into by 50 stout women under the direction of the Department of Health. The newspapers reported the varying weights of the contestants, printed their menus, described and illustrated their exercises, and quoted from advice given them by the supervising health officer. At the same exposition considerable publicity was secured through the participation of some of the newspapers as exhibitors, each displaying the work of one of its departments and using not only this particular department but its news columns as well to promote the exposition. One newspaper showed its life extension work, another its outdoor life department, and a third conducted a baby contest.

While the exposition is in progress it can supply news from the program, the exhibitors, the stunts, and the visitors. In Boston the Evening Transcript on the opening day of the Health Exposition of 1923 brought out a special Health Show Section with articles about the Exposition, popular scientific and historical papers on various phases of medicine and hygiene, messages from prominent citizens, and many illustrations.

There is perhaps no other type of exposition news so obviously ready at hand and so sure of acceptance as a program including noted speakers and distinguished musical or dramatic performances. We have pointed out, however, that the program by drawing persons away from the exhibits, may actually lower the educational value of the exposition as a whole. It might be well, therefore, to consider whether it cannot be omitted and some other way found to take its place as a source of news.

One alternative would be the use of news-creating devices in connection with the exhibits themselves, thus playing up the attractions of the exhibition instead of placing other features in competition with them. The announcement that prominent people will visit certain booths on special days is likely to draw reporters as well as visitors. Games and stunts often develop good newspaper stories. Activities suitable for use in connection with exhibits are described in Chapter XV, Dramatic Methods and also in Chapter XVI, Fairs.

Special visiting days assigned to certain organizations or to selected districts or nearby towns serve to bring out people seldom, if ever, reached through other forms of popular education, as well as many busy persons—leaders in the political, business, labor, and social worlds—who might otherwise postpone coming until they fail to come at all. Advertising is done in advance for the purpose of interesting these groups and plans are made for giving them special entertainment and representation on the program of the day. This method helps also to distribute the attendance over the week, thus preventing congestion during the last days of the exposition.

The advance sale or free distribution of tickets is another method of getting large and selected audiences. In the Cincinnati Health Exposition, 25,000 tickets were sold before it opened. Many of these were bought in quantity lots by employers for distribution among their employes. The Associated Charities distributed 500 tickets to its clients. A generous attendance of parents was assured by the distribution to school children of free tickets, each good for one admission if the child was accompanied by an adult who purchased a ticket. This plan not only increased the sale of tickets to adults but largely eliminated the difficulty of having crowds of unattended children blocking the aisles and clamoring for souvenirs.

At one exposition in order to reach people who might want to attend but would hesitate to spend 25 cents, tickets made up in lots of 500 were sold in advance to large business houses at a special rate of 15 cents.

Continued Publicity Needed. Inexperienced exposition leaders are likely to overestimate the effectiveness of their publicity work and to slacken their efforts at the time when it is most important to keep the event before the public. Being themselves in touch with all the publicity sent out and hearing many of their friends and acquaintances talking about the exposition, they think that everybody is interested and is planning to attend. Personal contacts like these, however, number only a few hundred persons at most, while a large attendance is measured in thousands. Again, many people may be aware of an exposition without feeling a definite desire to visit it. Publicity and promotion efforts need to continue until the closing day.

ADMINISTRATION

The standards maintained for the exposition depend in the last analysis on the executive committee or other responsible leaders of the enterprise. Whether or not things are done and said which they would not endorse as individuals depends largely on whether or not the leaders take their responsibility seriously. Unless they give time and thought to the project, they cannot sponsor it without incurring the risk of backing something that may be in actual opposition to much of the teaching which they wish to have brought before the community.

Organization of Local Forces. Any plan should recognize the importance of local initiative, local hard work, and reasonable time allowance for preparation. If the local workers put but few of their own ideas and little effort into the affair, they will not take a lively interest in it, for interest goes with participation, and the follow-up work, which is necessary if the exposition is to amount to anything more than a flash in the pan, is pretty sure to be neglected.

The usefulness of local workers depends upon good committee organization. The best results will be secured if there are enough committees so that none will be assigned too many tasks and if all are given as definite instructions as possible regarding what is expected of them and the method of going about it. There is something for everybody to do, for those with artistic, dramatic, or administrative talent, and for those with no special gifts. Volunteers, working under direction, may gather information, take photographs, draw sketches, make models and mechanical devices, distribute literature, act as attendants, organize co-operating committees, or help with clerical tasks.

To simplify the work of organization it is helpful to make a card catalog of "useful people,"[1] listing the address, telephone number, and special abilities of each person. From this catalog a committee on committees makes up the assignments.

The Cincinnati Health Exposition, already referred to, was run with a very generous use of committees. The boosters' committee, consisting of prominent business men, assisted in the sale of commercial space. A committee on motion pictures secured lists of motion pictures from many sources, obtaining pictures to fit into each program, and examining each picture in advance to be sure that it was suitable and in good physical condition. Service in taking care of the films and in displaying them was obtained

[1] For details, see The A B C of Exhibit Planning. p. 201.

through a motion picture exchange. A committee on advance sale of tickets disposed of 25,000 tickets. A special committee on music, consisting of representatives of the different colleges of music, the director of music in the public schools, and others, supplied a musical program daily. Various contests which furnished effective publicity were carried out by a committee on contests along lines outlined for them in advance.

Besides giving assistance in carrying out the exposition plans, volunteer committees increase public interest in the affair because of the inclusion of so many persons locally well known. Many forms of publicity and promotion which are beyond the reach of a primarily commercial enterprise become possible to a social welfare exposition through the co-operation of numerous committees. Another advantage is that the use of local forces brings together individual workers in different social agencies, many of whom would ordinarily have little contact with one another, and it may also result in better understanding and closer acquaintance between the social agencies and the business people of the community.

Management. An experienced and successful campaign manager can make an important contribution to the exposition on the organizing side. He knows how to select committees, how to put them to work, and how to get the value of widespread participation and individual initiative without slowing up the machinery of operation. With the assistance of an exhibit specialist and a business manager he may be the best person to direct the whole affair.

The business items of exposition management are numerous: handling of financial matters, including sale of space, admissions, contracts and keeping accounts; all arrangements for getting work done in the exposition hall, such as the decoration, setting up booths, lettering titles and signs, the installation and packing of exhibits, service to exhibitors in the way of sign-making, cartage and connections for electricity, steam, gas, and water; arrangements for fire and police protection, and for paid attendants at the hall.

On the business management side there are several groups of commercial organizers and promoters of expositions who may sometimes be called in for a welfare exposition. A few specialize on business shows or food shows or industrial expositions. Others devote themselves to the organization of affairs in which there is a combination of educational with commercial exhibits.

Financing. The method of financing has a distinct influence upon the character of an exposition. When the support comes only through paid admissions, voluntary contributions, and possibly, an appropriation from the city, no entangling alliances are involved and consequently the show may be strictly educational, and, within the limits of the talent and money available, the project may be worked out without restraint. The effort to cover part of the expenses through the sale of space, which is characteristic of the joint educational and commercial affair, tends to create opposition between the need for getting money and the desire to make a success of the educational features. The effort to make a profit through space selling turns the exposition into a commercial enterprise where educational features which receive free space are likely to be subordinated and exhibiting social agencies may have little voice in the management.

Selling space is not easy. In any exposition endorsed or backed by social organizations it is complicated by two limitations: first, the commercial exhibits should have some relation to the subject of the exposition; second, they should not contradict the standards set by the social agencies.

Merchants and manufacturers are often skeptical about the advertising value of expositions. Some of them take space because they find it difficult to refuse, although they may prefer instead to make an outright contribution. The social agency which contemplates going into any exposition scheme where the selling of space is an important item would do well to ascertain in advance the feeling of the local merchants on the subject.

AN EVALUATION OF EXPOSITIONS

A general statement either that an exposition is a waste of effort or, on the other hand, that it is a good thing for social agencies to undertake would be without basis in fact.

On the negative side, it has been pointed out that expositions offer information under distinctly unfavorable conditions, namely, crowding, noise, confusion, the fatigue of long standing, and the presentation of new and unrelated ideas in rapid succession. Again, an individual exhibitor too often fails to select his material wisely and to design and arrange the exhibit so that its meaning can be quickly grasped. Perhaps he has consented to take space in a particular exposition only because he does not wish to be left out, and so puts as little time and money into the exhibit as possible.

The joint commercial and educational enterprise places many difficulties in the way of those who wish to maintain high standards of accuracy and soundness in whatever educational propaganda they sponsor. The lack of development of a suitable technique for designing, promoting, and managing enterprises of this type is still another argument against taking part in them.

It is not always possible to evaluate an exposition by comparing it with other methods of public information. In many instances, although some other form of publicity might be more suitable, no choice between alternative methods takes place. In most cases an invitation to take part in an exhibition presents itself as a definite opportunity about which a decision must be made without delay. Many of those who agree to go into the project would have done very little to inform the public about their work if this occasion for doing so had not been placed in their way.

However, there is more to be said in support of the exposition than this somewhat negative argument that it is better than nothing. At its best, it presents information in an impressive setting. Again, the exhibitor, with his booth on an aisle along which crowds pass, has the same advantage that a merchant seeks in choosing a busy corner for his store. If he has something to say to a large miscellaneous crowd and can say it quickly, here is an unusually good chance. Moreover, as a news-creating event, the exposition provides a wealth of excellent material and continues to be a source of news for a period of months before, during, and after the show itself. Through the large scale on which its publicity work is done, through the picturesqueness of some of its features, and through its very bigness, the exposition reaches people whom it would be difficult, if indeed it would be at all possible, to reach by any other method within the means of the social agency, with the possible exception of the intensive campaign.

Such benefits as have been named are by no means necessary

or even usual accompaniments of expositions, but they are entirely possible of attainment. Future expositions may overcome many of the handicaps which have caused expositions to fail educationally. It should be possible, as has been pointed out, to plan an exposition in which a few impressions are piled up until they take a firm hold on the attention and the memory of visitors.

A question to be raised before undertaking an exposition is whether it will serve the purpose as well as an intensive campaign. The main difference between these two forms of educational publicity is that the exposition brings throngs of people to one spot to see a spectacular presentation, while the intensive campaign reaches out into the neighborhoods and homes where the people are and varies the presentation of its message to meet the interests or degree of education of different sections of the community. The intensive campaign is described in some detail in the part that follows.

PART VI: THE INTENSIVE CAMPAIGN

CHAPTER XVIII

ELEMENTS OF THE CAMPAIGN

THE intensive campaign concentrates into a given number of days, usually a week, the greatest volume and variety of publicity which the campaign organization can achieve. Banners, posters, and exhibits decorate the town; campaign stories and pictures have a prominent place in the daily newspapers; talks are given on the streets, in churches, business houses, and industrial plants; spectacular stunts are carried on wherever crowds pass or are easily gathered. Hundreds and sometimes thousands of workers unite to carry the campaign idea into every household and place of business.

That a method of this kind should have come into use, in cities especially, is not surprising. The complexity of living conditions, the rapid succession of events, and the tremendous competition among those who seek public attention lead to the use of more and more striking and insistent methods of forcing a cause or an idea on people's notice. Campaign leaders aim to make the affair while it lasts the biggest piece of news and the liveliest event in the community, a celebration in which everybody has an interest.

Many intensive campaigns are annual affairs. Some are national in scope, like the sale of Christmas seals of the National Tuberculosis Association, the Red Cross Roll Call, Thrift Week, and Fire Prevention Week. Others, local in character, but similar to these in method, are the community fund campaigns, baby weeks, and safety weeks. Many rather mild spurts in an effort to engage public interest, called intensive campaigns by the agencies undertaking them, are not such in the sense in which the term is used here. What marks the intensive campaign as a distinct form of publicity is its conspicuousness as a community-wide event.

The word "drive," which is sometimes applied to a money-raising campaign, suggests a machine-like force operating ruthlessly to obtain subscriptions through means quite apart from convincing givers that the cause is a good one. The business man approached by an associate or a customer often subscribes in order to gain, or at least not to lose, his goodwill. The employe, asked to contribute, sometimes feels that his job may be at stake if he fails to do so. The more effectively a drive of this kind is organized and the more pressure that is brought to bear on individuals, the less important is public information, since results do not depend upon understanding, but upon the skill with which resistance is overcome.

On the other hand, an intensive publicity campaign, if rightly conducted, centers the force of its drive on compelling public attention, so that no one can fail to be aware of conditions to be corrected, for instance, the overcrowding in hospitals and the need for a new one, or the number of children killed playing in the public streets, and the need to vote "Yes" on a playground referendum. Such a campaign may employ dramatic methods for awakening enthusiasm and follow them with an efficiently organized canvass to collect subscriptions or to get people to go to the polls, but it does not include any efforts to compel them to act through fear or to persuade them through strong emotional appeals which blind their judgment.

Conditions Necessary for Undertaking a Campaign

The decision to undertake a campaign should be based on an assurance that there is a need for it and that it has a fair chance to succeed. A canvass of the situation to determine these points includes a discussion of the series of questions which follow. The answers are dependent on local conditions but their consideration is important for national organizations as well as for local agencies, since, in ignorance of them, the national organization may lead its branches into ill-advised undertakings.

Is the Cause of General Interest? The first condition to be recognized is that the campaign must center about some cause or reform in which the majority of people in the territory covered are personally concerned, or must propose some action which they can easily perform. Reducing the number of street accidents is the concern of everyone who walks or who drives a car. The Red Cross Roll Call, with its dollar memberships, and a community fund campaign, which welcomes even the smallest contributions, are matters in which the whole community can share. A vaccination campaign combines something definite for everyone to do with important results for the whole community to be achieved by their doing it. Destructive fires are misfortunes from which anyone may suffer, so the fire prevention slogan, "It Might Be You," applies to everybody. It is the responsibility of every voter to pass upon the proposals and measures placed upon the ballots on election day. On the other hand, legislative action which is only indirectly the problem of the individual voter is difficult to promote through an intensive campaign. So also are those undertakings intended to benefit directly a comparatively small group of people as, for example, those who are feeble-minded or recent immigrants.

Is It Favorably Known? Conspicuous success should not be expected unless widespread goodwill toward the organization or objective in the interest of which the campaign is proposed already exists or can be created in advance of the undertaking. Community fund leaders had hard work at first to put over the idea of "one fund for all" and in any place not yet accustomed to the method the conception of the sick, the lame, the old, and the poor as community responsibilities has to be widely and deeply impressed upon the public before a campaign can be safely launched.

An intensive effort to get large numbers of persons to sign up for a health examination during the week set aside for it is likely to be coldly received unless the nature of a health examination has been made clear to them in advance.

Is It Part of a Continuous Program? The campaign to forward improved hospital facilities, for instance, which stands alone as the one publicity project of the year on the subject deserves the criticism that it is little more than a flash in the pan. Walt Mason only slightly exaggerates the facts when he describes humorously the reaction which naturally follows a sporadic attempt at reform:

Our village had a "Safety Week," when autos slowly ran, and victims were not heard to shriek—it was a splendid plan; all over town a gent must seek to find a mangled man. With windshields labeled "Safety First," our trusty horns we blew, and curbed all wild desires to burst such speed laws as we knew; and no pedestrians were hearsed until the week was through. The smiling voter went his way and had no broken spine; no accident in seven days! A record truly fine. And rival towns, in stark amaze, beheld that record shine. But when the Safety Week was done the boys stepped on the gas; so swiftly did the motors run they burned up all the grass; as shot from some Big Bertha gun, we saw the autos pass. Our Safety Week had strained the nerves of speed fiends and their kin; a stretch of virtue often serves to start a stretch of sin; and cars went whooping round the curves, fine cars, and cars of tin.[1]

Perhaps Walt Mason's village had no improvement society, much less a chamber of commerce with a safety committee. Or perhaps, if it had, the society or the committee grew as indifferent as the citizens after the one big effort was over. Otherwise, the village should have harvested from steady follow-up work a better standard of law enforcement or a better law to enforce against those who "whoop round the curves."

The intensive campaign finds its greatest usefulness as the high point, or the wind-up of an educational program. In the attempt to teach safety it is often employed as the attention device with which a program of continuous educational publicity is launched. Clean-up Week and Thrift Week may be high points in all the year round propaganda. The first takes advantage of the spring house-cleaning season to win new recruits and jog people into fresh activity; the second uses Benjamin Franklin's birthday annually as the inspiration for beginning a week of special effort to urge people to lay aside money. The money-raising or vote-getting campaign is generally the climax of a year of active though less intense publicity.

CREATING ATMOSPHERE THROUGH DISPLAY

When the campaign begins, elaborate and colorful display affords visible evidence of community-wide celebration. To recall the Liberty Loan drives brings to mind a vivid picture of the festive appearance of streets and public squares during those periods. Flags were flying from windows and flagpoles; strings of electric lights or of banners carrying slogans stretched across the main streets; and electric signs flashed a message from the walls or tops of buildings. Booths, platforms, or courts of honor were

[1] George Matthew Adams Service, Inc., New York.

erected in public squares and open places; billboards were covered with striking posters; store windows along the business streets vied with one another in conspicuous and appropriate displays.

The lavish decorations of the war period are beyond the means and the needs of most social organizations. Indeed in some annual campaigns the tendency is to reduce the street display after the community has accepted the idea. Where the campaign idea is new, however, profuse display is often very helpful in the task of introducing it, and with good taste and careful planning, effective decorations can be secured without undue expense.

Each detail of display has its use. Banners, flags, and pennants proclaim the campaign a big event. Electric signs and searchlights may be used to illumine the celebration at night. During Baby Week pennants have been flown from the windows of private houses to show what homes have babies in them. Streets and corners, public squares, small parks, plazas, broad steps, and corridors of public buildings make excellent settings for conspicuous decorations and stunts. In one city during Milk Week milk bottles 10 feet high flanked the entrance to the city hall. Gaily decorated street booths where Christmas seals are sold are often features of these sales.

In money-raising campaigns a huge clock face has sometimes been placed in the business center of the town, the hands being moved forward as the collections and pledges are reported each day. During a certain community fund campaign daily totals were recorded on the cloth tube of a thermometer 14 feet high and four feet broad, with figures illuminated at night by a red light. Along the side of the tube were such phrases as "low temperature," "high temperature," "fever heat"; when the campaign reached the climax, the thermometer broke and a red light shone at the top of the tube. New and ingenious devices for recording progress are continually being introduced into campaigns.

With the co-operation of the police department it may be possible to carry display even into the middle of traffic. In some campaigns the traffic stations or the "Stop—Go" Signals have been decorated with the campaign emblem. Traffic policemen have regulated traffic for one day with the double-barred cross of the tuberculosis movement.

Posters. Posters not only furnish decoration but also give the keynote of the spirit and purpose of a campaign. In different sizes they are displayed on billboards, on public buildings, in windows, and on street cars, delivery wagons, and trucks. Their importance is placed high among campaign features.

Charles Matlack Price, in telling what a poster should be and do, brings out certain elements of particular significance in the campaign poster. He quotes Hamilton King, a poster artist, as saying:

> The poster should seize a moment—exploit a situation with one daring sweep of the pencil or brush. The poster is not a portrait, nor a study—it is an impression—a flash of line, a sweep of color . . . all that can be told of a tale in the passing of an instant.[1]

When the poster attempts to give more than a single impression, the charm and simplicity which are its most valued characteristics are lost. A widely inclusive campaign topic presents many difficulties to the artist. Common faults of posters are the use of many human figures to indicate that people of all ages or of all classes are among those to be benefited; the choice of an idea that gives a one-sided or inadequate interpretation of the theme; and the use of too many words. A way out of the perplexity caused by a complex subject is sometimes found by using one figure to represent the sorrow to be dispelled, or the happiness or power to be obtained from carrying out the campaign objective.

Slogans. Slogans appear not only on posters but on windshield stickers, slides, streamers, in advertisements, and in window displays. Since the slogan is, or should be, repeated oftener than any other campaign expression, it should give as concretely as possible whatever suggestion or idea is to be spread most widely. Usually, it contains a statement of what people are asked to do. "Open Your Windows" and "Join the Red Cross" say definitely what is wanted. So also do "Vote 'Yes' on the $150,000 Bond Issue for the Public Library," and "Cross Streets at the Crossings."

Slogans such as "Measure Your Giving by the Golden Rule," "Prevent Fires," "Save Babies," and "Open Your Heart" are too broad to inspire the average individual to definite, intelligent

[1] Poster Design. George W. Bricka, New York, 1922, p. 2.

action. They may be effective, however, in campaigns of the type of the community fund, where thoroughly organized personal work insures that the suggestions will be reinforced by clear, widely distributed information telling people definitely just what is desired of them. In these circumstances the campaign slogan often suggests an inspiration or a motive rather than a definite act: "It's Everybody's Job," "Suppose Nobody Cared," "Safety or Sorrow." Slogans like these are often used independently but their effectiveness is enhanced if they are accompanied by an appealing picture.

Window Displays. Exhibits relating to the campaign topic are usually placed in the windows of leading stores and banks. People have formed the habit of looking at store windows to see what new things are being shown, and the campaign gains in importance if they find that many merchants have given window space to the cause. The strength of the total impression made by the campaign is greater if each window display is made part of a scheme of decoration and interpretation.

It is generally easier and more desirable to visualize the immediate objective of the campaign or some one aspect of the exhibiting organization than it is to attempt to show the whole program or purpose of an agency.

Any attempt to tell a complicated or detailed story by means of a window display is likely to result in weakness and confusion. One effort of this sort in a community fund campaign showed a dozen illuminated, boxed placards, bearing such captions as "The Hungry," "Too Old to Work," "The Industrially Unfit," "The Sick" and "In Domestic Difficulty," arranged irregularly on the floor, with lengths of cloth rumpled in and out among them to break the angles of the placards. In the center background was a small, lighted window with a poster below it carrying the plea "Keep the Light Burning—Give to the Community Fund," while three other posters gave general information regarding the exhibiting agency. The confusion of such a display greatly enfeebled the force of the publicity. The effect was somewhat as if a merchant should hang in his window the announcement "We have 50,000 yards of material," and instead of showing his goods should display placards with such captions as "Flannel," "Velvet,"

"Georgette Crêpe," and so forth. Most merchants, however, find it more worth while to make an attractive display of a few samples from their stock than to proclaim the contents of their stores by means of placards or by crowding the window space with every kind of material. The social agency, following this method, will find it profitable to choose some one service or need which can be interpreted effectively in the space at its disposal.

The following descriptions suggest attractive window exhibits, each simple in design as well as in theme:

To show visiting nurse work.—At the back of the window a painted street scene shows a row of houses or tenements. A cut-out photograph of a nurse, or a painted figure of thin wood or cardboard dressed in nurse's uniform, is knocking at the door of one of the houses. The caption reads—"Visiting nurses last year knocked on the doors of . . . homes while on your errands of service."

For a family welfare agency.—A mechanical device in motion, or a cartoon, placed in the foreground of a window shows money being poured through a sieve. In the background is a row of silhouetted figures representing family visitors. The caption reads: "To give money without service is like pouring water through a sieve. Our trained workers are giving friendly service to families in trouble."

For an institution.—The window is heaped with loaves of bread, preferably wrapped, only the outside loaves being real. A sign reads: "It took . . . loaves of bread to serve the boys in the Kingswell Home in 1924." Other foods could be used in similar fashion.

In several community fund campaigns good window displays were secured by enlarging photographs of persons engaged in some interesting occupation until the figures were nearly life size. The windows were arranged with the appropriate settings and these cut-out photographs took the place of the usually expressionless and unconvincing doll figures. Some remarkable effects were secured, and, although the method was expensive, it was considered to be justified by the results.

Some occasions and some causes offer greater possibilities for decorative effects than others. May Day, which the American Child Health Association has dedicated to child health, is especially adapted to attractive displays. The Christmas Seal Sale, coming at Christmas time, is another occasion for bright, alluring window

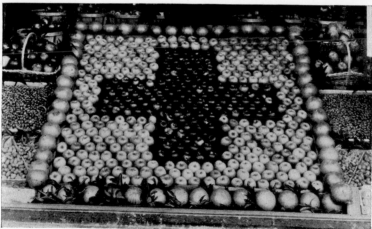

WINDOW DISPLAYS DURING INTENSIVE CAMPAIGNS

Above: The national costumes of the "Mothers of All Nations" may be depended upon to draw attention to the information on the placards about Baby Week.

Below: How a fruiterer of Northampton, Mass., displayed the emblem of the Red Cross to passersby during a Red Cross Roll Call.

exhibits. One design shows a Christmas tree in the foreground and at the back a fireplace hung with stockings. Packages, some opened, others wrapped, but all bearing Christmas seals, lie about the floor, hang from the tree, and stick out from the tops of the bulging stockings.

Combining campaign publicity with articles from the stock of the merchant who lends the window is sometimes a workable arrangement if the social agencies are careful that the merchant's material is used to carry out their purpose and not to obscure it. Fire Prevention Week offers many possibilities of this sort:

> Dealers in builders' supplies should feature fire-resistive materials; hardware dealers, metal waste and ash cans and incinerators showing results of hot ashes in wooden barrels, etc.; dry cleaners, the dangers of gasoline cleaning at home; clothing stores, the advantage of woolen clothing, which is much safer than light cotton material; electrical dealers, the superiority of the flashlight over the candle or match for inspecting dark closets.[1]

Like exhibits at fairs and expositions, window displays are especially attractive when they are animated.[2] Something alive or moving draws more observers and holds attention longer than a stationary display.

DRAMATIC METHODS [3]

Against the background of generous display such as has been pictured in the foregoing paragraphs, street events staged at frequent intervals or carried on continuously give life to the occasion. These events may be humorous, novel, artistic, or solemn so long as they are in harmony with the theme of the campaign and call attention to its object rather than to themselves.

In a No Accident Week a street car decorated with safety slogans, with a siren whistle heralding its coming, traveled through the streets. Attached to the car was a trailer carrying a wrecked automobile with a figure in Devil's costume at the wheel. In other safety weeks groups of Boy Scouts have been assigned to

[1] Fire Prevention Week Handbook. National Fire Protection Association, Boston, Revised 1926, p. 29.

[2] See p. 295.

[3] For earlier discussion and examples, see Chap. XV, Dramatic Methods, p. 259.

the police force to help regulate traffic. An attractive feature of some clean-up weeks has been tree planting on a large scale on a given day or days.

Come and see tours such as were described in Chapter XV, Dramatic Methods,[1] are used with excellent results in improvement weeks and in money-raising drives. Seeing for oneself the good work of institutions needing support or the menace of unsightly and insanitary conditions makes a stronger impression than any argument expressed in words. In some cities factory employes, during community fund campaigns, select a committee from among themselves to visit and report on the agencies represented in the campaign. Visits of boys to industrial plants, commercial establishments, and the offices of local civic officials are among the successful events of Boys' Week.

At least once during a campaign there may well be a big and impressive outdoor event, a parade, festival, or pageant. The parade sums up better than the festival or the pageant all the elements characteristic of a campaign. It has color and life, great possibilities in interpreting the subject of the drive, news value for both the newspapers and the motion picture weekly, the opportunity for large numbers of persons to take part and a reasonable chance in a community of average size for the marchers and banners to be seen by a considerable number of the population. In Minneapolis one of the community fund campaigns opened with a parade including among the hundreds of marchers a column of musicians drawn from various bands and orchestras of the city and a section made up of the entire uniformed nurses' corps of the Visiting Nurse Association and the Infant Welfare Society. The parade ended at a hall where some 1,500 workers assembled at luncheon.

An announcement of events scheduled for one of the celebrations of May Day as Child Health Day stated that the Governor of Ohio and his official staff would head a parade of 3,000 Blue Ribbon children in Mansfield, Ohio. Mansfield was the community chosen by the National Child Health Council for a demonstration of what could be done to improve the health of children. The 3,000 Blue Ribbon boys and girls, selected for their fine showing

[1] See p. 273.

328

in health examinations, were regarded as convincing evidence of the results achieved.

THE NEWSPAPER AND THE CAMPAIGN

The value of a campaign as a source of news has already been discussed. News items, feature stories, and pictures begin to appear in the newspapers several weeks before the drive opens, thus arousing anticipation of coming events. During the week of the campaign streamers across the top of the front page announce its presence and groups of pictures show campaign leaders, glimpses of the work of social agencies, and campaign events staged especially for the news photographer. The names and committee assignments of participants published from day to day may run into many columns of space. A rotogravure supplement devoted entirely to the campaign may be distributed with the Sunday papers. Many advertisers give emphasis to the drive by inserting mention of it in their regular copy, and paid space varying from a quarter to a full page may be devoted to appeals for contributions or to information about the work of social agencies. From the mayor's opening proclamation to the final announcement of the returns or the closing events of the week, an amazing volume of news is created. As a rule, campaigns being community events as well as live news, newspaper editors are quite as much a part of the movement as anyone else, and give space generously to their happenings.

Intensive campaigns of more limited appeal absorb much less space than do community fund campaigns. Even the least vigorous, however, usually manages to receive some notice, since the fact that a campaign is being staged is in itself regarded as news.

Although the space given to campaign news measured in inches may count up to an impressive total, it does not always follow that readers become better informed about the work of the social agency conducting it. The complete file of newspaper clippings from one successful community fund campaign contains only such vague references to the object of the drive as are found in these quotations from speakers:

> We have got to go through with this thing. If we don't there will be more poor, more sick, crippled, homeless and abandoned children and people on our streets than I care to think about.

We must go over the top. It means salvation from poverty and from loneliness and from fear as well.

We look to you men and women composing this great organization which is established to abate the crime and poverty of our city, to collect from those. . . .

During a fire prevention week a prominent newspaper published on its society page an article entitled "Fire Prevention Week Brings Memories of Society's Volunteer Firemen." The text told of the early volunteer fire companies giving the names and often something of the genealogy of the socially prominent members. It contained no practical information about fire prevention. Yet the conspicuous title, mentioning this specialized week in a part of the newspaper where otherwise it probably would not have appeared, had undoubted publicity value.

The bulk of the news naturally centers about the campaign events and the names of the men and women connected with them. However, one may weave important social information into news reports of these events. An account of what a workers' committee saw on a come and see tour, or what the mayor said to the purchasers when he presided at the auction of the first Christmas seals to be sold may contain some of the social information newspaper readers should have.

SPEAKING

Campaign speaking frequently begins with special sermons or announcements in the churches on the Sunday of the week in which the event opens. Sometimes these start a week or two in advance of the campaign.

A campaign speech may well be made before almost any kind of audience. Speakers have addressed such diverse groups as a state legislature, county commissioners, the city council, and the board of education; a college commencement gathering, professional schools, public schools, kindergartens; mothers' meetings; an army post, a naval station, the crew on a battleship; even penitentiary, jail, and state penal farm inmates; a bridge club, an art club, a choral society in the midst of a rehearsal; and an evangelistic meeting. One speaker says that he has talked

NEWSPAPER NOTICE OF A CAMPAIGN

Over 12 columns of campaign publicity appeared in the Cleveland Plain Dealer on the Sunday before a community fund campaign opened. There was also a full page of pictures in the rotogravure section.

about tuberculosis between bouts at a wrestling match. Street crowds gathered at busy corners are told why they should vote in favor of a bond issue for a hospital.

Speakers do not find it easy to break in upon a mood of care-free enjoyment with a tale of suffering, upon a spirit of worship with practical considerations of sanitary measures, or upon a cold business meeting with an emotional appeal. The chances of being well received depend upon a speaker's ability to adapt his talk to the occasion. The manner of his introduction to the audience and the extent to which the urgency of the subject has been accepted by the public because of other forms of publicity also have much to do with his success.

Even the most adaptable speakers are likely to find it difficult to get a response from speeches delivered between acts at a theatrical performance. Many campaign leaders have discontinued the practice of sending speakers to theaters.

The campaign speeches addressed to these miscellaneous gatherings are usually brief. They express the spirit of the campaign and seek to give the audience a realization of their responsibility to see the thing through. The persuasive but not always thoroughly informed speaker is likely to be chosen for this type of speech. He may have no connection with the organizations represented in the campaign, a point often in his favor since his unselfish and enthusiastic belief in the cause sets an example for his audiences. It is probably better for this type of speaker not to attempt to give any but the simplest information. If he goes into detail about social work methods, his statements may be hazy or inaccurate. Few campaign speakers are likely to have at their command any but the simplest facts, despite the handbooks they are supposed to have read, or their attendance at meetings of instruction. We frequently find handbooks for campaign speakers filled with technical material evidently set down without any thought of the speaker's ability or willingness to grapple with it. One which proposes that a labor leader address his own union offers for his use information about prevention of disease which only a trained health worker could discuss with assurance and accuracy.

In a campaign a speakers' bureau can be of great help by showing speakers some of the social problems they are to describe. A method is demonstrated for them or they are taken to visit the place where work to be referred to is carried on. These contacts give speakers a sense of reality which makes them more confident.

Perhaps no part of a campaign is worth more educationally than a series of talks by well-informed speakers to carefully selected audiences. This form of publicity has been skilfully and successfully used in many cities during Cancer Week. Much sifting of important points to select what is suited to each audience is an important element of success in making such talks interesting. Baby Week Campaigns, a handbook issued by the United States Children's Bureau, contains material for messages to fathers about their responsibility toward mother and baby; to older brothers and sisters of babies; to clubs whose members are asked to support work for saving infant lives and so on.[1] But adequate preparation to relate talks to the special interests of different types of audiences goes far beyond anything attempted by the usual campaign organization.

USE OF THE RADIO

Because the intensive campaign is a conspicuous event, it seems to be fairly easy to arrange to broadcast campaign information or appeals. Reports from about 30 cities widely scattered over the country indicate that a campaign can almost always obtain a place on the programs of a local station for five or ten-minute talks, if not daily, at least once or twice a week.

Devices designed to induce people to tune in may be needed to obtain the maximum number of listeners. In a Cincinnati community chest campaign a character called "Cincinnatus," impersonated by an anonymous speaker, acted as interrogator in a dialogue concerning the work of the various social agencies in which a succession of their leaders took part. A monologue in dialect was given during an improvement week in one city. During a community fund campaign in Cleveland the director of the local Red Cross chapter reproduced the radio call for help that it had received a few months earlier from a nearby town which had been

[1] Baby Week Campaigns. Children's Bureau, Washington, Revised 1917, pp. 38–41, 138–141.

hit by a tornado. Then he reproduced the radio reply Cleveland sent and he followed this by a dramatic account of the swift rallying of forces throughout the night to bring help to those in need.

In drives where team rivalry is a factor, reports from team captains are announced to radio audiences, or still better, their daily luncheon meeting is broadcast. Other numbers for radio programs include a competition among high school boys and girls for the selection of campaign radio speakers, a program of music by bands or choruses from settlements and institutions introduced by a short talk, and the broadcasting of a one-act play.

SCHOOL PARTICIPATION

The school is an important element in many intensive campaigns. In some it is the center of activities. Instructed in advance, verbally and through handbooks prepared for them, teachers carry the campaign message into all classes where it can be applied. Work in connection with the school is generally begun the week before the campaign opens, so that when the affair is in progress the pupils may understand its purpose and co-operate intelligently.

Bulletins issued to teachers by the Cleveland Community Fund suggest practicable ways for introducing the idea of community service into their various courses, especially in connection with English, mathematics, and civics. To test the students' knowledge of the social resources of the city, questions are asked such as:

Where is the nearest hospital to your school?

Does it have a dispensary?

What is a dispensary?

Where can you send a man who asks, on the street or at your back door, for money, for food and lodging?

Where would you go for legal advice if you could not afford to pay for it?

What would you do if you were lost in a strange city?

The Fire Prevention Week Handbook, issued by the National Fire Protection Association, contains a home inspection blank for school children. Some of the questions are:

How many stories high is your house? How many families occupy it?

333

Is anything kept on the fire-escape landing or steps?
What kind of matches do you use?
Are there any gas jets near windows that curtains can blow against?
Are the curtains so secured as not to blow loose?
How are ashes disposed of? Do you ever put them in wooden barrels
or boxes?

School exercises to which parents and friends are invited, letters from the children to their parents, competitions, and distribution of literature are means of enlisting school children to help carry information out into the community.

Motion Pictures

At motion picture theaters we may find many of that elusive section of the public whose members read little and seldom attend meetings.

The preferred picture of social work for these audiences is a short "trailer," usually three or four hundred feet of film. A picture used by the Cleveland Community Fund in one campaign was an animated cartoon called "The Ten Little Dollars"; each of the dollars was shown running around performing all sorts of service. The Christmas Seal Sale has used an animated cartoon in which characters appearing in the design of the Christmas seal or the campaign poster are brought to life and become actors in a play. A longer film, to be acceptable to the theater audience, needs to be exceptionally entertaining or to show well-known local people and scenes.

A type of motion picture apparently popular for campaign purposes shows situations which it is desirable that the audience should experience, actually or in imagination. A film for use in a health examination campaign, Working for Dear Life, produced by the Metropolitan Life Insurance Company, centers about a vigorous young man scornful of the suggestion that there could be anything the matter with his health. The film shows how he is induced to have an examination and how the experience leads him to become an ardent advocate of health work.

Dividends in Happiness, used by the Providence District Nursing Association, opens with a young woman collector asking a contribution from a business man who inquires "What dividends do you pay?" The scenes following show how the woman answers his question to his entire satisfaction by having a nurse take him with her on her daily rounds, an experience shared by the audience.

In many of the campaign films, the incidents are stereotyped and not infrequently forced. Scenario writers seem to put most of their ingenuity into the effort to hold disconnected scenes together. In one instance the mechanism employed to give dramatic form to the picture was a dream in which a man went through a number of obviously built-up misfortunes from which he was rescued by various relief agencies. In another a huge "Kindness Cup" relieved a number of typical distressing situations with remarkable facility by pouring out its contents: "Better Health," "Family Welfare," "Child Welfare." A fantastic device is one that causes a social worker to change into a gipsy who shows the scenes through crystal gazing. Sometimes the incidents are presented through imaginary and wholly unfamiliar characters personifying a quality or an idea. All these devices easily lapse into strained and futile efforts at effect.

Good campaign scenarios will probably come in time from writers who have first-hand contact and genuine sympathy with the people whose problems and activities are dramatized. Meanwhile, motion picture plays illustrating some aspect of social service might be adapted from the best of the spoken dramas based on the same theme. At Ellis Island, The First of May, and From House to House[1] contain good material for films and may suggest other situations which can be pictured in an original, informing, and entertaining manner.

Campaign Literature

Regarding the desirability of putting out campaign literature in enormous quantities, opinions differ. There appears to be a growing preference for using only a few kinds, each serving a specific purpose. Nevertheless, the handbills, novelties, folders, booklets, and other printed matter used in most campaigns run into prodigal amounts. In a drive for a million dollar bond issue for a county hospital, 4,000,000 pieces were printed, an average of 30 to every vote cast in the election.

[1] See p. 261.

In some money-raising campaigns the attempt is made to put something into the hands of every adult member of the population and every school child. In some of the large cities community funds during their annual drives issue a picture or news sheet somewhat similar to the graphic section of city newspapers, which is distributed from house to house before the canvass of solicitors is begun so that everyone asked to subscribe will have received information about the campaign. The Minneapolis Council of Social Agencies issued a rotogravure pamphlet printed and folded on the outside to resemble a bond. In a city of about 40,000 inhabitants a broadside was mailed to nearly every household.

In some campaigns, a selected list, usually including about 10 per cent of the population, receives a letter making an appeal on the basis of service rendered which is described in a folder or on the inside pages of a four-page letterhead. In community fund campaigns a similar list, including about the same proportion of the population, receives an attractive illustrated booklet of from 16 to 32 pages, describing the year's work of the social agencies included in the fund.

Other forms of printed matter adapted in size and in quantity to available methods of distribution are also used. Leaflets and small folders are prepared for enclosure with bills sent out by public utility corporations, as well as in pay envelopes and packages delivered by laundries and stores. Blotters carrying some brief appeal or bit of information are distributed in office buildings, or in check-book size are sent out by banks and trust companies with their monthly statements. The slogan or some other reminder of the campaign appears on paper bags and tops of milk bottles, or is hung from door knobs. Folders or handbills are distributed at meetings. A daily news bulletin and a handbook of instruction are issued to campaign workers.

The free literature can perform several distinct services. It can carry into every household and place of business the name, date, and slogan of the campaign. By showing, "set down in black and white," a list of expenditures, a summary of work done, and the endorsement of prominent people, it can spread confidence that the cause has reliable backing. It can give in handy form announcements of the times and places of campaign events, or such directions as how to dispose of waste in Clean-up Week or where to go for examination in Health Examination Week. It can present a brief appeal.

The booklet prepared for distribution to a selected list is perhaps the most important element in the campaign from the educational standpoint. In its 8, 12, or more pages there is room to tell in some detail the story of work done, to describe needs to be met, or to give practical instruction. If the booklet is impressive in appearance, well written, and pleasingly illustrated, it is likely to be widely read; at least the circumstances are favorable to its being read because its subject matter is news and the person receiving it is probably being pressed for a decision as to his own response to the appeal of the campaign.

A weakness characteristic of campaign literature is that it is so often written in a spirit of argument or admonition. The writer seems to expect that the reader will disagree with him or be reluctant to read what he has to say. Since the existence of widespread goodwill is a premise of the campaign, now, even more than at other times, it is wise to assume friendliness and sympathy.

PERSONAL CANVASS

Personal visits to homes and offices are the surest means of achieving the campaign purpose, whether it be to obtain votes or money, or to spread information. The visitor has an opportunity to answer questions and to adapt statements or appeals to the understanding and point of view of each person approached.

In a campaign to defeat four anti-public health measures offered to the voters of California, the Metropolitan Life Insurance Company sent hundreds of its agents into the homes of policy holders to inform them of the meaning of the proposed legislation.

In Framingham, Massachusetts, in a drive to get everyone in town to submit to a general health examination, personal visits were made to the homes and the whole matter talked over with each family. Personal inspections by school children of their own premises to find possible fire hazards provide a feature of Fire Prevention Week.

The backbone of the community fund campaign is the personal canvass. The organization of teams of solicitors, the collection of pledges, and obtaining of daily reports which are among its chief features do not come within the scope of this discussion. Yet the picture of an intensive money-raising campaign as a publicity method is incomplete without including in it the informative work of the collectors. Even though their main purpose is to obtain signatures to pledges, solicitors are also expected to inform the persons they approach about the cause for which soliciting is done. They are equipped for their task not only with pledge cards but also with handbooks or folders containing answers to questions which they may expect to be asked. In some instances they carry with them on their rounds portfolios of pictures illustrating the work of social agencies.

SIGNIFICANCE OF THE GOAL

Volunteer workers enter with zest into the team rivalries and the speeding-up elements of the campaign which consist in a drive toward a fixed goal. The conception of the campaign as a race is strikingly illustrated in the following headlines, quoted from Cincinnati newspapers in the order in which they appear over daily reports of one of the community chest campaigns:

First Rally Is Held. Several Teams Ready to Start at Word Go.

All Ready. Teams Await "Go." Thousand Chest Workers Attend Big Rally.

They're Off! Chest Drive Is On. 6,000 Workers Face Flag at Start. Success Is Up to Liberal-Hearted Citizens. Goal Two Million for Cause of Charity.

Cheers of Workers Ring as Captains Report Ten Per Cent of Quotas. First Day's Pledges Total $173,234. High Percentage Honor Is Won by Team E.

Half Million Mark Passed in Subscriptions to the Chest. Total for Two Days $347,757.

Fund Near Million Mark. Half Way Stage Is to Be Passed Today. Team E Heads List with 62 Per Cent.

Fund Is Swelled by $255,787. War-time Pep is Revived.

Gifts Drop into Chest. Team Workers Eager to Resume Quest. Results in Residential District Gratifying.

338

Danger to Chest Scented. Warning Is Sounded at Meeting of Workers. All Large Gifts Are Said to Be in Hand. Small Givers Expected to Insure Success.

Last Lap of Drive Entered. Final Reports to Be Made Tomorrow. Sum Still Required for Quota Is $364,000. Number of Pledges 30,000 Short.

Last Call Sounded.

Goal Missed by $51,000.

Small Deficit Remains as Campaign Closes. Last Day's Report of $312,342 Greeted with Cheers. Three Teams Exceed Required Amount.

Headings like these, spectacular records of progress, and daily rallies excite in workers and public much the same emotions as those felt at an athletic contest; confidence, uncertainty, too great assurance of success, then doubt and suspense, and at last the climax when time is called and the final result announced.

The daily rally of workers at luncheon or dinner is the main driving force which keeps team activity at high pressure. At these meetings, there are roll calls to which team captains respond by announcing amounts collected in the last twenty-four hours; cheers and good-natured heckling greet the reports; rivalry is fostered by awarding banners to the teams with the best showing; amounts received are posted on a large bulletin board; and short speeches fire the enthusiasm of the workers for carrying on their work with increased zeal and energy.

The canvassing and the daily rallies provide the high point of interest in the money-raising campaign, and so tend to absorb attention for themselves instead of directing it toward social information. On this account, it might seem that campaigns of this type do little to increase public interest in social work. Yet even though the piling up of quotas holds the center of the stage, the cause for which money is sought can be kept in the picture at all times. In the weeks immediately preceding the period devoted to solicitation, social information is placed in the way of thousands of persons who are more likely to notice it now than at other times because they are participants, or because the drive is such a conspicuous event. Avenues for spreading ideas not open to social agencies at other times are now at their disposal. These include front-page space in newspapers, the opportunity to show motion pictures at the theaters, display space in prominent store windows, and invitations to speak at many gatherings.

No doubt some money-raising campaigns that are successful in obtaining the funds sought accomplish very little in the way of public education, but there is no reason inherent in the method itself why this should be so.

The dramatic element of striving to win a race may be a feature of other types of campaigns besides those directed toward raising funds. In the political campaign there is a battle not only against time and possible indifference, but also against active opposition. An important advantage of setting an objective to be reached at the end of the campaign period is that it serves to hold campaign leaders to an aim possible of achievement. In contrast to the rallying force of the fixed goal, an energetic but scattered effort to spread in a single week information about many phases of a broad subject, such as child welfare, safety, or education, is like a great deal of shouting, which accomplishes little more than to make a loud noise. Leaders of campaigns of these specialized weeks lose themselves in an endless variety of topics and admonitions. With the mistaken idea that they are "concentrating public attention," they say in effect "Look at this on Monday," "at that on Tuesday," and so on throughout the week, and the chances are that by the end of the week Monday's topic will be forgotten by all except those who were already interested in it before the campaign opened.

An example of this tendency to cover too broad a field in an intensive educational campaign is found in a set of instructions for Health Week sent out by a state health department. The local worker is advised to give the public information about contagious diseases; flies, typhoid, general health, patent medicines; children's books; books on story telling; older children's good and poor books; and the benefit to be derived from physical examination. There is obviously no possibility of anyone's thinking to definite purpose on such a confused mass of material as this. Attention is scattered, not concentrated.

The Children's Bureau recognizes the value of a concrete purpose in proposing plans for Baby Week, suggesting that the campaign emphasize:

340

. . . some one phase of infant welfare work which is needed in the community, such as the establishment of a public nursing service, or an infant welfare station, or a prenatal clinic, or a county center for maternal and infant welfare; the employment of a full-time health officer; the establishment of a division or bureau of child hygiene in the local health department; . . . the systematic after-care of infantile paralysis; . . .[1]

The promoters of No Accident Week in a number of communities have urged that a record of no lives lost through street accidents during the seven days of the campaign be attempted and the record has been attained in some instances. In Clean-up Week the clearing of rubbish from yards, lots, alleys, and parks may be spurred by dividing the town into districts and setting as a climax to the week Inspection Day, when the standing of rival districts will be compared and prizes awarded.

When no goal is set for the public to reach, the campaign leaders can at least avoid broadcasting a miscellaneous assortment of facts and ideas by setting up a reasonable aim beyond which they determine not to go. Cancer Week accomplished a great deal merely by concentrating for seven days on the one vital fact that cancer in its early stages can be cured. A tangible result of holding to this definite and limited topic was observed in the greatly increased numbers of persons who applied at hospitals and clinics for examinations immediately after the campaign.

Even a single easily grasped idea as a high spot of interest does not rally the support of volunteer workers or take hold of public attention with the same arresting force as a concrete and immediate purpose whether this be obtaining a sum of money, winning an election, cleaning up a city, or reducing accidents.

FEWER AND BETTER CAMPAIGNS

"Fewer and Better Campaigns" might well be a slogan for social workers to follow. When an intensive campaign follows too closely upon the heels of a similar affair, the method loses whatever advantages it may have over other forms of publicity. Indeed, when it becomes a commonplace the avenues of publicity which make it spectacular are closed. A celebration which is like many others

[1] Baby Week Campaigns. p. 70.

PUBLICITY FOR SOCIAL WORK

has not enough news value to secure front-page space for a week. The merchant who responds cordially perhaps two or three times a year to the request for special window displays may feel imposed upon and possibly refuse altogether after he has been deluged with such appeals. The schools cannot break into their routine for a continuous succession of special lessons and exercises, and ministers, who usually have their programs planned in advance, grow weary of requests to celebrate some cause nearly every Sunday in the year.

The prestige of the plan is threatened partly by overuse and partly by having its name attached to unimportant affairs. A slightly increased effort to obtain publicity should not be confused with a campaign which throws the spotlight on some condition or fact so as actually to focus the attention of the community on it. If weeks or campaigns were projected only when their promoters were definitely prepared to do the hard work needed to make an impression on the community, the number of such campaigns would be automatically reduced. The intensive campaign is, after all, only one way to gain support for social programs and activities. and is by no means an appropriate method for every need.

CHAPTER XIX

ORGANIZING AND MANAGING THE CAMPAIGN

OUTSTANDING examples of a workable campaign technique developed and improved over a period of years are found in the community fund campaigns and Christmas Seal Sale from which many of the illustrations in the preceding chapter have been drawn, as well as in the Red Cross Roll Call and a few of the annual improvement weeks. Many of the details of planning and management used in these and other campaigns originated in hospital and Young Men's Christian Association building campaigns, and in membership drives of chambers of commerce. From a study of these enterprises we may reach a few conclusions as to how a campaign is successfully promoted, how it is directed, and how the work is done.

PRINCIPLES OF CAMPAIGN ORGANIZATION

Charts of intensive campaign organization usually take the shape of the one shown on page 344. The broad line across the top indicates the representative character of the enterprise—the religious, industrial, and other community groups whose backing is needed and from whose members the advisory committee is drawn; the small unit or units in the center indicate concentration of management in the hands of the executive committee, and the director; the many lines extending downward from this unit lead to the names of various working committees. These are usually made up of volunteers, in some cases assisted or directed by paid secretaries.

Advisory or Honorary Committee. Members of this committee are selected because of their influence with the groups they represent, as well as for their personal standing in the community. Sometimes they meet once to launch the campaign project and appoint an executive committee, but usually they are not called upon to take committee action and have no responsibility for campaign policies. The reason for this is obvious, in that a group

343

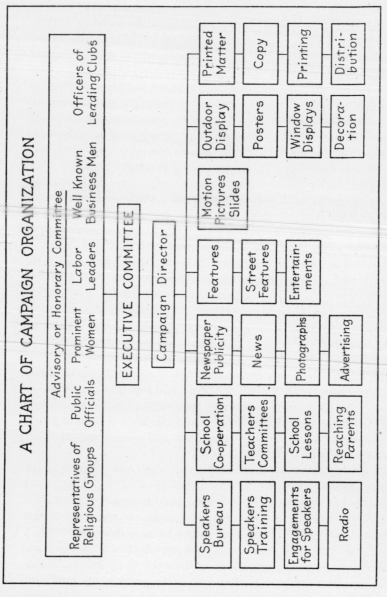

A CHART OF CAMPAIGN ORGANIZATION

Advisory or Honorary Committee

| Representatives of Religious Groups | Public Officials | Prominent Women | Labor Leaders | Well Known Business Men | Officers of Leading Clubs |

EXECUTIVE COMMITTEE

Campaign Director

Speakers Bureau	School Co-operation	Newspaper Publicity	Features	Motion Pictures Slides	Outdoor Display	Printed Matter
Speakers Training	Teachers Committees	News	Street Features		Posters	Copy
Engagements for Speakers	School Lessons	Photographs	Entertainments		Window Displays	Printing
Radio	Reaching Parents	Advertising			Decoration	Distribution

This chart indicates the main activities usually adopted. The grouping and the development of sub-committees are subject to many variations, largely in accordance with the interests and experience of the executive committee or campaign director.

representing so many different interests, however united it might be in aim and motive, would find co-operation difficult when it came to arranging details. The primary function of the committee is by its existence to give solidarity and breadth to the enterprise and to obtain recognition for it as a real community event.

As individuals, the members advise about problems coming up in their own fields during the campaign, make statements or comments for quotation in the newspapers, sign letters or messages addressed to their constituencies, and occasionally use their influence to secure desirable concessions or services.

Executive Committee. The executive committee is a small group characterized by the ability of its members to work well together and with the director. If they represent a wide range of interests in the community, so much the better, but their chief qualification is that they can "keep things moving," losing no time through the multiplication of individual opinions, dissensions, or futile talk which so often hamper the efforts of a large committee. The special circumstances of any given campaign determine whether the members divide among themselves responsibility for the different branches of work, or whether they simply represent group judgment and backing for the director.

A magnetic personality and wide popularity are among the best assets of the campaign chairman. Prestige and influence are helpful but contagious enthusiasm and a sense of humor have greater rallying power. The chairman need not, in most organizations, take the initiative nor give much attention to details, but he must understand the principles and methods of the campaign sufficiently to know what is being done and to exercise judgment about it.

Campaign Director. The enthusiasm roused by the executive chairman is put to work by the campaign director. The directing of intensive campaigns is a recognized occupation to this extent—that there exist a considerable number of men and women who make a business of doing it on the basis of experience in such work. On the other hand, many successful campaigns are managed by the executive secretaries of the agencies sponsoring them. Their qualifications, aside from a general aptitude for publicity, are chiefly the gift of getting people to work together and a familiarity with methods in common use; for the technique of the campaign director is, so far as we know, included in no curriculum nor even set down anywhere in detail. No training, even if it were to be had, could take the place of experience, because one of the most important factors in the smooth running of a campaign is that much of the detail should not have to be thought out for each particular occasion. Such tasks as setting up the campaign office, organizing lists, and laying out channels of distribution for publicity become a matter of routine to the experienced director.

The sort of person most successful in directing campaigns is curiously opposite to the type one might naturally associate with an enterprise of this kind. Whereas the drive is spectacular, the director is likely to be retiring, or at least self-effacing, giving the credit and the center of the stage to his committee members, who, on their part, are often amazed and fascinated by the way the wires are worked behind the scenes. Their confidence that he understands his business makes them work hard for him.

Other qualities the director needs are vitality and endurance because of the high tension of the drive.

Paid Staff. The size of the paid staff varies. An adequate office force is indispensable, since a campaign involves a tremendous amount of clerical work. Usually the campaign director is assisted by a publicity manager who takes entire responsibility for the publicity and leaves the director free for administrative work. In some community fund campaigns paid secretaries assist the more important committees. The amount of detailed work to be accomplished may be very great. Thus, in one campaign, the secretary of the committee in charge of the radio program, gave full time to the work for six weeks and enlisted nearly 100 persons to take part.

Working Committees. The number of volunteers who can be put to work effectively depends to a large extent on the size and efficiency of the paid staff and the energy of the division chairmen.

The canvassers, organized into teams under captains, who, in turn, are under division heads, absorb the largest number of volunteers in the campaign worked out on the team basis. In many cities where the community fund or other organized drive is an annual affair, the team organization has become as machine-like

346

as an army formation. Any large campaign feature may provide for participation of hundreds of workers. Such undertakings as a parade, a pageant, or a series of come and see tours are in themselves miniature campaigns in which many diverse tasks must be carried out.

Sometimes a group already organized is made a committee to take charge of some special task. For example, in a community fund campaign in Toledo firemen tied strings to 60,000 tags, incidentally furnishing an excellent news story besides accomplishing a necessary chore. In another city a woman's club undertook the responsibility of telephoning a number of people to remind them to attend a tuberculosis exhibition. Boy Scouts are frequently enlisted for various tasks.

The participation of large numbers of people is perhaps the most distinctive single characteristic of an intensive campaign. In a report of one of the drives of the Community Fund of Norfolk, Virginia, the director lists the types of service for which volunteers were used:

> More than 900 persons served in the soliciting organization, or as speakers, or on active committees, or at campaign headquarters. Nine hundred teachers and officials in the public schools assisted the schools section. Two hundred and fifty colored workers participated in their section. More than 200 women from various churches helped with the luncheons. Many ministers presented the cause in their churches. The representatives appointed by 150 of the larger firms of the city assisted solicitors in their respective firms. All told, between 2,400 and 2,500 individuals gave personal service to the campaign.

Whereas in a business enterprise the aim is to get work done by the fewest persons who can accomplish it, in the campaign, ability to find suitable tasks for as many people as possible is a requirement of good leadership.

Interesting and informing such a varied group is in itself an important achievement, and one for which the conditions are unusually favorable, since people are much more likely to give thoughtful attention to new facts when they know they will have immediate use for them.

Utilizing Ability

The campaign scheme should be flexible enough to utilize exceptional ability wherever it is found. The assignment of such tasks as writing copy, designing window displays, or producing a motion picture scenario is largely a matter of personal equation. In one city a famous humorist wrote a campaign folder; in another a clever designer planned the window displays. A series of exceptionally artistic tableaux was made possible in one campaign just because the right person to do this kind of thing happened to be interested and available. Not only talent but such necessary resources as delivery service, billboard space, transportation facilities, and so forth are obtained in one way or another according to whether or not persons controlling such resources happen to be interested in the campaign.

Some improvement weeks have objectives in which business groups are directly interested. Thrift Week, an enterprise of the National Council of the Young Men's Christian Association receives co-operation and support from banks and insurance companies. The paint industry gives much assistance to civic associations in carrying on clean-up and paint-up weeks.

Definite Instruction for Everybody

Definite written or printed instructions issued by the director and the executive committee to the chairmen of the working committees simplify the carrying out of details. These state what is to be done; the time to do it; the method of procedure; and who is to do it.

In a referendum campaign for the establishment of a civic center in Buffalo, a printed list of 29 main tasks was circulated among the workers. The name of the individual responsible for each item appeared in bold-face type opposite a description of the assigned task.

An advantage of definite instruction is its effect upon the morale of the workers. Their sense of responsibility and their respect for the undertaking is increased by evidences of well-organized, smooth-working machinery. They recognize possibilities of a well-directed effort and enjoy sharing in it.

348

"The Best Laid Schemes"

The value of thorough organization can best be realized by considering how easily campaign schemes "gang aft a-gley," how many gaps may occur between plan and accomplishment. An illustration of this is afforded by a health week undertaken a few years ago by a community improvement league in a city of 100,000 population. The plans provided for extensive publicity through newspapers, distribution of slides, street features, window displays, car cards, talks, form letters, and an exposition as the main event. Having seen the ambitious plans in advance, we later witnessed the event. Here are a few of the slips which occurred there and which are liable to happen in any campaign which is loosely organized and without vigorous, experienced leadership.

Advertisers in local papers were asked to mention Health Week in their daily copy and many of them promised to do so. No one reminded them of this promise at the proper time, nor were they supplied with copy for insertion. Consequently, only one advertiser carried out the plan.

Slides and motion picture films to be used in the motion picture theaters were not ready on time and even those which might have been delivered later were forgotten in the confusion of the final days. No person or committee was charged with the duty of distributing the slides to the theaters.

Cards and announcements for display in store windows were prepared and distributed, but no one being appointed to see that they were actually placed in the windows, very few were in evidence during Health Week.

The placards for street cars were not made in the size to fit the available spaces. This mistake was corrected when the week was nearly over.

Under the franking privilege of the state bureau of venereal diseases, 20,000 voters were to receive a circular letter and pamphlet from the bureau, with which would be enclosed a program of the week. Boy Scouts addressed the envelopes, which were then arranged by postal delivery routes. The pamphlet was late in arriving, and when it came the Boy Scouts were no longer available to fill the envelopes. The school children who took their places

349

mixed the mailing routes. Under the pressure of work that fell upon the director because the committees were not well organized, the time never arrived to straighten out this confusion and a large part of the material remained unmailed until two days before the close of the week. The program of events had to be omitted entirely from the mailing because it was not printed in time.

Numerous factory talks and other lectures which had a prominent place on the planned program were not given, while several public conferences which sounded most significant on paper were a failure because audiences failed to appear.

PREPARING A CAMPAIGN CALENDAR

About the best means of escaping a last minute stampede to get things done with a resulting fiasco like that described in the preceding paragraphs is the preparation and use of a campaign calendar listing actual dates or a period during which certain steps are to be taken.

A campaign bulletin issued by the Evansville, Indiana, Community Chest contains this item about the way the work has been scheduled:

> . . . the mass of detailed work has been so planned and scheduled that the campaign calendar has taken the form of a time-table in its exactness, continuity and correlating of technical detail.
>
> With mechanical nicety, each necessary item of organizing technique is planned to achieve the maximum effectiveness. Non-essentials have been stripped from the program altogether. Committees are working under concise and definite instructions.

The calendar may be prepared in two divisions, the first scheduling the things to be done in advance, and the second specifying the dates on which each piece of publicity should be released and each event staged. Some organizations conducting annual campaigns begin preparation a year in advance. Not every campaign is begun so far ahead, but whatever the time allowance, the preparations are much the same and usually observe the sequence followed below.

The first item on the schedule may well be "Find out existing prejudices and misunderstandings," and there is no better time for this than the period immediately after a vigorous campaign.

happened to be on hand was considered good enough to use. Forehandedness is especially needful in obtaining "before and after" pictures. Conditions that will change, buildings to be torn down, or lots and alleys to be cleaned up, should be photographed, so that when the change is effected the contrast can be shown; pictures should be taken of ailing babies when they are brought to the clinic and later when they have responded to treatment. Seasonal pictures obviously fix their own time for being taken. The choice of subjects for photographs depends upon the particular slant the campaign is to take, another reason why the ideas to be emphasized should be selected early.

Assuming that the last three months will be a rush period when things must move swiftly and details will pile up, certain essential material should be in readiness for this period. Anywhere from a year to six months in advance of the campaign is none too early to begin the revision of lists of all kinds; mailing lists, if these are to be used; a directory of organizations; and a catalog of useful people[1] who may be called upon for committee service or special assignments of work.

The bulk of campaign publicity shows evidence of hasty preparation. This is unavoidable when many of the facts to be used are not available until the last minute. But there is no doubt that the mediocre exhibits, printed matter, and news stories only too commonly found in campaigns could be vastly improved if more time were allowed for preparation. If the material is produced locally, a period should be assigned early on the calendar for writing copy, choosing a slogan, designing the poster and window displays, and planning the dramatic features. Such supplies as posters, slides, buttons, and so on, if they are obtained from a national organization, need to be ordered months in advance.

About three months ahead of the drive committees should be organized and the pre-campaign publicity determined. Additional staff members should be taken on, full-time work begun, and the campaign machinery made ready to function.

It may be interesting to see some of the details of an actual

[1] For detailed description, see Routzahn, Evart G., and Routzahn, Mary Swain, The A B C of Exhibit Planning. Russell Sage Foundation, New York, 1918, pp. 208–211, 201–202.

calendar. The following calendar for the Christmas Seal Sale is quoted in condensed form from the 1924 handbook sent to local branches by the National Tuberculosis Association. While not altogether related to publicity, this calendar furnishes an admirable example of the kind of detailed schedule needed in any campaign:

January: Hold a "post mortem" on methods used in last campaign, i. e., compare results obtained by mail sale, personal solicitation, telephone sale, booth sale, sale by school children, etc. Find out, if possible, how better results may be obtained by each of these methods.

Begin to revise the general list, taking out the names of people who have moved away, died, or who for other reasons should be eliminated.

February: Secure winter photographs for use in connection with publicity campaign for next seal sale.

March: Continue the revision of the general list.

April: Begin personal cultivation of key people for next seal sale.

May or June: Place order for Christmas seal supplies.

June: Secure photographs of summer work and have special feature stories and articles written for use in publicity during next seal sale. Begin drafting mail sale letter.

July: Submit draft of mail sale letter to mail sale experts for criticism.

August: Get letter in final form and place order for printing or multigraphing mail sale letters.

September: Begin publicity campaign with carefully prepared "pre-campaign" stories.

Start organizing campaign committee.

October: Complete the revision and compilation of the general list.

Make arrangements for addressing mail sale envelopes.

Begin to intensify publicity, giving facts regarding the work of the association. Do not feature the forthcoming seal sale.

Organize special committee for securing large gifts.

Organize a special publicity committee and begin to enroll team captains.

November: Organize industrial committee, booth sale committee, "telephone-order" committee, and arrange with school authorities for whatever co-operation is to be given by teachers and school children.

Intensify effort to secure team captains and workers.

Arrange with ministers to appeal to their congregations on Sunday, November 30th. Provide ministers with talking points.

Start selling publicity during week of Thanksgiving Day. Get some of first posters up this same week.

Hold meetings of volunteer workers for personal solicitation on Saturday, November 29th or Monday, December 1st.

December 1: Begin personal solicitation.

A second part of the calendar, giving dates for the many tasks crowding into the campaign period, is of special value to the director in checking up the innumerable details assigned to committees. With the calendar before him, he knows just how the work is going from day to day and the possibility of hitch or lagging is reduced to a minimum.

NATIONAL ORGANIZATION OF CAMPAIGNS

Although conspicuous local celebration is an essential characteristic of the true intensive campaign, nevertheless, most of the campaigns upon which we have drawn for illustration are national in scope. They are either conducted in all parts of the country during the same period, each local celebration being part of the national event, or else the campaign is mapped out in a national office and put on at different times in different cities.

There are many advantages to the local campaign in having national backing. These are well illustrated in the Christmas Seal Sale, which is comparable to any large business enterprise for the nation-wide distribution of products. In the national office are centered the administrative resources which make possible economy and practicability in the preparation of literature, posters, exhibits, publications, and other educational materials. Long before the local association has begun to think of the next campaign, the national body has completed its work of selecting designs, placing orders for printing, and writing copy for leaflets and articles.

Many elements of a campaign are distinctly national in character: articles, photographs and cartoons placed in newspapers by syndicates; magazine articles; news sent out through press associations; magazine cover designs representing the campaign; and films routed through national distributing channels.

State Participation. Perhaps the most significant feature in the machinery of the annual sale of seals is the way that it functions through thoroughly organized state offices. Each state secretary is in charge of organizing and promoting the state-wide sale of the seals, formulating plans and methods of sale, providing state-wide publicity, arranging for district conferences of campaign workers in various parts of the state, and securing and distributing the Christmas seals and campaign material.

With the help supplied by the state and national bodies the campaign comes very nearly ready made to the local committee, which may, however, exercise initiative and originate ideas freely within prescribed limits. All the year round the state organization sends out occasional bulletins reminding the committees that the time has come to take this or that step in preparation for the campaign. During the last few months before the campaign begins these bulletins come with greater and greater frequency. They contain needed information about such matters as post office rulings, the regulations of the state department of education in regard to the participation of schools, and state rulings about the placing of windshield stickers on automobiles, ideas for window displays, paragraphs to incorporate in the mayor's proclamation, outlines for news stories, and an exchange of information and ideas among local branches of the state organization. Sometimes material of this kind is put up in what is called a "publicity kit," which is similar to a campaign handbook.

Another function as useful as that of supplying the material and the ideas is the stirring up of competition between towns and counties, which has somewhat the same value that team rivalry has in the local campaigns.

The following paragraphs are taken from one of the campaign bulletins of the Indiana Tuberculosis Association, which stimulates activity by reporting daily the clever ideas and the achievements of various bodies:

> What county in Indiana eventually will be accorded the honor of having sold the first health bond? Vincennes, Knox County, comes forward with the first claim, with a sale of a $25 bond on the morning of November 25. Let's hear from you.
>
> More than twenty automobile loads of Peru business men toured Miami County and the city of Peru on Tuberculosis Sunday selling seals and health bonds. They did it because the death-rate from tuber-

culosis is not decreasing fast enough to suit real business men there. Is there a thought in this for your town?

The laundry owners of Marion County are placing in each package of laundry this week a slip advertising Christmas seals and health bonds. There are some laundries in your town.

The Need for Local Enthusiasm. Although the national and, in turn, the state organization may supply material, ideas, and leadership, the life of a campaign must always come from within the community where it is held. Many of the nation-wide campaigns raise money to support local activities designed to meet local needs. The enthusiasm which local committees put into these drives is largely due to this fact.

This is something to be remembered by the secretaries or committees who project campaigns from distant offices believing that by means of a proclamation, a slogan, a handbook, and some campaign supplies they can produce local celebrations in quantity, each having sufficient life to make an impression on the community in which it occurs. Here and there such an enterprise will strike fire because some local group is prepared for it, but as a rule there must be in existence or there must be created in each community an organization and a sentiment for the campaign strong enough to make the fire that has been kindled spread into a real conflagration.

CONCLUSION

CHAPTER XX

THE PUBLICITY PROGRAM

THE analysis and planning of a publicity program for social work are considered at the end of this volume because the technique to be employed must be understood before procedure can be discussed. The task of social publicity is to make a sufficiently strong impression on the human mind to awaken new thought and to influence action. To accomplish this, a well-organized plan is necessary. Knowledge of the subject matter of social work and skill in applying the principles of publicity to its presentation are not enough. The promoter of a successful publicity program is one who can bring his experience to bear on each particular situation, and can relate the separate parts of a program to the whole.

The meager statements commonly prepared by social agencies in advance of a particular undertaking or at the beginning of the year's work scarcely deserve to be called plans. They consist chiefly of a consideration of the means to be employed, with a rough estimate of their cost. If advice is sought before a plan is made, the questions asked too often reveal a belief on the part of questioners that methods can be evaluated quite apart from the circumstances under which they will be used. The following questions are typical: Does a house organ pay for the effort and money expended? What are the merits of portable projection machines? Are posters effective? Again, a novel idea initiated in one community is frequently put to work in another without any searching test of its appropriateness. It is necessary in appraising any particular method to take into account its relation to the publicity program of which it is to be a part.

ELEMENTS OF PLANNED PUBLICITY

The analysis of a publicity problem which is the basis for drafting a plan may be resolved very much like the lead of a news story into

359

the five following factors: why, what, who and where, how, and when. Thus:

1. Why: The immediate and specific, as well as the broad, general purpose for which the particular publicity is to be used.
2. What: The soundness, timeliness, and value of the information that is to be made public, as well as its accessibility when required.
3. Who and Where: Identification of the persons to be reached, their numbers, where they may be found, and their present attitude toward the matter in hand.
4. How: The choice and combination of publicity methods, also the particular incentives to attention and interest, and the forms of appeal most appropriate to the subject and the audience. We should add to this list another "how," namely, how to get the work done.
5. When: The period of time allowed for the undertaking and the schedule or calendar for preparing and releasing each form of publicity.

In certain instances some of the above factors may not require much thought because they represent fixed conditions, the premises with which one starts in deciding to spread information. Other factors may have been determined before the details of a publicity plan come up for consideration. The important thing is to make sure that each factor deserving study or planning receives it. This is brought out in the discussion that follows.

Analysis of Known and Unknown Factors. For example, let us suppose that publicity is needed for the findings of a state-wide survey of poor relief that has been conducted by a state department of public welfare. An impressive body of facts has been gathered by trained investigators that show that the existing system of public care for the sick and indigent poor is costly, inhumane, and antiquated. The facts about the abuses are disclosed and the recommendations for remedying them are embodied in the printed report of the survey, which contains tables of figures, diagrams, spot maps, photographs, and well-written accounts of what the investigators observed. A workable program of reform, based on the recognition that almshouse inmates are chiefly the chronically ill and infirm, is presented, showing how the present poorhouse farms may be replaced by institutions primarily hospitals.

At this point a plan for publicity is considered and an analysis of its elements is made. The immediate purpose is readily seen to be the use of the information in the report as a means of arousing the citizens of the different counties to secure the passage of laws abolishing their dilapidated and insanitary poor farms and providing for county homes of a modern and suitable type. To accomplish this, the premise with which the planner starts is the report that contains the facts about the existing system and the ideas about the projected one that have been set forth in a concise and convenient form. These are the "why" and "what" of his problem. Other elements, however, require thought and study. For instance, although the information about the almshouses should ultimately reach all the voters, it may be more effective and practical to attempt first to interest those citizens who will be willing and competent to take the lead in getting the proposed program fully considered by the people of the state. So the question arises: Who are the individuals and the organized groups of people that can be sufficiently aroused to a sense of the importance of the situation to undertake this leadership and where are they to be found?

In searching for a responsive audience for the first effort of publicity, the initial step may be an attempt to view the facts and proposals contained in the report as they are likely to appear to different types of citizens. For instance, information about the neglect, waste, and insanitation existing in almshouses; the failure to provide reasonable comforts; and the use of outworn, ineffectual methods of care will appeal to those who have a humanitarian interest in the relief of suffering. These facts, therefore, should be called to the attention of social workers, members of churches, women's clubs, and so forth. Members of the medical and nursing professions might be interested primarily in the proper medical care of the inmates; business men might be concerned in improving the system because they see the waste of public funds through maintaining many small and poorly equipped almshouses which might be combined into a few suitably built and well-managed institutions. The facts should also be widely made known to the general public in order to arouse the interest of citizens not ordinarily active in social welfare. Among the special groups, as also among the larger body of the general public, might be found citizens who would become leaders to develop a plan for good almshouse care.

The question of how the facts brought out by the survey should be presented also requires study. The information must be given so that the persons addressed will realize its public importance. Examination of the report issued reveals excellent material for news, feature articles, interviews, and editorials in which the significance of the findings can be impressively brought out. Again personal letters may be addressed to individuals who should be asked to identify themselves with the movement for better public care of the indigent poor. It will be desirable to place articles in the professional and trade publications read by the groups named above and to prepare for the various editors suitable abstracts of the report taking account of their interests.

Looking at the report again we find pictures and diagrams which may be used in illustrated talks to ready-made audiences.[1] Tours of inspection by small groups of people to certain county almshouses are another phase of the campaign to be planned. Some of the worst and some of the best institutions may be chosen.

To cover the last point in the outline, "when," a time schedule for distributing the publicity is of particular importance. It will be necessary to launch a number of local campaigns in different counties, and the state welfare department, which will probably have a limited personnel, must arrange the many tasks involved in carrying out the planned publicity so that the time of its staff members can be used to best advantage.

Thus, step by step, a plan begins to take shape in which each special article, speech or set of illustrations has its definite place and purpose.

Clarifying the Purpose. In the instance just cited of publicity for a survey of almshouses no doubt or confusion existed as to the purpose in undertaking the campaign. Frequently, however, the main objects of publicity are not clearly visualized. They require definition and in some instances modification in order to form a practical basis for an intelligently planned educational campaign.

This was the case with a labor union in a large city which had

[1] See discussion of such audiences, p. 237.

received a gift of $10,000 to be spent on the health education of its 50,000 members, too small a sum with which to do a good job. Distributing it evenly would give but 20 cents with which to "educate" each member in the broad topic of health, at best allowing for a booklet or a series of folders to send to each. How then could the money be devoted to some attainable end which would satisfy the conditions of the gift? Persuading members to make better use of the facilities of a health center maintained by the union was discussed as a workable project, which would certainly be a step in the direction of health education. Since it would not do to use the fund for the benefit of a part of the membership, ignoring the rest, publicity might be directed to leaders of the locals or to shop chairmen of plants who could relay it to their fellow-workers. Again, the whole sum might be spent for posters and motion pictures with the understanding that other sources of income should be drawn upon for the salary of a publicity worker who would make possible the effective use of these forms of graphic material.

At any rate it seemed clear that unless a plan of some kind based on a reasonable estimate of what could be accomplished with $10,000 was determined upon the money would be wasted by spreading the instruction out too thinly.

Investigation a Preliminary Step. A sound analysis of the elements in a publicity program usually requires, in addition to clear thinking, the collection of data on which to base decisions. Thus, a committee representing civic organizations and departments of the local government is formed in a large city to undertake an "anti-litter campaign" in the parks. Their task is to teach people to throw their lunch-boxes, banana and orange skins, newspapers, cigarette wrappers, and so forth into receptacles and not on the ground. Here at least is a concrete and simple purpose. In order to devise an intelligent scheme to accomplish it, one should learn among other things:

What members of the city's population are chiefly responsible for the litter?
At what seasons, on what days, and at what places is the litter greatest?
Of what does it consist?
How can it be disposed of most easily and satisfactorily?

What motives for taking the trouble to put waste into the cans provided would be likely to appeal to those who now fail to do so?

What experiments could be tried through the use of different appeals such as pride in a clean city, or greater personal enjoyment of the parks, or holding offenders up to reproach or ridicule?

Where might reminders be placed so that they would be observed by persons on the way to parks or already in them? What dramatic methods, such as an inter-park contest, might be conducted?

How should various efforts of publicity be timed so that they will have a cumulative effect and yet not dull interest by too much repetition?

Is it desirable to make a clean-park demonstration in one park or to make the effort city wide?

What service and publicity materials suited to the purpose might be contributed by advertisers, transportation companies, newspapers, and social agencies? For example, could an advertising club be interested to provide a committee to direct or at least to advise about the enterprise?

What publicity must be paid for?

Since such study is a somewhat time-consuming and difficult process, guesswork regarding unknown factors frequently takes its place. The committee in charge of the enterprise would need to undertake studies to find the right answers to all these questions. If it is a typical committee the members will probably omit the study and depend for guidance on their own casual observations and opinions. They may in this way hit upon successful methods, but a genuine effort to obtain the right answers to the questions listed above would be much more certain to secure the results desired.

ADVANTAGES OF SPECIFIC PROJECTS

A specific project such as the anti-litter campaign integrates activities and directs them in an orderly way toward an objective to be reached within a fairly brief period, a year or a few years at most. A project lends itself more readily to analysis and planning of the kind we have suggested than does a continuous program of spreading information with the hope that it will gradually penetrate far enough into people's thoughts to bear fruit eventually in a changed public opinion or in a changed social custom. The latter procedure is in much more general use than the project method, however. Given a set of ideas to promulgate, most publicity workers strike out vigorously, using all channels, all occasions indiscriminately, so long as they get their ideas into circulation.

For example, a family welfare society seeking to keep its work before the public publishes a monthly news bulletin; sends stories occasionally to the newspaper (when a legacy is received, a new staff member engaged, or a coal shortage during a severe winter creates an emergency); publishes an annual report; holds an annual meeting; asks a representative once in a while to address church societies and men's luncheon clubs; and, if the opportunity can be secured, arranges for one or more speeches over the radio.

While such a program may succeed in maintaining a general awareness of the society's existence and a vague sort of goodwill toward it, this routine publicity might be supplemented to advantage by a series of clearly defined projects, all a part of the larger purpose of increasing public understanding and support.

Thus, one project would be to increase the information of a picked group, the ministers or teachers of a community, on how family work is done and how they can best co-operate with the society, as well as how the society can co-operate with them. A second project directed toward givers who have helped particular families would seek to strengthen the contacts of these givers with the organization by interesting them, for instance, in its preventive work. A third would make known throughout the entire community how and where to report cases of persons in trouble.

Undertakings like these need not make up the whole publicity program of an organization. It would be highly impracticable for some organizations to put all their resources, even temporarily, into a special effort for making one of several equally important ideas known to one part of the population. In the meantime news occurs and must be reported; a house organ once started must be issued at stated periods, although it has no place in the special project. Information of various kinds must be reiterated in order that it may not be forgotten. A certain routine must be followed for the sake of economy or for other practical considerations.

Some of the best planned all-the-year-round publicity includes continuous distribution of information combined with one or more projects which form the high points of the year's program. A council of social agencies may, during the year, conduct a campaign of publicity following a survey of the local hospitals, or child-caring agencies; may co-operate with a newspaper in offering "opportunities for volunteers"; may hold a clean-up week in the spring; and may co-operate in the usual intensive money-raising campaign in the autumn. Each of these efforts may be so planned as to accomplish a specific result, and to this extent may constitute a separate project. At the same time routine publicity need not be neglected.

Dissatisfaction with the slow advance along the whole front of social effort toward a far-off destination, such as the elimination of a disease or illiteracy, is seen in the growing tendency of social agencies to seek lesser goals that can be reached more quickly and, when attained, carry them by definitely marked stages toward their more distant aims. This tendency is illustrated in "demonstrations," which consist in the application of thoroughness in a selected town or neighborhood to undertakings that are often only half accomplished because too much is attempted in view of the resources available. It seems possible that similar demonstrations or projects in popular health education or indeed in any other form of social publicity might be undertaken experimentally by some of the organizations that are at present committed to the use of "general publicity." The specific project gives a sense of satisfaction in that one sees where he is going and in some cases, at least, can within a reasonable time find out where he has arrived.

FUNDAMENTAL DEFECTS DISCLOSED BY ANALYSIS

The demand that publicity shall arrive somewhere instead of going ahead aimlessly inevitably leads to a critical examination of one's materials and methods. So long as "informing the public" is the sole end in view, it is easy to make vague and impracticable proposals. But if one seeks concrete results, questions as to how the persons to whom advice is offered can act on it must be met. People cannot obey the injunction "have a general health examination" if they cannot afford to pay doctors to make such examinations, or, if doctors, as is true in some instances, are not prepared to make them. They cannot be expected to sleep with their windows open in cold weather if they are unable to afford sufficient bed covering to keep them warm. If we are thinking through the steps in a process of teaching, we are sure to come upon difficulties like these which raise doubts as to the feasibility of offering the public a particular bit of advice when the facilities or conditions which make it possible for them to take the advice do not exist.

Analyzing a publicity problem with a view to planning a specific project may lead us even farther than this facing of practical considerations and may raise questions regarding the soundness of the undertaking of which the publicity is a part. A first step in seeking to establish better relations between the different elements of a community, for instance, teachers or ministers and a family welfare society, would be to find what members of these professions already think and know about family work. In the course of such an inquiry, the publicity worker may come up against unexpected criticisms of the society, some of which may be well deserved. Under these circumstances, winning co-operation becomes something more than enlightening a group of people. The policies and methods of the society must be revised before the publicity worker can hope by any efforts of his own to gain confidence in them.

Again, although the sponsors of some social or civic reform may have supposed that they had a strong case, the search for suitable facts and arguments to present to the public in support of the undertaking may reveal that those in hand are too meager and that careful study is needed in order to supply them. Recently a campaign was launched to arouse the public to do something to reduce crime. Beginning with much indignation and a strong desire for action, the leaders of the movement soon found themselves involved in a mass of conflicting opinions about what should be done. They later postponed the attempt to arouse public opinion until such time as further investigations into the causes of crime and their effective treatment could be completed.

Publicity for social work is an integral part of social work; its quality is dependent on the quality of the service it seeks to make known. If a specific cause is honest and its work well organized, much is to be gained by examining it to discover the best methods of presentation. If the work is poor, but has some excellent aspects, the only straightforward course for the publicity worker is to refuse to present it or else to emphasize its good points and to call the attention of the public to what is being done toward correcting its weaknesses. At any rate, the analysis which precedes good planning must include a careful evaluation of the facts, social service, or whatever is to be presented. While this is not in most instances a task for the publicity worker, it is essential to the effectiveness of his work that he should make sure that it is done by competent persons.

STAYING ON THE TRACK

Still another advantage of the planned campaign is that it holds the publicity worker on the main track leading to his goal and prevents him from straying off into tempting by-paths. When he has nothing more definite in view than to bring his organization before the public he may easily be led into making success in "the game" of publicity his destination. Triumphs in the way of securing front-page space, a famous singer or actress to take part in a meeting, or the use of windows in leading stores in which to display exhibits—all these are very alluring. Nor are they unimportant, but they are easily over-rated and lead to the neglect of less spectacular but more effective means of spreading information.

Frequently the secretary of a social agency who thinks he has no time to map out a program ultimately devotes more hours than planning would have required to an undertaking whose sole purpose is to utilize an unsought opportunity for free publicity. For instance, the manager of a motion picture theater offers the use of his theater for any meeting the agency may like to have in it and the secretary arranges a motion picture program largely to show his appreciation of the offer. This is to subordinate the aims of publicity to the promotion of cordial relations. It may be advisable to do so, but accepting an offer in the form and at the time that it is made is not always necessary in order to obtain goodwill.

Whims and impulses are sometimes allowed to decide the choice of publicity methods when no line of action has been previously determined. A director of the organization has attended an exposition during a visit to another city and proposes that his own organization undertake a similar affair; a member of the staff has delivered an address at a state or national meeting and money is appropriated by the organization to print and circulate it which

368

might better be spent on some other form of publicity; the executive secretary has been struck with an idea for a scenario and would like to produce a picture built around it. "Bright ideas" and the unconscious desire for self-expression are will-o'-the-wisps that lead many workers off the main road. Testing an idea by seeing how it will fit into a plan of campaign will do much to forestall the adoption of inappropriate methods.

THE PLACE OF PUBLICITY IN THE PROGRAM OF A SOCIAL AGENCY

The factors thus far suggested as elements of good planning are mainly questions of how to obtain results. Behind this type of planning there should be a policy of wider scope, based on a clear conception of the place of publicity in the whole program of the organization. Very few social agencies exist for the sole purpose of spreading information. Those that do are usually of a temporary nature like the committees brought together to conduct an anti-litter campaign or a health exposition. Publicity in most organizations is combined with individual instruction, fact-finding, personal service, and treatment in an effort to accomplish some end —for example, to save sight, to prevent juvenile delinquency, or to restore families to independence. The social organization must form judgments about the relation of publicity to these different forms of effort in order to apportion suitably its budget and the working time of the members of its staff. Should publicity have a major or minor place on the program and should it be conducted independently or in close co-ordination with fact-finding or with personal service? In reaching a decision on these questions, one needs to consider to what extent the lay public, once its members have become informed, can and should participate in bringing about the desired results.

For instance, we are reasonably sure that response in such matters as eating the right foods, driving automobiles cautiously, assuming correct posture, and a number of other observances can be accomplished through competent mass instruction and persistent reminders. Publicity then might be relied upon to carry the heavy end of the load in movements in which the habits and conduct of men and women figure largely as causes of disease, accidents, and death. In some cases it should be closely allied to

369

patient, individual instruction, such as is given to mothers in the care of babies. This is especially true when the general advice and necessary teaching are complicated and must be modified to suit the understanding and different circumstances of the persons who need instruction and when this instruction cannot be sufficiently simplified to use on posters, folders, and in group work.

Organizations that seek to change the conditions under which we live rather than to influence the behavior of individuals find it necessary to mobilize public support for legislation or other means of putting these changes into effect. Laws requiring that tenements shall have plenty of light and air, or limiting the working hours of women, can be secured and enforced only through the backing of public opinion, and this in turn must be obtained through the popular presentation of facts. Theoretically at least, in programs directed toward replacing existing customs and institutions with new ones, publicity takes equal rank with fact-finding and experimentation. In practice, however, leaders of organizations concerned with social changes show far more vision and competence in studying conditions and devising improvements than in seeking popular understanding of their carefully thought out expedients. Organizations which gather data and prepare plans for social betterment need to round out their service with programs of publicity as intelligently planned and vigorously executed as are the other parts of their task.

Occasionally one organization devotes itself exclusively to surveys and investigations while others take the responsibility for presenting to the public the findings of such investigations. Perhaps a government bureau makes a survey and issues a technical report of it, and at this point one or more voluntary societies take over the work of popularizing the information. This is an excellent division of labor and has brought about some notable results, as in the field of maternity care and child health in which the Children's Bureau of the United States Department of Labor has cooperated with women's clubs of the country.

Service to individuals is by far the largest section of the field of social work. The great majority of social agencies are engaged in child placing, home nursing, assisting families in trouble, personally supervising delinquent adults and children who have been placed on probation, and giving care in hospitals and other institutions. While publicity has rightly a subordinate place in the programs of these agencies, a greater appreciation of the value of keeping the public informed about the nature of their work would lighten the load of those who are giving personal service. As visitors to homes where they are not personally known or the services they offer understood, they are often obliged individually to break down hostility or suspicion toward the organizations they represent before they are in a position to be helpful. They encounter misunderstandings and prejudices common to a national group or to one section of the community that complicate the problems of families within the group.

Carefully planned educational publicity, can, for instance, make parents understand more readily what the probation officer is trying to do for their delinquent boy, or can teach pregnant women or mothers of infants the importance of supervision by the public health nurse. It can help to build up a general attitude of acceptance of these and other types of service in the community as a whole and thus simplify the visitor's task in winning the confidence of its individual members. Not only the persons who are to be assisted but those who may be consulted or asked to help carry out a plan of relief for a family and its restoration to normal living, such as employers, policemen, city officials, lawyers, and members of church societies will co-operate more intelligently and with less delay if they already understand something of the methods and principles which guide the case worker.

However, we do not mean to imply that publicity always deserves a more important place in the program of an organization than it receives. The opposite conclusion might be reached after a study of the question. An organization may lose the confidence of the public by seeking continually to obtain favorable mention of its achievements. Then there is the problem of keeping the demand for service in accord with the amount that an agency can supply. If making itself better known brings a family welfare society more applications from persons in need of help than it can take care of, the society may undertake to comply with all

371

requests and so do a poor quality of work. When this happens, the reaction of both its clients and the public will be one of distrust. The giving of information to the public by a society should keep pace so far as possible with its capacity to extend its service, neither incurring the danger of outrunning this capacity nor yet withholding the enlargement of usefulness that waits only upon public understanding.

The Terms on Which Support May Be Obtained

Another question of policy broader than the immediate and practical one of how to get results is: What are the most creditable and far-seeing methods of obtaining public attention and support? Those who make the programs of social organizations have not as yet gone far enough in formulating well-grounded policies as to the terms on which they are willing to secure responses to their appeals or admonitions. For example, the workers interested in raising money for a community fund when they make their annual appeal find that they can obtain much more money to support child-caring institutions than to investigate causes of juvenile delinquency; more for the support of old people's homes than for movements to enable old persons to stay in their own homes; more, indeed, for all the old familiar forms of relieving distress than for any of the newer kinds of constructive and preventive measures. Both the popular and unpopular kinds of work are carried on by agencies supported by the community fund. The appeals may quite honestly place in the foreground of the picture those forms of service with which the public sympathizes readily, for as yet these are quantitatively, at least, by far the largest part of the work undertaken by social agencies. But how will the public advance in its conception of what social work should be, if the most conspicuous effort of publicity that is made in the community, the annual money-raising campaign, intensifies wrong views by ignoring or minimizing the importance of the more significant and progressive but less appealing forms of service?

The solution of the problem is to be found in part in the more skilful presentation of the human elements in those forms of work which are less familiar and which seem on the surface less dramatic.

Whereas the plea for the crippled child brings a quick and almost universal response, we can by a vigorous effort to increase understanding create a like sympathy for the child whose chance in life is crippled by the "blind alley" job. This latter plea, however, to be effective requires the giver to have a knowledge of the true aims of social work, one of which is the development in the individual of the power to be self-supporting. Such a knowledge is in fact the only basis of sound and continuous financial support for any welfare program.

Social work is built on a weak and shaky foundation when it leaves the public far behind in understanding present developments merely because by not disturbing established beliefs it is easier to get support.

Another problem in the relation of an agency to the public it serves or from which it needs support has to do with the reasonableness of its claims on the time and attention of people for matters which are only a very small part of all that concerns them as members of a community. This question raises a number of perplexing problems. Yet with the increase of all sorts of enterprises to attract the attention of people, we cannot avoid a thoughtful consideration of this competition.

We may insist that we desire from the public a reasoned, intelligent response, and to this end we give out information on which people may make their own decisions. But how much thinking is it reasonable to expect the ordinary citizen to give to each of the host of social questions with which he is confronted? A man who is a representative member of the public that supports charitable or educational efforts is equally a member of other groups and as such is besought to take an interest in many other matters. He is addressed as a voter, a parent, a buyer, a member of a trade or profession, a baseball fan, a taxpayer, a Protestant or Catholic, a pedestrian or the driver of a car, a tenant or property owner, a 100 per cent American, a giver, and so on. In each of these capacities he receives quantities of information, appeals, requests, and advertising through letters, articles in trade papers, regular meetings of this or that club, and various other approaches.

But granting the impossibility of an individual's forming an independent opinion on so many matters, should that deter us from placing our information before him in the hope that out of all this welter of proposals and assertions he will choose ours for careful consideration?

If we relax our pressure because we are sorry for the man who is so harassed by the many and varied demands upon him, do we not yield too easily to his desire to be let alone, to be allowed to ignore the misery of the world, and to evade the responsibilities that go with community life? How shall we draw the line between respecting his right to choose what he will give attention to and recognizing that persuasion is necessary to interest him in an unfamiliar subject or to stir him to a personal sacrifice? How shall we estimate fairly his thoughtfulness, his independence of judgment, and unselfishness so that our approaches to him shall be neither too many nor too few and on neither too high nor too low a plane?

While these questions take us into complex problems of human relationships much broader than any discussed in this book on publicity for social work, nevertheless those who make publicity programs should be deeply concerned with them. To separate the methods of obtaining public support from consideration of the kind of relationship that should exist between a social agency and its public is unsound.

RESPONSIBILITY FOR PUBLICITY PROGRAMS

As social work is organized at present, it is hard to find in its ranks persons who are in a position to think their way through these questions. The executive and his board of directors would appear to be the logical ones to decide the place of publicity in the program of the organization and to set standards by which to judge the plan of work which they or someone employed for the purpose may prepare. Probably there are many executives and board members to whom it has never occurred that they should have a policy about their relations with the public. Indeed, since few have prepared publicity programs it is not surprising that but a small number have formed judgments about the value of this relationship. Executives are so pressed by the urgency of detailed administrative problems that they do not find time to think about these matters. Their special training in social case work, psychiatry, criminology, or medicine may not have included any study of publicity or preparation for using it. Administrators who have not the training or aptitude for publicity must recognize the importance of looking about for someone to help them to plan it intelligently.

Not until the demand for this service increases will it be easy to secure persons equipped to give it, whether as consultants or as staff members. In large cities a number of agencies specialize in publicity directed only toward money raising. Very few as yet are prepared to advise on methods of developing campaigns of public information directed toward another end than that of obtaining funds. Moreover, executives of social work organizations are naturally wary about engaging this kind of service because they have no criteria by which to determine whether or not the agency can supply sufficient wisdom and skill to justify its employment.

An increasing number of national, state, and large city organizations have full-time publicity directors on their staffs. As was stated in the Preface to this volume, there is as yet no established source of supply for such workers. There are no training schools to prepare them and no generally accepted ideas as to what should be their duties or their qualifications for the task. Some of those already in the field have worked on newspapers; others have acquired facility in writing, speaking, designing, printing, or in some other means of spreading information. This insufficient and not well-rounded preparation in the principles and methods of publicity does not equip them to become competent advisers. Again, comparatively few escape from the pressure to produce results by the quickest, and often the most trivial methods.

Those who have been engaged in social publicity work for a few years and have acquired a keen perception of the value of their task are likely to grow dissatisfied with the superficial nature of their efforts. Their interest in the principles and aims of the organization they serve and of the larger social movement makes them see possibilities of more lasting and solid achievements than merely the placing of an impressive amount of publicity in circulation. When they reach this stage in the development of their experience and outlook, they should be given the opportunity to devote time and thought to framing policies and shaping programs.

Those who are ready for this larger responsibility, however,

375

must first persuade executive officers and directors of social agencies to revise their attitude toward publicity. At present many directors and officers disparage and distrust it, perceiving as they do its use for selfish ends and its alarming power to stifle thinking and dominate the minds of people. The evidences of the mediocrity they must appeal to in people as revealed by the success of crude and childish devices in winning attention and interest are also discouraging to them.

The best type of publicity for social work seeks to make the enlightenment of the public and the gaining of its active interest important factors in accomplishing human betterment. Its aim is a wider and more understanding participation by all the community in such movements. When the leaders of social work fasten their attention on the highest attainments of publicity rather than on its worst manifestations, they will not only call upon the few specialists now engaged in it to show the best that they can do, but they will stimulate greater effort by developing a more critical attitude toward the quality of the work. They will demand as a matter of course that publicity be based on orderly and practicable plans, and they will test these plans by a clearly formulated philosophy about the relations that it is desirable and possible for a social agency to establish with the public.

INDEX

INDEX

Abbreviations and nicknames, 34

A B C of Exhibit Planning, The, by
E. G. and M. S. Routzahn, 239, 294,
311, 352 *notes*

"A Cat May Look at a Kaiser in the
Camera's Best Sellers," by C. P.
Cushing, 90 *note*

Access to news sources, opportunities
for, imperative, 94

Accuracy: need for, viii; avoiding in-
accuracy, 32

Achilles, P. S., 60 *note*

Acknowledgments, viii–ix

Addams, Jane, 28

Administration of an exposition, 310–
313

Administrative work as a source of
news, 112–115

Advertisements: in railway or street
cars, 7; double-page, 8; of Metropolitan Life Insurance Company, 14,
54–55; humor in, 26; to sell nostrums, 37; motive recognized by advertisers, 48; advertising tests, 59;
buying space in newspapers for, 91,
93; for social work, *illus.*, 92; type
face for, 160; pictures found in, 181;
offering free literature, 206, cost of,
206

Advertising and Selling, by H. L.
Hollingworth, 46, 161 *notes*

Advertising—Its Principles and Practice, by Tipper, Hotchkiss, Hollingworth, and Parsons, 171 *note*

Alabama, school conditions as a news
source in, 103

Almanacs, 144

American Child Health Association, 26,
48, 133, 178, 270, 326

American City, 277 *note*

American Journal of Public Health, vi,
164, 247 *notes*

American Journal of Sociology, 60 *note*

American Museum of Natural History,
231

American Newspaper Annual, 122 *note*

American Peace Award, 237

American Public Health Association:
Section on Public Health Education,

v; Committee on Municipal Health
Department Practice, 103 *note*

American Red Cross, v, 8, 206, 267,
271, 286, 288, 320, 343

American Social Hygiene Association:
contribution of publicity material
from, iv; 26, 48, 51, 60, 123, 133, 199,
207, 209; investigations by, 60;
booklets advertised by, 206

American Society for the Control of
Cancer, 72, 133

Analyzing and planning a publicity program, 359–376

Annual meetings, 236, 246

Annual reports: value of, 39; cover-
pages for, *illus.*, 143; organization of
subject matter, 191. *See also* Reports

"Another Germ Bites the Dust," by
Ernest Gruenig, 20 *note*

Anti-litter campaign, planning for, 363

Appeals: selecting the appeal, 43–59;
testing, 59–60; psychological reports
on, 60, 65 *note;* inappropriate in
news stories, 77; in photographs, 90;
advertising, 91; of pictures, 174;
policy in making, 372, 373. *See also*
Motives

Appreciation, expression of, *illus.*, 38

Argument versus persuasion, 57

ARRANGING AND CONDUCTING MEET-
INGS, 236–255

Art work: in layout or dummy, 152;
ordering, 180; reproduction of, 188;
as copy, 189. *See also* Cartoons; Decoration; Illustrations; Silhouettes;
Sketches; Thumbnail sketches

At Ellis Island, by Cecilia Razovsky, 262

Atlantic Monthly, 164

Atmosphere created through display,
322

Attendance: at meetings, 245–250;
how to secure, at expositions, 308

Attendant at exhibits, 298, 299

Attention: ability to secure, 6–7; how
sought, 7; counter attractions, 7;
through intensity, 8–9; through contrast or novelty, 9–11; familiarity
attracts, 11–14; *illus.*, 12; through
ease of comprehension, 14; studying

379

4 26

INDEX

Habits: of attention, studying, 15; of
reading, 65; aim of printed matter to
change, 134; of speakers, 220
Half-tones: plates for, how made, 164,
166, 188; quality of paper for, 164,
166; adapted to the paper, *illus.*, 165
Hall, F. S., 105 *note*
Handbills: use of, 136; *illus.*, 138, 139;
in campaigns, 336
Handbook for Newspaper Workers, by
G. M. Hyde, 120 *note*
Handbook of Public Speaking, A, by
John Dolman, Jr., 221, 225 *notes*
Handbooks for speakers, 331
Harrison, S. M., 105 *note*
Hart, H. H., 106
Headings, section and paragraph, 191
Headlines: on news releases, 120; as
copy, 189
Health: state boards of, visits made to,
iv; suspense the basis of talk on, 23–
24; humorous stories and cartoons
for, 26; obtaining goodwill, and responsibility in appeals for, 32–33, 43–
61; publicity for, in West Virginia,
92; rating of health departments as
news, 103; quantity of literature on,
133; cartoons, 178, 180; distribution
of literature by health departments,
204, 206; use of properties by speakers on, 231–232; meetings, and
ready-made audiences, 237; arrangements for meetings by state departments of, 249–250; program of a
health meeting, 252; plays, 259–260;
parades in China, 270; baby health
contests, 276; side shows at fairs, 281;
Health Fortune Teller, 282, 292; department's control of food at fairs,
288; expositions chiefly on, 294–315;
Health Week, 340. *See also* United
States Public Health Service
Health demonstration, contest for
securing, 277
"Health Education and Publicity," by
William Feather, 164 *note*
Health Fortune Teller, 282, 292
Health News, of New York State De-
partment of Health, 238 *note*
Health Show Comes to Town, The, by
E. G. Routzahn, 24 *note*
Healthgrams, 91, 93
"Here Is a Thing Worth Fighting For,"
by E. D. Biggers, 56 *note*
Higham, Sir Charles, 54 *note*
Hill, H. W., 196 *note*
Hoboken Observer, 100 *note*

Holding Attention, 17–31
Holding attention: by clear mental
pictures, 17–21; by personal application of ideas, 21; through the element
of suspense, 22–25; with light or
humorous treatment, 25–28; by per-
sonal contact, 28; variety a factor in,
29; by change of emphasis, 30
Hollingworth, H. L., 46; 161, 171 *notes*
Holmes, O. W., 87
Home Mission Council, 262 *note*
Hoover, Herbert, 57
Hosmer, Mrs. F. M., 76
Hotchkiss, G. B., 65, 171 *notes*
House organs: use of, vii, 145; promote
goodwill, 39; a source of news, 115
"How Calkins and Holden Use Humor-
ous Advertising," by E. E. Calkins,
26 *note*
How England Is Meeting the Housing
Shortage, by Lawrence Veiller, 272
note
How to Write Special Feature Articles,
by W. G. Bleyer, 86, 114 *notes*
Howe, Dr. E. C., 231
Howland, P. B., 261
Human interest in news, 73
Humanizing of Knowledge, The, by
J. H. Robinson, vii, 199 *note*
Humor: attracts attention, 25–28;
illus., 27, 53; in cartoons, 178
Hyde, G. M., 120 *note*

Illinois: Tuberculosis Association window display, 44; Chicago United
Charities appeal, 49; Social Hygiene
League, 193; State Department of
Health, 281, 291
Illustrated talks: material and properties for, 228–234; charts and maps
used in, 229, *illus.*, 230; lantern slides
for, 232–234
Illustrations: in dummy or layout,
152; for printed matter, 169–188;
examples of, 170, 171, 173, 175; to
convey information, 172–174; pictures that appeal, 174; cartoons,
176–180; artists who contribute, 180–
181; ordering, 181; borrowing, and
objections to, 181; maps, diagrams
and charts for, 182; photographs for,
185–187; reproduction of, 188; as
copy, 189
Immigrants, social service plays, 262
Indiana: Community Fund publicity
in Indianapolis, 246; State Department of Health, 281; Evansville

384

INDEX

Mechanical devices: how to attract attention by, 9; illuminated map, 231; at expositions, 297, 301, 303. *See also* Exhibits; Models

Meetings: suspense in, 23–24; variety in, 30; as a source of news, 106; distribution of printed matter at, 212; arranging and conducting, 236–255; ready-made audiences for, 237–245; card catalogs of organizations an aid in arranging, 239; speakers' bureaus for, 238–245; shop, 242; assembling audiences for, 245–250; advance publicity for, 246–248; invitations increase attendance at, 248; careless arrangements for, illustrated, 249–250; securing best conditions for, 251–255; chairman's functions at, 251; programs for, 252; discussion at, 254; overcrowding programs, 254–255. *See also* Public speaking; Speakers

Meier, N. C., 60 *note*
Mental Hygiene, 57 *note*
Mental pictures, 17
Metropolitan Life Insurance Company, 14, 55 *note*, 133, 213, 334, 337
Michigan: Detroit health club, 71; State Department of Health news release, 72; Detroit Tuberculosis Association, 283
Midway methods at county fairs, 281–284
Milk Week, 110–111, 272, 323
Minnesota: news value cited, 71; speakers' bureau of St. Paul, 244; Hennepin County Tuberculosis Association, 282 *note;* fair exhibits, 291, 301; Minneapolis campaign parade, 328; Minneapolis Visiting Nurse Association, 328; Minneapolis Infant Welfare Society, 328; Minneapolis Council of Social Agencies, 336
Missouri, school conditions as a news source in, 103
Models: to illustrate talks, 231; used at expositions, 297, 298, 302; miniature, *illus.*, 300. *See also* Exhibits; Mechanical devices
Morley, L. H., 207 *note*
Mosher, J. A., 220
Mother contest, 276
Motion pictures: significance of, vii; conditions visualized by, 18–19; cartoon films, 26; poor use of, at meetings, 252; at fairs, 284; at expositions, 296; preferred types of, in campaigns, 334–335

Motives. *See* Challenge; Duty; Economic; Fear; Love of children; Neighborliness; Pleasurable feeling; Pride in appearance; Public spirit; Ridicule; Social custom. *See also* Appeals; Response
"Motives in Voting: A Study in Public Opinion," by N. C. Meier, 60 *note*
Municipal Health Department Practice of the American Public Health Association, Report of the Committee on, 103 *note*

Names. *See* Prominent names
Narrow Door, The, by G. M. P. Baird, 260, 264
National Broadcasting Company of America, 234
National Child Health Council, 328
National Conference of Social Work, v *note*, 226
National Fire Protection Association, 327 *note*
National Housing Association, 272
National Information Bureau, 37
National Kindergarten Association, 22, 197
National organizations: aid in this study, iv; relations with newspapers, 121; printed matter issued by, 133, 201; assistance to fairs, 292; at expositions, 301; campaign work of, 319, 320; national organization of campaigns, 354
National Society for the Prevention of Blindness, 122
National Tuberculosis Association, iv, 8, 34, 86, 133, 265, 353
Nation's Health, The, 115 *note*
Neighborliness, 54–55
New Jersey, health exposition in Newark, 302
New York: American Red Cross Chapter contributed to study, v; United Hospital Fund, 13, 79; People's Institute of Brooklyn, 26; Charity Organization Society, 28, 38, 41, 71, 84, 194; State Department of Markets, 28; State Charities Aid Association, 75; Auburn welfare news, 76; Maternity Association, 87; Travelers Aid Society, 97; Rochester Health news, 108, 110; Young Men's Christian Association, 130; American Museum of Natural History food exhibits, 231; National Broadcasting Company of America, 234; State

386

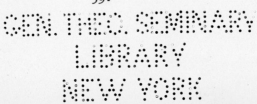

The fact that a subject is prominently before the public brings out opinions regarding it which might not otherwise be expressed. Canvassers for funds have to meet and answer even yet the objection "I do not believe in organized charity," and they are constantly encountering other misconceptions which, if reported in time, can be combated before the next drive.

Another important item in the early planning of campaign talking points is to work out a balance between old and new information. The director may find it well worth while to spread out on his desk a set of samples of publicity material from the recently ended campaign—the poster, photographs of the window displays, a scenario of the motion picture, a list of facts and arguments used by speakers, and a set of newspaper clippings. Then let him try to estimate what was the probable effect of all this publicity on a few given persons—his letter carrier, his banker, the man who repairs his shoes, a saleswoman, a minister. He may assume for the purpose of experiment that these representative persons were thoroughly "exposed" to the publicity, that is to say that during the campaign they read the newspapers, walked about the streets, attended a motion picture show, and otherwise received as much information about the drive as was intended for them.

Reviewing the output as it might appear to the individuals thus encountering it, the director may perhaps find reasonable assurance that certain facts must have made a lasting impression because they were vividly presented at many different times and places. These points, then, may be subordinated in the next campaign or at least presented from a new angle so as to avoid monotony. On the other hand, other equally important facts may not have appeared nearly so often or so conspicuously as had been intended, or they may have been presented in such dull or obscure terms that the persons would probably fail to notice them. In planning the next campaign these points will need more emphasis and better treatment. In the meantime, they could be given a prominent place in the all-year-round publicity.

"Get photographs" is another item that comes early on the calendar. The importance of appropriate photographs is better realized today than it was a few years ago, when anything that